LETTERS FROM EGYPT

TRAVELLERS AND EXPLORERS
General Editor: Robin Hallett

MAP TO ILLUSTRATE 'LETTERS FROM EGYPT'

LETTERS FROM EGYPT
(1862–1869)

LADY DUFF GORDON

RE-EDITED WITH

ADDITIONAL LETTERS BY

Gordon Waterfield

FREDERICK A. PRAEGER, *Publishers*

New York · Washington

BOOKS THAT MATTER

Published in the United States of America in 1969
by Frederick A. Praeger, Inc., Publishers
111 Fourth Avenue, New York, N.Y. 10003

© 1969 in London, England, by Gordon Waterfield

Library of Congress Catalog Card Number: 71–83973

Printed in Great Britain

'The letters of Lady Duff Gordon are an introduction
to her in person . . . [she] was of the order of women
of whom a man of many years may say that their
like is to be met but once or twice in a
lifetime.'

George Meredith, 1902

'As to interest and enjoyment I don't think Italy
or Greece can equal the sacred Nile, the perfect freshness
of the gigantic buildings, the beauty of the sculptures
and the charm of the people. . . . This country is a palimpsest
in which the Bible is written over Herodotus and the Koran
over that.'

'The blind rapacity of the present ruler [Ismail Pasha]
will make him astonish the Franks one day . . . It is
no secret to any but those Europeans whose interests
keep their eyes tightly shut and they will soon have them
opened.' 1865.

Lady Duff Gordon

Contents

CONTENTS

CONTENTS

Illustrations

xi

Note: Except where otherwise stated, the illustrations are by the Scottish painter, David Roberts (1796-1864), who made a tour of Egypt, Palestine and Syria in 1838, publishing *Sketches in the Holy Land and Syria* in 1842-49, containing two volumes of Egyptian drawings. The places had changed very little, if at all, at the time that Lucie Duff Gordon visited them.

The quotations under the illustrations, where not attributed, are from Lucie Duff Gordon's letters.

Preface

LUCIE DUFF GORDON'S *Letters from Egypt* was first published in May 1865 by Macmillan and was so successful that it went into three impressions before the end of the year; it was edited by her mother, Sarah Austin. *Last Letters from Egypt*, with *Letters from the Cape* (reprinted from 'Vacation Tourists' of 1864), was edited by her daughter, Janet Ross, and published in 1875; a second impression followed in 1876. Janet Ross published a fuller edition of *Letters from Egypt* in 1902 (R. Brimley Johnson), and since then there has been no new edition of this delightful book.

This new edition has been checked against a copy of the original letters which are in the possession of my family and contains a number of unpublished letters which had been considered too outspoken to be printed. Some of these were included in my biography of Lucie Duff Gordon, published by John Murray in 1937.

The *Letters from Egypt* cover the period from October 1862 to her death in July 1869. They follow the *Letters from the Cape* which start in July 1861 and end in July 1862. I had thought of combining the two groups of letters in one volume but, owing to the length, it would have meant cutting down on both and I preferred to issue as full a text of the *Letters from Egypt* as was of interest and to be able to add the new material.

If these letters should prove as popular today as they were following the earlier editions, it might be considered that there was sufficient demand for a new edition of *Letters from the Cape*.

In certain cases I have rearranged Lady Duff Gordon's letters so that they follow the sequence of her travels and this is not always in keeping with the date sequence of her letters. I have also brought some of the letters together in relation to the subjects they illustrate, but this rearrangement has only been made with letters which were written within a few days or weeks of one another.

The letters are to her mother, husband and children; they were generally passed round the family and I have only included the name of the recipient where it seemed necessary.

The spelling of Arabic names and places which she employed have, in some cases, been retained.

The material which has not been published in any previous editions of Lady Duff Gordon's *Letters from Egypt* is the following:

Chapter XXIV about Sally and Omar having a baby; some of chapter XXXIV about the problem of having European maids; chapter XLVIII about Maurice and the Belgian tutor, and the quarrel between Lucie and her husband, Sir Alexander Duff Gordon, about a dragoman in chapter XLIX.

I wish to thank Mrs Doreen Ingrams for advice on Arab customs and phrases and for compiling the index, also Mrs Joan St George Saunders for research, Mr D. J. S. Thomson for his help with German phrases and Mr Memduh Zeki for checking Arabic words. For his valuable general advice I wish to thank the Editor of the series, Mr Robin Hallett.

G. W.

Introduction

I read my great-grandmother's *Letters from Egypt* before going to Alexandria in the 1920's to learn about cotton, and I was enchanted at the prospect of meeting Egyptians who were described so charmingly and vividly by Lucie Duff Gordon. I was like the American who visited Luxor in the 1860's and told Lucie's Egyptian friends that he felt very friendly towards them because he had read an American edition of Lady Duff Gordon's *Letters from Egypt*.

But the cotton-broker uncle, who was sending me abroad to train for his business in Manchester, objected to my reading the letters; the Egyptians, he said, were no longer as she had described them and I would be disappointed. It was enough for me, however, that they had existed and came alive in her pages, and later I realized that my uncle's knowledge of Egypt was largely confined to the cotton centre of Alexandria, which was full of British, French, Italians, Greeks, Cypriots and Maltese. Even in the 1860's Lucie had considered Alexandria to be very different from the rest of Egypt: 'the European ideas and customs have extinguished the Arab altogether, and those who remain are not improved by the contact'.

It is true that the average visitor to Egypt today would have to persevere to find the kind of people Lucie knew as her friends, but they still exist, in spite of the stresses and frustrations of the last hundred years. The Egyptians she knew had not yet been overwhelmed by the impact of the West. The French occupation under Bonaparte had only lasted three years, from 1798 to 1801, but had begun to point the way to a new knowledge and science from Europe, and Mohammed Ali Pasha, the Viceroy, had encouraged the new learning by sending missions to Paris. Later came the ruinous westernization under Ismail Pasha, the revolt of Ahmed Arabi and the British occupation, which lasted through two world wars when the main centres were occupied by

British and Allied troops; great bitterness, too, has been aroused by western encouragement of the formation of the State of Israel and by the Anglo-French Suez adventure of 1956.

Egyptians have suffered wounding and frustrating experiences since Lucie's day, arousing fear, intolerance and a strong nationalism. But basically the Egyptians are the same, for they have as background and inspiration two remarkable civilizations—Pharaonic and Arab, which have given them pride, standards of morality and great courtesy. It would be a mistake for anyone reading these letters to think that Lucie Duff Gordon was exaggerating the kindness and goodness she found among the people of Luxor or that she was carried away by emotions of sympathy. 'She inherited from her father the judicial mind', wrote George Meredith, 'and her fine conscience brought it to bear on herself as well as on the world . . . Hers was the charity which is perceptive and embracing; we may feel sure that she was never a dupe of the poor souls, Christian and Muslim, whose tales of simple misery or injustice moved her to friendly service.'[1]

Ill with consumption Lucie Duff Gordon had to leave a happy social and family life in England in 1861 to travel to the Cape and then to Egypt where she lived for seven years, most of the time at Luxor when it was still a ramshackle village, in an old house built over the ancient Egyptian temple. She died in Cairo in 1869 at the age of forty-seven and was buried there.

The letters to her family reveal her lively curiosity and interest in her neighbours. Her approach to people was direct and sympathetic. 'It is to this large and tolerant humanity', wrote her mother Sarah Austin in the preface to the first edition of Letters from Egypt published in 1865, 'that the writer owes her power of understanding and interpreting thoughts and feelings unintelligible to most Europeans . . . If they [the letters] should awaken any sentiments like those which inspired them, on behalf of races of men who come in contact with civilization only to feel its resistless force and its haughty indifference or contempt, it will be some consolation to those who are enduring the bitterness of the separation to which they owe their existence.'

The English and the Egyptians

'The English would be a little surprised at Arab judgements on

---

[1] Preface by George Meredith to the 1902 edition of Letters from Egypt, edited by Janet Ross. Later comments by Meredith on Lucie Duff Gordon are also from this Preface.

them', wrote Lucie; 'they admire our veracity and honesty, and like us on the whole, but they blame the men for their conduct to women. They are shocked at the way Englishmen talk about hareem among themselves, and think the English hard and unkind to their wives, and to women in general . . . Omar [her servant] mentioned some Englishman who had divorced his wife and made her frailty public. You should have seen him spit on the floor in abhorrence. "What once he sleep in bed with her, and after show her face black before the people like Europeans. Never!" . . . Here it is quite blackguard not to forfeit the money and take all the blame in a divorce. There are a good many things about hareem here which I am barbarian enough to think extremely good and rational. An old Turk of Cairo, who had been in Europe, was talking to an Englishman a short time ago, who politely chaffed him about Mussulman license. The venerable Muslim replied, "pray how many women have you, who are quite young, seen (that is the Eastern phrase) in your whole life?" The Englishman could not count—of course not. "Well, young man, I am old and was married at twelve, and I have seen in all my life seven women; four are dead, and three are happy and comfortable in my house. *Where are all yours?*" '

She found her Arab friends to be a great deal more tolerant on religious questions than many of the British Protestants and Roman Catholics; the Muslims believed that the Christians were still inspired by the old spirit of the Crusades. 'I have been really amazed at several instances of English fanaticism this year [1865]. Why do people come to a Mussulman country with such bitter hatred "in their stomachs" as I have seen three or four times . . . Why do the English talk of the beautiful sentiment of the Bible and pretend to feel it so much, and when they come and see the same life before them, they ridicule it.'

In the book written by her cousin, Harriet Martineau, *Eastern Life Present and Past* describing her visit to Egypt in 1846, Lucie considered that the descriptions were excellent, 'but she evidently knew and cared nothing about the people, and had the feeling of most English people here, that the difference in manners is a sort of impassable gulf, the truth being that their feelings and passions are just like our own. It is curious that the old books of travel that I have read mention the natives of strange countries in a far more natural tone, and with far more attempt to discriminate character, than modern ones, e.g., Niebuhr's Travels here and in Arabia, Cook's Voyages, and many others. Have we grown so *very* civilized since a hundred years that outlandish people seem like mere puppets, and not like real human

B

beings'. The word 'civilized' was not always used in a favourable sense, any more than 'barbarian' was necessarily pejorative.

Lucie cared a great deal about the people, especially those who suffered as the Egyptians did under the rule of the Viceroy Ismail Pasha in the 1860's. She was the only European who had lived long enough in Upper Egypt at that time to get to know the people and to gauge the effects of taking men from their fields to work on de Lesseps' Canal or to fight in Crete against the Christians who had revolted, or to carry out so-called reforms for the Viceroy which were intended to impress Europe. 'The system of wholesale extortion and spoliation has reached a point beyond which it would be difficult to go', she wrote in January 1865, 'The story of Naboth's vineyard is repeated daily on the largest scale. I grieve for Abdallah el Habbashi and men of high position like him, sent to die by disease (or murder) in Fazogli [in the Sudan], but I grieve still more over the daily anguish of the poor fellaheen, who are forced to take the bread from the mouths of their starving families and to eat it while toiling for the private profit of one man. Egypt is one vast "plantation" where the master works his slaves without even feeding them. From my window now I see the men limping about among the poor camels that are waiting for the Pasha's boats to take them, and the great heaps of maize which they are forced to take for their food. I can tell you the tears such a sight brings to one's eyes are hot and bitter. These are no sentimental grievances; hunger and pain, and labour without reward, and the constant bitterness of impotent resentment. To you all this must sound remote and almost fabulous . . . I know the cruel old platitudes about governing the orientals by fear which the English pick up like mocking birds from the Turks. I know all about "the stick" and "vigour" and all that—but—"I sit among the people" and I know, too, that Mohammed feels just as John Smith or Tom Brown would feel in his place . . . . However, in Cairo and more still in Alexandria, all is quite different. There, the same system, which has been so successfully copied in France, prevails. The capital is petted at the expense of the fellaheen. Prices are regulated in Cairo for meat and bread, as they are or were in Paris, and the "dangerous classes" enjoy all sorts of exemptions . . . Yussuf says: "What the Turkish Government[1] fears is not for *your* safety, but lest we should learn to love you too well", and it is true. Here there is but one voice: "Let the Franks come, let us have the laws

[1] As Egypt was then part of the Ottoman Empire, the Government was often called Turkish and the people Turks.

4

of the Christians". In Cairo the Franks have dispelled this *douce illusion* and done the Turk's work as if they were paid for it. But here come only travellers who pay with money and not with stick. . . . When I remember [she wrote in May 1867], the lovely smiling landscape which I first beheld from my windows, swarming with beasts and men, and look at the dreary waste now, I feel the "foot of the Turk" heavy indeed. Where there were fifty donkeys there is but one; camels, horses, all are gone; not only the horned cattle, even the dogs are more than decimated, and the hawks and vultures seem to me fewer; mankind has no food to spare for hangers-on.'

Prophetic Statements

Not all these criticisms of Ismail's Government and the behaviour of Europeans were published in the early edition of *Letters from Egypt* during Lady Duff Gordon's lifetime, but enough was stated to lead to her being watched by Ismail's spies and many of her letters home were tampered with or 'lost'. A fuller edition of the letters was not published until 1902, after the British navy had bombarded Alexandria in 1882, Ahmed Arabi had been defeated at Tel el Kebir and Cromer had been installed as virtual ruler of Egypt. Her letters to her family make it clear why Arabi and the other nationalists had such an enthusiastic following among the fellaheen who had been frustrated and tormented for twenty years. Arabi's revolt was much more than a military one, though the British Consul Malet was not able to see that. During the 1860's and later, hardly anyone, besides Lucie Duff Gordon, bothered about the state of mind of the people and the British Consuls only knew the large towns.

'I could tell you a little of the value of Consular information!' she wrote, 'but what is the use? Europe is enchanted with the "enlightened" Pasha who has ruined this poor country.' After giving an account of the operations carried out by the Viceroy Ismail, she wrote to her husband: 'I wish you to publish these facts; they are no secret to any but those Europeans whose interests keep their eyes tightly shut, and they will soon have them opened. The blind rapacity of the present ruler will make him astonish the Franks some day.' But when the crisis came and Ismail was deposed, the British Government based its decisions on a misunderstanding of the situation partly due to ill-informed and biased consular reports.

Governments, however, have to pay attention to the reports of their

5

Consuls and such accounts as Lucie gave were probably not taken too seriously, perhaps being regarded as the outpourings of a sentimental radical. One of the letters from Cairo of May 21 1863, included in the 1865 edition, was very much to the point and should have been heeded. Lucie recounts a conversation she had with a well-informed neighbour, Hekekian Bey, but does not give his name lest he should get into trouble. 'His heart is sore with disinterested grief for the sufferings of the people. "Don't they deserve to be decently governed—to be allowed a little happiness and prosperity? They are so docile, so contented; are they not a good people?" Those were his words as he was recounting some new iniquity. Of course, half these acts are done under pretext of improving and civilizing, and the Europeans applaud and say, "Oh, but nothing could be done without forced labour", and the poor fellaheen are marched off in gangs like convicts, and their families starve, and (who would have thought it?) the population keeps diminishing . . .

'You know that I don't see things quite as our countrymen generally do, for mine is another *standpunkt,* and my heart is with the Arabs. I care less about opening up trade with the Sudan, or about all the new railways, and I should like to see person and property safe, which no one's is here—Europeans, of course, excepted . . . What is wanted here is hands to till the soil; wages are very high; food, of course, gets dearer, the forced labour inflicts more suffering than before and the population will decrease yet faster. This appears to me a state of things in which it is of no use to say that public works *must* be made at any cost. I daresay the wealth will be increased if, meanwhile, the people are not exterminated. Then every new Pasha builds a huge new palace, whilst those of his predecessors fall to ruin . . .; so money is constantly wasted more utterly than if it were thrown into the Nile, for then the fellaheen would not have to spend their time, so much wanted for agriculture, in building hideous barrack-like so-called palaces. What chokes me is to hear Englishmen talk of the stick being "the only way to manage Arabs", as if there could be any doubt that it is the easiest way to manage anybody, where it can be used with impunity.'

Lucie's son-in-law, Henry Ross, who was a director of the Egyptian Commercial and Trading Company formed in 1863, took no heed of her clear warnings that the company was trying to carry out too many developments and putting too much trust in princes and in dishonest employees. She believed the Company would get into serious difficulties and it eventually went bankrupt as did many other companies,

6

until a point was reached when the Khedive Ismail could raise no more money; Egypt itself was bankrupt and the European creditors began to take political control. The big population of Greeks, Maltese and Italians in Egypt and all who had the protection of a European Consul were able to defy the laws of Egypt and each be judged by his own country's laws through the Consul. 'It would be hard to exaggerate the amount of injustice, or the hideous administrative confusion, arising from this state of things' wrote Sir Alfred Milner in 1899 in *England in Egypt*, and others wrote in much stronger terms. Lucie had written in 1867, fourteen years before the British bombardment of Alexandria and the occupation of Egypt: 'I wonder when Europe will drop the absurd delusion about Christians being persecuted by Muslims. It is absolutely the other way . . . The Christians know that they will always get backed by some Consul or other, and it is the Muslims who go to the wall invariably.'

Lucie was describing the first stirrings of a peasant revolt which, owing to the British occupation, was not revealed again, after the Arabi movement, until 1919 under Saad Zaghlul, and then in 1952 under Gamal Nasser. Under Cromer the conditions of the fellaheen was much improved with the abolition of forced labour and an enlarged irrigation system, but these benefits were to a great extent forgotten for various reasons to do with politics, nationalism and dislike of Cromer who made it clear that he had a low opinion of Egyptians. One of the main reasons for the strong Egyptian reaction against the Cromer regime resulted from the harsh and unjust sentences passed on the people of Denshawi[1] in the Egyptian Delta, following incidents in June 1906 when the villagers objected to a group of British officers shooting their pigeons. This practice had been carried on by Europeans for very many years and aroused much ill-feeling. In February 1864 Lucie wrote from Luxor that 'she had been called by some poor men who want me to speak to the English travellers about shooting their pigeons. Here, where there are never less than eight or ten boats lying for full three months, the loss to the fellaheen is serious and our Consul, Mustapha Agha, is afraid to say anything. I have given my neighbours permission to call the pigeons mine, as they roost in flocks on my roof and to go out and say that the Sitt objects to her poultry being shot, especially as I have had them shot off my balcony as they sat there.'

---

[1] As a result of the trouble at Denshawi a British Officer and a villager died and a special tribunal condemned four out of the fifty-two villagers arrested to be hanged; others were beaten or sentenced to long terms of imprisonment.

It was the insensitivity of the British and of other foreigners which annoyed Lucie and she would have agreed with a statement written one hundred years later. 'In the many-sided impact of imperialism, it is the injury to self-respect that hurts most. It is the resentment aroused by spiritual humiliation that gives rise to an irrational response to rational exploitation.'[1]

The Taylors of Norwich

Born on June 24 1821 Lucie was the only child of remarkable parents. Her father, John Austin, author of *Province of Jurisprudence Determined*, created a great impression on his contemporaries such as Jeremy Bentham, James Mill, George Grote and others for his intellect, wide knowledge and conversational powers, but he suffered from melancholia and had such a passion for perfection in his attempts to establish a science of law that he wrote very little. 'If John Austin had had health', stated Lord Brougham, 'neither Lyndhurst nor I would have been Chancellor.'

[1] *Bankers and Pashas*, by D. S. Landes, London, 1958.

In 1814, the year before the Battle of Waterloo, he fell in love with Sarah Taylor, the daughter of John and Susannah Taylor who came of a large and distinguished Norwich family. Mrs John Taylor was an exceptional woman, shrewd and with a sense of humour as can be seen in the drawing of her opposite. She was known for her wisdom and used to discuss politics and literature with eminent Whigs of Norfolk such as Lord Albermarle and Coke of Holkham. When news came of the Fall of the Bastille in 1789 there was rejoicing in the Taylor family; Susannah planted a Tree of Liberty in her garden and danced round it with the erudite Dr Samuel Parr, while her husband wrote a stirring song with the refrain 'Fall, tyrants fall. These are the days of Liberty'. She believed that it was in the middle classes that 'true elegance as well as information' were to be found, and expressed her hostility to those in the House of Lords who had 'ridiculed the advocates of the oppressed negroes'.

Sarah inherited Susannah's talents and was taught good French, German, Italian, Latin and Greek; sensible advice came in letters from her mother: 'A well educated young woman may always provide for herself, while girls that are but half instructed have too much cultivation for one sort of life and too little for another. Besides that, the stiff aristocratical carriage produced by the idea that they are born to be young ladies and to spend their time in frivolous occupations is an impediment to everything valuable, for we must mix kindly and cordially with our fellow creatures in order to be useful to them or to make them useful to us ... The way to stand well with people is not to make them feel your consequence but their own, and while you are conversing with them to take an interest in whatever interests them.'

The views of the large Taylor family and of their relations, the Martineaus, were an important background to both Sarah and Lucie. There was a strong sense of unity and there used to be family meetings attended by over sixty members.

Sarah Taylor's family and friends did not think at first that she would engage herself to the handsome but serious young Austin. She had many admirers, being beautiful, flirtatious and full of vitality. Young Austin's excessive honesty was liable to annoy people, and his remarkable letter of proposal[1] to Sarah might well have intimidated her if she had not had confidence, courage and been in love. It was a long and formidable document, like a legal treatise, pointing out many

---

[1] Austin's letter of proposal is published in *Lucie Duff Gordon*, by Gordon Waterfield, Murray, 1937.

reasons why their marriage might be a failure; John Austen then required her 'to submit to a self-examination which may perhaps severely wound your vanity, but which you must triumphantly encounter before I can dare to hang the fate of my feelings upon the chance of your consistency'.

After an engagement of four years John Austin was called to the Bar in 1818 when he was twenty-eight and she was three years younger. They were married the next year and went to live at No. 1 Queen Square, Westminster, a house next to Austin's friend, James Mill, and not far from Jeremy Bentham's. Janet Ross was to write of her Austin grandparents: 'Two people more unlike it would have been difficult to find—Mr Austin, habitually grave and despondent; his wife, brilliantly handsome, fond of society, in which she shone, and with an almost superabundance of energy and animal spirits.'[1] It should be added, however, that Austin was sometimes moved to passion in his eloquent denunciations of society and the law. But he had to give up practice at the Bar because of ill health and Sarah maintained the family budget by publishing articles on education and books translated from German, a language she knew well. It was fortunate that her mother had encouraged her to study: 'The character of girls', she had written to Sarah, 'must depend upon their reading as much as upon the company they keep. Besides the intrinsic pleasure to be derived from solid knowledge, a woman ought to consider it as her best resource against poverty.' Lucie was born two years after the marriage.

Sarah was very busy looking after Lucie, encouraging her husband, helping Italian refugees who flocked to the Austin house, publishing translations of German classics and entertaining many radical friends, such as Sir Francis Burdett, Daniel O'Connell, Macaulay, Molesworth, Roebuck, Charles Buller, John Sterling, John Stuart Mill, Sydney Smith, Francis Jeffrey and John Austin's successful brother, Charles, who made £40,000 during a short time at the Bar and retired to enjoy life. 'It was', wrote *The Times*, 'as remarkable an assemblage of persons as ever met in a London drawing-room.'[2]

It was not however, much fun for the small Lucie who had to find her own amusements. 'She has an insatiable love of reading', wrote Sarah. 'Her original way of thinking will save her, I hope, from a trivial or vulgar taste. John Mill is ever my dearest child and friend and

[1] *Memoirs and Correspondence of Mrs John Taylor, Mrs Sarah Austin and Lady Duff Gordon*, by Janet Ross, 2 vols., John Murray, 1888.
[2] *The Times*, August 12 1867.

he really doats on Lucie, and can do anything with her. She is a monstrous great girl, but, though she has admirable qualities, I am not satisfied with her. She is too wild, undisciplined and independent; and though she knows a great deal, it is in a strange, wild way. She reads everything; composes German verses, has imagined and put together a fairy world, dress, language, music, everything and talks to them in the garden; but she is sadly negligent of her own appearance.' Lucie kept mice and canaries and collected newts from the Regent Canal or she played next door with John Stuart Mill or in Jeremy Bentham's garden, but had to be careful not to disturb the tapes which marked out his famous ideal prison. Inside the house her father would be arguing with Jeremy Bentham, who was then over eighty but still full of plans for reforming the world.

'From this early and intense loneliness probably sprung much of that independence and concentration of thought which marked the progressive stages of her rapidly maturing intellect,' wrote Lucie's friend Caroline Norton. 'A great reader, a great thinker, very original in her conclusions, very eager in impressing her opinions, her mind was not like those of many women, filled with echoes of other folks' sayings . . . From the aspect of nature, and the study of human nature such as she found it, she drew her unassisted lessons of knowledge. As life advanced, as the field of her experience widened, many of these conclusions became modified; and commerce with her kind taught her the wide indulgence and sympathy she afterwards showed for all who suffered or struggled in the up-hill labour of life.'[1] 'Perhaps no woman of our own time, except perhaps Mrs Somerville and Mrs Browning, in their different styles, combined so much erudition with so much natural ability.'[2]

Lucie learned German when she went with her parents to Bonn. Austin wanted to meet the German philosophers to prepare for the lectures he was to deliver at the newly founded University of London to which he had been appointed Professor of Jurisprudence. Austin's lectures, which he began to deliver in 1828, were packed with information but so over-elaborated that his pupils dwindled away until by November 1831 he had none left and resigned. 'That was', wrote Sarah later, 'the blow from which he never recovered; in a temper so little sanguine as his there could be no second spring.' He did, however,

---

[1] 'Lady Duff Gordon and her Works', by the Hon. Mrs Norton, *Macmillans Magazine*, Vol. 20, September 1869.
[2] *The Times*, July 26 1869.

manage to put together the first of his lectures in his book *The Province of Jurisprudence Determined* which was published in 1832, the year of the Reform Bill. To Lord Melbourne, it was 'the dullest book he had ever read and full of truism elaborately set forth', but to those who understood jurisprudence it was regarded as a most valuable contribution to the philosophy of law and legislation.

As John Austin had no salary the family moved to cheaper lodgings in Bayswater where Sarah continued to write and entertain. She was comforted by the friendship of Thomas and Jane Carlyle. 'To my wife', Carlyle wrote. 'I believe you are the best of all woman-kind; neither for me is there any figure in that huge city, whom I can remember with purer satisfaction . . . Continue to bear yourself like a brave, true woman, and know that friendly eyes and hearts are upon you . . . On the whole, my dear Heroine, there is no rest for us in this world which subsists by toil.' While Sarah was worrying about money and Lucie's education she became distracted by a strange love affair she carried on by post with Prince Hermann Puckler Muskau whom she had not met but whose book she had decided to translate;[1] it described a tour he had made of England, Ireland and France, a book which had been praised by Goethe and Heine. The Prince was a wild, amorous, adventurous and romantic figure owning the estates of Muskau, Groditz and Branitz which included the castle at Muskau and forty-five villages. He stood for many of the emotions and passions which Sarah had missed with John Austin and they wrote love letters to each other with remarkable freedom. But it was a worrying time for Sarah and she dreaded lest her letters to Hermann, whose reputation was none too high, might become known. 'I am half killed', she wrote, 'with expenses, anxiety, sorrow and physical fatigue. . . . If I were not high-spirited I could not go through with it and stand where I do in our purse-proud, aristocratic society.' In spite of the risk Sarah went on writing. 'I have the most intimate persuasion that we should live together in a sort of oneness such as is not to be found twice. I have all your tastes, animal, social, intellectual—above all, the urge for loving and being loved, *au suprême degré* and in that which is the life of life and the sense of my whole being, Oh! how have I been bitterly disappointed.' Lucie knew nothing of this romantic intrigue and wrote to the Prince in German thanking him for verses he had sent to her. 'Since I received them I have been to Cornwall and was very happy

---

[1] Sarah Austin called it *Tour of a German Prince* from the original four volumes, *Briefe eines Verstorbenen*, published 1830–31.

there. I have brought home a sweet little dove. Its mother was killed by a cat when it was only a few hours old and I have brought it up. Now he perches on my shoulder and chirps its love into my ear, for it loves me very much and I love it too'.

Lucie at twelve began to find friends of her own age and became very fond of Alice Spring-Rice, whose father, later Lord Monteagle, was in the Colonial Office; but she was to find that a wealthy and social family, such as the Spring-Rices, lived such a different life that it was not easy to maintain a friendship. Henry Taylor, who later married Alice Spring-Rice, observed of Lucie: 'She is upon the whole a very curious and interesting, dark, pale, twelve-year-old young lady, solid, independent and self-possessed. . . . She is rather handsome and very striking, with a stern, determined expression of countenance which might qualify her to sit for the picture of Cassandra or Clytemnestra.'

In 1833 a Royal Commission was appointed to draw up a digest of the criminal law and procedure and Austin was a member, but he was distressed because the commission's scope was so limited, for he considered it was necessary entirely to recast the criminal law which was, indeed, full of injustices. When that work was concluded the family was without sufficient means to live in England and Lucie, aged thirteen, went with them to live at Boulogne. Sydney Smith,[1] then over sixty, wrote on her departure: 'Lucie, Lucie, my dear child, don't tear your frocks: tearing frocks is not of itself a proof of genius. But write as your mother writes, act as your mother acts; be frank, loyal, affectionate, simple, honest, and then integrity or laceration of frocks is of little import. And Lucie, dear child, mind your arithmetic. You know in the first sum I ever saw there was a mistake. You carried two (as a cab is licensed to do), and you ought, dear Lucie, to have carried but one. Is this a trifle? What would life be without arithmetic but a scene of horrors? You are going to Boulogne, the city of debts, peopled by men who have never understood arithmetic. By the time you return, I shall probably have received my first paralytic stroke, and shall have lost all recollection of you. Therefore I now give you my parting advice—don't marry anyone who has not a tolerable understanding and a thousand a year. And God Bless you dear child.'

[1] Sydney Smith, 1771–1845, well known for his wit and trenchant writings on Catholic Emancipation and parliamentary reform; for many years he wrote brilliant articles for the *Edinburgh Review*, which he had helped to found and was its first editor.
Sarah Austin, who was devoted to him, edited an early edition of his letters in 1855—*A Memoir of the Reverend Sydney Smith by his daughter, Lady Holland, with a Selection of his letters edited by Mrs Austin.*

Sarah had been invited with her husband and Lucie to stay at Muskau castle; 'who knows what would happen', wrote Hermann. Sarah knew very well, and decided that she would have to put up with poverty in Boulogne and devote herself to her family. In Boulogne she was known as '*La Belle Anglaise*' and both she and Lucie were very popular with the fishermen; Sarah was admired, too, for her courage. One stormy night in December she and Lucie were called out because a large sailing ship was sinking off the shore; this was the *Amphitrite* taking women convicts to Botany Bay. They did what they could; Sarah dashed into the sea to rescue a drowning woman and helped to save three sailors who had been washed ashore insensible. As a mark of her bravery the Royal Humane Society presented her with the Life Saving Medal.

Lucie enjoyed her life with the fishermen; she had long talks with Heinrich Heine who was staying at the same inn and she wrote letters to Alice Spring-Rice on life, the theatre and religion: 'My family are all Unitarians, that is on my mother's side, and amongst them I got an idea of Christianity, but the Aunt that told me about it was a bigoted and intolerant Unitarian, and I thought to myself, if this religion is to produce hatred my own is better, for I believed that all good people of religion *quelconque* were acceptable to God. I got an intense love for Jesus Christ, whom I considered as the best man ever born and a great philosopher who had constructed the highest code of morality, which I determined to follow to the best of my power. I can *prier Dieu* just as well in one church or chapel as another, and I cannot say that I belong to any particular sect ... I daresay you have always heard religion spoken of as a thing to be believed in without a doubt and not to be reasoned upon, well, you must make allowances for the great difference in what I have heard.' Lucie loved Alice, and she knew that such letters on religion would shock her very devout friend but it was important to her to try to sort out her religious ideas. With Janet Shuttleworth who had been strictly brought up in the Church of England, Lucie had similar arguments: 'Really, dear Janet, our views are, and likely to remain, so entirely opposite, that it is but vanity and vexation of spirit to have any more discussion on the subject ...; my idea of the importance of *doctrines* is absolutely nothing.'

After nearly eighteen months in Boulogne her parents went to Malta in June 1836 and Lucie was sent to a boarding school at Bromley. John Austin had been chosen as a member of a Commission of two to inquire into Maltese grievances; the other commissioner was George Cornewall Lewis, later Chancellor of the Exchequer.

Sarah was welcomed by the Maltese who liked her friendly ways and she considered that much of the discontent 'arose from the insolence, prejudice and want of breeding of the English. If they bully, where they are on sufferance (as on the Continent), what will they do where *chaque petit employé se croit un roi.*' In the *Athenaeum* she wrote that 'the English offend by a cool indifference, a haughty ignorance'; she considered that the effect of English manners was more serious than was generally imagined 'and that a great deal of asperity has been added to the envy and jealousy excited by the commercial greatness of England, by the impertinent, sneering remarks, the affronting comparisons and the insolent wonder of purse-proud travellers. . . .' Later from the Cape and from Egypt it was always to her mother that Lucie wrote most freely about the attitude of English people abroad, for she knew that Sarah would understand and not be shocked.

Lucie at School

Lucie was fifteen when she went to school; the drawing of her done by a schoolfriend at the time gives her a Cassandra-like look. She missed her life of freedom—when she had been able to read and write what she wished and flirt with French fishermen—so that she found the restrictions at school almost unbearable. She was 'prodigiously dragooned' and not allowed to write even to her mother without Miss Shepherd, the headmistress, seeing her letters. But gradually she began to adapt herself to school life and to come to terms with Miss Shepherd and her own religious beliefs. Christmas 1837, when she was sixteen, she stayed for the holidays with Mrs and Mr North, who was Whig M.P. for Hastings and when their baby daughter, Catherine (later Mrs John Addington Symonds) was due to be baptized into the Church of England, Lucie decided, on her own responsibility, that she would also be baptized. Mrs North considered that she should wait to hear from her parents, but Lucie replied that she honoured her parents by confident trust that they would sanction her action, which they later did. But her Unitarian relations were furious and even Mrs Grote, to whom Lucie was devoted, wrote her a sarcastic and cutting letter. But Lucie was confident that if she had not taken the decision she would have 'probably remained in the same painfully unsatisfied state of mind' that had so long been hers.

Lucie spent many holidays with the Norths while her parents were in Malta and Marianne North (later the traveller and naturalist) who was then seven years old, wrote: 'The person who made the strongest impression on me was Lucie Austin . . . Her grand eyes and deep-toned voice, her entire fearlessness and contempt for what people thought of her, charmed me. Then she had a tame snake, and surely must have been more than a woman to tame a snake! She used to carry her pet about with her, wound round her arm (inside the large baggy sleeves which were then the fashion), and it would put its slender head out of the wrist hole, and lap milk out of the palm of her hand with its little forked tongue . . . Sometimes Lucie would twist the pretty bronze creature in the great plait of her hair she wore round her head, and once she threatened to come down to a dinner-party of rather stiff people, thus decorated, and only gave it up when my mother entreated her with tears in her eyes not to do so. She used to sit for hours together in a rocking-chair reading Shakespeare to us, and acting and declaiming her favourite parts over and over again, till I knew them by heart myself, and Beatrice and Portia became my personal friends.'

Sarah wrote a number of letters from Malta to ask for help and advice from Mr Nassau Senior,[1] who had been a member of the Poor Law Commission of 1832, and it was arranged that Lucie should go to stay with them during some of her holidays. 'She was tall, handsome, precocious and self-confident', wrote Miss Senior of Lucie, 'but so good-natured and amusing that we submitted willingly to her temporary rule.'[2]

Marriage

In July 1838 the Austins returned from Malta after two years as a change of Government in England had brought the work of the Commission to a close, but nearly every measure recommended was adopted.[3] That summer Lucie left school and began to go to balls in

---

[1] Some of Sarah Austin's informative letters from Malta are published in *Three Generations of English Women* by Janet Ross. When she arrived there was only one school in the island and when she left two years later her activity resulted in an increase to ten. The poverty was terrible 'where marriage is so criminally and disgustingly early and so dreadfully prolific'. There was great ignorance about hygiene and disease and four thousand died of cholera while she was there; she was thankful that Lucie had not come with them.

[2] *Many Memories of Many People*, by M. C. M. Simpson, London 1898.

[3] 'No Commission ever did its work more carefully, and its reports to the Colonial Office are remarkable papers, dealing with great ability and thoroughness with some of the most important questions of political economy and jurisprudence';—Dictionary of National Biography. (John Austin.)

London. At her first ball at Lansdowne House she met Sir Alexander Duff Gordon;[1] they fell in love and were married on May 16 1840 when Lucie was nearly nineteen and Alexander was twenty-nine. There had been some delay because the Dowager Lady Gordon had at first opposed the marriage of her son to a young woman with no dowry; John Austin was against it as he was ill and nervous, and Alexander had very little money being a clerk in the Treasury. 'Alexander has nothing', wrote Sarah, 'but a small salary, his handsome person, excellent and sweet character, and his title (a great misfortune).' After marriage they went to live at No. 8 Queen Square, not far from where Lucie had been brought up as a child.

The Duff Gordons were a handsome and hospitable couple with many friends. Tennyson used to come and read his poems and he was later to say that he was thinking of Lucie when he wrote *The Princess* because of her beauty and erudition; Sydney Smith used to visit them, Macaulay, Charles Austin, Tom Moore, Henry Reeve, Dickens, Thackeray, Dicky Doyle, and Tom Taylor, later Editor of Punch. Lucie liked especially to hear accounts of travel and William Kinglake was often at her house describing his impressions of the Middle East which were to be published in his book *Eothen*. 'The classical form of her features', he wrote of Lucie, 'the noble poise of her head and neck, her stately height, her uncoloured yet pure complexion, caused some of the beholders to call her beauty statuesque, and others to call it majestic, some pronouncing it even to be imperious. But she was so intellectual, so keen, so autocratic, sometimes even so impassioned in speech, that nobody, feeling her powers, could well go on feebly comparing her to a mere Queen or Empress.'

Having at first only a small income, the Duff Gordons lived happily and quietly, a rather bohemian life for those days; sometimes they went to dinner with Lord Lansdowne who admired Lucie for her 'sense and beauty', and Lucie would go also to take part in charades at Charles Dickens', or to a theatre with Caroline Norton and Lord Melbourne. But a great deal of their evenings were spent in reading and writing, for Alexander shared Lucie's interest in German literature and was himself a good scholar of German. Lucie began to make a little money by writing, and translated Barthold Niebuhr's *Stories of the Gods and Heroes of Greece*—the stories Niebuhr used to tell his small son with

---

[1] He was son of Sir William Duff Gordon who married Caroline, daughter of Sir George Cornewall, and grandson of William Gordon, 2nd earl of Aberdeen, who had married Anne, daughter of Alexander the 2nd Duke of Gordon.

whom Lucie had played thirteen years before when she was in Germany with her parents; the book was published under her mother's name in 1842, the year that her daughter Janet was born.

In 1844 John Murray published Lucie's translation of Wilhelm Meinhold's *Maria Schweidler die Bernsteinhexe*, under the title *Mary Schweidler: The Amber Witch*, which went through three impressions in the first year. Lucie's translation was used in the 1927 edition of the World's Classic series. 'It is of its kind a masterpiece', wrote Mr J. W. Mackail in the Preface, 'and the translator was one of the most remarkable women of the time; . . . she achieved a rarity, a translation equal, and in some respects, superior to the original.' Lucie was very thorough and studied all she could find about witchcraft in the seventeenth century before embarking on her translation. The next year her *French in Algiers* was published in Murray's Colonial and Home Library.[1] She was also working on a long German book by Anselm Ritter von Feuerbach in which this well-known judge and legislator set out the interesting criminal cases which had come within his experience. The cases had a bearing on the need for law reform and she read through numbers of the *Law Magazine* and the liberal Quarterlies which dealt with this question; she consulted her father who had always regretted his inability to make the first Commission on Criminal Law more effective. 'The reader', wrote Lucie in her preface to her selection from Feuerbach's *Remarkable Criminal Trials*, 'who may be inclined altogether to condemn this German prolixity and deliberation of the Bavarian system of justice, should remember that in the year 1827 no fewer than six persons, who had been convicted of capital crimes at the Old Bailey and left for execution, were proved to be innocent and saved by the zeal and activity of the Sheriff.' The *Law Magazine* wrote in a review of the book which appeared in 1846: 'the present collection of criminal cases form, as far as we are aware, the most interesting specimen existing in our language.'

With her very full social life and her translation work, one wonders how much time she was able to spare for her daughter, Janet. When Janet was three, however, there arrived in the house, much to her delight, a jet black Nubian boy of about twelve years of age, Hassan el-Bakkeet, known as Hatty, who had been taken as a slave. He had

---

[1] The first part is an account by a young Lieutenant in the Oldenburg service, Clemens Lamping, who went to Algeria in 1839 and joined the Foreign Legion; the second part is the story of five months captivity with the Arabs of Algeria by a Lieutenant in the French Navy, de Franco.

learned good English, rather Biblical in style, from British missionaries who had found him; somehow he had become 'owned' by one of the Italian refugees who were befriended by Sarah Austin and Hassan used to bring notes from his master to the Austins and to the Duff Gordons. The Italian had turned him out of doors when it appeared that he was going blind and Hassan sought refuge with Lucie, known to have a kind heart for anyone in trouble. She took him into her service and had his eyes cured by a good oculist, who was so impressed by his intelligence and charm that he offered him £12 a year and a scarlet uniform to take service with him. Lucie advised him to accept what was then a good offer, but Hatty threw himself at her feet and tearfully begged her not to send him away from her. He remained in Lucie's household until he died in Alexander's arms from congestion of the lungs on Christmas Day 1850.

Hatty became a well-known character in the Duff-Gordon's house and was popular with everyone. When Lucie brought into her household a girl who had had an illegitimate baby she assembled the servants and warned them that anyone would be instantly dismissed who was unkind to the girl because of her difficulties. 'Poor Hassan', wrote Kinglake, 'small, black as jet, but possessing an idea of the dignity of his sex, conceived it his duty to become the spokesman of the household, and, accordingly, advancing a little in front of the neat-aproned, tall, wholesome maidservants, he promised in his and their name a full and careful obedience to his mistress's order; then wringing his hands and raising them above his head he added: "What a lesson to us all, milady." ' When Lucie gave birth to a second child, Hatty announced triumphantly to all callers, 'we have a boy', but the baby died within a few months.

To Janet, Hassan was her 'beloved playfellow' and Lucie and Alexander were devoted to him. 'I distinctly recollect', wrote Janet later,[1] 'Mr Hilliard, the American author, being shocked at seeing me in Hatty's arms, and my rage when he asked my mother how she could let a negro touch her child. Whereupon she called us to her, and kissed me first and Hatty afterwards.' Later when Hatty was ill in bed the doctor ordered leeches to be applied to his chest and Lucie instructed a newly recruited maid what she was to do. 'Lawks, my lady,' she replied in horror, 'I could not touch either of them'. 'I can see now', wrote Janet, 'the look of pitying scorn with which my mother turned from the girl, which softened into deep affection as she bent over

[1] *The Fourth Generation. Reminiscences,* by Janet Ross, Constable, 1912.

Hatty, and with her white hands placed the leeches on his black chest.'

In 1846 Alexander nearly died of cholera and Lucie became very nervous about his health which was never particularly good. To help him recover Lord Lansdowne lent the Duff Gordons his villa at Richmond, which was, wrote Lucie, 'Bowood on a diminished scale'; Hassan was 'an inch taller for our grandeur—*peu s'en faute*, he thinks me a great lady and himself a great butler'. The Duff Gordons were able to entertain more while there; Mary and Agnes Berry lived near, Nassau Senior came for week-ends, Landseer, Eastlake, Dwarkanauth Tagore, Kinglake and others. Kinglake left them to visit Algeria 'where', wrote Lucie, 'he hopes to join Abd-el-Kader if possible'. She arranged for him to visit her parents who were living in Paris and wrote to her mother: 'He is both shy and reserved. But when the ice is broken he is very amusing, and he nursed Alick and cheered me with the gentleness and kindness of a woman.'

To celebrate Janet's fifth birthday the next year there was a dinner party at the Duff Gordons' house in Queen Square with Lord Lansdowne, Thackeray, Tom Taylor, Richard Doyle, Caroline Norton and C. J. Bayley who was lodging with the Duff Gordons and was known for his hard-hitting leading articles in *The Times*. Janet was rather spoilt, brought up as she was among her parents' friends who all petted her. She used to climb on to Macaulay's knee and tell him to talk which he needed no invitation to do; she told Carlyle not to be rude to her mother; Thackeray gave her her first oyster at the age of five and she insisted on having two more of his; and Dicky Doyle drew pictures for her, such as Orpheus taming the animals with his music.

Caroline Norton was especially admired by Janet who wrote, 'no one could tell a story better, and then it gained so much by being told in that rich, low-toned voice'. Lucie admired her wit, independence and beauty and was angered at the way that society had treated her after the Melbourne case.[1] The Duff Gordons always refused to go to any party to which Caroline had not been invited, if the Melbourne case was the reason for not inviting her.

William Lamb, 2nd Viscount Melbourne, had had many troubles including his marriage to another Caroline from whom he had separated in 1825 after her notorious affair with Byron. At the time that Lucie used to go out to dinner and theatre parties with Caroline Norton and Lord Melbourne, he was unhappy at having lost the premiership in 1841 and because he was no longer in close contact with Queen Victoria; the one thing he dreaded was being bored, but with Caroline and Lucie he enjoyed himself. Lucie took pleasure in his company because, as Greville wrote of him he was 'a keen observer of the follies and vices of mankind, taking the world as he found it, and content to extract as much pleasure and diversion as he could from it'.

One evening that the three of them spent together Melbourne failed to be amused. He had invited Caroline and Lucie to a box at the St. James's Theatre to see Charles Dickens' production of Ben Jonson's *Every Man in his Humour;* Dickens was to take the chief part of Bobadil and London society was eager to have tickets. Lucie had been invited to dinner by Dickens, a few nights before the final production, because there had been a quarrel with Thackeray, and Dickens wanted her, as a mutual friend, to use her influence to smooth things over before the night of the performance. Thackeray was hurt because he had offered to sing during the intervals between the acts and no one

[1] Caroline Norton was one of the three beautiful grand-daughters of Richard Brinsley Sheridan. In 1827, at the age of seventeen, she married a Tory, George Norton, who quarrelled with her over politics, as she was a staunch Whig, and also made life unbearable for her in the home. In 1836 London society was shocked by an action brought by George Norton against Lord Melbourne, the Prime Minister, on the charge of seducing his wife, but there was no case and the jury had no difficulty in deciding against Norton. Wives, however, were not allowed in those days to make any statement to the Court or have Counsel and sufficient gossip had been reported in Court to lead to Caroline being ostracized by many in society.

had wanted him to; it had also been reported that Dickens' friend, John Forster, had described Thackeray as 'false as hell'. The quarrel between the rival novelists might have been embarrassing to both if it had continued, but Lucie succeeded in calming everyone down. She and Caroline enjoyed Ben Jonson's play but Melbourne was very restless and during the first interval he exclaimed in a loud voice, which could be heard throughout the theatre, 'I knew this play would be dull, but that it should be so damnably dull as this, I did not suppose. '

Caroline and Lucie saw a great deal of each other, having much in common. 'Both were used to the conversation of brilliant and distinguished men; both had wider interests than the ordinary run of their contemporaries. Also, they both loved literature and the arts . . . But it was for the nobility of her character that Caroline loved her. Lady Duff Gordon was very unselfish and sympathetic. The wish to help was the mainspring of her existence.'[1] But that did not mean that she went out of her way to look for the poor and the destitute. She led a normal family and social life. Like her father and mother she enjoyed conversation and could even out-talk Carlyle on German literature; these friends who came to the Duff Gordon house were great talkers, too—Macaulay, Sydney Smith and Charles Austin—and she would go to the Sunday breakfasts presided over by Samuel Rogers at his house in St James's Place where conversation lasted sometime until lunch-time. Rogers was a better host than poet. 'When he is delivered of a couplet with infinite labour and pain,' wrote Sydney Smith, 'he takes to his bed, has straw laid down, the knocker tied up, expects his friends to call and make enquiries, and the answer at the door invariably is: "Mr Rogers and his little couplet are as well as can be expected". '

Lucie did not suffer from the stresses and strains that Sarah underwent in supporting a home and encouraging her husband. Sarah had lost much of her former gaiety and Kinglake remarked, rather unkindly, that 'a joke of any kind was to her a detestable interruption of serious reasoning'. Sarah became more and more earnest about trying to improve the world, a matter on which Lucie was not indifferent but did not feel that it was her business, though she spoke out vehemently against injustices. Lucie found enjoyment in being with people of every walk in life, while Sarah, for her husband's sake and because of their poverty, considered that she had to cultivate men of influence.

[1] *Caroline Norton,* by Alice Ackland, Constable 1948.

The Austins had had to move abroad and Sydney Smith wrote that he considered that Sarah, from what she told him, had too many distinguished people in her Paris Salon and he would have preferred more of a mixture. Heinrich Heine persuaded his publisher, Herr Laube, to come with him to Sarah Austin's 'famous' salon, where he might even meet Guizot, the Prime Minister, 'and you have no idea how proud he is. When he goes up to Heaven he will start by complimenting the Almighty on having created him so well'. But the revolution of 1848 changed everything; Louis Philippe lost his throne and Guizot had to flee to England disguised as someone's servant. The Austins, too, had to leave and Guizot sought refuge at the Duff Gordon's house in London.

John Austin had been horrified by what he had seen of mob violence in Paris and had turned away from his early radicalism. 'I can assure you that my fear of socialism (or communism) is anything but fanciful', he wrote to Lucie. 'The socialist tendencies in England, though less flagrant [than in France] are sufficiently manifest . . . Look at the language held by Lord Ashley and other of our ignorant humanitarians; language calculated to persuade the workmen that their privations and severe labour are caused by the selfishness of their masters.' Sarah was not prepared to go as far as that; nor did either she or John Austin approve of such injustices as the transportation to Australia in 1834 of the six farm labourers of Tolpuddle for forming a Trade Union. But Sarah, too, had changed many of her radical views, having been, with her husband, 'too near witness of terrific political convulsions not to have modified many opinions and questioned many axioms'.

Lucie, however, considered that much of the resentment among the working classes was, indeed, due to the attitude of the employers and to the injustice of the laws against the Trade Unions. She had faith in the people, whereas her parents had become apprehensive of the mob after what they had witnessed abroad. Lucie came to know the men in the workshops at Bow run by a friend, William Bridges Adams, and started a library there. When the Chartist march on London in 1848 caused panic among some of the citizens, forty of the men from the workshops came to the Duff Gordon's house to see that no harm came to 'their lady'. While Alexander patrolled the streets having enrolled as a special constable, there was a supper party of cold beef and beer with songs and speeches at Queen Square. 'I never wish to see forty better gentlemen', commented Lucie.

23

In March 1849 Lucie gave birth to a son, Maurice, and Caroline Norton was asked to be godmother; she accepted in a letter in which she drew a 'design to replace the statue of Queen Anne on the wall of the house of Sir Alex. D. Gordon Bart', and signed it Flaxman. Soon after the birth of Maurice, Lucie became ill and the Duff Gordons moved out of London to stay with John and Sarah Austin in a cottage at Weybridge, where Lucie nearly died of bronchitis and intermittent fever. The Duff Gordons then moved to Esher and Lucie wrote to C. J. Bayley, who had been appointed as Secretary to the Government of Mauritius: 'We have moved all our goods and ourselves to a very nice, pretty, old-fashioned house on the very top of a high hill close to Claremont, which indeed joins our garden and field, and where bachelor beds can be given to our friends. I only wish you were installed in one of them, dear Lodger, for if a constant longing to see you and have your company again constitutes being very much in love, as you seem to think, I also must "own the soft impeachment" . . . Your place as lodger is now filled by Azimullah Khan [an emissary of Nana Sahib who was later one of the leaders in the Indian Mutiny]. He calls me his European Mother as the civillest thing he can say! When do you think you will come back and resume your duties as a lodger? I have pretty maids, and Janet will be old enough to flirt with by the time you return . . . I fear you would think me very much altered since my illness; I have lost much of my hair, all my complexion and all my flesh and look thin and old and my hair is growing grey. This I consider hard on a woman just over her thirtieth birthday'.

Consumption had begun to take a hold on her but she continued to lead an active life entertaining friends at her house, known as 'The Gordon Arms', translating books, riding about the countryside with Alexander. She was very distressed in January 1852 when news came of the death of their friend, Eliot Warburton (author of *The Crescent and the Cross*), on board a ship called the *Amazon* which caught fire at sea. 'Kinglake, too, is terribly cut up', wrote Alexander to his mother. 'He was such a joyous fellow and one cannot associate anything so horrid as a long lingering agony with him . . . He was seen on deck, dressed and assisting the Captain, by some men who escaped in one of the boats'. A long time later there arrived a drawing of Lucie made by a schoolfriend, which Warburton had kept and which he asked someone who was leaving in one of the boats to send to the family.

Henry W. Phillips, who had fallen down the stairs at Waterloo station and broken his knee-cap, came to stay with the Duff Gordons and painted a portrait of Lucie. 'Phillips has made a glorious picture of Lucie which yesterday he bestowed upon me', wrote Alexander to his mother. 'He will just finish it in time for the exhibition and tomorrow Watts comes to inspect and advise upon it. We have also struck up a friendship with Layard, who is most pleasant and seems to take amazingly to the "Gordon Arms" and ours *sans façon* way of life.'[1] Phillips stayed four months off and on and Alexander considered that he had been much improved 'by living with a family, seeing the necessity of giving way to others, being bored by children etc. which,

[1] Henry Layard, the discoverer of Nimrud and Nineveh, had just resigned from his post as Under-Secretary of State for Foreign Affairs, a post he had held under Lord John Russell, the Prime Minister, and Lord Granville, Foreign Minister. In February Palmerston had defeated Russell over the Militia Bill, part of the defence against a possible invasion of England by Louis Napoleon.

otherwise, a single man—completely his own master—could never have seen. He looks with horror at living a bachelor life again'.

In 1854 when Gladstone was succeeded as Chancellor of the Exchequer by Sir George Cornewall Lewis, there was rejoicing at the 'Gordon Arms' because Lewis appointed his cousin, Alexander, as his secretary; this meant more money and an interesting post. The Crimean War, however, cast a shadow on all and Lucie regretted the absence of Kinglake visiting the Crimea to consider writing an account and to defend the British Commander-in-Chief, Lord Raglan, who was bitterly attacked by the Press for the conduct of the war. 'Flesh and blood cannot endure the incessant baiting', wrote Sarah Austin. 'The next despotism the world will have to undergo is that of the Press.'

Lucie heard another side of the story from Layard, who had visited the Crimea with Kinglake and Delane of *The Times*. Both Layard and Delane were violent critics of the Aberdeen Government for its management of the war. One of Lucie's friends was Monsieur Joly de Bammeville, who came to stay with the Duff Gordons in 1855 and assured them that within eighteen months there would be a mutiny in India. He knew a number of prominent Indians, who had visited the Crimea and had been so impressed by the talk of the British officers there about the disastrous state of the British army, that they were returning to India certain that the moment had come to revolt against the British Raj. Bammeville was a remarkable man, a great linguist and connoisseur of art; Alexander was so interested by his story that he informed Lord Palmerston, who had succeeded Aberdeen as Prime Minister in February 1855, but Palmerston took no notice. After peace had been declared in 1856 Alexander was given the post of Commissioner of Inland Revenue which meant travelling for about a month to six weeks each year. The Duff Gordons made a number of journeys to Paris to see their friends.

Lucie used to visit there a friend whom she had met as a child at Boulogne, Heinrich Heine, and wrote a moving account of her visits to him for Monckton Milnes (Lord Houghton). 'I, for my part could hardly speak to him, so shocked was I by his appearance. He lay on a pile of mattresses, his body wasted so that it seemed no bigger than a child under the sheet that covered him . . . His voice was weak and I was astonished by the animation with which he talked; evidently his mind had wholly survived his body. He raised his powerless eye-lids with his thin white fingers, and exclaimed: *"Gott! die kleine Lucie ist gross geworden, und hat einen Mann; dass ist eigen!"* (God! little Lucie has grown up, and has a husband; that is odd!)' Some time later she saw him two or three times a week during a two months' stay in Paris. ' "I have now made peace with the whole world", said Heine, "and at last also with God, who sends thee to me as a beautiful angel of death: I shall certainly soon die" . . . He said that what he liked so much was that I laughed so heartily, which the French could not do . . . He had so little feeling for what I liked best in the French that I could see he must have lived only with those who "sit in the scorner's seat"; whereas, while he laughed at Germany, it was with *des larmes dans la voix*. He also talked a good deal about his religious feelings; much displeased at the reports that he had turned Catholic . . . The impression he made on me was so deep, that I had great difficulty to restrain my tears till I had left the room the last few times I saw him, and shall never forget the sad, pale face and eager manner of poor Heine.'

In 1857, the year of the Indian Mutiny, the Duff Gordons let their house at Esher because they were overdrawn at the bank and went for several months to Paris where they lived in the Rue Chaillot. They then were visited by friends of the family such as Victor Cousin, Alfred de Vigny, Barthelmy St Hilaire, Auguste Comte, who died at the end of that year, and Leon de Wailly, whose *Stella and Vanessa* Lucie had translated and published in 1850. The Emperor, Louis Napoleon, who had been hospitably received by the Duff Gordons when he was in exile in London, several times offered to put one of his carriages at her disposal, but Lucie, and most of her French friends, strongly disapproved of the way he had come to power, and she always refused.

In 1858 Lucie gave birth to another child, Urania, who was to die at the age of nineteen, eight years after Lucie's death in 1869.

Lucie often visited her parents at Weybridge and found her father gloomy: 'I fear it is his normal state.' 'It is true that he was shamefully treated', wrote Sarah to Guizot, 'but you and I know that there is another way of avenging oneself on the injustice of men . . . He is to me sometimes as a god, sometimes as a sick and wayward child—an immense, powerful and beautiful machine, without the balance-wheel, which should keep it going constantly, evenly and justly.' Sarah had begun to work on the notes of his lectures and had been given £100 a year on the Civil List for her work on behalf of education, but she had changed many of her views. 'Poor France! Poor Germany!', she wrote to Gladstone. 'What is the result of their so excellent seeming systems? An ounce of education demanded is worth a pound imposed. This, you will observe, is a voluntary recantation on the part of the

zealous translator of Cousin.[1] I cannot say it costs me much, for it involves the recognition of the unspeakable superiority of England.' She was overwhelmed by her husband's death in 1859 at the age of seventy, and found little comfort in Lucie or her grandchildren. 'Children, dear as they are', she wrote, 'belong necessarily to another generation and another order of ideas and feeling.'

Lucie had spent many nights by her dying father 'as white as marble, her face set and stern, and her large eyes fixed on his face'. She had a great admiration for him and his death was a great blow to her; her vigils in the damp cottage at Weybridge hastened her consumption.

For three more years the 'Gordon Arms' at Esher remained a cheerful meeting place and Dicky Doyle drew a coat of arms depicting Alexander and Lucie on horseback with barrels of beer and the cigars that Lucie smoked to ease her cough. 'The hospitable house at Esher

[1] *Report on the State of Public Instruction in Prussia*, 1834, from the French of Victor Cousin.

gave its warm welcome', wrote George Meredith, 'not merely to men and women of distinction; the humble undistinguished were made joyous guests there . . . She [Lucie] had the laugh that rocks the frame, but it was usually with a triumphant smile that she greeted things good to the ear: and her manner of telling was concise, on the lines of the running subject, to carry it along, not to produce an effect . . . Quotation came when it sprang to the lips and was native. She was shrewd and cogent, invariably calm in argument, sitting over it, not making it a duel, as the argumentative are prone to do; and a strong point scored against her received the honours due to a noble enemy . . . While health was still with her there was one house where men and women conversed, when that house perforce was closed a light had gone out in our country.'

George Meredith came to live in a cottage near the Duff Gordons soon after separation from his wife, the daughter of Thomas Love Peacock. He had a great admiration for Lucie and described her in his novel *Evan Harrington*, or *He Would Be a Gentleman*, as it was first called when published in serial form; she was Lady Jocelyn and Janet was Rose, her daughter, the heroine of the novel; while Evan was George Meredith. Janet was then seventeen, very handsome and a good rider, while Meredith was thirty with a fine head which Rosetti had used as a model for one of his pictures of Christ. He was very much attached to Janet, perhaps in love with her, and they would go for long walks and discuss the novel; Janet knew that she was the heroine of it and after reading the story as it progressed, she would comment as to whether she would or would not have done or said what Meredith had written. The story is an elaboration of the difficulty that Evan Harrington, the son of a tradesman (as was Meredith), encountered in asking Rose to marry him. The question as to who was or was not a gentleman was much discussed at that time when members of the aristocracy were shocked at the way men with money from the middle classes were infiltrating into their society. But Lady Jocelyn did not think in these terms and it was not she, but the many relations who reacted violently against the idea of Rose marrying a tradesman's son. Rose in the novel tells Evan that her mother would forgive anything but lying: 'She will be our friend; she will never forsake us Evan, if we do not deceive her. Oh! Evan it never is of any use. But deceive her, and she cannot forgive you. It is not in her nature . . . You know she is called a philosopher; nobody knows how deep-hearted she is though. My mother is as true as steel.'

To Meredith, the Duff Gordons appeared as aristocrats; to people like Janet and the Rev. Henry Brookfield, who were sensitive to shades of class and the proprieties, the Duff Gordons were uncomfortably bohemian and had strange friends. After dinner at the 'Gordon Arms' Brookfield remarked that he had been a little shocked that Lady Duff Gordon should have herself dressed the salad in the kitchen. Lucie did not bother what sort of impression she made and had no desire to pose as an aristocrat. She was, indeed, critical of the arrogance of the 'upper classes', though there were exceptions such as Lord Lansdowne and Sidney Herbert. When at school she had been angered by the sudden coldness towards her shown by her former friend Alice Spring-Rice and she complained in a letter to Mrs Grote that another friend, Janet Shuttleworth, had been treated in much the same way though not quite so churlishly, 'for though she is too radical for them, she is an heiress of very tolerable family . . . But I do not accuse them, it is the fault of their station; it is what one must always be prepared for if one has anything to do with aristocrats. Mamma will think so too one day, though she would not be pleased at my entertaining such an opinion now'.

For those who did not know her well, it was not easy to assess where the beautiful and imperious Lucie stood in society. At a party at Lansdowne House a well-known clairvoyant, called Alexis, was having a great success reading thoughts and telling guests what kind of house each lived in. He told Lucie that she was thinking of Julius Caesar or Alexander the Great; no, she was thinking of her faithful black Hassan; when he described her house as like Lansdowne House with huge rooms and fine pictures, she laughed and told him that it was rather small and bourgeois. Alexis was annoyed and said that she lacked faith.

Her independence and refusal to be guided by the conventions meant that she had many detractors, mainly among women. 'In the circles named "upper" there was mention of women unsexing themselves', wrote Meredith. 'She preferred the society of men on the plain ground that they discuss matters of weight and are—the pick of them—of open speech, more liberal, more genial, better comrades.' He pointed out, however, that her intimate friendships were with women as well as men. 'The closest friend of this most manfully-minded of women was one of her sex, little resembling her, except in downright truthfulness, lovingness and heroic fortitude.'

This was a reference to Caroline Norton whom he had met on one occasion at the Duff Gordons and had heard much about her sad and dramatic life from Lucie; but she certainly did not give him the information which he was later to use in a novel about Caroline— *Diana of the Crossways*. If Lucie had been alive she would not have let him revive an old and untrue political scandal that Caroline Norton had 'betrayed' a cabinet secret in December 1845 to Delane of *The Times* who published an article, which caused a sensation, that Robert Peel's Cabinet had decided to repeal the Corn Laws.[1]

Lucie Duff Gordon was portrayed as Lady Dunsborough, an older friend and confidante of Diana, but without the liveliness and understanding of Lady Jocelyn in *Evan Harrington* and without the main springs of Lucie's character—independence and sympathy. Caroline Norton wrote of her: 'From the hours of her lone childhood to the hour of her lonelier death, the idea of not "lending a hand" when help of any sort was in her power, never appears to have crossed her imagination.' Perhaps the most striking example of this was during an epidemic at Luxor when there had been several deaths and much serious illness through stoppage of the bowels: she and Omar visited the sick in their huts administering enemas and saved many lives as a result of this practical help. 'The *lavement* machine I brought was an inspiration', she wrote. She also held unconventional views on sex.

Some of the qualities Lucie admired had been possessed by her father. She wrote of a woman friend, Jane Lewis; 'She is one of those rare people whom I especially love; those natures who seem truly "unspotted from the world"—and incapable of contamination— people whose instincts are wise and pure somehow independently of their intellects, and always walk in the straight path. I hope that Maurice [her son] has inherited that from my dear father, even if he has not his mental gifts.'

Lucie was distressed at Maurice's aversion to reading and study; she wrote to Alexander that other Etonians of Maurice's age, whom she had met doing the Nile tour, 'have exactly the same baronial view of life and hate the "cads" who are base enough to read books'. Maurice's

---

[1] The novel was also based on a story that Caroline and Sidney Herbert, before he married Elizabeth Ashe A'Court, had been lovers and that Herbert, who was Secretary at War in Peel's Cabinet in 1845, had given her the information about the repeal of the laws. Herbert, who became Lord Herbert of Lea, died in 1861 and Caroline Norton in 1877, before the novel was published in 1885; but Caroline's nephew, Lord Dufferin then Ambassador in Paris, and others made it known publicly that Caroline had not in any way been responsible for the leakage of secret information, and Meredith was obliged to insert a notice to that effect in later editions.

31

comment was that he enjoyed being with his mother but was rather ashamed that she was considered to be an intellectual: 'Why, you know, even the Governor', he told Lucie, 'says you talk like a blue-stocking.'

*   *   *

By the winter of 1861 Lucie was at times in great pain and had become so ill at Esher that the doctor advised that she should go abroad to try to recover her health in a warmer climate. It meant the break up of her home for a while at least and there was the problem of her baby Urania, but Lucie's aunt, Charlotte Austin, offered to look after her. Alexander was travelling a good deal as Inspector of Inland Revenue, Maurice was at Eton and Janet had become engaged at the age of eighteen to Henry Ross, who was twenty-two years her senior and a year older than Lucie, having been born in Malta in 1820. Ross had been a merchant and traveller in Mesopotamia where he had helped Henry Layard excavate Nimrud; in 1860 he was a Director of Briggs Bank in Alexandria. Friends were surprised at the engagement of the flighty and handsome Janet; her own account is very matter of fact. 'I took Mr Ross out with the Duc d'Aumale's harriers and was much impressed by his admirable riding, his pleasant conversation, and his kindly ways. The result was that I promised to marry him, to the dismay of many of my friends, who did not at all approve of my going to live in Egypt'.[1] They were married in December 1860.

Lucie did not follow her daughter to Egypt then, as Janet had hoped she would, but decided that she would visit South Africa, which was considered to be a good climate for those suffering from lung trouble. She hoped that she would get well enough to be able to settle once more with her family and friends in England, but, in fact, it was exile for eight years with only occasional visits home during the summer. It was a sad parting from husband, mother and children, especially from her baby daughter, Urania. On July 21 1861 Lucie sailed for the Cape with her maid Sally Naldrett and a goat to give milk in a new ship of 1200 tons register, the *St Lawrence*.

Her story for the next year, until her return to England in July 1862,

[1] Henry Ross's niece, Lina Duff Gordon, was later to write more enthusiastically: 'The quick determination of my uncle's mind, his calm, wide outlook on men and events together with a keen insight into the character of Orientals, and a love of everything beautiful upon earth, made his talk of unique interest and charm.'—Epilogue to *Letters from the East, 1837–1857* by Henry James Ross, London, 1902

is told in her lively letters to her family full of fine descriptions of the beauty of the country and shrewd comments on the Dutch, British, Kaffirs, Hottentots and Malays. The family found these letters so interesting that they asked if she would agree to publication. At first Lucie was taken aback by the idea and wrote to her husband: 'you must have fallen into second childhood to think of *printing* such rambling, hasty scrawls as I write. I never could write a good letter, and unless I gallop ahead as hard as I can and don't stop to think, I can say nothing, so all is confused and unconnected; only I fancy *you* will be amused by some of my impressions'. Eventually she decided that, as they were short of money with the expense of her journey and with Maurice at Eton, Alexander should ask George Meredith for his advice. 'The Cape Diary', he wrote, 'is immensely amusing and shews her fine manly nature admirably.' The letters were published and were very popular, reaching a far wider public than her careful translations, because she wrote as she talked and she talked eloquently. In spite of ill-health and separation from her friends and family she was immensely interested in all she saw. 'To those who think voyages and travels tiresome', she wrote home, 'my delight in the new birds and beasts and people must seem very stupid. I can't help it if it does, and am not ashamed to confess that I feel the old sort of enchanted wonder with which I used to read Cook's voyages and the like, as a child.'

Lucie Duff Gordon herself conveys that enchanted wonder in her accounts; the voyage and the climate gave her new life. 'No one *can* conceive what it is, after two years of prison and utter languor, to stand on top of a mountain pass and enjoy physical existence for a few hours at a time. I felt it was quite selfish to enjoy anything so much when you were all so anxious about me at home.'

On the voyage from London to the Cape, which took two months, it would have been difficult for a stranger to realize how ill Lucie had been and still was. She and Sally were among the very few passengers who enjoyed the rough seas. Lucie continued to smoke the cigars she liked and was in the dining-room for her meals even in the roughest weather. The Captain told her she was a great help to him as she set an example in punctuality and discipline. Her cabin was 'water-tight as to big splashes but damp and dribbling' and she felt 'almost ashamed to like such miseries so much. The forecastle is under water with every lurch, and the motion quite incredible to one only acquainted with steamers. If one can sit this ship, which bounds like a tiger, one should be able to sit any leap over a haystack. Evidently I can never be sea-sick, but holding on is hard work and writing harder ...

'We had a most stormy voyage, and I recommend a fortnight's heavy gale in the South Atlantic, lat. 34 or so S., and long. 25, as the best cure for a blasé state of mind. It can't be described;—the sound, the sense of being hurled along utterly regardless of "side uppermost", the beauty of the whole scene, and the occasional crack and bear-away of sails and spars; the officer trying to "sing out" quite in vain, and the boatswain's whistle quite inaudible. I got lashed near the wheel for as long as I could bear it every day and was enchanted . . . For three days we ran under close-reefed (four reefs) topsails before a sea, which Sally said looked like Oxshott hills. The gale in the Bay of Biscay was a little shaking up in a puddle (a dirty one) compared to that glorious South Atlantic in all its majestic fury. The intensely blue waves, crowned with fantastic crests of bright emeralds, and with spray blowing about like wild dishevelled hair, came after us to swallow us up at a mouthful, but took us up on their backs, and hurried us along as if our ship were a cork.'

During a collision with a large ship Sally was 'as cool as an icicle' and Lucie remained in her cabin preferring to go down 'comfortably' in her cot. The other women rushed out like maniacs and one of the passengers, Mrs Polson, was 'shrieking and hystericking' and clinging to all the officers; 'I had no idea that women could behave so ill—such bare, abject cowardice'. The First Lieutenant, who regarded passengers as 'odious cargo', became friendly and reported to the Captain that Lady Gordon had not caused any trouble nor asked any questions—'that's beautiful'. During the voyage the Polson daughter and another passenger, Mr Adams, fell in love, but when they arrived in Capetown and she told her parents that she was going to be married they beat her and eventually turned her out of doors. It was, of course, to Lucie that she went for help, and Lucie put her up for a week while negotiations were conducted with the parents; 'but as they would do nothing but curse and threaten to lock her up if they caught her, Mr Adams married her three days ago. My story sounds crazy ... only Balzac could imagine such a family'.

Lucie wrote that Capetown, where she arrived on September 17 1861, was picturesque and the old Dutch buildings 'handsome and peculiar', but all was falling to decay. 'As it is neither paved nor drained it won't do in hot weather, and I shall migrate up-country to a Dutch village ... This is a dreary place for strangers, as people have no idea of hospitality. Except Mrs Jamison, not a soul of all the people to whom I had letters have done more than leave a card.'[1] 'Yesterday', she wrote on November 6, 'I had a dreadful heartache after Rainie [Urania then three years old] on her little birthday, and even these lovely ranges of distant mountains, coloured like opals in the sunset, did not delight me.' 'She is not worse', wrote Sarah Austin to a friend, 'the blood-spitting has not returned, but she writes in a depressed tone, and seems to feel her absence and privations very painfully. Her longing for home is almost an illness. God help us through this miserable time.'

Lucie became happier when she found friends among the community of Malays who had originally been brought across the Indian Ocean as slaves by the Dutch East Indies Company, but had been freed under the British Slave Emancipation Act of 1834. She visited their mosques, attended a Malay funeral and saw them at the Capetown races where half the crowd was Malay as they were extremely fond of horse-racing. 'There were dozens of carts crowded with the bright-eyed women, in petticoats of every most brilliant colour, white muslin jackets, and gold daggers in the great coils of shiny black hair. All most *anständig*, as they always are. Their pleasure is driving about *en famille*; the men have no separate amusements. Every spare corner in the cart is filled by the little soft round faces of the intelligent-looking quiet children, who seem amused and happy, and never make a noise or have the fidgets. I cannot make out why they are so well behaved. It favours Alick's theory of the expediency of utter spoiling, for one never hears any educational process going on.'

When Lucie went up-country to Caledon she travelled for three days with Sally in a light cart with two wheels and four horses driven by a charming Malay called Choslullah with his seven-year-old nephew Mohammed, 'a miniature of himself . . . so small and handy that he would be worth his weight in jewels as a tiger . . . Tiny Mohammed never spoke but when he was spoken to, and was always happy and alert. I observed that his uncle spoke to him like a grown man, and never ordered him about, or rebuked him in the least . . . The Malay coolies have a grave courtesy which contrasts most strikingly with both European vulgarity and negro jollity.' Her favourite Malay friends were Abdul Jamaalee and his wife Betty, 'a couple of old folks who were slaves to Dutch owners, and now keep a fruit-shop of a rough sort, with "Betsy, fruiterer" painted on the back

[1] Dorothea Fairbridge, who annotated an edition of *Letters from the Cape* (Oxford University Press, 1927) commented with surprise on this lack of hospitality.

of an old tin tray which hangs on the door of the house. Abdul first bought himself and then his wife, whose "Missis" generously "lumped in" Betsy's bed-ridden old mother. He is a fine handsome old man, and has confided to me that £5,000 would not buy what he is worth now. I have also read the letters written by his son, Abdul Rachman, now a student in Cairo, who has been away five years, four passed at Mecca. The young theologian writes to his "*Hoog eerbare Moeder*" a fond request for money, and promises to return soon. I am invited to the feast wherewith he will be welcomed. Old Abdul Jamaalee thinks it will divert my mind, and prove to me that Allah will take me home safe to my children, about whom he and his wife ask many questions.'

Lucie was trusted and was popular with the Malays because she ate and drank with them and found that Abdul's herb tea eased her cough. When Lucie continued to drink the tea at her lodgings the Dutch landlady and the white servants warned her that she would be poisoned; 'them nasty Malays can make it work months after you take it'. 'They also possess the evil eye', she wrote of the Malays, 'and a talent for love potions. As the men are very handsome and neat, I incline to believe that part of it.' Lucie was told that Choslullah had reported well on her because of her 'plenty good behaviour'—that she spoke to him just as to a white gentleman and did not 'laugh and talk nonsense talk' or say 'Here you black fellow'. 'The English when they mean to be good-natured, are generally offensively familiar, and talk "nonsense talk", i.e. imitate the Dutch English of the Malays and blacks . . . The Malays, who are intelligent and proud, of course feel the annoyance of vulgar familiarity more than the blacks, who are rather awe-struck by civility, though they like and admire it.'

Lucie liked the friendliness of the blacks and the beauty of the Caffres or Kaffirs. 'There is nothing like a Caffre for power and grace; and the face, though *very* African, has a sort of grandeur which makes it utterly unlike that of the negro . . . The Caffres are also very clean and very clever as servants, I hear, learning cookery etc. in a wonderfully short time. When they have saved money enough to buy cattle in Kaffraria, off they go, cast aside civilization and clothes, and enjoy life in naked luxury . . . The Farnese Hercules is literally true. I saw him in the street two days ago, and he was a Caffre coolie. The proportions of the head and throat were more wonderful in flesh, or muscle rather, than in marble . . . The Hottentots, as they are called—that is, those of mixed Dutch and Hottentot origin (correctly, "bastaards")—have a sort of blackguard elegance in their gait and figure which is peculiar to

them; a mixture of negro or Mozambique blood alters it altogether . . .
A mixture of black blood often gives real beauty, but takes off from the
"air" and generally from the talent; but then the blacks are so pleasant
and the Hottentots are taciturn and reserved.' At the Moravian Mission
at Genadenthal, near Caledon, she met a pure Hottentot who was over
a hundred years old and conversed in Dutch. 'You cannot conceive
the effect of looking on the last of a race once the owners of all this
land, and now utterly gone.'

'The Dutch round Capetown . . . are sulky and dispirited; they
regret the slave days, and can't bear to pay wages. They have sold all
their fine houses in town to merchants etc. and let their handsome
country places go to pieces and the land lie fallow, rather than hire the
men they used to own. They hate the Malays, who were their slaves and
whose "insolent prosperity" annoys them, and they don't like the
vulgar, bustling English. The English complain that the Dutch won't
die, "and that they are the curse of the colony" (a statement for which
they can never give a reason). But they, too, curse the emancipation,
long to flog the niggers, and hate the Malays, who work hard and
don't drink . . . The Africanders (Dutch and negro mixed in various
proportions) are more or less lazy, dirty and dressy, and the beautiful
girls wear pork-pie hats, and look very winning and rather fierce.'

Among a few people up-country she found a happy relationship
between former master and former slave. In the house of the postmaster at Caledon, Heer Wilhelm Klein, she met a handsome Malay
with a basket of shell-fish. 'Old Klein told me they were sent him by a
Malay who was born in his father's house, a slave, and had been *his boy*
and playfellow. Now, the slave is far richer than the old young master,
and no waggon comes without a little gift—oranges, fish etc—for
"Wilhelm" . . . "Good boy!" said old Klein; "good people the
Malays." It is a relief after the horrors one has heard of Dutch cruelty,
to see such an *idyllisches Vehältniss* [idyllic relationship]. I have heard
other instances of the same fidelity from Malays, but they were utterly
unappreciated, and only told to prove the excellence of slavery and
"how well the rascals must have been off". '

The relationship, however, had not always been satisfactory for old
Klein, who poured out to Lucie the misery he had undergone from the
'ingratitude' of Rosina who had been a slave-girl of his. 'She was in her
youth handsome, clever, the best horse-breaker, bullock-trainer and
driver, and hardest worker in the district. She had two children by
Klein, then a young fellow; six by another white man, and a few more

by two husbands of her own race! But she was a rebellious spirit, and took to drink. After the emancipation, she used to go in front of Klein's windows and read the statute in a loud voice on every anniversary of the day; and, if that did not enrage him enough, she pertinaciously (whenever she was a little drunk) kissed him by main force every time she met him in the street, exclaiming, "Aha! when I young and pretty slave-girl you make kiss me then; now I ugly, drunk, dirty and free woman, I kiss you!" Frightful retributive justice!'

The climate, Lucie thought, was good for invalids because it was bracing as well as warm and dry, but care was needed, as it was not as warm as she had expected, 'the southern icebergs are at no great distance, and they ice the S.E. wind for us'. She found that the constant eating of grapes had done her good but she was surprised at the primitive methods of wine-making and she wrote home to obtain details of the Spanish process.[1] 'They literally know nothing about wine-making here, and with such matchless grapes I am sure it ought to be good.'

When the weather became warmer in May, Lucie prepared for her return to England. Her health had not improved as much as she had hoped it would; 'I fear I shall have to fly from next winter again, and certainly will go with Janet to Egypt, which seems to me like next door.' In July 1862 she arrived in England and there was a great welcome for her from her family and friends. Alexander was as ever calm, amiable and handsome; Maurice was much grown, Urania at the delightful age of four; Sarah was old and failing in health and Janet was nearing the time of having a child. Lucie was bitterly disappointed when the doctors told her that she should not stay long in England; they recommended Eaux Bonnes in the south of France and then a hot climate, such as Egypt, for the winter. She asked if she would ever be able to live a normal life with her family and the reply was that if she did what she was told she might be restored to health in two years time.

It was a great disappointment to have to leave before Janet had her baby. The day after she left for France, Henry Ross, who was staying with the Duff Gordons, became seriously ill with typhoid fever within a few days of Janet's confinement. Sarah was heart-broken at Lucie's departure but wrote: 'I have but one consolation. Janet is all I could wish. This young woman, apparently so giddy, seemingly caring for no one, only thinking of her own amusement, shows a devotion and

[1] Duff Gordon relations were making wine and sherry in Spain and the 'Duff Gordon,' sherry is still popular today.

courage [nursing Henry Ross] which astonishes everyone. Never a word of complaint, never an allusion to her own condition.' This time the Duff Gordon house at Esher was dismantled. 'Of all that happy group', added Sarah, 'none are left save the poor old grandmother'.

At Eaux Bonnes Lucie nearly died of the cold and damp. 'I hear the drip, drip, drip of Eaux Bonnes', she wrote later, 'when I am chilly and oppressed in my sleep.' Egypt, however, in the autumn of 1862 gave her new life and she was delighted to go to a country about which she had read much in the *Arabian Nights*, Herodotus, *Eothen* and the Bible.

Owing to the trust aroused by her understanding and compassion during her seven years in Egypt, and because of her humour, enjoyment and lively curiosity, Lucie Duff Gordon wrote a new classic on the 'Manners and Customs of the Modern Egyptians' —more personal and circumscribed than Edward Lane's. Illness overtook her intention of writing a thorough study and she argued that her husband was wrong to fear she would be 'cut up' by the learned: 'the learned know books and I know men and, what is more difficult, women.'

Her own remarkable character and her original views on life and people are also revealed in her letters and, on her death in Cairo in July 1896, she left 'a memory of her greatness and goodness such as no other European woman acquired in that country'.

Tenterden, 1969   GORDON WATERFIELD

I

Lucie's servant Omar 'graceful and pleasing'

Alexandria, October 27 1862. I arrived here all right having lost a day by the *giorno di festa* at Leghorn, where we shipped a curious motley crew—French *café chantant* women, an Italian opera troupe, a Spanish Consul the image of Don Quixote, four Levantine ladies with fifty peacock power of voice and the best natured creatures possible, Italians, Algerines, Egyptians, I for England and one poor Parisienne on her way to sing at Cairo, a very nice person but so put out by the *méridonaux*. No discipline, nor order but plenty of good nature.

I was as comfortable in the boat as French want of order will permit. I had a cabin to myself, and the food was excellent and the beds clean though hard. But I found the motion of the screw most distressing; it became like the slow torture of the drop of water.

The filly arrived here all right and I am told that the Arabs are wild about her and swear she is no English horse but a noble Beduin mare and will fetch any price here. I have not been about much, walking is fearfully dusty and Janet's[1] horses are too vicious. I tried twice to drive, but once they kicked and nearly ran over several people and the next day one horse lay down in the street, so, as I had no mind to stand the risk of broken knees or springs, I begged to be excused any further attempt at driving.

---

[1] Janet Duff Gordon, Lucie's daughter, had arrived in Egypt in January 1861 as the wife of Henry Ross, who was a director of Briggs Bank.

The filly was sent to Janet by her father. When Halim Pasha, the uncle of Said Pasha, the Viceroy, saw Janet Ross riding the horse he insisted on buying it which Henry Ross agreed to because he was doing a great deal of business with Halim Pasha.

I shall go on to Cairo in a few days. I am dismayed at the noise and turbulence of the people here, after the soft voices and gentle ways of the Cape blacks. The difference of atmosphere between Europe and Africa is wonderful; even Malta wants the clearness of Egypt, and this is far more misty than the Cape, but equally beautiful in a different way. I was delighted with Valetta, which seemed to me the most beautiful town I ever saw—all so handsome and solid.

I am now going with the eldest Levantine girl to Said Pasha's[1] hareem, where she is very intimate. She told the Princess that I had been very kind to her at sea when she was sick, and I was consequently invited to go to see the hareem.

I am frightened at the dearness of everything here. I found it quite impossible to get on without a servant able to speak English. The janissary of Mr Thayer, the American Consul-General,[2] recommended to me a youth called Omar (surnamed 'the Father of sweets'), whom I have taken. He is graceful and pleasing and seems to deserve his name. He will do all I ask for £3 a month and a greatcoat (if we get a boat). He is an enthusiast about the Nile; and if Cairo has a cheap boat, Omar will take it. I don't think I should get much good out of life in an Eastern town; the dust is intolerable, and the stuffiness indoors very unwholesome. There is none of the out-doors existence which was so healthy at the Cape. My cough is bad, but Omar says I shall lose it and 'eat plenty' as soon as I see a crocodile.

Yesterday I went with Mr Thayer, who is equally kind and agreeable, and Hekekian Bey[3] to see a few palaces; oh, what ignoble,

[1] Said Pasha, the favourite son of Mohammed Ali Pasha, had become Viceroy of Egypt in July 1854 when he succeeded his nephew, Abbas Pasha, who had been murdered by two of his slaves.

[2] William Thayer kept a diary in which he described Lucie as 'handsome, bright and forty and a capital traveller. She knows the literary people of England but does not gossip about them'. (Extracts from his diary are published in the biography *Lucie Duff Gordon* by Gordon Waterfield, Murray 1937.)

[3] Hekekian Bey and his family had taken a prominent part in Egyptian affairs under Mohammed Ali Pasha. He was Director of the *Ecole des Arts et Métiers;* one of his brothers-in-law, Kosrew Bey, was First Dragoman to the Viceroy and another brother-in-law, Artin Bey, was Prime Minister; but all members of the family were dismissed by Abbas Pasha who got rid of all the friends of his great uncle, Mohammed Ali Pasha. Hekekian Bey was a tall, handsome man of high intelligence who looked rather like an Italian. He had been introduced to Lucie by Nassau Senior, the economist, who had been invited to Egypt by de Lesseps to accompany the Commissioners drawn from various countries to determine the line of the Ship or Suez Canal; they arrived in Egypt at the end of 1855. Senior reported a number of interesting conversations he had with Hekekian Bey in his *Conversations and Journals in Egypt and Malta*, which were not published until 1882, after Senior's death.

shabby-genteel! One of them is merely a 'Yankee notion' bought piecemeal from New York, and stuck up by the sea.

There is none of the pleasant *avenante* manner and smiling look to which I grew familiar at the Cape; but the people are prodigiously handsome—lads like John of Bologna's Mercury, with divine legs, and young women so lovely in their dirt and scanty drapery; and among the Beduin men I have seen the two handsomest men I ever beheld. Likewise the camels enchant me, and the date-palms.

But on the other hand, all is profoundly melancholy; the people's faces, the surface of the country, the dirt, the horrible wretchedness, the whacking of the little boys and girls who do all the work which Irish hodmen do with us. Such is my first impression of the land of Egypt; but Omar's eager description of Cairo and the Nile makes me expect something much more agreeable. If we reach Nubia, we are to take a present of salt from Shaheen, Janet's nice red servant (for he is in form and colour the exact likeness of a hieroglyphic figure), to his parents; likewise to give them money on his account, should they need it. He has the dearest little brother, who is for ever in the hall here and the Boab's bench is the scene of incessant study. An old white-bearded man teaches reading and writing to Shaheen and a select circle of friends, and Shaheen's white slate looks very creditable indeed to my ignorant eye. The children are mostly hideous here, and cry incessantly.

In the hut under the bedroom window, a poor woman is dying of consumption, which seems to be very common here, judging from the faces one sees and the coughs one hears; a baby, too, is ill. The anxious distress of the friends is very affecting, and quite contrary to the commonplace talk about Eastern apathy, hardness, etc. Their faces and behaviour show ten times the feeling of the common people in some parts of Europe; what is not pleasant, is the absence of all brightness or gaiety, even from young and childish faces. The very blacks here can't get up so much as a broad smile; a good laugh I have not yet heard. A stronger contrast than my present henchman, Omar, with his soft but anxious eyes and supple figure, and my last year's driver at the Cape, Choslullah, the world could not afford. The Malay's sturdy figure and beaming smile spoke independence as plainly as possible, while these young men, Omar and Shaheen, are more servile in look and gesture than is pleasant to me.

I regret more than I can say that I ever came here, for I fear it will be utterly impossible to live as cheaply as I had hoped. I will do my utmost, be sure, but I find all so dear and so troublesome to a stranger not knowing the language; and a servant I could not anyhow do without. If I find Cairo agrees with me as ill as this place, and the boats are too dear, I will see whether I can get to Algiers, or if not, to Palermo. Kiss my darling Rainy for me. It is wretched to think that she is four today [November 5] and how little I have seen of her.

II

'Cairo is the Real Arabian Nights'

Grand Cairo, November 11 1862. Dearest Mother. I write to you out of the real Arabian Nights. Well may the Prophet (whose name be exalted) smile when he looks on Cairo. It is a golden existence, all sunshine and poetry, and, I must add, kindness and civility. I came up last Thursday by railway with the American Consul-General and had to stay at this horrid Shepheard's Hotel. But I do little but sleep here. Hekekian Bey, a learned old Armenian, takes care of me every day, and the American Vice-Consul is my sacrifice.

I went on Sunday to his child's christening, and heard Sakna, the 'Restorer of Hearts'. She is wonderfully like Rachel,[1] and her singing is *hinreisend* [delightful] from expression and passion. Mr Wilkinson [the British Consul] is a Levantine, and his wife Armenian, so they had a grand fantasia; people feasted all over the house and in the street. Arab music clanged, women yelled the *zaghareet*, black servants served sweetmeats, pipes, and coffee, and behaved as if they belonged to the company, and I was strongly under the impression that I was at Nurreddin's wedding with the Vizier's daughter.

My servant Omar turns out a jewel. He has discovered an excellent boat for the Nile voyage, and I am to be mistress of a captain, a mate, eight men and a cabin boy for £25 a month. I went to Boulaq, the port of Cairo, and saw various boats, and admired the way in which the English travellers pay for their insolence and caprices. Similar boats cost people with dragomans £50 to £65. But, then, 'I shall lick the fellows,' etc., is what I hear all round. The dragoman, I conclude, pockets the difference.

[1] The stage name of the French actress Elizabeth Felix who won a European reputation for her acting in Racine's *Phédre* in 1843.

44

The owner of the boat, Sid Ahmad el-Berberi, asked £30, where-upon I touched my breast, mouth and eyes, and stated through Omar that I was not, like other Ingeleez, made of money, but would give £20. He then showed another boat at £20, very much worse, and I departed (with fresh civilities) and looked at others, and saw two more for £20; but neither was clean, and neither had a little boat for land-ing. Meanwhile Sid Ahmad came after me and explained that, if I was not like other Ingeleez in money, I likewise differed in politeness, and had refrained from abuse, etc., etc., and I should have the boat for £25. It was so very excellent in all fittings, and so much larger, that I thought it would make a great difference in health, so I said if he would go before the American Vice-Consul (who is looked on as a sharp hand) and would promise all he said to me before him, it should be well.

It was pleasant to find that Hekekian Bey and the American Vice-Consul exactly confirmed all that Omar had told me about what I must take and what it would cost; they thought I might perfectly trust him. He put everything at just one-fourth of what the Alexandrian English told me, and even less. Moreover, he will cook on board; the kitchen, which is a hole in the bow where the cook must sit cross-legged, would be impossible for a woman to crouch down in. Besides, Omar will avoid everything unclean, and make the food such as he may law-fully eat. He is a pleasant, cheerful young fellow, and I think he rather likes the importance of taking care of me, and showing that he can do as well as a dragoman at £12 a month. It is characteristic that he turned his month's wages and the '£2 pounds for a coat' into a bracelet for his little wife before leaving home. That is the Arab savings-bank.

I dined at Hekekian Bey's after the excursion yesterday. He is a most kind, friendly man, and very pleasant and cultivated. He dresses like an Englishman, speaks English like ourselves, and is quite like an uncle to me already.

Mr Thayer, the American Consul-General, gives me letters to every consular agent depending on him; and two Coptic merchants whom I met at the fantasia have already begged me to 'honour their houses.' I rather think the poor agents, who are all Armenians and Copts, will think I am the republic in person. The weather has been all this time like a splendid English August, and I hope I shall get rid of my cough in time, but it has been very bad. There is no cold at night here as at the Cape, but it is nothing like so clear and bright.

Omar took Sally[1] sightseeing all day while I was away, into several mosques; in one he begged her to wait a minute while he said a prayer. They compare notes about their respective countries and are great friends; but he is put out at my not having provided her with a husband long ago, as is one's duty towards a 'female servant,' which almost always here means a slave.

Of all the falsehoods I have heard about the East, that about women being old hags at thirty is the biggest. Among the poor fellah women it may be true enough, but not nearly as much as in Germany; and I have now seen a considerable number of Levantine ladies looking very handsome, or at least comely, till fifty. Sakna, the Arab Grisi,[2] is fifty-five—an ugly face, I am told (she was veiled and one only saw the eyes and glimpses of her mouth when she drank water), but the figure of a leopard, all grace and beauty, and a splendid voice of its kind, harsh but thrilling like Malibran's. I guessed her about thirty, or perhaps thirty-five. When she improvised, the finesse and grace of her whole *Wesen* [manner] were ravishing. I was on the point of shouting out 'Wallah!' as heartily as the natives. The eight younger *Halmeh* (*i.e.*, learned women, which the English call *Almeh* and think is an improper word) were ugly and screeched. Sakna was treated with great consideration and quite as a friend by the Armenian ladies with whom she talked between her songs. She is a Muslimeh and very rich and charitable; she gets £50 for a night's singing at least.

It would be very easy to learn colloquial Arabic, as they all speak with perfect distinctness that one can follow the sentences and catch the words one knows as they are repeated. I think I know forty or fifty words already.

The reverse of the brilliant side of the medal is sad enough: deserted palaces, and crowded hovels scarce good enough for pigstyes. 'One day man see his dinner, and one other day none at all,' as Omar observes; and the children are shocking to look at from bad food, dirt and overwork, but the little pot-bellied, blear-eyed wretches grow up into noble young men and women under all their difficulties. The faces are all sad and rather what the Scotch call 'dour' not *méchant* at all, but harsh, like their voices. All the melody is in walk and gesture;

[1] Sally was Lucie's maid who had accompanied her to South Africa. Her sister, Ellen, was Janet Ross's maid in Alexandria.

[2] Judith and Julia Grisi were well-known Italian singers and another cousin was an actress and it was probably to her that Lucie referred. Malibran (Mlle Garcia) was a famous French singer who died in Manchester at the age of twenty-eight.

46

they are as graceful as cats, and the women have exactly the 'breasts like pomegranates' of their poetry.

A tall Beduin woman came up to us in the field yesterday to shake hands and look at us. She wore a white sackcloth shift and veil, and nothing else. She asked Mrs Hekekian a good many questions about me, looked at my face and hands, but took no notice of my rather smart gown which the village women admired so much, shook hands again with the air of a princess, wished me health and happiness, and strode off across the graveyard like a stately ghost. She was on a journey all alone, and somehow it looked very solemn and affecting to see her walking away towards the desert in the setting sun like Hagar. All is so Scriptural in the country here. Sally called out in the railroad, 'There is Boaz, sitting in the cornfield'; and so it was, and there he has sat for how many thousand years, and in one war-song Sakna sang as Miriam, the prophetess, may have done when she took a timbrel in her hand and went out to meet the host.

Wednesday.—My contract was drawn up and signed by the American Vice-Consul today, and my Reis kissed my hand in due form, after which I went to the bazaar to buy the needful pots and pans. The transaction lasted an hour. The copper is so much per oka, the workmanship so much; every article is weighed by a sworn weigher and a ticket sent with it. More Arabian Nights. The shopkeeper compares notes with me about numerals, and is as much amused as I. He treats me to coffee and a pipe from a neighbouring shop while Omar eloquently depreciates the goods and offers half the value. A waterseller offers a brass cup of water; I drink, and give the huge sum of twopence, and he distributes the contents of his skin to the crowd (there always is a crowd) in my honour. It seems I have done a pious action. Finally a boy is called to carry the *batterie de cuisine*, while Omar brandishes a gigantic kettle which he has picked up a little bruised for four shillings. The boy has a donkey which I mount astride *à l Arabe*, while the boy carries all the copper things on his head. We are rather a grand procession, and quite enjoy the fury of the dragomans and other leeches, who hang on the English, at such independent proceedings, and Omar gets reviled for spoiling the trade by being cook and dragoman all in one.

III

'The beauty of Arab architecture'

November 11. I went this morning with Hekekian Bey to the two earliest mosques. The Tulun is exquisite—noble, simple, and what ornament there is is the most delicate lacework and embossing in stone and wood.[1] This Arab architecture is even more lovely than our Gothic. The mosque of Sultan Hassan (early in our fourteenth century) is, I think, the most majestic building I ever saw, and the beauty of the details quite beyond belief to European eyes; the huge gates to his tomb are one mass of the finest enamel ornaments, as you may discover by rubbing the dirt off with your glove. No one has said a tenth part enough of the beauty of Arab architecture.[2] The Hassaneeyeh is even grander than a Gothic cathedral, and all is in the noblest taste.

The Mosque of the Citadel (Mohammed Ali's)—where the English broke the lamps—is like a fine modern Italian Church; but Abbas Pasha stole the alabaster columns and replaced them by painted wood.

---

[1] Lucie does not give the name of the second early mosque she visited but it may have been that of 'Amr, built in the winter of 641–2 A.D., the year after 'Amr led the Arabs to the conquest of Egypt.

The Tulun was completed in the spring of 879 A.D. built by one of the greatest rulers of Egypt, ibn Tulun, son of an enfranchised slave. It is the finest monument of early Muslim architecture in Cairo. 'The mosque of ibn Tulun impresses one by its great size and by the noble simplicity of its plan', wrote K. A. C. Creswell in *Early Muslim Architecture*.

The fine, austere and monumental mosque of Sultan Hassan was built about five hundred years later, in 1356 A.D., and is perhaps the finest example of the later mediaeval art in Cairo.

[2] It is true that hardly any of the eighteenth- and nineteenth-century travellers showed much interest in Islamic architecture. Lucie's friends such as William Kinglake stated in *Eothen* 'there is not much in the way of public buildings to admire at Cairo', and Eliot Warburton in the *Crescent and the Cross* referred to 'the filthy, intricate lanes and alleys' of Cairo.

Friday.—I went today on a donkey to a mosque in the bazaar, of what we call Arabesque style, like the Alhambra, very handsome. The *Kibleh*[1] was very beautiful, and as I was admiring it Omar pulled a lemon out of his breast and smeared it on the porphyry pillar on one side of the arch, and then entreated me to lick it. It cures all diseases. The old man who showed the mosque pulled eagerly at my arm to make me perform this absurd ceremony, and I thought I should have been forced to do it. The base of the pillar was clogged with lemon-juice.

I then went to the tombs of the Khalifah;[2] one of the great ones had such arches and such wondrous cupolas but all in ruins. There are scores of these noble buildings, any one of which is a treasure, falling to decay. The next, strange to say, was in perfect repair. I got off the donkey, and Omar fidgeted and hesitated a little and consulted with a woman who had the key. As there were no overshoes I pulled my boots off, and was rewarded by seeing the footprints of Mohammed on two black stones, and a lovely little mosque, a sort of *Sainte Chapelle*. Omar prayed with ardent fervour and went out backwards, saluting the Prophet aloud. To my surprise the woman was highly pleased with sixpence, and did not ask for more. When I remarked this, Omar said that no Frank had ever been inside to his knowledge. A mosque-keeper of the sterner sex would not have let me in.

I returned home through endless streets and squares of Muslim tombs, those of the Mamelukes among them. It was very striking; and it was getting so dark that I thought of Nurreddin Bey, and wondered if a Jinn would take me anywhere if I took up my night's lodging in one of the comfortable little cupola-covered buildings.

The Tulun is now a vast poorhouse, a nest of paupers. I went into three of their lodgings. Several Turkish families were in a large

---

[1] The *Kibleh* or *Qibla* denotes the direction in which Muslims should pray towards Mecca and is shown by the position of a beautifully ornamented niche generally on the south wall of the mosque, known as the *Mihrab* or *Qibla*.

[2] This eastern cemetery below the Mokhattam hills is certainly known as the 'Tombs of the Khalifah' but no Khalif is buried there. They are the tombs of the Mameluke rulers, the Circassians of the last period from the 14th to the early 16th centuries. 'Here are some of the finest buildings in Cairo spread out over a period of rather more than a hundred years', wrote Dorothea Russell. 'These impressive monuments are the product of a great age, of great riches, of forceful men, but of an age that was soon to perish . . . These mosques and tombs did not stand alone, and the 'City of the Dead' was far from being the ghostly place that it is now, for a busy life went on around the great tombs, and many living, as well as the dead, had their habitation here. An immense personnel was attached to the service of these tombs and mosques. (*Medieval Cairo* by Dorothea Russell, Weidenfeld and Nicolson, 1962.)

square room neatly divided into little partitions with old mats hung on ropes. In each were as many bits of carpet, mat and patchwork as the poor owner could collect, and a small chest and a little brick cooking-place in one corner of the room with three earthern pipkins for I don't know how many people—that was all—they possess no sort of furniture, but all was scrupulously clean and no bad smell whatever.

A little boy seized my hand and showed where he slept, ate and cooked with the most expressive pantomime. As there were women, Hekekian could not come in, but when I came out an old man told us they received three loaves (cakes as big as a sailor's biscuit), four piastres a month—*i.e.*, eightpence per adult—a suit of clothes a year, and on festive occasions lentil soup. Such is the almshouse here.

A little crowd belonging to the house had collected, and I gave sixpence to an old man, who transferred it to the first old man to be *divided* among them all, ten or twelve people at least, mostly blind or lame. The poverty wrings my heart. We took leave with salaams and politeness like the best society, and then turned into an Arab hut stuck against the lovely arches. I stooped low under the door, and several women crowded in. This was still poorer, for there were no mats or rags of carpet, a still worse cooking-place, a sort of dog-kennel piled up of loose stones to sleep in, which contained a small chest and the print of human forms on the stone floor. It was, however, quite free from dust, and perfectly sweet. I gave the young woman who had led me in sixpence, and here the difference between Turk and Arab appeared. The division of this created a perfect storm of noise, and we left the five or six Arab women out-shrieking a whole rookery. I ought to say that no one begged at all.

My Coptic friend has just called in to say that his brother expects me at Keneh. I find nothing but civility and a desire to please. My boat is the *Zint el Bahreyn*, and I carry the English flag and a small American distinguishing pennant as a signal to my consular agents.

1. Sarah Austin, *by J. Linnell, 1839*
'Handsome, fond of society . . . with an almost superabundance of
energy and animal spirits.' – Janet Ross, her grand-daughter.

2. Lucie Austin by a school friend. Described at the time by Henry Taylor as 'handsome and very striking with a stern, determined expression of countenance, which might qualify her to sit for the picture of Cassandra or Clytemnestra'

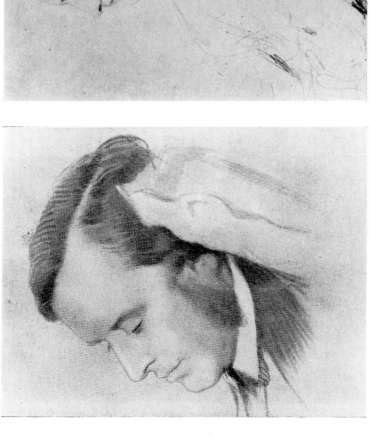

'3. (a) Sir Alexander Duff Gordon Bt., *by G. F. Watts, R.A.*   3. (b) Lucie Duff Gordon after marriage, *by G. F. Watts R.A.*

'Alexander has nothing but a small salary, his handsome person, excellent and sweet character and his title (a great misfortune!)' – Sarah Austin

4. Lucie's daughter, Janet, and her 'beloved playfellow', Hassan
el-Bakkeet, *by Caroline Norton*

5. Caroline Norton, *by John Haytor*. Lucie admired her wit, independence and beauty and was angered by the way society had treated her after the Melbourne case

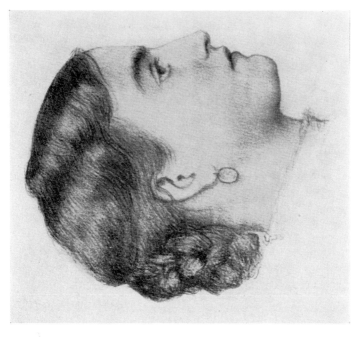

6. (b) Janet Ross, *by Val Prinsep, 1865*

6. (a) Henry Ross, *by G. F. Watts*, at the time that he married Janet
Duff Gordon in 1860

7. Lucie Duff Gordon, *painted by Henry W. Phillips* in 1852.
'She was radiantly beautiful with dark brows on a brilliant com-
plexion, the head of a Roman and features of
Grecian line' – George Meredith

8. Omar Abu Halawy, Lucie's faithful servant
and companion in Egypt

9. Cairo. 'It is a golden existence, all sunshine and poetry'

10. Mosque of Sultan Hassan and entrance to the Citadel – 'even grander than a Gothic Cathedral, and all is in the noblest taste'

11. Interior of Mosque of Sultan Hassan

12. (a) Tombs of the Mamelukes – 'there are scores of these noble buildings. . . falling to decay'

12. (b) The ferry at Gizeh

13. The 'Holy Tree' at Matarych, near Cairo – 'the tree and the well
where Sittina Mariam (the Virgin Mary) rested with Sayyidna Issa
(Jesus) in her arms during the flight into Egypt'

14. 'In the street they are so noisy, but get the same men in a coffee-
shop. . . and they are the quietest of mankind'

15. 'The more I see the back-slums of Cairo,
the more in love I am with it'

16. Luxor from the Nile

IV

Sailing to Nubia

On board the boat off Embabeh, November 21 1862. **Dearest Alick.**
We embarked yesterday, and after the fashion of Eastern caravans
are abiding today at a village opposite Cairo; it is Friday, and therefore would be improper and unlucky to set out on our journey.

The scenes on the river are wonderfully diverting and curious, so
much life and movement. My crew have all sported new white
drawers in honour of the Sitti Ingleezee's supposed modesty—of
course compensation will be expected. Poor fellows! they are very
well mannered and quiet in their rags and misery, and their queer
little humming song is rather pretty, '*Eyah Mohammad, eyah Mohammad*', *ad infinitum*, except when an energetic man cries, '*Yallah!*'—
i.e., 'O God!'—which means 'go it' in everyday life. Omar is gone
to fetch one or two more 'unconsidered trifles', and I have been explaining the defects to be remedied in the cabin door, broken window,
etc., to my Reis with the help of six words of Arabic and dumb show,
which they understand and answer with wonderful quickness.

The air on the river is certainly quite celestial—totally unlike the
damp, chilly feeling of the hotel and Frank quarter of Cairo.

Next winter I shall stay with you. If this voyage does me as much
good as it has done to others, I shall be well enough for anything.
If not, it is not worth while to drag on a sickly existence at so much
expense of money and annoyance to others. I am so glad to hear
such good accounts of Maurice and Rainie. If I die soon you will
have as much happiness as most people in such nice children. I will
write from wherever there are consular agents.

I shall go up to the second Cataract[1] as fast as possible, and return

---

[1] This was near Wadi Halfa. The first cataract was near Aswan where no barrage or
dam had as yet been built.

E

back at leisure. Hekekian Bey came to take leave yesterday, and lent me several books; pray tell Senior what a kindness his introduction was. It would have been rather dismal in Cairo—if one could be dismal there—without a soul to speak to. I was sorry to know no Turks or Arabs, and have no opportunity of seeing any but the tradesman of whom I bought my stores but that was very amusing. The young man of whom I bought my cups was so handsome, elegant and melancholy that I know he was the lover of the Sultan's favourite slave.

How I wish you were here to enjoy all this, so new, so beautiful, and yet so familiar, life—and you would like the people, poor things! they are complete children, but amiable children. I went into the village here, where I was a curiosity, and some women took me into their houses and showed me their sleeping-place, cookery, poultry, etc.; and a man followed me to keep off the children, but no back-sheesh was asked for, which showed that Europeans were rare there. The utter destitution is terrible to see, though in this climate of course it matters less, but the much-talked-of dirt is simply utter poverty. The poor souls are as clean as Nile mud and water will make their bodies, and they have not a second shirt, or any bed but dried mud.

Give my love to my darlings, and don't be uneasy if you don't get letters. My cough has been better now for five days without a bad return of it, so I hope it is really better; it is the first reprieve for so long. The sun is so hot, a regular broil; November 21, and all doors and windows open in the cabin—a delicious breeze.

Feshn, Monday November 30. Dearest Mother. I have now been enjoying this most delightful way of life for ten days, and am certainly much better. I begin to eat and sleep again, and cough less.

My crew are a great amusement to me. They are mostly men from near the first Cataract above Aswan, sleek-skinned, gentle, patient, merry black fellows. The little black Reis is the very picture of good-nature and full of fun, 'chaffing' the girls as we pass the villages, and always smiling. The steersman is of lighter complexion, also very cheery, but decidedly pious. He prays five times a day and utters ejaculations to the apostle Rusool continually. He hurt his ankle on one leg and his instep on the other with a rusty nail, and they festered. I dressed them with poultices, and then with lint and strapping, with perfect success, to the great admiration of all hands, and he announced how much better he felt, '*Alhamdulillah*. Praise be to God and thanks without end O Lady', and everyone echoed.

The most important person is the 'weled'—boy—Ahmad. The most merry, clever, omnipresent little rascal, with an ugly little pug face, a shape like an antique Cupid, liberally displayed, and a skin of dark brown velvet. His voice, shrill and clear, is always heard foremost; he cooks for the crew, he jumps overboard with the rope and gives advice on all occasions, grinds the coffee with the end of a stick in a mortar, which he holds between his feet, and uses the same large stick to walk proudly before me, brandishing it if I go ashore for a minute, and ordering everybody out of the way. 'Ya Ahmad!, resounds all day whenever anybody wants anything, and the 'weled' is always ready and able.

My favourite is Osman, a tall, long-limbed black who seems to have stepped out of a hieroglyphical drawing, shirt, skull-cap and all. He has only these two garments, and how anyone contrives to look so inconceivably 'neat and respectable' (as Sally truly remarked) in that costume is a mystery. He is always at work, always cheerful, but rather silent—in short, the able seaman and steady, respectable 'hand' *par excellence*. Then we have El Zankalonee from near Cairo, an old fellow of white complexion and a valuable person, an inexhaustible teller of stories at night and always *en train*, full of jokes and remarkable for a dry humour much relished by the crew. There is a certain Shereef who does nothing but laugh and work and be obliging; helps Omar with one hand and Sally with the other, and looks like a great innocent black child. The rest of the dozen are of various colours, sizes and ages, some quite old, but all very quiet and well-behaved.

We have had either dead calm or contrary wind all the time and the men have worked very hard at the tow-rope. On Friday I proclaimed a halt in the afternoon at a village at prayer-time for the pious Muslims to go to the mosque; this gave great satisfaction, though only five went, Reis, steersman, Zankalonee and two old men. The up-river men never pray at all, and Osman occupied himself by buying salt out of another boat and stowing it away to take up to his family, as it is terribly dear high up the river.

At Benisuef we halted to buy meat and bread; it is *comme qui dirait* an assize town, there is one butcher who kills one sheep a day. I walked about the streets escorted by Omar in front and two sailors with huge staves behind, and created a sensation accordingly. It is a dull little country town with a wretched palace of Said Pasha.

V

'The kindness of the Copts'

November 30 1862. We halted at Bibbeh, where I caught sight of a large Coptic church and sallied forth to see whether they would let me in. The road lay past the house of the headman of the village, and there 'in the gate' sat a patriarch, surrounded by his servants and his cattle. Over the gateway were crosses and queer constellations of dots, more like Mithraic symbols than anything Christian, but Girgis was a Copt, though the chosen head of the Muslim village. He rose as I came up, stepped out and salaamed, then took my hand and said I must go into his house before I saw the church and enter the hareem. His old mother, who looked a hundred, and his pretty wife, were very friendly; but, as I had to leave Omar at the door, our talk soon came to an end, and Girgis took me out into the divan, without the sacred precincts of the hareem. Of course we had pipes and coffee, and he pressed me to stay some days, to eat with him every day and to accept all his house contained. I took the milk he offered, and asked him to visit me in the boat, saying I must return before sunset when it gets cold, as I was ill. The house was a curious specimen of a wealthy man's house—I could not describe it if I tried, but I felt I was acting a passage of the Old Testament.

We went to the church, which outside looked like nine beehives in a box. Inside, the nine domes resting on square pillars were very handsome. Girgis was putting it into thorough repair at his own expense, and it will cost a good deal, I think, to repair and renew the fine old wood panelling of such minute and intricate workmanship. The church is divided by three screens; one in front of the eastern three domes is impervious and conceals the holy of holies.

He opened the horseshoe door for me to look in, but explained that no hareem might cross the threshold.

To the right of this sanctum is the tomb of a Muslim saint enclosed under the adjoining dome! Here we went in and Girgis kissed the tomb on one side while Omar salaamed it on the other—a pleasant sight. They were much more particular about our shoes than in the mosques. Omar wanted to tie handkerchiefs over my boots like at Cairo, but the priest objected and made me take them off and march about in the brick and mortar rubbish in my stockings.

The hareem sit behind a third screen, furthest removed from the holy screen, where also was the font, locked up and shaped like a Muslim tomb in little. ('Hareem' is used here just like the German *Frauenzimmer* [womenfolk], to mean a respectable woman; Girgis spoke of me to Omar as 'hareem'.) The Copts have but one wife, but they shut her up much closer than the Arabs. The children were sweetly pretty, so unlike the Arab brats, and the men very good-looking. They did not seem to acknowledge me at all as a *co-religionnaire*, and asked whether we of the English religion did not marry our brothers and sisters.[1]

The priest then asked me to drink coffee at his house close by, and there I 'sat in the gate'—*i.e.*, in a large sort of den raised two feet from the ground and matted, to the left of the gate. A crowd of Copts collected and squatted about, and we were joined by the mason who was repairing the church, a fine, burly, rough-bearded old Mussulman, who told how Mar Girghis (St George), buried in the church of Bibbeh, had appeared to him three nights running at Cairo and ordered him to leave his work and go to Bibbeh and mend his church, and how he came and offered to do so without pay if the Copts would find the materials. He spoke with evident pride, as one who had received a Divine command, and the Copts all confirmed the story and everyone was highly gratified by the miracle.

It is not often that a dead saint contrives to be equally agreeable to Christians and Mussulmans, and here was the staunch old 'true believer' working away in the sanctuary which they would not allow an English fellow-Christian to enter!

---

[1] The Copts have remained separate from other Christian communities because they are of the monophysite faith, teaching that Christ had one nature made up of the divine and human; their belief, as they repeat, is that 'His Divinity was not separated from his Manhood for one moment or for the twinkling of an eye'. They are strict monogomists; males are circumcised before baptism and it was long the practice to circumcise females also.

Whilst we sat hearing all these wonders, the sheep and cattle pushed in between us, coming home at eve. The venerable old priest looked so like Father Abraham, and the whole scene was so pastoral and Biblical that I felt quite as if my wish was fulfilled to live a little a few thousands of years ago. They wanted me to stay many days, and then Girgis said I must stop at Feshn where he had a fine house and garden, and he would go on horseback and meet me there, and would give me a whole troop of Fellaheen to pull the boat up quick. Omar's eyes twinkled with fun as he translated this, and said he knew the Sitt would cry out, as she always did about the fellaheen, as if she were hurt herself. He told Girgis that the English customs did not allow people to work without pay, which evidently seemed very absurd to the whole party.

December 1 1862. The thing that strikes me most is the tolerant spirit that I see everywhere. They say, 'Ah! It is your custom', and express no sort of condemnation, and Muslims and Christians appear perfectly good friends, as my story of Bibbeh goes to prove. I have yet to see the much-talked-of fanaticism, at present I have not met with a sympton of it. There were thirteen Copt families at Bibbeh and a considerable Muslim population, who had elected Girgis their headman and kissed his hand very heartily as our procession moved through the streets. Omar said he was a very good man and much liked.

The villages look like slight elevations in the mud banks cut into square shapes. The best houses have neither paint, whitewash, plaster, bricks nor windows, nor any visible roofs. They don't give one the notion of human dwellings at all at first, but soon the eye gets used to the absence of all that constitutes a house in Europe, the impression of wretchedness wears off, and one sees how picturesque they are, with palm-trees and tall pigeon-houses, and here and there the dome over a saint's tomb.

The men at work on the river-banks are exactly the same colour as the Nile mud, with just the warmer hue of the blood circulating beneath the skin. Prometheus has just formed them out of the universal material at hand, and the sun breathed life into them. Poor fellows—even the boatmen, ragged crew as they are—say, 'Ah, fellaheen!' with a contemptuous pity when they see me watch the villagers at work.

The other day four huge barges passed us towed by a steamer and crammed with hundreds of the poor souls torn from their homes to work at the Isthmus of Suez, or some palace of the Pasha's, for a nominal piastre a day, and find their own bread and water and cloak.[1] One of my crew, Andrasool, a black savage whose function is always to jump overboard whenever the rope gets entangled or anything is wanted, recognised some relations of his from a village close to Aswan. There was much shouting and poor Andrasool looked very mournful all day. It may be his turn next.

When I call my crew black, don't think of negroes. They are elegantly-shaped Arabs and all gentlemen in manners, and the black is transparent, with amber *reflets* under it in the sunshine; a negro looks *blue* beside them.

Assiut, December 10. I could not send a letter from Minieh, where we stopped. I visited a sugar manufactory and a gentlemanly Turk, who superintended the district, the Mudir. I heard a boy singing a *Zikr* (the ninety-nine attributes of God) to a party of dervishes in a mosque, and I think I never heard anything more beautiful and affecting. Ordinary Arab singing is harsh and nasal, but it can be wonderfully moving.

Wassef, a Copt here, lent me his superb donkey to go up to the tomb in the mountain. The tomb is a mere cavern, so defaced, but the view of beautiful Assiut standing in the midst of a loop of the Nile was ravishing. A green deeper and brighter than England, graceful minarets in crowds, a picturesque bridge, gardens, palm-trees, then the river beyond it, the barren yellow cliffs as a frame all around that. At our feet a woman was being carried to the grave, and the boys' voices rang out the Koran full and clear as the long procession—first white turbans and then black veils and robes—wound along.

It is all a dream to me. You can't think what an odd effect it is to take up an English book and read it and then look up and hear the

[1] Janet Ross had visited the work on the Suez Canal with de Lesseps and wrote to her mother on March 1 1862 while Lucie was still at the Cape: 'You may imagine what a hole has to be made in the sand when I tell you that the canal is to be 189 feet broad and 28 feet deep. I pitied the poor *fellaheen* their treadmill labour. Up and down the sliding sand-banks from sunrise to sunset, and a lick over the back when they did not go fast enough ... Eight thousand of the men came from the Upper Nile between Philae and Khartum, a far finer race then the Lower Egyptians and better and faster workers. There was more animation in their section, much talking and some laughter, while the *Beheré* looked dispirited and melancholy.' (*The Fourth Generation, Reminiscences* by Janet Ross, pp 126,7, Constable, 1912.)

men cry, 'Yah Mohammed'. 'Bless thee, Bottom, how art thou translated'; it is the reverse of all one's former life when one sat in England and read of the East. *'Und nun sitz ich mitton drein'* [and now I sit in the middle of it all], in the real, true Arabian Nights, and don't know whether 'I be I as I suppose I be' or not.

I do so long for my Rainie. The little Copt girls are like her, only pale; but they don't let you admire them for fear of the evil-eye.

Thebes, December 20. I have had a long, dawdling voyage up here, but enjoyed it much, and have seen and heard many curious things. I only stop here for letters and shall go on at once to Wadi Halfa, as the weather is very cold still, and I shall be better able to enjoy the ruins when I return about a month hence, and shall certainly prefer the tropics now.

I can't describe the kindness of the Copts. The men I met at a party in Cairo wrote to all their friends and relations to be civil to me. Wassef's attentions consisted first in lending me his superb donkey and accompanying me about all day. Next morning arrived a procession headed by his clerk, a gentlemanly young Copt, and consisting of five black mamelukes carrying a live sheep, a huge basket of the most delicious bread, a pile of cricket-balls of creamy butter, a large copper cauldron of milk and a cage of poultry. I was confounded, and tried to give a good baksheesh to the clerk, but he utterly declined.

At Girgeh one Mishreghi was waiting for me, and was in despair because he had only time to get a few hundred eggs, two turkeys, a heap of butter and a can of milk. At Keneh one Issa (Jesus) also lent a donkey, and sent me three boxes of delicious Mecca dates, which Omar thought stingy. Such attentions are agreeable here where good food is not to be had except as a gift. They all made me promise to see them again on my return and dine at their houses, and Wassef wanted to make a fantasia and have dancing girls.

How you would love the Arab women in the country villages. I wandered off the other day alone, while the men were mending the rudder, and fell in with a troop of them carrying water-jars—such sweet, graceful beings, all smiles and grace. One beautiful woman pointed to the village and made signs of eating and took my hand to lead me. I went with her, admiring them as they walked. Omar came running after and wondered I was not afraid. I laughed, and said they were much too pretty and kindly-looking to frighten anyone, which amused them immensely when he told them so. They all wanted me to go and eat in their houses, and I had a great mind to it, but the wind was fair and the boat waiting, so I bid my beautiful friends farewell. They asked if we wanted anything—milk or eggs— for they would give it with pleasure, it was not their custom to sell things, they said; I offered a bit of money to a little naked child, but his mother would not let him take it.

I shall never forget the sweet, engaging creatures at that little village, or the dignified politeness of an old weaver whose loom I walked in to look at, and who also wished to 'set a piece of bread before me'.

It is the true poetical pastoral life of the Bible in the villages where the English have not been, and happily they don't land at the little places. Thebes[1] has become an English watering-place. There are now nine boats laying here, and the great object is to *do the Nile* as fast as possible. It is a race up to Wadi Halfa or Aswan. All the English stay here and 'make Christmas', as Omar calls it, but I shall go on and do my devotions with the Copts at Esneh or Edfu. I found that their seeming disinclination to let one attend their service arose from an idea that we English would not recognise them as Christians.

In a week I shall be in Nubia.[2] Some year we must all make this voyage; you would revel in it. Kiss my darlings for me.

[1] Lucie was at Luxor but she often dated her letters as from Thebes, the name given by the Greeks to the ancient capital of Upper Egypt—Homer refers to it in the Iliad. This grea tmetropolis had temples and tombs on both banks of the Nile, including the well-known temples of Karnac and Luxor on the east bank. It is four hundred and fifty miles by river from Cairo.

She also dated her letters as from el-Uksur, Arabic for 'the Castles', and the origin of the name Luxor.

[2] The Nubia Lucie is referring to is the region between the first cataract at Aswan and the second cataract below Wadi Halfa. John Lewis Burckhardt and other travellers' besides Lucie Duff Gordon, have found the Nubians an attractive people; although great travellers they have nearly always returned to their home—the long strip of Nile Valley enclosed by barren sandstone hills. Many of them have now had to be moved elsewhere because of the huge lake, known as Nasser's lake, which is being formed by the building of the High Dam at Aswan.

VI

'Black as ink and handsome
as the Greek Bacchus'

February 11 1863. At Aswan I had been strolling about in that most
poetically melancholy spot, the granite quarry of old Egypt and
burial-place of Muslim martyrs, and as I came homewards along the
bank a party of slave merchants, who had just loaded their goods for
Senaar from the boat on the camels, asked me to dinner, and, oh! how
delicious it felt to sit on a mat among the camels and strange bales
of goods and eat the hot tough bread, sour milk and dates, offered
with such stately courtesy. We got quite intimate over our leather
cup of sherbet (brown sugar and water), and the handsome jet-black
men, with features as beautiful as those of the young Bacchus,
described the distant lands in a way which would have charmed
Herodotus. They proposed to me to join them, 'they had food
enough', and Omar and I were equally inclined to go.

It is of no use to talk of the ruins; everybody has said, I suppose,
all that can be said . . . The scribbling of names is quite infamous,
beautiful paintings are defaced by Tomkins and Hobson, but worst
of all Prince Pückler Muskau[1] has engraved his and his *Ordenskreuz*
in huge letters on the naked breast of that august and pathetic giant

---

[1] Prince Von Hermann Puckler-Muskau, 1785-1871, was a strange character who wrote
a number of accounts of his travels including one on Egypt at the time of Mohammed Ali
and one on his tour of England, Ireland and France which was translated by Sarah Austin
as *Tour of a German Prince*. A correspondence began and Sarah fell in love with him by
post but was disappointed when she finally met him. It is unlikely that Lucie knew anything about her mother's infatuation with a Prince who had a very bad reputation in
England. 'They call you even to me', wrote Sarah to him, 'a liar and a swindler, and
adventurer, a coward' etc. See Introduction p. 12.

who sits at Abu Simbel.[1] I wish someone would kick him for his profanity.

I have eaten many odd things with odd people in queer places, dined in a respectable Nubian family (the castor-oil was trying), been to a Nubian wedding—such a dance I saw. Made friends with a man much looked up to in his place (Kalabshee—notorious for cutting throats), inasmuch as he had killed several intrusive tax-gatherers and recruiting officers. He was very gentlemanly and kind and carried me up a place so steep I could not have reached it. Just below the cataract—by-the-by going up is nothing but noise and shouting, but coming down is fine fun—*Fantasia khateer* as my excellent little Nubian pilot said. My sailors all prayed away manfully and were horribly frightened. I confess my pulse quickened, but I don't think it was fear.

Below the cataract I stopped for a religious fête, and went to a holy tomb with the dervish, so extraordinarily handsome and graceful. He took care of me through the crowd, who never had seen a Frank woman before and crowded fearfully, and pushed the true believers unmercifully to make way for me. He was particularly pleased at my not being afraid of Arabs; I laughed, and asked if he was afraid of us. 'Oh no! he would like to come to England; when there he would work to eat and drink, and then sit and sleep in the church'. I was positively ashamed to tell my religious friend that with us the 'house of God' is not the house of the poor stranger. I asked him to eat with me but he was holding a preliminary Ramadan (it begins next week), and could not; but he brought his handsome sister, who was richly dressed, and begged me to visit him and eat of his bread, cheese and milk.

Such is the treatment one finds if one leaves the highroad and the backsheesh-hunting parasites. There are plenty of 'gentlemen' bare-footed and clad in a shirt and cloak ready to pay attentions which you may return with a civil look and greeting, and if you offer a cup of coffee and a seat on the floor you give great pleasure, still more if you eat the dourah and dates, or bread and sour milk with an appetite.

[1] Rameses II (about 1250 B.C.) The rock-hewn colossi stand sixty-five feet high but much of the temple was buried in sand when visited by Lucie, as shown in the illustration by David Roberts. It had aroused the interest of J. L. Burckhardt who encouraged Belzoni to excavate the temple which he did in 1817. The monuments have now been raised to higher ground as the building of the huge Nasser Dam at Aswan would have submerged them.

At Kom Ombo we met a Rifaee dervish with his basket of tame snakes. After a little talk he proposed to initiate me, and so we sat down and held hands like people marrying. Omar sat behind me and repeated the words as my 'Wakeel', then the Rifaee twisted a cobra round our joined hands and requested me to spit on it, he did the same and I was pronounced safe and enveloped in snakes. My sailors groaned and Omar shuddered as the snakes put out their tongues—the darweesh and I smiled at each other like Roman augurs. I need not say the creatures were toothless[1].

It is worthwhile going to Nubia to see the girls. Up to twelve or thirteen they are neatly dressed in a bead necklace and a leather fringe four inches wide round the loins, and anything so absolutely perfect as their shapes or so sweetly innocent as their look can't be conceived.

My pilot's little girl came in the dress mentioned before, carrying a present of cooked fish on her head and some fresh eggs; she was four years old and so *klug*. I gave her a captain's biscuit and some figs, and the little pet sat with her little legs tucked under her, and ate it so *manierlich* and was so long over it, and wrapped up some more white biscuit to take home in a little rag of a veil so carefully. I longed to steal her, she was such a darling.

Two beautiful young Nubian women visited me in my boat, with hair in little plaits finished off with lumps of yellow clay burnished like golden tags, soft, deep bronze skins, and lips and eyes fit for Isis and Hathor. Their very dress and ornaments were the same as those represented in the tombs, and I felt inclined to ask them how many thousand years old they were. In their house I sat on an ancient Egyptian couch with the semicircular head-rest, and drank out of crockery which looked antique, and they brought a present of dates in a basket such as you may see in the British Museum. They are dressed in drapery like Greek statues, and are as perfect, but have hard, bold faces, and, though far handsomer, lack the charm of the Arab women; and the men, except at Kalabshee and those from far up the country, are not such gentlemen as the Arabs.

At Aswan I dined on the shore with the 'blameless Ethiopians', merchants from Sudan, black as ink and handsome as the Greek Bacchus. The bas-reliefs in the tombs are accurate representations of the country people of the present day—especially the Nubians and Copts. Most ancient of all though are the Copts, and last Sunday in

[1] Lucie knew about snakes as she had kept one as a girl, see Introduction p. 16.

their church I saw a procession carrying babies three times round it, copied from the temple of Athor at Dendera. The slightly aquiline nose and long eye are the very same as the profiles of the tombs and temples, and also like the very earliest Byzantine pictures; *du reste,* the face is handsome, but generally sallow and rather inclined to puffiness, and the figure wants the grace of the Arabs. Nor has any Copt the thoroughbred, *distingué* look of the meanest man or woman of good Arab blood. Their feet are the long-toed, flattish foot of the Egyptian statue, while the Arab foot is classically perfect and you could put your hand under the instep. The beauty of the Ababdeh, black, naked and shaggy-haired, is quite marvellous. I never saw such delicate limbs and features, or such eyes and teeth.

I have seen all the temples in Nubia and nine of the tombs at Thebes. Some are wonderfully beautiful—Abu Simbel, Kalabshee, Kom Ombo—a little temple at El Kab, lovely—three tombs at Thebes and most of all Abydos; Edfu and Dendera are the most perfect, Edfu quite perfect, but far less beautiful. But the most lovely object my eyes ever saw is the island of Philæ. It gives one quite the supernatural feeling of Claude's best landscapes, only not the least like them—*ganz anders* [quite different]. The Arabs say that Ans el Wagud, the most beautiful of men, built it for his most beautiful beloved, and there they lived in perfect beauty and happiness all alone. If the weather had not been so cold while I was there I should have lived in the temple, in a chamber sculptured with the mystery of Osiris' burial and resurrection. Omar cleaned it out and meant to move my things there for a few days, but it was too cold to sleep in a room without a door.

Sally's delight at the ancient temples was boundless and she rode a dozen miles on a donkey, without saddle or bridle, to see them intrepidly. It was droll to hear my boatmen coaxing her to give them soap, or needles and thread. 'Ya Sara' was the constant cry. She has enjoyed her travels thoroughly and is as fond of the Arabs as I am; she and Omar are great friends.

A clever old dragoman I met at Philæ offers to lend me furniture for a lodging or a tent for the desert, and when I hesitated he said he was very well off and it was not his business to sell things, but only to be paid for his services by rich people, and that if I did not accept it as he meant it he should be quite hurt. This is what I have met with from everything Arab—nothing but kindness and politeness. I shall say farewell to Egypt with real feeling; among other things, it will be quite a pang to part with Omar who has been my shadow all this time and for whom I have quite an affection, he is so thoroughly good and amiable.

Mustapha Agha, the [British] consular agent at Thebes, has offered me a house of his, up among the tombs in the finest air, if ever I want it. He was very kind and hospitable indeed to all the English there. I went into his hareem, and liked his wife's manners very much. It was charming to see that she henpecked her handsome old husband completely. They had fine children and his boy, about thirteen or so, rode and played Jereed one day when Abdallah Pasha had ordered the people of the neighbourhood to do it for General Parker. I never saw so beautiful a performance. The old General and I were quite excited, and he tried it to the great amusement of the Shaikh el Beled. Some young Englishmen were rather grand about it, but declined mounting the horses and trying a throw. The Shaikh and young Hassan and then old Mustapha wheeled round and round like beautiful hawks, and caught the palm-sticks thrown at them as they dashed round. It was superb, and the horses were good, though the saddles and bridles were rags and ends of rope, and the men mere tatterdemalions.

VII

'One is constantly reminded of Herodotus'

February 1863. Nothing is more striking to me than the way in which one is constantly reminded of Herodotus. The Christianity and the Islam of this country are full of the ancient worship, and the sacred animals have all taken service with Muslim saints. At Minieh one reigns over crocodiles; higher up I saw the hole of Æsculapius' serpent at Gebel Sheykh Hereedee, and I fed the birds—as did Herodotus—who used to tear the cordage of boats which refused to feed them, and who are now the servants of Shaikh Naooneh, and still come on board by scores for the bread which no Reis dares refuse them. Bubastis' cats are still fed in the Cadi's court at public expense in Cairo, and behave with singular decorum when 'the servant of the cats' serves them their dinner.

Mar Girgis is simply Ammon Ra, the God of the Sun and great serpent-slayer, who is still revered in Egypt by all sects, and Seyd el-Bedawee is as certainly one form of Osiris. His festivals, held twice a year at Tanta, still display the symbol of the Creator of all things. All is thus here—the women wail the dead, as on the old sculptures; they offer sacrifices to the Nile, and walk round ancient statues in order to have children. The ceremonies at births and burials are not Muslim, but ancient Egyptian. All the ceremonies are pagan, and would shock an Indian Mussulman as much as his objection to eat with a Christian shocks an Arab. This country is a palimpsest, in which the Bible is written over Herodotus, and the Koran over that. In the towns the Koran is most visible, in the country Herodotus. I fancy it is most marked and most curious among the Copts, whose churches are shaped like the ancient temples, but they are so much less accessible than the Arabs that I know less of their customs.

As to interest and enjoyment, I don't think Italy or Greece can equal the sacred Nile, the perfect freshness of the gigantic buildings, the beauty of the sculptures, and the charm of the people.

Omar wanted to hear all the news you sent about the children and was quite delighted to hear of Maurice's good report at school and is much interested about Eton. He thinks that the 'father of the children'—you to wit—will send a sheep to the master who teaches Maurice. I hope and trust I shall soon hear more news as good as the last. I always thought he was made of good stuff and not the stupid boy you and Janet voted him. My darling Rainie! How I did wish for her to play with Ahmad in the boat and see the pretty Nubian boys and girls. I shall stay here ten days [1] or so and then return slowly to get to Cairo on the 10th of March, the last day of Ramadan. I will stay a short time in Cairo and then take a little boat and drop down to Alexandria and see Janet.

I have learned a new code of propriety altogether—*célà a du bon et du mauvais*, like ours. When I said 'my husband' Omar blushed and gently corrected me; when my donkey fell in the streets he cried with vexation, and on my mentioning the fall to Hekekian Bey he was quite indignant. 'Why you say it, ma'am? that shame'—a *faux pas* in fact. On the other hand they mention all that belongs to the production of children with perfect satisfaction and pleasure. A very pleasing, modest and handsome Nubian young woman, wishing to give me the best present she could think of, brought me a mat of her own making, and which had been her marriage-bed. It was a gift both friendly and honourable and I treasure it accordingly. Omar translated her message with equal modesty and directness. He likewise gave me an exact description of his own marriage—the whole ceremony in detail and did not drop any curtain at all—appealing to my sympathy about the distress of absence from his wife. I intimated that English people were not accustomed to some words and might be shocked, on which he said, 'Of course I speak not of my hareem to English gentleman, but to good Lady can speak it'.

Everyone is cursing the French here. Forty thousand men always at work at the Suez Canal at starvation-point, does not endear them to the Arabs. There is great excitement as to what the new Pasha

[1] Lucie is writing from Luxor to her husband.

will do. If he ceases to give forced labour, the Canal, I suppose, must be given up.[1]

A few miles below Girgeh, March 7 1863. I am wonderfully better; the fine air of Nubia seemed to suit me as well as that of Caledon. It has the same merits, and the same drawback of violent winds. Fancy that meat kept ten and fourteen days under a sun which even I was forced to cover my head before! In Cairo you must cook your meat in two days and in Alexandria, as soon as it is killed—and the sun is nothing there. But in Nubia I walked till I wore out my shoes and roasted my feet, and was as dry as a chip. In Cairo the winter has been terribly cold and damp, as the Coptic priest told me yesterday at Girgeh, so I don't repent the expense of the boat, for I am *all* the money the better, and really think of getting well.

Now that I know the ways of this country a little, which Herodotus truly says is like no other,[2] I see that I might have gone and lived at Thebes or at Keneh or Aswan on next to nothing, but then how could I know it? The English have raised a mirage of false wants and extravagance which the servants of the country of course, some from interest and others from mere ignorance, do their best to keep up. As soon as I had succeeded in really persuading Omar that I was not as rich as a Pasha and had no wish to be thought so, he immediately turned over a new leaf as to what must be had and said, 'Oh, if I could have thought an English lady would have eaten and lived and done the least like Arab people, I might have hired a house at Keneh for you, and we might have gone up in a clean passenger boat, but I thought no English could bear it'.

At Cairo, where we shall be, *Inshallah*, on the 19th, Omar will

[1] Ismail, the new Pasha or Viceroy (the Sultan of Turkey did not make him Khedive until later), succeeded his uncle, Said Pasha, in January 1863. Ismail, noted William Thayer in his diary, was short but strongly built; he had 'reddish, sandy hair with whiskers neatly trimmed'.

At a meeting with the Consular representatives of Foreign Powers soon after his accession, Ismail made a short speech in good French, stating that he would reverse the extravagant policy of his predecessors, a promise he did not keep.

Ismail also stated that he would abolish the system of forced labour (the corvée), whereupon the French Consul quickly interrupted to ask that it should not be abolished for work on the Suez Canal, to which Ismail agreed. (From the American Consul's diary published in *Lucie Duff Gordon* by Gordon Waterfield, Murray 1937.)

[2] There are the well-known chapters 35 and 36 in which Herodotus enlarges on his statement that 'just as the climate of Egypt and its river differ from all others, so the customs and laws of the Egyptians are contrary to those of other men in almost all respects'. Herodotus went to Egypt as a tourist in about 450 B.C. and stayed from August to December and his delightful account is contained in Book II of the nine books of his history.

F

get a lodging and borrow a few mattresses and a table and chair and, as he says, 'keep the money in our pockets instead of giving it to the hotel'.

A little below Thebes I stopped, and walked inland to Koos to see a noble old mosque falling to ruin. No English had ever been there and we were surrounded by a crowd in the bazaar. Instantly five or six tall fellows with long sticks improvised themselves our bodyguard and kept the people off, who *du reste* were perfectly civil and only curious to see such strange 'hareem,' and, after seeing us well out of the town, evaporated as quietly as they came without a word. I gave about tenpence to buy oil, as it is Ramadan, and the mosque ought to be lighted, and the old servant of the mosque kindly promised me full justice at the Day of Judgment, as I was one of those Nasranee of whom the Lord Mohammed said that they are not proud and wish well to the Muslimeen. Mohammed Ali Pasha had confiscated all the lands belonging to the mosque, and allowed 300 piastres—not £2 a month—for all expenses; of course the noble old building with its beautiful carving and arabesque mouldings must fall down. There was a smaller one beside it, where he declared that anciently forty girls live unmarried and recited the Koran.

Some way above Bellianeh Omar asked eagerly leave to stop the boat as a great Shaikh had called to us, and we should inevitably have some disaster if we disobeyed. So we stopped and Omar said, 'come and see the Shaikh, ma'am'. I walked off and presently found about thirty people, including all my own men, sitting on the ground round St Simon Stylites—without the column. A hideous old man like Polyphemus, utterly naked, with the skin of a rhinoceros all cracked with the weather, sat there, and had sat day and night, summer and winter, motionless for twenty years. He never prays, he never washes, he does not keep Ramadan, and yet he is a saint.

Of course I expected a good hearty curse from such a man, but he was delighted with my visit, asked me to sit down, ordered his servant to bring me sugar-cane, asked my name and tried to repeat it over and over again, and was quite talkative and full of jokes and compliments, and took no notice of anyone else. Omar and my crew smiled and nodded, and all congratulated me heartily. Such a distinction proves my own excellence (as the Shaikh knows all people's thoughts), and is sure to be followed by good fortune. Finally Omar proposed to say the *Fathah* in which all joined except the

Shaikh, who looked rather bored by the interruption, and desired us not to go so soon, unless I were in a hurry.

A party of Beduin came up on camels with presents for the holy man, but he took no notice of them, and went on questioning Omar about me, and answering my questions. What struck me was the total absence of any sanctimonious air about the old fellow, he was quite worldly and jocose; I suppose he knew that his position was secure, and thought his dirt and nakedness proved his holiness enough. Omar then recited the *Fathah* again, and we rose and gave the servants a few foddahs—the saint takes no notice of this part of the proceeding—but he asked me to send him twice my hand full of rice for his dinner, an honour so great that there was a murmur of congratulation through the whole assembly.

I asked Omar how a man could be a saint who neglected all the duties of a Muslim, and I found that he fully believed that Shaikh Seleem could be in two places at once, that while he sits there on the shore he is also at Mecca, performing every sacred function and dressed all in green. 'Many people have seen him there, ma'am, quite true.'

From Bellianeh we rode on pack-donkeys without bridles to Abydos,[1] six miles through the most beautiful crops ever seen. The absence of weeds and blight is wonderful, and the green of Egypt, where it is green, would make English green look black. Beautiful cattle, sheep and camels were eating the delicious clover, while their owners camped there in reed huts during the time the crops are growing. Such a lovely scene, all sweetness and plenty. We ate our bread and dates in Osiris' temple, and a woman offered us buffalo milk on our way home, which we drank warm out of the huge earthen pan it had been milked in.

Assiut, March 9. I found here letters from Alick, telling me of dear Lord Lansdowne's death.[2] Of course I know that his time was come, but the thought that I shall never see his face again, that all

---

[1] Abydos is one of the most ancient cities of Upper Egypt and became, during the XIIth dynasty, the place of pilgrimage and worship of Osiris, whose sacred head was stated to be preserved there. Temples were built on the site from the time of the 1st dynasty for about four thousand years.

[2] Henry Petty Fitzmaurice, third marquess of Lansdowne, was born in 1780 and died in January 1863 as a result of a fall at Bowood. He was a prominent leader of the Whig Party for over fifty years and had wide influence. Bowood and Lansdowne House were meeting places for politicians and those interested in literature and painting.

that kindness and affection is gone out of my life, is a great blow. No friend could leave such a blank to me as that old and faithful one, though the death of younger ones might be more tragic; but so many things seem gone with him into the grave. Many indeed will mourn that kind, wise, steadfast man—*Antiqua fides*. No one nowadays will be so noble with such unconsciousness and simplicity. I have bought two Coptic turbans to make a black dress out of. I thought I should like to wear it for him—here, where 'compliment' is out of the question.

March 10. I have got a superb illumination tonight, improvised by Omar in honour of the Prince of Wales's marriage, and consequently am writing with flaring candles, my lantern being on duty at the masthead, and the men are singing an epithalamium and beating the tarabookeh as loud as they can. Omar wishes he could know exactly when the Prince 'takes his wife's face' that we might shriek for joy according to Arab fashion.

I dined and spent the day with Wassef and his hareem, such an amiable, kindly household. I was charmed with their manner to each other, to the slaves and family. The slaves (all Muslims) told Omar what an excellent master they had. He had meant to make a dance-fantasia, but as I had not good news it was countermanded. Poor Wassef ate his boiled beans rather ruefully, while his wife and I had an excellent dinner, she being excused fasting on account of a coming baby.

The Copt fast is no joke, neither butter, milk, eggs nor fish being allowed for fifty-five days. They made Sally dine with us, and Omar was admitted to wait and interpret. Wassef's younger brother waited on him as in the Bible, and his clerk, a nice young fellow, assisted. Black slaves brought the dishes in, and capital the food was. There was plenty of joking between the lady and Omar about Ramadan, which he had broken, and the Nasranee fast, and also about the number of wives allowed, the young clerk intimating that he rather liked that point in Islam. I have promised to spend ten or twelve days at their house if ever I go up the Nile again. I have also promised to send Wassef all particulars as to the expense, etc. of educating his boy in England, and to look after him and have him to our house in the holidays. I can't describe how anxiously kind these people were to me. One gets such a wonderful amount of sympathy and real hearty kindness here.

A curious instance of the affinity of the British mind for prejudice is the way in which every Englishman I have seen scorns the Eastern Christians, and droll enough that sinners like Kinglake and I should be the only people to feel the tie of the 'common faith' (*vide* 'Eothen'). A very pious Scotch gentleman wondered that I could think of entering a Copt's house, adding that they were the publicans (tax-gatherers) of this country, which is partly true. I felt inclined to mention that better company than he or I had dined with publicans, and even sinners.

VIII

'I have a black slave—Zeynab'

Cairo, March and April 1863. After leaving Assiut I caught cold. The worst of going up the Nile is that one must come down again and find horrid fogs, and cold nights with sultry days. So I did not attempt Sakhara and the Pyramids, but came a day before my appointed time to Cairo. Up here in the town it is much warmer and dryer, and my cough is better already. I found all your letters in many volumes, and was so excited over reading them that I could not sleep one moment last night, so excuse dullness, but I thought you'd like to know I was safe in Briggs' bank, and expecting Janet and Ross tonight.

I have had a very severe attack of bronchitis. As I seemed to be getting worse after Janet and Ross left for Alexandria, Omar very wisely sent for Hekekian Bey, who came at once bringing De Leo Bey, the surgeon-in-chief of the Pasha's troops, and also the doctor to the hareem. He has been most kind, coming two and three times a day at first. He won't take any fee, *sous prétexte* that he is *officier du Pasha;* I must send him a present from England. As to Hekekian Bey, he is absolutely the Good Samaritan, and these Orientals do their kindnesses with such an air of enjoyment to themselves that it seems quite a favour to let them wait upon one. It had an odd, dreamy effect to hear old Hekekian Bey and my doctor discoursing in Turkish at my bedside. I shall always fancy the good Samaritan in a tarbush and white beard and very long eyes. Hekekian comes in every day with his handsome old face and a budget of news, all the gossip of the Sultan and his doings.

The Sultan's coming is a kind of riddle. Noone knows what he wants. Ismail Pasha has ordered all the women of the lower orders to keep indoors while he is here, as Arab women are outspoken and might shout out their grievances. The Sultan and his suite have not eaten bread here; all their food and even water to drink has to be brought from Constantinople. I heard that from Hekekian Bey, who formerly owned the eunuch who is now Kislar Aghasy to the Sultan himself, and Hekekian had the honour of kissing his old slave's hand.[1]

I have a black slave—a real one.[2] I looked at her little ears wondering they had not been bored for rings. She fancied I wished them bored (she was sitting on the floor close at my side), and in a minute she stood up and showed me her ear with a great pin through it: 'Is that well, lady?' The creature is eight years old. The shock nearly

[1] The Sultan, Abdel Aziz, had succeeded his brother Abdel Majid on his death in 1861, and came to Egypt to see for himself a country which was stated to be more advanced than his own and where foreigners were investing money. He wished to see what he could gain from Egypt. 'The Sultan, and still more the Sultan's ministers, cannot bear to think that of the large revenue of Egypt not a tenth comes to his hands. They believe that if it were a completely dependent province, like Syria, they would have the spending and the plundering for themselves of the sums that are spent here for Egyptian purposes.

'They are continually intriguing against the Viceroy's quasi-independence. He is surrounded even in his harem by Turkish agents and spies. This naturally throws him on foreign support. Abbas lent on England—Said leans on France. I trust that the time may not come when an Egyptian Viceroy may lean on Russia.

'One of the expedients adopted by each is to get Egypt talked about. The policy of the Porte, in public and in private matters, is always to insulate those whom it means to destroy. Let the man be forgotten and then you may safely hand to him the cup of coffee. The transit and the railway and the Canal are all means by which Egypt is kept before the eyes of the world.

'You will understand much better the policy of both Turkey and Egypt if you bear in mind that many of the measures of each country, though professedly matters of local legislation, are in fact adopted with a view to their effect in Europe.' (Hekekian to Nassau Senior in *Conversations and Journals in Egypt and Malta*.)

[2] It was not the first time that Lucie had looked after a slave (see Introduction p.19). It was true that Said Pasha, the Viceroy, had prohibited the entrance of slaves into Egypt across the frontiers and towards the end of 1855 had issued an edict compelling every master to free any slave who asked for freedom.

Not many, however, wanted to be free because of the difficulty of earning a living and because they were treated well in many of the households. Sabbatier, the French Consul before M. Tastu, had a young slave whom he had bought in Nubia and the boy looked down on the hired servants who could be dismissed at any moment—'*moi, je suis de la maison*', he said.

The new law was not taken very seriously even by the Viceroy whose mother gave him a present of a white slave-girl every year. 'The cases in which the law has been put into force are very few', stated Hekekian Bey. 'You must recollect that our slavery does not resemble that of America or of the West Indies; it is not degrading. For centuries Egypt has been ruled by slaves, almost all its nobles and great men have been slaves or the sons of slaves. Said's mother was a slave, so was Abbas's, so was Halim's, so were almost everybodys'.' (Hekekian to Nassau Senior *Conversations*.)

73

made me faint. What extremities of terror had reduced that little mind to such a state. When she first came, she tells me, she thought I should eat her; now her one dread is that I should leave her behind. She sings a wild song of joy to Maurice's picture and about the little Sitt. [Urania.]

She was sent from Khartoum as a present to Mr Thayer, who has no woman-servant at all. He fetched me to look at her, and when I saw the terror-stricken creature being coarsely pulled about by his cook and groom, I said I would take her for the present. She sings quaint little Kordofan songs all day. She had never seen a needle, and in a fortnight sews very neatly and quickly. She wails aloud when Omar tells her she is not my slave. Zeynab is very quiet and gentle, poor little savage, but blacker than ebony. The utter slavishness of the poor little soul quite upsets me. She has absolutely no will of her own.

Cairo, April 13. I have been out twice for a drive, and saw the sacred Camel bearing the Holy Mahmal rest for its first station outside the town. No words can describe the departure of the Holy Mahmal and the pilgrims for Mecca. I sat for hours in a Beduin tent in a sort of dream. It is the most beautiful sight of man and beast and colour and movement; and their first encampment is in a glorious spot, among the domes and minarets of the ruined tombs of the Mameluke Sultans.

It is a deeply affecting sight, when one thinks of the hardships all these men are prepared to endure. Omar's eyes were full of tears and his voice husky with emotion as he talked about it, and pointed out the Mahmal and the Shaikh-el-Gemel, who leads the Sacred Camel, naked to the waist with flowing hair.

Muslim piety is so unlike what Europeans think it is, so full of tender emotions, so much more sentimental than we imagine—and it is wonderfully strong. I used to hear Omar praying outside my door while I was so ill, 'O God, make her better. O my God, let her sleep,' as naturally as we should say, 'I hope she'll have a good night.'

May 29. Do write and tell me what you wish me to do. If it were not that I cannot endure not to see you and the children, I would stay here and take a house at the Abbassieh in the desert; but I could not endure it. Nor can I endure this wandering life much longer. I must come home and die in peace if I don't get really better.

It would be delightful to have you at Cairo now I have pots and pans and all needful for a house, but a carpet and a few mattresses, if you could camp with me *à l'Arabe*.

How you would revel in old Masr el-Kahira, peep up at lattice windows, gape like a *ghasheem* (green one) in the bazaar, go wild over the mosques, laugh at portly Turks and dignified Shaikhs on their white donkeys, drink sherbet in the streets, ride wildly about on a donkey, peer under black veils at beautiful eyes and feel generally intoxicated! I am quite a good cicerone now of the glorious old city. Omar is in raptures at the idea that the Sidi el Kebir (the Great Master) might come, and still more if he brought the 'little master'. How our hearts would be dilated!

IX

'The days of the beauty of Cairo
are numbered'

May 25 1863. I went out to the tombs yesterday. Fancy that Omar
witnessed the destruction of some sixty-eight or so of the most
exquisite buildings—the tombs and mosques of the Arab Khaleefah,
which Said Pasha used to divert himself with bombarding for practice
for his artillery. Omar was then in the boy corps of camel artillery,
now disbanded. Thus the Pasha added the piquancy of sacrilege to
barbarity.

Our street and neighbours would divert you. Opposite lives a
Christian dyer who must be a seventh brother of the admirable
barber. The same impertinence, loquacity and love of meddling in
everybody's business. I long to see him thrashed, though he is a
constant comedy. My delightful servant Omar Abu-el-Halaweh
(the father of sweets)—his family are pastrycooks—is the type of all
the amiable *jeune premiers* of the stories. I am privately of opinion
that he is Bedr-ed-Deen Hassan, the more that he can make cream
tarts and there is no pepper in them. Cream tarts are not very good,
but lamb stuffed with pistachio nuts fulfils all one's dreams of excellence. The Arabs next door and the Levantines opposite are quiet
enough, but how *do* they eat all the cucumbers they buy off the man
who cries them every morning as 'fruit gathered by sweet girls in
the garden with the early dew'.

The more I see of the back slums of Cairo, the more in love I am
with them. The dirtiest lane of Cairo is far sweeter than the best
street of Paris. Here there is the dirt of negligence, and the dust of
a land without rain, but nothing disgusting; decent Arabs are as

76

clean in their personal habits as English gentlemen. As to the beauty of Cairo, *that* no words can describe. The oldest European towns are tame and regular in comparison, and the people are so pleasant. If you smile at anything that amuses you, you get the kindest, brightest smiles in return; they give hospitality with their faces, and if one brings out a few words, 'Mashallah! what Arabic the Sitt Ingleez speaks'.

The Arabs are clever enough to understand the amusement of a stranger and to enter into it, and are amused in turn, and they are wonderfully unprejudiced. When Omar explains to me their views on various matters, he adds: 'The Arab people think so—I know not if right'; and the way in which the Arab merchants work the electric telegraph, and the eagerness of the fellaheen for steam-ploughs, are quite extraordinary.

They are extremely clever and nice children, easily amused, easily roused into a fury which lasts five minutes and leaves no malice, and half the lying and cheating of which they are accused comes from misunderstanding and ignorance.

The Beduin and the Mughrabi and their noble-looking women are magnificent, and the irregular Turkish and Arab horsemen, so superior to the drilled cavalry, are wildly picturesque. To see a Beduin and his wife walk through the streets of Cairo is superb. Her hand resting on his shoulder, and scarcely deigning to cover her haughty face, she looks down on the Egyptian veiled woman who carries the heavy burden and walks behind her lord and master.

If you have any power over any artists, send them to paint here. No words can describe either the picturesque beauty of Cairo or the splendid forms of the people in Upper Egypt, and above all in Nubia. I was in raptures at seeing how superb an animal man (and woman) really is.

If I could afford it I would have a sketch of a beloved old mosque of mine, falling to decay with three palm trees growing in the middle of it—indeed, I would have a book full, for all is exquisite and, alas, all is going. The old Copt quarter is *entamé* and hideous, shabby French houses are being run up like the one I live in. In this weather how much better would be the Arab courtyard with its *mastabah* and fountain.

The days of the beauty of Cairo are numbered. The mosques are falling to decay, the exquisite lattice windows rotting away and re-placed by European glass and *jalousies*. Only the people and the Government remain unchanged.

If anyone tries to make you believe any bosh about civilization in Egypt, laugh at it. The real life and the real people are exactly as described in the most veracious of books, the 'Thousand and One Nights'; the tyranny is the same, the people are not altered—and very charming people they are. If I could but speak the language I could get into Arab society here through two or three different people, and see more than many Europeans who have lived here all their lives. The Arabs are keenly alive to the least prejudice against them, but when they feel quite safe on that point they rather like the amusement of a stranger.

Alick is quite right that I am in love with the Arab ways and I have contrived to see and know more of family life than many Europeans who have lived here for years.

In a few days I shall go down to Alexandria, if it makes me ill again I must return to Europe or go to Beirut. I can't get a boat under £12. Thus do the Arabs understand competition; the owner of boats said so few were wanted, times were bad on account of the railway, etc., he must have double what he used to charge. In vain Omar argued that that was not the way to get employment. '*Maalesh!*' (Never mind!), and so I must go by rail. Is not that Eastern? Up the river, where there is no railroad, I might have had it at half that rate. All you have ever told me as most Spanish in Spain is in full vigour here, and also I am reminded of Ireland at every turn; the same causes produce the same effects.

Alexandria, May 1863. I have been here a fortnight, but the climate, although very warm, disagrees with me so much that I am going back to Cairo at once, by the advice of the French doctor of the Suez Canal. I fancy I can stay at Cairo a month perhaps, and then I hope to go home, or, if not well enough for that, to go somewhere in the south of Europe. I cannot at all shake off the cough here. The American Consul kindly lends me his nice little bachelor-house, and I take Omar. It is very hot here, but with a sea-breeze which strikes me like ice. Strong people enjoy it, but it gives even Janet cold in the head.

She is *Times'* correspondent and does it very well and gets £100 a year besides its being good for Henry's position. Their prospects are very flourishing indeed since the accession of Ismail Pasha [as Viceroy] and the increased influence of Halim Pasha. If only Henry can keep his health he will do a great business here.

I am terribly disappointed at not being as materially better as I hoped I should be, while in Upper Egypt. I cannot express the longing I have for home and my children, and how much I feel the sort of suspense my illness causes to you all. Perhaps Cairo will cure this cough, and then I may venture home in July—via Liverpool is only £16. Next winter will cost very little, as all my cooking things and boat-furniture are safe at Cairo with my washerwoman, and Mustapha will lend me a house at Thebes, and there will be steamers up the Nile then; so I shall save all the boat expenses which are so great, and shall live for nothing up there. When I went yesterday to deposit my goods at the worthy old woman's house, the neighbours seeing me arrive on my donkey, followed by a cargo of pots and pans, thought I was come to live there, and came running out. I was patted on the back and welcomed, and overwhelmed with offers of service to help to clean my house, etc. Of course all rushed upstairs, and my washerwoman was put to a great expense in pipes and coffee.

X

'The social equality which prevails here'

Alexandria, May 1863. Dearest Mother, I think you would enjoy, as I do, the peculiar sort of social equality which prevails here; it is the exact contrary of French *égalité*. There are the great and powerful people, much honoured (outwardly, at all events), but nobody has *inferiors*. A man comes in and kisses my hand, and sits down *off* the carpet out of respect; but he smokes his pipe, drinks his coffee, laughs, talks and asks questions as freely as if he were an Effendi or I were a fellah; he is not my inferior, he is my poor brother.

The servants in my friends' houses receive me with profound demonstrations of respect, and wait at dinner reverently, but they mix freely in the conversation and take part in all amusements, music, dancing-girls or reading of the Koran. Even the dancing-girl is not an outcast; she is free to talk to me, and it is highly irreligious to show any contempt or aversion. The rules of politeness are the same for all. The passer-by greets the one sitting still, or the one who comes into a room those who are already there, without distinction of rank. When I have greeted the men they always rise, but if I pass without, they take no notice of me.

One must come to the East to understand social equality. As there is no education and no reason why the donkey-boy who runs behind me may not become a great man, and as all Muslims are *ipso facto* equal;[1] money and rank are looked on as mere accidents, and my *savoir vivre* was highly thought of because I sat down with fellaheen and treated everyone as they treat each other.

[1] Edhem Pasha, a previous Governor of Cairo, had started in Egypt as a donkey-boy. He had been a Janissary in Constantinople and had escaped to Alexandria where he ran errands; he was employed in one of Mohammed Ali's factories and eventually became head of a cannon foundry and then Minister of Foreign Affairs under Said Pasha.

All this is very pleasant and graceful, though it is connected with much that is evil. The fact that any man may be a Bey or a Pasha tomorrow is not a good fact, for the promotion is more likely to fall on a bad slave than on a good or intelligent free man. Thus, the only honourable class are those who have nothing to hope from the great—I won't say anything to fear, for all have cause for that. Hence the high respectability and *gentility* of the merchants, who are the most independent of the Government.

In Alexandria all that is changed. The European ideas and customs have extinguished the Arab altogether, and those who remain are not improved by the contact. Only the Beduin preserve their haughty *nonchalance*. I found the Mughrabi bazaar full of them when I went to buy a white cloak, and was amused at the way in which one splendid bronze figure, who lay on the shop-front, moved one leg to let me sit down. They got interested in my purchase, and assisted in making the bargain and wrapping the cloak round me Beduin fashion, and they too complimented me on having 'the face of the Arab', which means Beduin. I wanted a little Arab dress for Rainie, but could not find one, as at her age none are worn in the desert.

I dined one day with Omar, or rather I ate at his house, for he would not eat with me. His sister-in-law cooked a most admirable dinner, and everyone was delighted. It was an interesting family circle. A very respectable elder brother a confectioner, whose elder wife was a black woman, a really remarkable person, who speaks Italian perfectly, and gave me a great deal of information and asked such intelligent questions. She ruled the house but had no children, so he had married a fair, gentle-looking Arab woman who had six children, and all lived in perfect harmony.

Omar's wife is a tall, handsome girl of his own age, with very good manners. She had been outside the door of the close little court which constituted the house *once* since her marriage. I now begin to understand all about womankind. There is a good deal of chivalry in some respects, and in the respectable lower and middle classes the result is not so bad. I suspect that among the rich few are very happy. I will go and see the black woman again and hear more; her conversation was really interesting.

When I first took Omar he was by way of 'ten pounds, twenty pounds', being nothing for my dignity. But as soon as I told him that 'my master was a Bey who got £100 a month and no backsheesh', he was as careful as if for himself. They see us come here and do what only their greatest Pashas do, hire a boat to ourselves, and, of course, think our wealth is boundless. The lying is mostly from fright. They dare not suggest a difference of opinion to a European, and lie to get out of scrapes which blind obedience has often got them into. As to the charges of shopkeepers, that is the custom, and the haggling a ceremony you must submit to. It is for the purchaser or employer to offer a price and fix wages—the reverse of Europe—and if you inquire the price they ask something fabulous at random.

Cairo, May 21. I have attached an excellent donkey and his master, a delightful youth called Hassan, to my household for fifteen piastres (under two shillings) a day. They live at the door, and Hassan cleans the stairs and goes errands during the heat of the day, and I ride out very early, at six or seven, and again at five. The air is delicious now. It is very hot for a few hours, but not stifling, and the breeze does not chill one as it does at Alexandria. I live all day and all night with open windows, and plenty of fresh warm air is the best of remedies. I can do no better than stay here till the heat becomes too great.

I left little Zeynab at Alexandria with Janet's maid Ellen who quite loves her, and begged to keep her 'for company', and also to help in their removal to the new house. She clung about me and made me promise to come back to her, but was content to stop with Ellen, whose affection she of course returns. It was pleasant to see her so happy, and how she relished being 'put to bed' with a kiss by Ellen or Sally.

The fault of my lodging here is the noise. We are on the road from the railway and there is no quiet except in the few hot hours, when nothing is heard but the cool tinkle of the Sakka's brass cup as he sells water in the street, or perchance *ark as-sous* (liquorice-water) or caroub or raisin sherbet. The *ark as-sous* is rather bitter and very good. I drink it a good deal, for drink one must; a gulleh of water is soon gone. A gulleh is a wide-mouthed porous jar, and Nile water drunk out of it without the intervention of a glass is delicious.

Omar goes to market every morning with a donkey—I went too, and was much amused—and cooks, and in the evening goes out with me if I want him. I told him I had recommended him highly, and hoped he would get good employment; but he declares that he will go with no one else so long as I come to Egypt, whatever the difference of wages may be. 'The bread I eat with you is sweet'—a pretty little unconscious antithesis to Dante.

I have been advising his brother Hajjee Ali to start a hotel at Thebes for invalids, and he has already set about getting a house there; there is *one*. Next winter there will be steamers twice a week— to Aswan! Juvenal's distant Syene, where he died in banishment.

My old washerwoman sent me a fervent entreaty through Omar that I would dine with her one day, since I had made Cairo delightful with my presence. If one will only devour these people's food, they are enchanted; they like that much better than a present. So I will honour her house some day. Good old Hannah, she is divorced for being too fat and old, and replaced by a young Turk whose family sponge on Hajjee Ali and are condescending.

There is a quarrel now in the street; how they talk and gesticulate, and everybody puts in a word; a boy has upset a cake-seller's tray; he claims six piastres damages, and everyone gives an opinion *pour ou contre*. We all look out of the window; my opposite neighbour, the pretty Armenian woman, leans out, and her diamond head-oranments and ear-rings glitter as she laughs like a child. The Christian dyer is also very active in the row, which, like all Arab rows, ends in nothing; it evaporates in fine theatrical gestures and lots of talk. Curious! In the street they are so noisy, but get the same men in a coffee-shop or anywhere, and they are the quietest of mankind. Only one man speaks at a time, the rest listen, and never interrupt; twenty men don't make the noise of three Europeans.

I hope to go home next month as soon as it gets too hot here and is likely to be warm in England. I do so long to see the children again. Mother writes me melancholy letters, but Alexander seems very happy. Lord Lansdowne's legacy of £5,000 to Maurice is a real kindness as it secures him a good education, come what may. Alexander's new arrangements have enabled him to repay Mother and I hope to leave Maurice's money to accumulate till he gets to college and wants more than £200 a year. Thanks very much to Omar's good management I have spent little more than £250 of which £120 were for the boat alone.

XI

'Put not thy trust in Princes'

May 1863. Read Janet's letter to *The Times*. Ross is director of the Sudan scheme, and hand-in-glove with all the Pasha's affairs. If things go on as now, he stands to win pots of money. But Egypt will no longer be the poetical land it is with weekly steamers up to remote Aswan and a railway through Nubia. Thank goodness that I have seen the old things.[1]

[1] Janet Ross described the formation of the 'Egyptian Commercial and Trading Company' (at first known as the Sudan Company) of which her husband was one of the directors, in several despatches in which she expressed, very naturally, her enthusiasm for the venture. Indeed, at first it seemed that there was no reason to have any serious misgivings. Lucie was the first to have them and commented later that she did not think that Henry Ross, in spite of his knowledge of the East, understood the situation in Egypt.

David S. Landes in *Bankers and Pashas* (Heinemann 1958) refers to the despatch published from their Alexandria Correspondent on May 29 1863—'even the cautious *Times* predicted a brilliant future for the new firm'. Janet Ross was not by nature cautious and revealed that the Trading Company's expectations were very high and that it planned to become involved in many ventures.

This despatch is given here since some of Lucie's comments in her letters were reactions to the plans. Janet Ross wrote: 'The company I mentioned in my last letter (published in *The Times*, April 7 1863) as having been formed to trade with Upper Egypt, the Sudan and the Red Sea, has brilliant prospects. It is under the patronage of the Viceroy, who takes a lively interest in it and has promised a telegraph above Khartum in five months' time and, it is understood, will eventually extend the railway thither from Cairo. Halim Pasha, his uncle and the second in succession, is president . . .

'Individuals have traded in that country for sometime [Upper Egypt and the Sudan], and have made an average profit of 200 per cent per annum; so that a company with the advantages of large capital, a telegraph, the line of steamers on the Nile and on the Red Sea, ought to be very successful . . . The intention of the company is to commence its operations in Upper Egypt and, as success crowns its efforts, gradually extend them to the Sudan and Abyssinia . . . The products consist of gums in very large quantities, elephant's teeth, ostrich feathers, bees-wax, ox-hides and gold-dust. On the White Nile incredible quantities of fine cattle are reared at a cost of £1 per head, and there is no doubt but that,

Janet and Henry are very eager for you to put Maurice's money [from Lord Lansdowne] into Halim Pasha's loan. I can have no opinion, as, of course, I only hear one side of the question, but the Bible text, 'put not thy trust in princes', rings with Eastern significance in my ears. A Muslim is the best of debtors, but are these half Frenchi-fied, wine-bibbing Turks, Muslims indeed? I should think the affair quite safe myself, but it is a great question whether one's peace of mind is not worth more than eight per cent. I should wish, if possible, to let Maurice's money accumulate till he has to go to college. We shall feel the increased expense more then, and at present we can do without, can't we?

I will do as cheaply as ever I can. I am quite vexed at how much I have spent, but you will see I shall not cost *nearly* so much again now I know so much better how to manage. Janet's cook in Cairo ruined me and I could not help myself, but now I go with Omar and Sally, and though his wages seem high he saves more by his care and honesty.

May 21. Hekekian Bey is my near neighbour, and he comes in and we *fronder* the Government. His heart is sore with disinterested grief for the sufferings of the people. 'Don't they deserve to be decently governed, to be allowed a little happiness and prosperity? They are so docile, so contented; are they not a good people?' Those were his words as he was recounting some new iniquity. Of course half these acts are done under pretext of improving and civilizing, and the Europeans applaud and say, 'Oh, but nothing could be done without forced labour', and the poor fellaheen are marched off in gangs like convicts, and their families starve, and (who'd have thought it) the population keeps diminishing. No wonder the cry is, 'Let the English Queen come and take us'.

You see, I don't see things quite as Ross does, but mine is another

---

with improved communications, a large and valuable trade will be established in live-stock, as the same cattle are worth £20 to £30 a head in Egypt.

'Later on, as business relations are formed with Abyssinia, Massowah would be another port [Suez and Suakin had been mentioned] and at the same time the company projects business with the coffee stations on the opposite shores of the Red Sea, and intends encouraging the culture of cotton in Upper Egypt and the Sudan and establishing cotton gins in various places. The cotton now grown there is sold for a mere trifle for want of means of transport; that of the Sudan, unlike the Egyptian, is a short staple cotton and the introduction of American seed, skilled labour and machinery will improve the quality, and no doubt bring it to high perfection and cause it to become a large article of commerce.'

standpunkt, and my heart is with the Arabs. I care less about opening up the trade with the Sudan and all the new railways, and I should like to see person and property safe, which no one's is here (Europeans, of course, excepted). Ismail Pasha got the Sultan to allow him to take 90,000 feddans of uncultivated land for himself as private property; very well, but the late Viceroy Said granted eight years ago certain uncultivated lands to a good many Turks, his *employés,* in hopes of founding a landed aristocracy and inducing them to spend their capital in cultivation. They did so, and now Ismail Pasha takes their improved land and gives them feddan for feddan of his new land, which will take five years to bring into cultivation, instead. He forces them to sign a *voluntary* deed of exchange, or they go off to Fazogli, a hot Siberia whence none return.

The Sultan also left a large sum of money for religious institutions and charities—Muslim, Jew and Christian. None have received a foddah. It is true the Sultan and his suite plundered the Pasha and the people here; but from all I hear the Sultan really wishes to do good.

What is wanted here is hands to till the ground, and wages are very high; food, of course, gets dearer, and the forced labour inflicts more suffering than before, and the population will decrease yet faster. This appears to me to be a state of things in which it is no use to say that public works must be made at any cost. The wealth will perhaps be increased, if meanwhile the people are not exterminated. Then, every new Pasha builds a huge new palace while those of his predecessors fall to ruin. Mohammed Ali's sons even cut down the trees of his beautiful botanical garden and planted beans there; so money is constantly wasted more than if it were thrown into the Nile, for then the fellaheen would not have to spend their time, so much wanted for agriculture, in building hideous barrack-like so-called palaces.

What chokes me is to hear English people talk of the stick being 'the only way to manage Arabs' as if anyone could doubt that it is the easiest way to manage any people where it can be used with impunity.

May 24. I went to a large unfinished new Coptic church this morning. Omar went with me up to the women's gallery, and was discreetly going back when he saw me in the right place, but the Coptic women began to talk to him and asked questions about me all the time I was looking down on the strange scene below. I believe they celebrate the ancient mysteries still. The clashing of cymbals, the chanting, a humming unlike any sound I ever heard, the strange yellow copes covered with stranger devices—it was *wunderlich*.

At the end everyone went away, and I went down and took off my shoes to go and look at the church. While I was doing so a side-door opened and a procession entered. A priest dressed in the usual black robe and turban of all Copts carrying a trident-shaped sort of candlestick, another with cymbals, a lot of little boys, and two young ecclesiastics of some sort in the yellow satin copes (contrasting queerly with the familiar tarbush of common life on their heads), these carried little babies and huge wax tapers, each a baby and a taper. They marched round and round three times, the cymbals going furiously, and chanting a jig tune. The dear little tiny boys marched just in front of the priest with such a pretty little solemn, consequential air. Then they all stopped in front of the sanctuary, and the priest untied a sort of broad-coloured tape which was round each of the babies, reciting something in Coptic all the time, and finally touched their foreheads and hands with water. This is a ceremony subsequent to baptism after I don't know how many days, but the priest ties and then unties the bands.

Then an old man gave a little round cake of bread, with a cabal-istic-looking pattern on it, both to Omar and to me, which was certainly baked for Isis. A lot of closely-veiled women stood on one side in the aisle, and among them the mothers of the babies who received them from the men in yellow copes at the end of the cere-mony. One of these young men was very handsome, and as he stood looking down and smiling on the baby he held, with the light of the torch sharpening the lines of his features, he would have made a lovely picture. The expression was sweeter than St Vincent de Paul, because his smile told that he could have played with the baby as well as have prayed for it.

In this country one gets to see how much more beautiful a per-fectly natural expression is than any degree of the mystical expression of the best painters, and it is so refreshing that no one tries to look pious. The Muslim looks serious, and often warlike, as he stands at prayer. The Christian just keeps his everyday face. When the Muslim gets into a state of devotional frenzy he does not think of making a face, and it is quite tremendous. I don't think the Copt has any such ardours, but the scene this morning was all the more touching that no one was 'behaving him or herself' at all. A little acolyte peeped into the sacramental cup and swigged off the drops left in it with the most innocent air, and no one rebuked him, and the quite little children ran about in the sanctuary—up to seven they are privileged—and only they and the priests enter it. It is a pretty commentary on the words, 'Suffer the little children', etc.

May 31 [to her aunt, Miss Charlotte Austin]. I hope to go home next month as soon as it gets too hot here and is likely to be warm enough in England. Alick proposes to me to spend this summer somewhere on the Continent, but I don't know where, and my horror of all I saw last autumn of the filth of the south of France and still worse of my glimpse of Italy, is intense. As to the beauty of Cairo, that no words can describe. There are perhaps finer buildings elsewhere, but nowhere such a vast number and such a variety in so small a space.

On board the steamer Venetian, *June 15 1863.* I feel much better since I have been at sea. We left on Thursday and are very comfortable, having the whole spacious ladies' cabin to ourselves and a very pleasant captain. Poor little Zeynab was terribly grieved at my leaving her and Omar shed some 'manly tears' like a great baby, as he kissed my hand on board ship and prayed for me to 'the Preserver'. Janet is remarkably well; Ross, I fear, is very delicate, but apparently likely to make much money.

I am longing to be home to see you all, especially my Rainie who must alter so fast now. I hope I shall not be very much in the way, but I conclude Mother could let me have half her house.

XII

Lucie's return to Egypt and the faithful Omar

Returning through France, October 1 1863. Dearest Mother. I find that people in France are very angry at the movement in Egypt against forced labour and lay it all to English intrigue against the Suez Canal. *Liberté, égalité, fraternité* must sound well to the tune of the *courbash* cracked upon the backs of the fellaheen! I told a Frenchman that I was disposed to be as great an *'intrigante'* as he could conceive if I had the power, if that was his notion of 'intrigue'. They are convinced that carrying earth in baskets for French masters is 'civilization'—*la drôle d'idée*!

I am tolerably well, but at Calais I coughed up a hard substance which I take to be tubercle and if so it confirms the worst opinion of my case. I cannot say I have much idea of ever recovering, but at any rate it is better to do all that is possible, and, painful as the separation is to myself, I believe it is much less to Alick than it would be to have me at home when he might think I should be better away and throwing away the chance of recovery. It is something, at least, to spare others the weary sight of lingering disease and of death if it is to come. Such an absence must break the violence of the pain and there is the knowledge that all has been done that can be done.

What weather! We are drowned here: what it must be on the Rhone. Floods seem the order of the day, old Father Nile and all. How amusing Janet's letter was of ten days ago or so. She does her work very well.[1] I wrote to her to say that I was coming on Monday's

[1] This was Janet's letter in *The Times* of September 28 1863 in which she described how the fellaheen were planting cotton wherever they could, and that the Viceroy, who had had 4,000 acres sown with cotton in 1862 had increased the cultivation to 19,000 acres in 1863.

The Egyptians were, indeed, going through a period of temporary prosperity. The

P & O boat, so Omar will meet us and see our luggage through the customs house and the turbulent porters who beset one on landing. It is quite winter here now, not very cold, but *so* damp.

The reference to her health upset her mother and Lucie replied from Alexandria, October 19. Your letter reached me here this morning. I feel quite grieved to have caused you so much anxiety, but I wished to say once what I feared was very possible. However, I am very well now: and that after a horrid voyage, good as to weather but wretched as to ship and odious as to company. Never again will I sail in French boats if I can help it.

I am competent to describe the horrors of the middle passage—hunger, suffocation, dirt and such *canaille*, high and low, on board. The only gentleman was a poor Moor going to Mecca (who stowed his wife and family in a spare boiler on deck). I saw him washing his children in the morning! *'Que c'est degoutant!'* was the cry of the French spectators. If an Arab washes he is a *sale cochon*—no wonder! A delicious man who sat near me on deck, when the sun came round to our side, growled between his clenched teeth: *'Voilà un tas d'intrigants a l'ombre tandis que le soleil me grille, moi,'* a good résumé of French politics, methinks.

On arriving at noon of Friday, I was consoled by seeing Janet come in a boat looking as fresh and bright and merry as ever she could look. She is remarkably well and greatly improved—so much kinder and more contented. And the faithful Omar was radiant with joy and affection. He has had an offer of a place as messenger with the mails to Suez and back, £60 a year; and also his brother wanted him for Lady Herbert of Lea, who has engaged Hajji Ali. Lady

---

American Civil War had reduced supplies of American cotton for Lancashire and elsewhere, so that there was a big demand for Egyptian cotton. The Viceroy was expecting to make about one million pounds on his cotton crop and doing his utmost to increase his acreage. 'As the price of cotton rose, his appetite for cultivable land became insatiable. No one, even relative or friend, was safe from his covetous eye. And when the Viceroy of Egypt offered what he felt was a reasonable price for a piece of land, the proprietor made haste to accept the honour, however much he may have been otherwise inclined'. (*Bankers and Pashas* by David S. Landes, Heinemann, 1958.)

The high prices paid for cotton led to very great inflation and Egypt, which had been an exporter of grain and beans, had to import foodstuffs. 'It is a strange thing', wrote Janet, 'to see this land of abundance forced to seek abroad for its daily food'. (*The Times*, February 2 1864.)

Herbert[1] offered Omar £8 a month to go with her. You may imagine
how Pietro [her courier, 'who is stupendously grand'] despised his
heathenish ignorance in preferring to stay with me for £3. It quite
confirmed him in his contempt for the Arabs. Omar said he could
not leave me: 'I think my God give her to me to take care of, how
then I leave her if she not very well and not very rich? I can't speak
to my God if I do bad things like that'. Ross has a very high opinion
of Omar, who helped in their removal and saved them much damage;
he seems to have behaved capitally and shown excellent feeling.

Lady Herbert will have trouble with her party, for Pietro told
Hajjee Ali before Sally that Mahommed was in hell and joked un-
pleasantly about his wife. Hajjee Ali went off rather rubbed the
wrong way. Here are no end of 'swells'. Duke of Rutland, Lord and
Lady Scarborough, etc., etc. Lord Howard and Lady Meux again
too. The poor old British Consul, Colquhoun, is in a seventh heaven
of toadydom.

Omar is gone to try to get a *dahabieh* to go up the river, as I hear
that the half-railway, half-steamer journey is dreadfully inconvenient
and fatiguing, and the sight of the overflowing Nile is said to be
magnificent, it is all over the land and eight miles of the railway gone.
Omar kisses your hand and is charmed with the knife, but far more that
my family should know his name and be satisfied with my servant.

Zeyneb is much grown and very active and intelligent, but a little
louder and bolder than she was owing to the maids here wanting to
christianize her, and taking her out unveiled, and letting her be
among the men. However, she is as affectionate as ever, and delighted
at the prospect of going with me. I have replaced the veil, and Sally
has checked her tongue and scolded her sister Ellen for want of
decorum, to the amazement of the latter. Sally went to Omar's house
yesterday and I go today to see the baby and the family and Hajjee
Hanna who has just come from Cairo. My donkey driver Hassan has
already sent me a message from Cairo hoping I do not forget that
he is my servant. Janet has a darling Nubian boy. Oh dear! what an
elegant person Omar seemed after the French 'gentleman', and how

[1] Widow of the handsome and talented Sidney Herbert, War Secretary 1852–55, who
had been a very close friend of Caroline Norton and London society had expected them
to marry. Instead he married Elizabeth A'Court. For his services during the Crimean War
he was made Lord Herbert of Lea and when he died in 1861, Lady Herbert, his widow,
began travelling and writing. George Meredith's novel *Diana of the Crossways* is based,
not very accurately, on the romance of Caroline Norton (Diana) and Sidney Herbert
(Percy Dacier). See Introduction p. 31.

noble was old Hamees's (Janet's doorkeeper) paternal but reverential blessing! It is a real comfort to live in a nation of truly well-bred people and to encounter kindness after the savage incivility of France.

Tuesday, October 20. Omar has got a boat for £12, which is not more than the railway would cost now that half must be done by steamer and a bit on donkeys or on foot. Poor Hajjee Hannah was quite knocked up by the journey down; I shall take her up in my boat. Two and a half hours to sit grilling at noon-day on the banks, and two miles to walk carrying one's own baggage is hard lines for a fat old woman.

Everything is almost double in price owing to the cattle murrain and the high Nile. Such an inundation as this year was never known before. Does the Nile God resent Speke's intrusion on his privacy?[1] It will be a glorious sight, but the damage to crops, and even to the last year's stacks of grain and beans, is frightful. One sails among the palm-trees and over the submerged cotton-fields.

Ismail Pasha has been very active, but, alas! his 'eye is bad', and there have been as many calamities as under Pharaoh in his short reign. The cattle murrain is fearful, and is now beginning in Cairo and Upper Egypt. Ross reckons the loss at twelve millions sterling in cattle. The gazelles in the desert have it too, but not horses, asses or goats.

Ellen is to marry Toderi at once [Janet Ross's Greek cook: 'my foolish housemaid insisted on marrying our Greek cook'].[2] The Greek padre worries their lives out, wanting to know how much money she has—backsheesh! Sally has been very ill again in the old way. I was quite alarmed about her a week ago, but she is better now. I think she was very anxious and unhappy at Ellen's marriage with a Greek, and that always affects those sort of diseases.

Kafr el-Zayat, October 31. We left Alexandria on Thursday about noon, and sailed with a fair wind along the Mahmoudieh Canal. My little boat flies like a bird, and my men are a capital set of fellows, bold and careful sailors. I have only seven in all, but they work well, and at a pinch Omar leaves the pots and pans and handles a rope or a pole manfully. We sailed all night and passed the locks at Atleh at four o'clock yesterday, and were greeted by old Nile tearing down

[1] John Hanning Speke had sent a telegram from Khartum at the beginning of 1863 announcing to the Royal Geographical Society that he had discovered the source of the Nile. When he arrived in Cairo he was received at the palace of Rhoda Island by Ismail Pasha.
[2] Janet Ross describes the Greek marriage ceremony in her drawing-room in *The Fourth Generation*, p. 147. Ellen Naldrett became Mrs Nicopolos.

like a torrent. The river is magnificent, 'seven men's height', my Reis says, above its usual pitch; it has gone down five or six feet and left a sad scene of havoc on either side. However what the Nile takes he repays with threefold interest, they say. The women are at work rebuilding their mud huts, and the men repairing the dykes.

A Frenchman told me he was on board a Pasha's steamer under M. de Lesseps' command, and they passed a flooded village where two hundred or so people stood on their roofs crying for help. Could you believe it: they passed on and left them to drown? None but an eye-witness could have made me believe such villainy.

All today we sailed in such heavenly weather—a sky like nothing but its most beautiful self. At the bend of the river just now we had a grand struggle to get around, and got entangled with a big timber boat. My crew became so vehement that I had to come out with an imperious request to everyone to bless the Prophet. Then the boat nearly pulled the men into the stream, and they pulled and hauled and struggled up to their waists in mud and water, and Omar brandished his pole and shouted, 'Islam el Islam!' which gave a fresh spirit to the poor fellows, and round we came with a dash and caught the breeze again. Now we have put up for the night, and shall pass the railway-bridge tomorrow. The railway is all under water from here up to Tantah—eight miles—and in many places higher up.

Cairo, November 14. Here I am at last in my old quarters at Thayer's house, after a tiresome negotiation with the Vice-Consul, who had taken possession. I was a week in Briggs' damp house, and too ill to write. The morning I arrived at Cairo I was seized with haemorrhage, and had two days of it; however, since then I am better. I was very foolish to stay a fortnight in Alexandria.

The passage under the railway-bridge at Tantah (which is only opened once in two days) was most exciting and pretty. Such a scramble and dash of boats—two or three hundred at least. Old Zedan, the steersman, slid under the noses of the big boats with my little *Cangia* and through the gates before they were well open, and we saw the rush and confusion behind us at our ease, and headed the whole fleet for a few miles. Then we stuck, and Zedan raged; but we got off in an hour and again overtook and passed all. And then we saw the spectacle of devastation—whole villages gone, submerged and melted, mud to mud, and the people with their animals encamped on spits of sand or on the dykes in long rows of ragged makeshift tents, while we sailed over where they had lived. Cotton rotting in all directions and the dry tops crackling under the bows of the boat.

When we stopped to buy milk, the poor woman exclaimed: 'Milk! from where? Do you want it out of my breasts?' However, she took our saucepan and went to get some from another family. No one refuses it if they have a drop left, for they all believe the murrain to be a punishment for churlishness to strangers—by whom committed no one can say. Nor would they fix a price, or take more than the old rate. But here everything had doubled in price.

Never did a present give such pleasure as Mme De Leo's bracelet. De Leo came quite overflowing with gratitude at my having remembered such a trifle as his attending me and coming three times a day! He thinks me looking better, and advises me to stay on here till I feel cold.

Mr Thayer's underling has been doing Levantine rogueries, selling the American protégé's claims to the Egyptian Government, and I witnessed a curious phase of Eastern life. Omar, when he found him in *my* house, went and ordered him out. I was ill in bed, and knew nothing till it was done, and when I asked Omar how he came to do it, he told me to be civil to him if I saw him as it was not for me to know what he was; that was his (Omar's) business. At the same time Mr Thayer's servant sent him a telegram so insolent that it amounted to a kicking. Such is the nemesis for being a rogue here. The servants know you, and let you feel it.

I was quite 'flabbergasted' at Omar, who is so reverential to me and to the Rosses and who I fancied trembled before every European, taking such a tone to a man in the position of a 'gentleman'. It is a fresh proof of the feeling of actual equality among men that lies at the bottom of such great inequality of position. Hekekian Bey has seen a Turkish Pasha's shins kicked by his own servants, who were cognizant of his misdeeds[1]. Finally, on Thursday we got the keys of

[1] Hekekian argued that it was the age of Egyptian civilization which gave the Egyptians their pride. 'Look', he stated to Nassau Senior, 'at an English peasant, or even an English shop-keeper, addressed by a peer. The Englishman knows that the man who is talking to him is his equal in the eyes of the law; that he dares not strike him, dares not touch him . . . yet he is timid, embarrassed and servile. Compare him with an Egyptian in the presence of a Turk. The Egyptian feels that the man before him is his master; that he can oppress him, bastinado him, and ruin him with impunity. Yet, he preserves towards this insolent tyrant the dignity of an equal, almost of a superior. There is nothing degraded in his submission, nothing abject in his fear. To what can this self-respect in misery, this grandeur in humiliation be owing, except to a civilization which has endured for hundreds of generations?' (*Conversations and Journals in Egypt and Malta* by Nassau William Senior.)

the house, and Omar came with two *farrashes* and shovelled out the Levantine dirt, and scoured and scrubbed; and on Friday afternoon (yesterday) we came in.

My friend, Mishragi the Copt from Assiut, is here and wanted to kiss my hand for having so vehemently exhorted him last winter not to give the presents which the Vice-Consul had been requiring of him, but to go straight to Alexandria to Mr Thayer about his business. The American Vice-Consul has just been cashiered ignominiously.

XIII

'There is no conceit like black conceit'

November 14 1863. Zeyneb has been very good ever since she has been with us, she will soon be a complete 'dragowoman', for she is learning Arabic from Omar and English from us fast. In Janet's house she only heard a sort of 'lingua franca' of Greek, Italian, Nubian and English. She asked me, 'How piccolo bint?' (How's the little girl?)—a fine specimen of Alexandrian. Ross is here, and will dine with me tonight before starting by an express train which Ismail Pasha gives him.[1]

On Thursday evening I rode to the Abbassieh, and met all the schoolboys going home for their Friday. Such a pretty sight! The little Turks on grand horses with velvet trappings and two or three grooms running before them, and the Arab boys fetched—some by proud fathers on handsome donkeys, some by trusty servants on foot, some by poor mothers astride on shabby donkeys and taking up their darlings before them, some two and three on one donkey, and crowds on foot. Such a number of lovely faces—all dressed in white European-cut clothes and red tarbushes.

The weather is delicious—much what we had at Bournemouth in summer—but there is a great deal of sickness, and I fear there will be more, from people burying dead cattle on their premises inside the town. It costs 100 *gersh* to bury one outside the town. All labour is rendered scarce, too, as well as food dear, and the streets are not

[1] Both Said and Ismail liked to order special trains on the line which had recently been constructed between Alexandria and Cairo. William Thayer described how Ismail Pasha had ordered a special train from Cairo to Alexandria for the sole purpose of bringing Thayer his uniform which he needed to attend a reception that Ismail was giving to the Consuls a fortnight after the death of Said Pasha. Thayer was shocked that an express train should have been provided to bring the uniform 130 miles from Cairo.

cleaned and water hard to get. My *sakka* comes very irregularly, and makes quite a favour of supplying us with water. All this must tell heavily on the poor. Hekekian's wife had seventy head of cattle on her farm—one wretched bullock is left; and, of seven to water the house in Cairo, also one left, and that expected to die.

Hajjee Ali has just been here, and offers me his tents if I like to go go up to Thebes and not live in a boat, so that I may not be dependent on getting a house there. He is engaged by Lady Herbert of Lea, so will not go to Syria this year and has all his tents to spare. I fancy I might be very comfortable among the tombs of the Kings or in the valley of Assaseef with good tents. It is never cold at all among the hills at Thebes—*au contraire*. On the sunny side of the valley you are broiled and stunned with heat in January, and in the shade it is heavenly.

How I do wish you could come too, how you would enjoy it! I shall rather like the change from a boat life to a Beduin one, with my own sheep and chickens and horse about the tent, and a small following of ragged retainers; moreover, it will be considerably cheaper, I think.

I have seen De Leo Bey who advises me not to live in a tent; it is too hot by day and too cold by night. So I will take a boat conditionally with leave to keep it for four months or to discharge it at Thebes if I find a lodging.

I was at the house of Hekekian Bey the other day when he received a parcel from his former slave, now the Sultan's chief eunuch. It contained a very fine photograph of Shureyk Bey (that is his name), whose face, though negro, is very intelligent and of charming expression—a present of illustrated English books, and some printed music composed by the Sultan, Abd el Aziz, himself. *O tempora! O mores!* one was a waltz.

Monday. I went yesterday to the port of Cairo, Boulaq, to see Hassaneyn Effendi about boats. He was gone up the Nile, and I sat with his wife—a very nice Turkish woman who speaks English to perfection—and heard all sorts of curious things. The Turkish ladies are taking to stays and the fashions of Constantinople are changing with fearful rapidity. Like all Eastern ladies that I have seen she complains of indigestion, and said she knew she ought to go out and to walk, but custom!—*e contro il nostro decoro.*

Tuesday. Since I have been here my cough is nearly gone, and I am better for having good food again. Omar manages to get good mutton, and I have discovered that some of the Nile fish is excellent. The *abyad*, six or eight feet long and very fat, is delicious, and I am told there are still better; the eels are delicate and good too. Maurice might hook an *abyad*, but how would he land him?

The worst is that everything is just double the price of last year, as, of course, no beef can be eaten at all, and the draught oxen being dead makes labour dear as well. The high Nile was a small misfortune compared to the murrain.

Cairo, December 1 1863. Zeyneb, after behaving very well for three weeks, has turned quietly sullen and displays great religious intolerance, in consequence of her association at Alexandria with the Berberi servants who have instilled religious conceit into her mind, poor child. She pretends not to be able to eat because she thinks everything is pig. Omar's eating the food does not convince her. There is no conceit like black conceit. I suppose the Nubians thought it right to preach Islam to her to neutralize Ellen's 'evil' teaching. As she evidently does not like us I will offer her to Mrs Hekekian Bey, and if she does not do there, in a household of black Mussulman slaves, they must pass her on to a Turkish house. She is very clever and I am sorry, but to keep a sullen face about me is more than I can endure, as I have shown her every possible kindness. I think she despises Omar for his affection towards me.

How much easier it is to instil the bad part of religion than the good; it is really a curious phenomenon in so young a child. She waits capitally at table, and can do most things, but she won't move if the fancy takes her except when ordered, and spends her time on the terrace. One thing is that the life is dull for a child, and I think she will be happier in a larger, more bustling house.

Omar performs wonders of marketing and cookery. I have not spent above ten shillings a day for the four of us and have excellent dinners—soup, fish, a *petit plat* or two and a roast every day. But butter and meat and milk are horribly dear. I never saw so good a servant as Omar and such a nice creature, so pleasant and good. When I hear and see what other people spend here in travelling and in living and what bother they have, I say, 'May God favour Omar and his descendants'.

Cairo, December 2. It is beginning to be cold here and I only await the results of my inquiries about possible houses at Thebes to hire a boat and depart. I have sent a request to the French Consul-General, Monsieur Tastu, to let me live in the French house over the temple at Thebes [i.e. the Temple of Luxor.] It is quite empty and would be most comfortable, indeed the only comfortable one there. Monsieur Tastu is the son of the charming poetess of that name whom my mother knew at Paris.

Yesterday I saw a camel go through the eye of a needle—*i.e.*, the low arched door of an enclosure; he must kneel and bow his head to creep through—and thus the rich man must humble himself. See how a false translation spoils a good metaphor, and turns a familiar simile into a ferociously communist sentiment.

I do look forward to next November and your coming here; I know you would donkey-ride all day in a state of ecstasy.

I stayed in bed yesterday for a cold, and my next-door neighbour, a Coptic merchant, kept me awake all night by auditing his accounts with his clerk. How would you like to chant your rows of figures? He had just bought lots of cotton, and I had to get into my door on Monday over a camel's back, the street being filled with bales.

XIV

'Arabs think the English unkind to women'

December 1863. I went to two hareems the other day in Alexandria with a little boy of Mustapha Aga's, and was much pleased. A very pleasant Turkish lady put out all her splendid bedding and dresses for me, and was most amiable. At another, a superb Arab with most *grande dame* manners, dressed in white cotton and with unpainted face, received me statelily. Her house would drive you wild, such antique enamelled tiles covering the panels of the walls, all divided by carved woods, and such carved screens and galleries, all very old and rather dilapidated, but superb, and the lady worthy of the house.

A bold-eyed slave girl with a baby put herself forward for admiration, and was ordered to bring coffee with such cool though polite imperiousness. The quiet scorn of the pale-faced, black-haired Arab was beyond any English powers. Then it was fun to open the lattice and make me look out on the square, and to wonder what the neighbours would say at the sight of my face and European hat. She asked about my children and blessed them repeatedly, and took my hand very kindly in doing so, for fear I should think her envious and fear her eye—as she is childless.

If I could describe all the details of an Arab, and still more of a Coptic, wedding, you would think I was relating the mysteries of Isis. At one house I saw the bride's father looking pale and anxious, and Omar said, 'I think he wants to hold his stomach with both hands till the women tell him if his daughter makes his face white'. It was such a good phrase for the sinking at heart of anxiety. It certainly seems more reasonable that a woman's misconduct should blacken her father's face than her husband's.

There are a good many things about hareem here which I am barbarian enough to think extremely good and rational. An old Turk of Cairo, who had been in Europe, was talking to an Englishman a short time ago, who politely chaffed him about Mussulman license. The venerable Muslim replied, 'Pray, how many women have you, who are quite young, seen (that is the Eastern phrase) in your whole life?' The Englishman could not count—of course not.

'Well, young man, I am old, and was married at twelve, and I have seen in all my life seven women; four are dead, and three are happy and comfortable in my house. *Where are all yours* ?' Hassaneyn Effendi heard the conversation, which passed in French, and was amused at the question.

I have learned a great deal that is curious from Omar's confidences, who tells me his family affairs and talks about the women of his family, which he would not to a man. He refused to speak to his brother, a very grand dragoman, who was with the Prince of Wales, and who came up to us in the hotel at Cairo and addressed Omar, who turned his back on him. I asked the reason, and Omar told me how his brother had a wife, 'An old wife, been with him long time, very good wife'. She had had three children—all dead. All at once the dragoman, who is much older than Omar, declared he would divorce her and marry a young woman. Omar said, 'No, don't do that; keep her in your house as head of your home, and take one of your two black slave girls as your hareem'. But the other insisted, and married a young Turkish wife; whereupon Omar took his poor old sister-in-law to live with him and his own young wife, and cut his grand brother dead.

See how characteristic!—the urging his brother to take the young slave girl 'as his hareem', like a respectable man—that would have been all right; but what he did was 'not good'. I'll trouble you (as Mrs Grote used to say) to settle these questions to everyone's satisfaction. I own Omar seemed to me to take a view against which I had nothing to say. His account of his other brother, a confectioner's household with two wives, was very curious. He and they, with his wife and sister-in-law, all live together, and one of the brother's wives has six children—three sleep with their own mother and three with their *other* mother—and all is quite harmonious.

The old father of my donkey-boy, Hassan, gave me a fine illustration of Arab feeling towards women today. I asked if Abd el-Kader[1] were coming here, as I had heard; he did not know, and asked me if he were not *Akh-ul-Benàt* (a brother of girls). I prosaically said I did not know if he had sisters. 'The Arabs, O lady, call that man a "brother of girls" to whom God has given a clean heart to love all women as his sisters, and strength and courage to fight for their protection.' Our European *galimatias* about the 'smiles of the fair', etc., look very mean beside *'Akh-ul-Benàt'*. Moreover, they carry it into common life. Omar was telling me of some little family tribulations, showing that he is not a little henpecked. His wife wanted all his money. I asked how much she had of her own, as I knew she had property. 'Oh, ma'am, I can't speak of that, shame for me if I ask what money she got.'

A man married at Alexandria, and took home the daily provisions for the first week, after that he neglected it for two days, and came home with a lemon in his hand. He asked for some dinner, and his wife placed the stool and the tray and the washing basin and napkin, and in the tray the lemon cut in quarters. 'Well, and the dinner?' 'Dinner! you want dinner? Where from? What man are you to want women when you don't keep them? I am going to the Cadi to be divorced from you'; and she did.

The man must provide all necessaries for his hareem, and if she has money or earns any she spends it in dress; if she makes him a skullcap or a handkerchief he must pay her for her work. *Tout n'est pas rosé* for these Eastern tyrants, not to speak of the unbridled license of tongue allowed to women and children. Zeyneb hectors Omar and I cannot persuade him to check her. 'How I say anything to it, that one child?' Of course, the children are insupportable, and, I fancy, the women little better.

The English would be a little surprised at Arab judgements of them; they admire our veracity and honesty, and like us on the whole, but they blame the men for their conduct to women. They are shocked at the way Englishmen talk about hareem among themselves, and think the English hard and unkind to their wives, and to women in

[1] Abdel Kader, Emir of Mascara, carried on resistance against the French invasion of Algiers from 1832 to 1847 when he was forced to submit. He was eventually allowed to go to Damascus where, in 1860, he helped to suppress the outbreak of Muslims against Christians and saved many lives, though it is stated that over three thousand were killed. He had visited Egypt in 1827 and is reported to have been impressed with the reforms carried out by Mohammed Ali Pasha with the help of Europeans. On this occasion he did not come to Egypt but visited London and Paris in 1865.

general. English hareemát is generally highly approved, and an Arab thinks himself a happy man if he can marry an English girl.

I think the influence of foreigners is much more real and much more useful on the Arabs than on the Turks, though the latter show it more in dress, etc. But all the engineers and physicians are Arabs, and very good ones, too. Not a Turk has learnt anything practical, and the dragomans and servants employed by the English have learnt a strong appreciation of the value of a character for honesty, deserved or no; but many do deserve it. Compared to the couriers and *laquais de place* of Europe, these men stand very high.

December 17. At last I hope I shall get off in a few days. On applying straight to the French Consulate at Alexandria, Janet got me the loan of the *Maison de France* at Thebes at once. M. Mounier, the agent to Halim Pasha, is going up to Esneh, and will let me travel in the steamer which is to tow his dahabieh. It will be dirty, but will cost little and take me out of this dreadful cold weather in five or six days. Monsieur Mounier is waiting in frantic impatience to set off, and I ditto; but Ismail Pasha keeps him from day to day. The worry of depending on anyone in the East is beyond belief.

You would have laughed to hear me buying a carpet. I saw an old broker with one on his shoulder in the bazaar, and asked the price, 'eight napoleons';[1] then it was unfolded and spread in the street, to the great inconvenience of passers-by, just in front of a coffee-shop. I look at it superciliously, and say, 'Three hundred piastres, O uncle'; the poor old broker cries out in despair to the men sitting outside the coffee-shop: 'O Muslims, hear that and look at this excellent carpet. Three hundred piastres! By the faith, it is worth two thousand!' But the men take my part and one mildly says: 'I wonder that an old man as thou art should tell us that this lady, who is a traveller and a person of experience, values it at three hundred—thinkest thou we will give thee more?' Then another suggests that if the lady will consent to give four napoleons, he had better take them, and that settles it. Everybody gives an opinion here, and the price is fixed by a sort of improvised jury.

Christmas Day. At last my departure is fixed. I embark tomorrow afternoon at Boulaq, and we sail—or steam, rather—on Sunday morning early, and expect to reach Thebes in eight days. I heard a curious illustration of Arab manners today. I met Hassan, the janissary of the American Consulate, a very respectable, good man. He told

---

[1] About £6 8s. 0d; the napoleon being worth sixteen shillings.

me he had married another wife since last year—I asked what for. It was the widow of his brother who had always lived with him in the same house, and who died leaving two boys. She is neither young nor handsome, but he considered it his duty to provide for her and the children, and not to let her marry a stranger.

So you see that polygamy is not always sensual indulgence, and a man may practise greater self-sacrifice so than by talking sentiment about deceased wives' sisters. Hassan has £3 a month, and two wives come expensive. I said, laughing, to Omar as we left him, that I did not think the two wives sounded very comfortable. 'Oh no! not comfortable at all for the man, but he take care of the women, that's what is proper—that is the good Mussulman.'

I shall have the company of a Turkish Effendi on my voyage—a Commissioner of Inland Revenue, in fact, going to look after the tax-gatherers in the Said [Upper Egypt]. I wonder whether he will be civil.

Sally is gone with some English servants out to the Virgin's tree, the great picnic frolic of Cairene Christians, and, indeed, of Muslimeen also at some seasons.

Omar is gone to a *Khatmeh*—a reading of the Koran—at Hassan the donkey-boy's house. I was asked, but am afraid of the night air. A good deal of religious celebration goes on now, the middle of the month of Regeb, six weeks before Ramadan. I rather dread Ramadan as Omar is sure to be faint and ill, and everybody else cross during the first five days or so; then their stomachs get into training.

The new passenger-steamers have been promised ever since the 6th, and will not now go till after the races—6th or 7th of next month. Fancy the Cairo races! It is growing dreadfully Cockney here, I must go to Timbuctoo: and we are to have a railway to Mecca, and take return tickets for the *Haj* from all parts of the world.

XV

Steamer travel with seven nationalities

Boulaq, on board a river steam-boat, December 27 1863. After infinite delays and worries, we are at last on board, and shall sail tomorrow morning. After all was comfortably settled, Ismail Pasha sent for *all* the steamers up to Rhoda, near Minieh, and at the same time ordered a Turkish General to come up instantly somehow. So Latif Pasha, the head of the steamers, had to turn me out of the best cabin, and if I had not come myself, and taken rather forcible possession of the forecastle cabin, the servants of the Turkish General would not have allowed Omar to embark the baggage. He had been waiting all the morning in despair on the bank; but at four I arrived, and ordered the *hammals* to carry the goods into the fore-cabin, and walked on board myself, where the Arab captain pantomimically placed me in his right eye and on the top of his head.

Once installed, this has become a hareem, and I may defy the Turkish Effendi with success. I have got a good-sized cabin with good, clean divans round three sides for Sally and myself. Omar will sleep on deck and cook where he can. A poor Turkish lady is to inhabit a sort of dusthole by the side of my cabin; if she seems decent, I will entertain her hospitably. There is no furniture of any sort but the divan, and we cook our own food, bring our own candles, jugs, basins, beds and everything. If Sally and I were not such complete Arabs we should think it very miserable; but as things stand this year we say, *Alhamdulillah* it is no worse.

Luckily it is a very warm night, so we can make our arrangements unchilled. There is no door to the cabin, so we nail up an old plaid, and, as no one ever looks into a hareem, it is quite enough. All on board are Arabs—captain, engineer and men. An English Sitt is a novelty, and the captain is unhappy that things are not *alla Franca* for me. We are to tow three dahabiehs—M. Mounier's, one belonging to the envoy from the Sultan of Darfur, and another. Three steamers were to have done it, but the Pasha had a fancy for all the boats, and so our poor little craft must do her best. Only fancy the Queen ordering all the river steamers up to Windsor!

At Minieh the Turkish General leaves us, and we shall have the boat to ourselves, so the captain has just been down to tell me. I should like to go with the gentlemen from Darfur, as you may suppose. See what strange combinations of people float on old Nile. Two English women, one French (Mme Mournier), one Frenchman, Turks, Arabs, Negroes, Circassians, and men from Darfur, all in one party; perhaps the third boat contains some other strange element. The Turks are from Constantinople and can't speak Arabic, and make faces at the muddy river water, which, indeed, I would rather have filtered.

I hope to have letters from home tomorrow morning. Hassan, my faithful donkey-boy, will go to the post as soon as it is open and bring them down to Boulaq. Darling Rainie sent me a card with a cock robin for Christmas; how terribly I miss her dear little face and talk! I am pretty well now; I only feel rather weaker than before and more easily tired. I send you a kind letter of Mme Tastu's, who got her son to lend me the house at Thebes.

Assiut, January 3 1864. We left Cairo last Sunday morning, and a wonderfully queer company we were. I had been promised all the steamer to myself, but owing to Ismail Pasha's caprices our little steamer had to do the work of three.

The best cabin was taken by a sulky old one-eyed Turkish Pasha, so I had the fore-cabin, luckily a large one, where I slept with Sally on one divan and I on the other, and Omar at my feet. He tried sleeping on deck, but the Pasha's Arnouts were too bad company, and the captain begged me to 'cover my face' and let my servant sleep at my feet. Besides, there was a poor old asthmatic Turkish Effendi going to collect the taxes, and a lot of women in the engine-room, and children also. It would have been insupportable but for the hearty politeness of the Arab captain, a regular 'old salt', and owing to his attention and care it was only very amusing.

At Benisuef, the first town above Cairo (seventy miles), we found no coals: the Pasha had been up and taken them all. So we kicked our heels on the bank all day, with the prospect of doing so for a week. The captain brought H.R.H. of Darfur to visit me, and to beg me to make him hear reason about the delay as I, being English, must know that a steamer could not go without coals.

H.R.H. was a pretty imperious little nigger about eleven or twelve, dressed in a yellow silk kuftan and a scarlet burnous, who cut the good old captain short by saying, 'Why, she is a woman; she can't talk to me'. 'Wallah! wallah! what a way to talk to English hareem!' shrieked the captain, who was about to lose his temper; but I had a happy idea and produced a box of French sweetmeats, which altered the young Prince's views at once. I asked if he had brothers. 'Who can count them? they are like mice'. He said that the Pasha had given him only a few presents, and was evidently not pleased. Some of his suite are the most formidable-looking wild beasts in human shape I ever beheld—bulldogs and wild-boars black as ink, red-eyed, and, ye gods! such jowls and throats and teeth!—others like monkeys, with arms down to their knees.

The Illyrian Arnouts on board our boat are revoltingly white— like fish or drowned people, no pink in the tallowy skin at all. There were Greeks also who left us at Minieh (second large town), and the old Pasha left this morning at Rodah.

The captain at once ordered all my goods into the cabin he had left and turned out the Turkish Effendi, who wanted to stay and sleep with us. No impropriety! He said he was an old man and sick, and my company would be agreeable to him; then he said he was ashamed before the people to be turned out by an English woman. So I was civil and begged him to pass the day and to dine with me, and that set all right, and now after dinner he has gone off quite pleasantly to the fore-cabin and left me here. I have a stern-cabin, a saloon and an anteroom here, so we are comfortable enough—only the fleas! Never till now did I know what fleas could be; even Omar groaned and tossed in his sleep, and Sally and I woke every ten minutes. Perhaps this cabin may be better, some fleas may have landed in the beds of the Turks.

I send a dish from my table every day henceforth to the captain; as I take the place of a Pasha it is part of my dignity to do so; and as I occupy the kitchen and burn the ship's coals, I may as well let the captain dine a little at my expense. In the day I go up and sit in his cabin on deck, and we talk as well as we can without an interpreter. The old fellow is sixty-seven, but does not look more than forty-five.

He has just the air and manner of a seafaring-man with us, and has been wrecked four times—the last in the Black Sea during the Crimean War, when he was taken prisoner by the Russians and sent to Moscow for three years, until the peace. He has a charming boy of eleven with him, and he tells me he has twelve children in all, but only one wife, and is as strict a monogamist as Dr Primrose, for he told me he should not marry again if she died, nor he believed would she. He is surprised at my grey hair.

There are a good many Copts on board too of a rather low class and not pleasant. The Christian gentlemen are very pleasant, but the low are *low* indeed compared to the Muslimeen, and one gets a feeling of dirtiness about them to see them eat all among the coals, and then squat there and pull out their beads to pray without washing their hands even. It does look nasty when compared to the Muslim coming up clean washed, and standing erect and manly—looking to his prayers; besides they are coarse in their manners and conversation and have not the Arab respect for women. I only speak of the common people—not of educated Copts. The best fun was to hear the Greeks (one of them spoke English) abusing the Copts—rogues, heretics, schismatics from the Greek Church, ignorant, rapacious, cunning, impudent, etc., etc. In short, they narrated the whole fable about their own sweet selves.

I am quite surprised to see how well these men manage their work. The boat is quite as clean as an English boat as crowded could be kept, and the engine in beautiful order. The head-engineer, Ahmad Effendi, and indeed all the crew and captain too, wear English clothes and use the universal, 'All right, stop her—fooreh (full) speed, half speed—turn her head', etc. I was delighted to hear, 'All right—go ahead—*el-Fathah*' in one breath. Here we always say the *Fathah* (first chapter of the Koran, nearly identical with the Lord's Prayer) when starting on a journey, concluding a bargain, etc. The combination was very quaint.

There are rats and fleas on board, but neither bugs nor cockroaches. Already the climate has changed, the air is sensibly drier and clearer and the weather much warmer, and we are not yet at Assiut. I remarked last year that the climate changed most at Keneh, forty miles below Thebes. The banks are terribly broken and washed away by the inundation, and the Nile far higher even now than it was six weeks earlier last year.

At Benisuef, which used to be the great cattle place, not a buffalo was left, and we could not get a drop of milk. But since we left Minieh we see them again, and I hear the disease is not spreading up the river. Omar told me that the poor people at Benisuef were complaining of the drought and prospect of scarcity, as they could no longer water the land for want of oxen. I paid ten napoleons passage-money, and shall give four or five more as backsheesh, as I have given a good deal of trouble with all my luggage, beddings, furniture, provisions for four months, etc., and the boat's people have been more than civil, really kind and attentive to us; but a bad *dahabieh* would have cost forty, so I am greatly the gainer.

Nothing can exceed the muddle, uncertainty and carelessness of the 'administration' at Cairo: no coals at the depots, boats announced to sail and dawdling on three weeks, no order and no care for anybody's convenience but the Pasha's own. But the subordinates on board the boats do their work perfectly well. We go only half as quickly as we ought because we have two very heavy *dahabiehs* in tow instead of one; but no time is lost, as long as the light lasts we go, and start again as soon as the moon rises.

January 5. Omar has just come in with coffee, and begs me to give his best salaam to his big master and his little master and lady, and not to forget to tell them he is their servant and my mameluke (slave) 'from one hand to the other' (the whole body).

How I do wish you were here to enjoy all the new and strange sights! I am sure it would amuse you, and as the fleas don't bite you there would be no drawback. Janet sent me a photo of dear little Rainie; it is ugly, but very like. Give her no end of kisses, and thank her for the cock robin, which pleased me quite as much as she thought it would.

We left Assiut this afternoon. The captain had announced that we should start at ten o'clock, so I did not go into the town, but sent Omar to buy food and give my letter and best salaam to Wassef. But the men of Darfur all went off declaring that they would stop, promising to cut off the captain's head if he went without them. Hassan Effendi, the Turk, was furious, and threatened to telegraph his complaints to Cairo if we did not go directly, and the poor captain was in a sad quandary. He appealed to me, peaceably sitting on the trunk of a palm-tree with some poor fellaheen. I uttered the longest sentence I could compose in Arabic, to the effect that he was captain, and that while on the boat we were all bound to obey him.

'*Mashallah!* one English hareem is worth more than ten men for sense; these Ingeleez have only one word both for themselves and for other people: *doghree—doghree* (right is right); this Ameereh is ready to obey like a mameluke, and when she has to command—whew!'— with a most expressive toss back of the head.

The bank was crowded with poor fellaheen who had been taken for soldiers and sent to await the Pasha's arrival at Girgeh; three weeks they lay there, and were then sent down to Sohag (the Pasha wanted to see them himself and pick out the men he liked); eight days more at Sohag, then to Assiut eight days more, and meanwhile Ismail Pasha has gone back to Cairo and the poor souls may wait indefinitely, for no one will venture to remind the Pasha of their trifling existence.

While I was walking on the bank with M. and Mme Mounier, a person came up and saluted them whose appearance puzzled me—an eccentric Bedawee young lady. She was eighteen or twenty at most, dressed like a young man, but small and feminine and rather pretty, except that one eye was blind. Her dress was handsome, and she had women's jewels, diamonds, etc., and a European watch and chain. Her manner was excellent, quite *ungenirt* [unabashed], and not the least impudent or swaggering, and I was told—indeed, I could hear— that her language was beautiful, a thing much esteemed among Arabs. She is a virgin and fond of travelling and of men's society, being very clever, so she has her dromedary and goes about quite alone. No one seemed surprised, no one stared, and when I asked if it was *proper*, our captain was surprised. 'Why not? If she does not wish to marry, she can go alone; if she does, she can marry—what harm? She is a virgin and free.'

She went to breakfast with the Mouniers on their boat (Mme M. is Egyptian born, and both speak Arabic perfectly), and the young lady had many things to ask them, she said. She expressed her opinions pretty freely as far as I could understand her. Mme Mounier had heard of her before, and said she was much respected and admired. M. Mounier had heard that she was a spy of the Pasha's, but the people on board the boat here say that the truth was that she went before Said Pasha herself to complain of some tyrannical Mudir who ground and imprisoned the fellaheen—a bold thing for a girl to do. To me she seems, anyhow, far the most curious thing I have yet seen.

Girgeh, January 9. We have put in here for the night. Today we took on board three convicts in chains, two bound for Fazogli, one for calumny and perjury, and one for manslaughter. Hard labour for life in that climate will soon dispose of them. The third is a petty thief from Keneh who has been a year in chains in the Custom-house of Alexandria, and is now being taken back to be shown in his own place in his chains. The *causes célèbres* of this country would be curious reading; they do their crimes so differently to us.

I find that the criminal convicted of calumny accused, together with twenty-nine others not in custody, the Shaikh-el-Beled of his place of murdering his servant, and produced a basket full of bones as proof, but the Shaikh-el-Beled produced the living man, and his detractor gets hard labour for life. The proceeding is characteristic of the childish *ruses* of this country. I inquired whether the thief who was dragged in chains through the streets would be able to find work, and was told, 'Oh, certainly; is he not a poor man? For the sake of God everyone will be ready to help him'. An absolute uncertainty of justice naturally leads to this result. Our captain was quite shocked to hear that in my country we did not like to employ a returned convict.

I made further inquiries about the Bedawee lady, who is older than she looks, for she has travelled constantly for ten years. She is rich and much respected, and received in all the best houses, where she sits with all the men all day and sleeps in the hareem. She has been in the interior of Africa and to Mecca, speaks Turkish, and M. Mounier says he found her extremely agreeable, full of interesting information about all the countries she had visited. As soon as I can talk I must try and find her out; she likes the company of Europeans.

Here is a contribution to folk-lore, new even to Lane I think. [1] When the coffee-seller lights his stove in the morning, he makes two cups of coffee of the best and nicely sugared, and pours them out all over the stove, saying, 'God bless or favour Shaikh Shadhilee and his descendants' [2]. The blessing on the saint who invented coffee of course I knew, and often utter, but the libation is new to me. You see the ancient religion crops up even through the severe faith of Islam.

Luxor, January 13 1864. We spent all the afternoon of Saturday

---

[1] Edward Lane, author of *Manners and Customs of the Modern Egyptians*, London, 1836.

[2] Coffee originated in Abyssinia, where it grew wild, and it was said to have been introduced into the Yemen about 1430 A.D. by Shaikh Ali Shadhilee ibn Omar. At first the drinking of coffee was forbidden by some of the orthodox Muslim leaders as it was considered an intoxicant and therefore contrary to the Koran, but in spite of this it became very popular and it was argued that it helped to prevent drowsiness during the long Muslim prayers. The result was that Mocha in Yemen became the world's centre for the coffee trade up to the beginning of the 19th century.

at Keneh, where I dined with the British Consular representative, a worthy old Arab, who also invited our captain, and we all sat round his copper tray on the floor and ate with our fingers, the captain, who sat next me, picking out the best bits and feeding me and Sally with them.

After dinner the French representative, a Copt, one Jesus Buktor, sent to invite me to a fantasia at his house, where I found the Mouniers, the Mudir, and some other Turks, and a disagreeable Italian, who stared at me as if I had been young and pretty, and put Omar into a great fury. I was glad to see the dancing-girls, but I liked old Seyyid Ahmad's patriarchal ways much better than the tone of the Frenchified Copt. At first I thought the dancing queer and dull. One girl was very handsome, but cold and uninteresting; one who sang was also very pretty and engaging, and a dear little thing. But the dancing was contortions, more or less graceful, *very* wonderful as gymnastic feats and no more. But the captain called out to one Latifeh, an ugly, clumsy-looking wench, to show the Sitt what she could do. And then it was revealed to me. The ugly girl started on her feet and became the 'serpent of old Nile'—the head, shoulders and arms eagerly bent forward, waist in, and haunches advanced on the bent knees—the posture of a cobra about to spring. I could not call it *voluptuous* any more than Racine's *Phèdre*. It is *Venus toute entière à sa proie attachée*, and to me seemed tragic. It is far more realistic than the 'fandango', and far less coquettish, because the thing represented is *au grande sérieux*, not travestied, *gaȝé*, or played with; and like all such things, the Arab men don't think it the least improper. Of course the girls don't commit any indecorums before European women, except the dance itself. Seyyid Ahmad would have given me a fantasia, but he feared I might have men with me, and he had had a great annoyance with two Englishmen who wanted to make the girls dance naked, which they objected to, and he had to turn them out of his house after hospitably entertaining them.

Our procession home to the boat was very droll. Mme Mounier could not ride an Arab saddle, so I lent her mine and *enfourché'd* my donkey, and away we went with men running with *meshhaals* (firebaskets on long poles) and lanterns, and the captain shouting out, 'Full speed!' and such English phrases all the way—like a regular old salt as he is.

XVI

'Settled in my Theban palace'

Luxor, January 13 1864. We got here last night, and this morning Mustapha Agha and the Nazir came down to conduct me up to my palace.

I have such a big rambling house all over the top of the temple of Luxor.[1] How I wish I had you and the chicks to fill it! We had about twenty fellaheen to clean the dust of three year's accumulation, and my room looks quite handsome with carpets and a divan. Mustapha's[2] little girl found her way here when she heard I was come, and it seemed quite pleasant to have her playing on the carpet with a dolly and some sugar-plums, and making a feast for dolly on a saucer, arranging the sugar-plums Arab fashion. She was monstrously pleased with Rainie's picture and kissed it. Such a quiet, nice little brown tot, and curiously like Rainie and walnut-juice.

The view all round my house is magnificent on every side, over the Nile in front facing north-west, and over a splendid range of green and distant orange buff hills to the south-east, where I have a

---

[1] The *Maison de France* was built over the Temple of Luxor about 1815 by Henry Salt, British Consul and 'archaeologist'; here Belzoni lived when Salt sent him to recover the huge bust of Memnon which is in the British Museum. Champollion and Rosellini lived in it in 1829, also the naval officers who were sent out two years later by the French Government to remove the obelisk which stands in the Place de la Concorde.

While Lucie lived there and, indeed, until excavations of the Temple of Luxor was begun by Maspero in 1884, little could be seen of the original Temple except the portico and the pylons on which the house was built; the level of the ground had been raised through the centuries to such an extent that the surrounding houses of the village of Luxor were built about fifty feet above the original pavement.

The Temple of Luxor was built by Amenophis III (1417-1379 B.C.) of the Eighteenth Dynasty, and dedicated to the Theban triad of Amen-ra, Mut (his consort) and Khons (their son). Other buildings were added by Rameses II and others.

[2] Mustapha Agha, Shaikh el-Beled of Luxor and British Consular representative.

spacious covered terrace. It is rough and dusty to the extreme, but will be very pleasant. Mustapha came in just now to offer me the loan of a horse, and to ask me to go to the mosque in a few nights to see the illumination in honour of a great Shaikh, a son of Sidi Hosseyn or Hassan. I asked whether my presence might not offend any Muslimeen, and he would not hear of such a thing. The sun set while he was here, and he asked if I objected to his praying in my presence, and went through his four *rekahs* very comfortably on my carpet. My next-door neighbour (across the courtyard all filled with antiquities) is a nice little Copt who looks like an antique statue himself. I shall *voisiner* with his family. He sent me coffee as soon as I arrived, and came to help.

Thursday. Now I am settled in my Theban palace, it seems more and more beautiful, and I am quite melancholy that you cannot be here to enjoy it. The house is very large and has good thick walls, the comfort of which we feel today for it blows a hurricane; but indoors it is not at all cold. I have glass windows and doors to some of the rooms. It is a lovely dwelling. Two funny little owls as big as my fist live in the wall under my window, and come up and peep in, walking on tip-toe, and looking inquisitive like the owls in the hieroglyphics; and a splendid horus (the sacred hawk) frequents my lofty balcony. Another of my contemplar gods I sacrilegiously killed last night, a whip snake. Omar is rather in consternation for fear it should be 'the snake of the house', for Islam has not dethroned the *Dii lares et tutelares.*

I have been 'sapping' at the *Alif Bey* (*A B C*) today, under the direction of Shaikh Yussuf, a graceful, sweet-looking young man, with a dark brown face and such fine manners, in his fellah dress—a coarse brown woollen shirt, a *libdeh,* or felt skull-cap, and a common red shawl round his head and shoulders; writing the wrong way is very hard work. Some men came to mend the staircase, which had fallen in and which consists of huge solid blocks of stone. One crushed his thumb and I had to operate on it. It is extraordinary how these people bear pain; he never winced in the least, and went off thanking God and the lady quite cheerfully.

Till today the weather has been quite heavenly; last night I sat with my window open, it was so warm. If only I had you all here! How Rainie would play in the temple, Maurice fish in the Nile, and you go about with your spectacles on your nose. I think you would discard Frangi dress and take to a brown shirt and a *libdeh,* and soon be as brown as any fellah. It was so curious to see Shaikh Yussuf blush from shyness when he came in first; it shows quite as much in the coffee-brown Arab skin as in the fairest European—quite unlike the much lighter-coloured mulatto or Malay, who never change colour at all.

A photographer who is living here showed me photographs done high up the White Nile. One negro girl is so splendid that I must get him to do me a copy to send you. She is not perfect like the Nubians, but so superbly strong and majestic. If I can get hold of a handsome fellahah here, I'll get her photographed to show you in Europe what a woman's breast can be, for I never knew it before I came here—it is the most beautiful thing in the world. The dancing-girl I saw moved her breasts by some extraordinary muscular effort, first one and then the other; they were just like pomegranates and gloriously independent of stays or any support.

January 20. Today was beautiful again, and I mounted old Mustapha's cob pony and jogged over his farm with him, and lunched on delicious sour cream and *fateereh* at a neighbouring village, to the great delight of the fellaheen. It was more Biblical than ever; the people were all relations of Mustapha's, and to see Sidi Omar, the head of the household, and the 'young men coming in from the field', and the 'flocks and herds and camels and asses', was like a beautiful dream. All these people are of high blood, and a sort of 'roll of Battle' is kept here for the genealogies of the noble Arabs who came in with Amr— the first Arab conqueror and lieutenant of Omar.

Not one of these brown men, who do not own a second shirt, would give his brown daughter to the greatest Turkish Pasha. This country *noblesse* is more interesting to me by far than the town people, though Omar, who is quite a Cockney, and piques himself on being 'delicate', turns up his nose at their beggarly pride, as Londoners used to do at bare-legged Highlanders. The air of perfect equality—except as to the respect due to the head of the clan—with which the villagers treated Mustapha, and which he fully returned, made it all seem so very gentlemanly. They are not so dazzled by a little show, and far more manly than the Cairenes.

I am on visiting terms with all the 'county families' resident in Luxor already. The Nazir (magistrate) is a very nice person, and my Shaikh Yussuf, who is of the highest blood (being descended from Abu-l-Hajjaj himself), is quite charming. There is an intelligent little German here as Austrian Consul, who draws nicely. I went into his house, and was startled by hearing a pretty Arab boy, his servant, inquire, '*Soll ich den Kaffee bringen?*' What next? They are all mad to learn languages, and Mustapha begs me and Sally to teach his little girl, Zeyneb, English.

Friday, January 22. Yesterday I rode over to Karnac,[1] with Mustapha's *sais* (groom) running by my side. Glorious hot sun and delicious air. To hear the *sais* chatter away, his tongue running as fast as his feet, made me deeply envious of his lungs. Mustapha joined me, and pressed me to go to visit the Shaikh's tomb for the benefit of my health, as he and Shaikh Yussuf wished to say a *Fathah* for me; but I must not drink wine at dinner. I made a little difficulty on the score of difference of religion, but Shaikh Yussuf, who came up, said he presumed I worshipped God, and not stones, and that sincere prayers were good anywhere. Clearly the bigotry would have been on my side if I had refused any longer. So in the evening I went with Mustapha.

It was a very curious sight, the little dome illuminated with as much oil as the mosque could afford, and the tombs of Abu-l-Hajjaj and his three sons.[2] A magnificent old man, like Father Abraham himself, dressed in white, sat on a carpet at the foot of the tomb; he was the head of the family of Abu-l-Hajjaj. He made me sit by him, and was extremely polite. Then came the Názir, the Cadi, a Turk travelling on Government business, and a few other gentlemen, who all sat down round us after kissing the hand of the old Shaikh. Everyone talked; in fact it was a *soirée* for the entertainment of the dead Shaikh.

A party of men sat at the further end of the place, with their faces to the *Kibleh*, and played on a *taraboukeh* (sort of small drum stretched on earthenware which gives a peculiar sound), a tambourine without bells, and little tinkling cymbals fitting on thumb and fingers (crotales), and chanted songs in honour of Mohammed and verses from the Psalms of David. Every now and then one of our party left off talking, and prayed a little or counted his beads. The old Shaikh sent for coffee, and gave me the first cup—a wonderful concession. At last the Názir proposed a *Fathah* for me, which the whole group round me repeated aloud, and then each said to me, 'Our Lord God bless and give thee

[1] The one and a half miles from the Temple of Luxor to Karnak is flanked with an avenue of sphinxes.

[2] The greater part of the Arab village was built within the temple courts and was known as Abu-l-Hajjaj after the Muslim saint of the 7th century; his tomb-mosque stands on a heap of debris about fifty feet above the original floor of the temple in the court built by Rameses II.

health and peace, to thee and thy family, and take thee back safe to thy master and thy children', one adding *Ameen* and giving the salaam with the hand. I returned it, and said, 'Our Lord reward thee and all the people of kindness to strangers', which was considered a very proper answer.

After that we went away, and the worthy Názir walked home with me to take a glass of sherbet, and enjoy a talk about his wife and eight children, who are all in Foum-el-Bachr, except two boys at school in Cairo. Government appointments are so precarious that it is not worth while to move them up here, as the expense would be too heavy on a salary of £15 a month, with the chance of recall any day. In Cairo or Lower Egypt it would be quite impossible for a Christian to enter a Shaikh's tomb at all—above all on his birthday festival and on the night of Friday.

Friday, January 29. The *moolid* (festival) of the Shaikh terminated last Saturday with a procession, in which the new cover of his tomb, and the ancient sacred boat, were carried on men's shoulders. It all seemed to have walked out of the royal tombs, only dusty and shabby instead of gorgeous. These festivals of the dead are such as Herodotus alludes to as held in honour of 'Him whose name he dares not mention —Him who sleeps in Philae', only the name is changed and the mummy is absent [i.e. Osiris].

For a fortnight everyone who had a horse and could ride came and 'made fantasia' every afternoon for two hours before sunset; and very pretty it was. The people here show their good blood in their riding. On the last three days all strangers were entertained with bread and cooked meat at the expense of the Luxor people; every house killed a sheep and baked bread. As I could not do that for want of servants enough, I sent 100 piastres (12s.) to the servants of Abu-l-Hajjaj at the mosque to pay for the oil burnt at the tomb, etc. I was not well and in bed, but I hear that my gift gave immense satisfaction, and that I was again well prayed for.

The Coptic Bishop came to see me, but he is a tipsy old monk and an impudent beggar. He sent for tea as he was ill, so I went to see him, and perceived that his disorder was arrak. He has a very nice black slave, a Christian (Abyssinian, I think), who is a friend of Omar's, and who sent Omar a handsome dinner all ready cooked; among other things a chicken stuffed with green wheat was excellent. Omar constantly gets dinners sent him, a lot of bread, some dates and cooked fowls or pigeons, and *fateereh* with honey, all tied up hot in a cloth. I gave an old fellow a pill and dose some days ago, but his *dura ilia* took no notice, and he came for more, and got castor-oil.

I have not seen him since, but his employer, fellah Omar, sent me a lot of delicious butter in return. I think it shows great intelligence in these people, how none of them will any longer consult an Arab *hakeem* if they can get a European to physic them. They now ask directly whether the Government doctors have been to Europe to learn *hekmeh,* and if not they don't trust them—for poor 'savages' and 'heathens' *ce n'est pas si bête.* I had to interrupt my lessons from illness, but Shaikh Yussuf came again last night.

I have much less cough and very little blood-spitting and little or no pain, but I am very weak and if I turn on my left side for one moment I suffocate and cough up a wonderful quantity of thin saltish fluid. Hitherto my right side has been the bad one, so now one side is uneasy and the other impossible to lie on and the loss of my good sound sleep tries me and so I don't seem well. We shall see what hot weather will do. If that fails I will give up the contest and come home to see as much as I shall have time for of you and my chicks.

I am so charmed with my house that I begin seriously to contemplate staying here all the time. Cairo is so dear now, and so many dead cattle are buried there, that I think I should do better in this place. There is a huge hall, so large and cold now as to be uninhabitable, which in summer would be glorious. My dear old captain of steamer XII would bring me up coffee and candles, and if I 'sap' and learn to talk to people, I shall have plenty of company.

The cattle disease has not extended above Minieh to any degree, and here there has not been a case. *Alhamdulillah!* Food is very good here, rather less than half Cairo prices even now; in summer it will be half that.

Sunday, February 7 1864. My poor Shaikh Yussuf is in great distress about his brother, also a young Shaikh (*i.e.,* one learned in theology and competent to preach in the mosque). Shaikh Mohammed is come home from studying in el-Azhar at Cairo—I fear to die. I went with Shaikh Yussuf, at his desire, to see if I could help him, and found him gasping for breath and very, very ill. I gave him a little soothing medicine, and put mustard plasters on him, and as it relieved him, I went again and repeated them. All the family and a lot of neighbours crowded in to look on. There he lay in a dark little den with bare mud walls, worse off, to our ideas, than any pauper; but these people do not feel the want of comforts, and one learns to think it quite natural to sit with perfect gentlemen in places inferior to our cattle-sheds. I pulled some blankets up against the wall, and put my arm behind Shaikh Mohammed's back to make him rest while the poultices were on him, whereupon he laid his green turban on my shoulder, and presently held up his delicate brown face for a kiss like an affectionate child. As I kissed him, a very pious old moollah said, '*Bismillah*' (In the name of God), with an approving nod, and Shaikh Mohammed's old father, a splendid old man in a green turban, thanked me with effusion, and prayed that my children might always find help and kindness.

I suppose if I confessed to kissing a 'dirty Arab' in a 'hovel' the English travellers would execrate me; but it shows how much there is in 'Mussulman bigotry, unconquerable hatred, etc.', for this family are Seyyids (descendents of the Prophet) and very pious. Shaikh Yussuf does not even smoke, and he preaches on Fridays. You would love these Saidis [Upper Egyptians], they are such thorough gentlemen.

I rode over to the village a few days ago to see a farmer named Omar. Of course I had to eat, and the people were enchanted at my going alone, as they are used to see the English armed and guarded. Sidi Omar, however, insisted on accompanying me home, which is the civil thing here. He piled a whole stack of green fodder on his little nimble donkey, and hoisted himself atop of it without saddle or bridle (the fodder was for Mustapha Agha), and we trotted home across the beautiful green barley fields, to the amazement of some European young men out shooting. We did look a curious pair, certainly, with my English saddle and bridle, habit, hat and feather, on horseback, and Sidi Omar's brown shirt, brown legs and white turban, guiding his donkey with his chibouque. We were laughing very merrily, too, over my blundering Arabic.

Tomorrow or next day Ramadan begins at the first sight of the new moon. It is a great nuisance, because everybody is cross. Omar did not keep it last year, but this year he will, and if he spoils my dinners, who can blame him?

There was a wedding close by here last night, and about ten o'clock all the women passed under my windows with cries of joy, 'ez-zaghareet', down to the river. I find, on inquiry, that in Upper Egypt, as soon as the bridegroom has 'taken the face' of his bride, the women take her down to 'see the Nile'. They have not yet forgotten that the old god is the giver of increase, it seems.

XVII

'Modern travellers show strange ignorance'

January 29 1864. Mr Arrowsmith called last night and got the information he wanted about cotton crops, tenure of land etc from Shaikh
Yussuf. He is a cotton spinner and came here to see what is really to be
hoped as to cotton from Egypt. He kindly gave me Miss Martineau's
book.[1] It is true as far as it goes, but there is the usual defect—the
people are not real people, only part of the scenery to her, as to most
Europeans. The descriptions are excellent, but she evidently knew and
cared nothing about the people, and had the feeling of most English
people here, that the difference of manners is a sort of impassable gulf,
the truth being that their feelings and passions are just like our own.

It is curious that all the old books of travels that I have read mention
the natives of strange countries in a far more natural tone, and with far
more attempt to discriminate character, than modern ones, *e.g.*,
Niebuhr's Travels here and in Arabia, Cook's Voyages, and many
others.[2] *Have* we grown so *very* civilized since a hundred years that
outlandish people seem like mere puppets, and not like real human
beings? Miss Martineau's bigotry against Copts and Greeks is droll
enough, compared to her very proper reverence for 'Him who sleeps

---

[1] The book, *Eastern Life Present and Past,* described Harriet Martineau's journey up
the Nile to the second cataract in Nubia and her visit to Syria and Palestine in 1846–7,
being published in 1848. Harriet Martineau was born in Norwich, the daughter of James
Martineau, the philosopher. The Martineaus and Taylors of Norwich were related and
were staunch Unitarians.

[2] Karsten Niebuhr (1733-1815) arrived in Egypt in January 1761 with members of the
scientific expedition sent by King Frederick V of Denmark, and then travelled to the
Yemen. He wrote several volumes, mostly on Arabia, between 1772 and 1778.

Captain James Cook (1728-1779) wrote *Account of a Voyage round the World in 1769-
1771, Voyage towards the South Pole and round the World . . . in 1772-1775,* and *A
Voyage to the Pacific Ocean . . . in 1776-1780.*

in Philæ,' and her attack upon hareems outrageous; she implies that they are brothels.

I must admit that I have not seen a Turkish hareem, and she apparently saw no other, and yet she fancies the morals of Turkey to be superior to those of Egypt. It is not possible for a woman to explain all the limitations to which ordinary people do subject themselves. Great men I know nothing of; but women can and do, without blame, sue their husbands in law for the full 'payment of debt,' and demand a divorce if they please in default. Very often a man marries a second wife out of duty to provide for a brother's widow and children, or the like. Of course licentious men act loosely as elsewhere. *Kulloohum Beni Adam* (we are all sons of Adam), as Shaikh Yussuf says constantly, 'bad-bad and good-good'; and modern travellers show strange ignorance in talking of foreign natives *in the lump*, as they nearly all do.

You may conceive how much we are naturalized when I tell you that I have received a serious offer of marriage for Sally. Mustapha Agha has requested me to 'give her to him' for his eldest son Seyyid, a nice lad of nineteen or twenty at most. As Mustapha is the richest and most considerable person here, it shows that the Arabs draw no unfavourable conclusions as to our morals from the freedom of our manners. He said of course she would keep her own religion and her own customs. Seyyid is still in Alexandria, so it will be time to refuse when he returns. I said she was too old, but they think that no objection at all. She will have to say that her father would not allow it, for of course a handsome offer deserves a civil refusal. Sally's proposals would be quite an ethnological study; Mustapha asked what I should require as dowry for her. Fancy Sally as hareem of the Shaikh-el-Beled of Luxor!

There are fifteen or sixteen English boats here now, a great many people coming and going, but I have only seen Lady Herbert and Lord and Lady Scarborough—very nice people—and now a Madame de Beaulaincourt, daughter of General Castellane who is here in one of the Khedive's steamers which he has lent her with an Effendi in attendance. She seems a clever woman. Lady Herbert is very attractive, full of life and energy. I am sorry she is going into Syria so soon with her delicate children; they will suffer from cold very much. Young Heathcote and Strutt called here but were hurrying on up the river. I shall see more of them when they come down. Young Strutt is so like his mother I knew him in the street.

I would like to give him a *fantasia*, but it is not proper for a woman to send for the dancing girls, and as I am a friend of the Maohn (Police

Magistrate), the Cadi and the respectable people here, I cannot do what is indecent in their eyes. It is quite enough that they approve my unveiled face and my association with men—that is 'my custom' and they think no harm of it. I will give Strutt and Heathcote a dinner when they come down, Arab fashion, and let them eat with their fingers. I have not forks and knives enough for more than two people at most, so I will borrow a copper tray and serve à l'Arabe.

Monday.—I have just heard that poor Shaikh Mohammed died yesterday, and was, as usual, buried at once. I had not been well for a few days, and Shaikh Yussuf took care that I should not know of his brother's death. He went to Mustapha Agha, and told him not to tell anyone in my house till I was better, because he knew 'what was in my stomach towards his family,' and feared I should be made worse by the news. And how often I have been advised not to meddle with sick Arabs, because they are sure to suspect a Christian of poisoning those who die! I do grieve for the graceful, handsome young creature and his old father. Omar was vexed at not knowing of his death, because he would have liked to help to carry him to the grave.

I have at last learned the alphabet in Arabic, and can write it quite tidily, but now I am in a fix for want of a dictionary, and have written to Hekekian Bey to buy me one in Cairo. Shaikh Yussuf knows not a word of English, and Omar can't read or write, and has no notion of grammar or of *word for word* interpretation, and it is very slow work. When I walk through the court of the mosque I give the customary coppers to the little boys who are spelling away loudly under the arcade, *Abba sheddeh o nusbeyteen, Ibbi sheddeh o kesreteyn,* etc., with a keen sympathy with their difficulties and well-smudged tin slates. An additional evil is that the Arabic books printed in England, and at English presses here, require a 40-horse power microscope to distinguish a letter.

I am just called away by some poor men who want me to speak to the English travellers about shooting their pigeons. It is very thoughtless, but it is in great measure the fault of the servants and dragomans who think they must not venture to tell their masters that pigeons are private property.[1] I have a great mind to put a notice on the wall of my house about it. Here, where there are never less than eight or ten boats lying for full three months, the loss to the fellaheen is serious, and our Consul Mustapha Agha is afraid to say anything. I have given my neighbours permission to call the pigeons mine, as they roost in flocks

[1] See Introduction p. 7 with reference to Denshawi.

on my roof, and to go out and say that the Sitt objects to her poultry being shot, especially as I have had them shot off my balcony as they sat there.

1 got a note from M. Mounier yesterday, inviting me to go and stay at El-Moutaneh, Halim Pasha's great estate, near Edfu, and offering to send his *dahabieh* for me. I certainly will go as soon as the weather is decidedly hot. It is now very warm and pleasant. If I find Thebes too hot as summer advances I must drop down and return to Cairo, or try Suez, which I hear is excellent in summer—bracing desert air. But it is very tempting to stay here—a splendid cool house, food extremely cheap; about £1 a week for three of us for fish, bread, butter, meat, milk, eggs and vegetables; all grocery, of course, I brought with me; no trouble, rest and civil neighbours. I feel very disinclined to move unless I am baked out, and it takes a good deal to bake me. The only fear is the Khamseen wind. I do not feel very well. I don't ail anything in particular; blood-spitting frequent, but very slight; much less cough; but I am so weak and good for nothing. I seldom feel able to go out or do more than sit in the balcony on one side or other of the house. I have no donkey here, the hired ones are so very bad and dear; but I have written Mounier to try and get me one at El-Moutaneh and send it down in one of Halim Pasha's corn-boats. There is no comfort like a donkey always ready. If I have to send for Mustapha's horse, I feel lazy and fancy it is too much trouble unless I can go just when I want.

Luxor, February 12. We are in Ramadan now, and Omar really enjoys a good opportunity of 'making his soul.' He fasts and washes vigorously, prays his five times a day, goes to mosque on Fridays, and is quite merry over it, and ready to cook infidels' dinners with exemplary good-humour. It is a great merit in Muslims that they are not at all grumpy over their piety. The weather has set in since five or six days quite like paradise. I sit on my lofty balcony and drink the sweet northerly breeze, and look at the glorious mountain opposite, and think if only you and the chicks were here it would be 'the best o' life.' The beauty of Egypt grows on one, and I think it far more lovely this year than I did last.

My great friend the Maōhn (he is *not* the Nazir, who is a fat little pig-eyed, jolly Turk) lives in a house which also has a superb view in another direction, and I often go and sit 'on the bench'—*i.e.,* the *mastabah* in front of his house—and do what little talk I can and see the people come with their grievances. I don't understand much of what goes on, as the *patois* is broad and doubles the difficulty, or I would send you a Theban police report; but the Maōhn is very pleasant in his manner to them, and they don't seem frightened.

We have appointed a very small boy our *bowàb*, or porter—or, rather, he has appointed himself—and his assumption of dignity is quite delicious. He has provided himself with a huge staff, and he behaves like the most tremendous janissary. He is about Rainie's size, as sharp as a needle, and possesses the remains of a brown shirt and a ragged kitchen duster as turban. I am very fond of little Ahmad, and like to see him doing *tableaux vivants* from Murillo with a plate of broken victuals. The children of this place have become so insufferable about *backsheesh* that I have complained to the Maōhn, and he will assemble a committee of parents and enforce better manners. It is only here and just where the English go. When I ride into the little villages I never hear the word, but am always offered milk to drink. I have taken it two or three times and not offered to pay, and the people always seem quite pleased.

Yesterday Shaikh Yussuf came again, the first time since his brother's death; he was evidently deeply affected, but spoke in the usual way, 'It is the will of God, we must all die,' etc. I wish you could see Shaikh Yussuf. I think he is the sweetest creature in look and manner I ever beheld—so refined and so simple, and with the animal grace of a gazelle. A high-bred Arab is as graceful as an Indian, but quite without the feline *Geschmeidigkeit* [flexibility] or the look of dissimulation; the eye is as clear and frank as a child's. Mr Ruchl, the Austrian Consul here, who knows Egypt and Arabia well, tells me that he thinks many of them quite as good as they look, and said of Shaikh Yussuf, *Er ist so gemüthlich*.

There is a German here deciphering hieroglyphics, Herr Dümichen,[1] a very agreeable man, but he has gone across the river to live at Gurna. He has been through Ethiopia in search of temples and inscriptions. I am to go over and visit him, and see some of the tombs again in his company, which I shall enjoy, as a good interpreter is sadly wanted in those mysterious regions.

My chest is wonderfully better these last six or seven days. It is quite clear that downright heat is what does me good. Moreover, I have just heard from M. Mounier that a good donkey is *en route* in a boat from El-Moutaneh—he will cost me between £4 and £5 and will enable me to be about far more than I can by merely borrowing

[1] Johannes Dümichen, 1833–1894, the German Egyptologist, was a pupil of Lepsius travelled widely in Egypt and published a number of books.

Mustapha's horse, about which I have scruples as he lends it to other lady travellers. Little Ahmad will be my *sais* as well as my door-keeper, I suppose.

I wish you would speak to Layard on behalf of Mustapha Agha. He has acted as English Consul here for something like thirty years, and he really is the slave of the travellers. He gives them dinners, mounts them, and does all the disagreeable business of wrangling with the reis and dragomans for them, makes himself a postmaster, takes care of their letters and sends them out to the boats, and does all manner of services for them, and lends his house for the infidels to pray in on Sundays when a clergyman is here. For this he has no remuneration at all, except such presents as the English see fit to make him, and I have seen enough to know that they are neither large nor always gracefully given.

The old fellow at Keneh who has nothing to do gets regular pay, and I think Mustapha ought to have something; he is now old and rather infirm, and has to keep a clerk to help him; and at least, his expenses should be covered. Please say this to Layard from me as my message to him. Don't forget it, please, for Mustapha is a really kind friend to me at all times and in all ways. [Later she wrote] If you see Layard tell him that Mustapha Agha had the whole Koran read for his benefit at the tomb of Abu-l-Hajjaj besides innumerable *fathahs* which he said for him himself. He consulted me as to the propriety of sending Layard a backsheesh, but I declared that Layard was an Emir of the Arabs and a giver, not a taker of backsheesh.[1]

My donkey came down last night, and I tried him today, and he is very satisfactory though alarmingly small, as the real Egyptian donkey always is; the big ones are from the Hejaz. But it is wonderful how the little creatures run along under one as easy as possible, and they have no will of their own. I rode mine out to Karnac and back, and he did not seem to think me at all heavy. When they are overworked and overgalloped they become bad on the legs and easily fall, and all those for hire are quite stumped up, poor beasts—they are so willing and docile that everyone overdrives them.

Mustapha told Omar that he expected Fadl Pasha, the Governor of

[1] Sir Henry Layard, discoverer of Nimrud and Nineveh, was an old friend of the family. Henry Ross had helped him with the excavations at Nimrud and Layard was to have been bestman at his wedding to Janet Duff Gordon, but was too busy with his work as Under-Secretary of Foreign Affairs. It is not clear whether he succeeded in getting Mustapha Agha his pay but he wrote to Colquhoun, the British Consul about it and it was for that that the Koran was read.

all Upper Egypt, to dinner and asked him to go and help to arrange the entertainment. Did not Omar bristle up? 'What'. Could his lady be left for some hours without her servant, on account of a Turkish Pasha? No, not for Effendina (the Viceroy) himself would he do such a thing. There is nothing like an Arab servant for asserting his master's or mistress's greatness, and I suspect a little sly pleasure in defying a big Turk from behind the protection of my dignity.

Dearest Alick. Young Strutt and Heathcote and Mustapha are to dine with me—my first entertainment in this country. What nice old-fashioned people Lord and Lady Scarborough are. Little Lord Pembroke is not pleasant, far too conscious of his own importance, and his tutor was quite a little snob. Lady Herbert seemed to me to have nasty people about her, though she is pleasant, and just what you would like, impetuous and impulsive and all that sort of thing. I quite enjoyed two long mornings which we spent together. She talked a great deal of Aunt Carrie [Caroline Norton] and in a very kind, generous spirit.[1] I think she has a good deal of ready feeling and plenty of good nature. Madame de Beaulaincourt and I struck up quite a friendship. She is a very pleasant sort of French woman, unaffected, very clever, a little *tranchante* in manner, but really kind, I fancy, at bottom. She has left me a letter for M. de Rougé, the great Egyptologist, whose steamer has just come down here; Mariette Bey is with him.[2] I hope they will turn out good company. I have seen several English travellers. One never hears peoples' names here; so, unless they call on me, the boats come and go and I don't know who is in them. The Arab servants never know their English masters' names, and never ask.

I am getting on with Arabic but it is very difficult. Shaikh Yussuf is bent on making an Alimeh of me and teaching me to speak elegantly with inflections, which are only used by the learned. Meanwhile my vocabulary increases slowly. Omar has not an idea of translating; he learned English too young to remember the process of learning, and

---

[1] See Introduction p. 21.

[2] Auguste Mariette Bey, later Pasha, was born in 1821, the same year as Lucie, and was sent by the French Government in 1850 to purchase Coptic, Syriac, Arabic and Ethiopic manuscripts. While in Egypt he did some archaeological exploration to see if he could find any buildings connected with ancient Egyptian worship of the bull at Memphis as mentioned by Pausanias and he discovered the huge Serapeum at Sakkara. He became Conservator of Egyptian monuments in 1858 and the Viceroy Ismail gave him a labour force of fifteen hundred men to excavate temples along the length of the Nile in Egypt. He died in Cairo in 1881.

Vicomte de Rougé was born in Paris in 1811 and became one of the early French Egyptologists under the influence of Champollion.

he can give no help because he talks too quick, and rattles out such a heap of illustrative sentences that one is bewildered.

February 18. I went the other day to a *fantasia* which Mustapha Agha gave to young Strutt and company, and was much amused; there was one very good dancer. Mariette Bey and M. de Rougé, came in with some dear old-fashioned English people, whose naïve wonder was irresistibly comic. A lady wondered how the women here could wear clothes 'so different from English females, poor things!' but they were not *malveillants*, only pitying and wonderstruck. What surprised them most was to see me going through the salaaming ceremonies with Seleem Effendi, the Maōhn, and our sitting down together on his carpet.

February 19. I have only time for a few lines to go down by Strutt and Heathcote's boat to Cairo; it is safer than the post which goes on foot all the way to Cairo. They are very good specimens and quite recognized as 'belonging to the higher people', because they 'do not make themselves big'.

I begin to feel the time before me to be away from you all very long indeed, but I do think my best chance is a long spell of real heat. I have got through this winter without once catching cold at all to signify, and now the fine weather is come. I am writing in Arabic from Shaikh Yussuf's dictation the dear old story of the barber's brother with the basket of glass. The Arabs are so diverted at hearing that we all know the *Alf Leyleh o Leyleh*, the 'Thousand Nights and a Night'. The want of a dictionary with a teacher knowing no word of English is terrible. I don't know how I learn at all. The post is pretty quick up to here. I got your letter within three weeks, you see, but I get no newspapers; the post is all on foot and can't carry anything so heavy.

February 26. Dearest Alick. You would be amused to see Omar bring me a letter and sit down on the floor till I tell him the family news, and then *Alhamdulillah*, we are so pleased, and he goes off to his pots and pans again.

Lord and Lady Spencer are here, and his sister, in two boats. The English 'Milord', extinct on the Continent, has revived in Egypt, and is greatly reverenced and usually much liked. 'These high English have mercy in their stomachs,' said one of my last year's sailors who came to kiss my hand—a pleasing fact in natural history! *Fee wahed Lord*, was little ragged Ahmad's announcement of Lord Spencer—'Here's a Lord'. They are very pleasant people. I heard from Janet today of *ice* at Cairo and at Shubra, and famine prices. I cannot attempt Cairo with meat at 1s. 3d. a pound.

I fear the loss of cattle has suspended irrigation to a fearful extent, and that the harvests of Lower Egypt of all kinds will be sadly scanty. The disease has not spread above Minieh, or very slightly; but, of course, cattle will rise in price here also. Already food is getting dearer here; meat is 4½ piastres—7d.—the *rötl* (a fraction less than a pound), and bread has risen considerably—I should say corn, for no bakers exist here. I pay a woman to grind and bake my wheat which I buy, and delicious bread it is.

Every act of life here is exactly like the early parts of the Bible and it seems totally new when one reads it here. Old Jacob's speech to Pharaoh really made me laugh (don't be shocked), because it is so exactly what a fellah says to a Pasha: 'Few and evil have been the days,' etc. (Jacob being a most prosperous man); but it is manners to say all that, and I feel quite kindly to Jacob, whom I used to think ungrateful and discontented; and when I go to Sidi Omar's farm, does he not say, 'Take now fine meal and bake cakes quickly,' and wants to kill a kid? *Fateereh* with plenty of butter is what the 'three men' who came to Abraham ate; and the way that Abraham's chief mameluke, acting as Vakeel, manages Isaac's marriage with Rebekah! All the vulgarized associations with Puritanism and abominable little 'Scripture tales and pictures' peel off here, and the inimitably truthful representation of life and character—not a flattering one certainly—comes out, and it feels like Homer. Joseph's tears and his love for the brother born of the *same mother* is so perfect. Only one sees what a bad inferior race the Beni Israel were compared to the Beni Ishmael or to the Egyptians. Leviticus and Deuteronomy are so very heathenish compared to the law of the Koran, or to the early days of Abraham. Verily the ancient Jews were a foul nation, judging by the police regulations needful for them.

XVIII

'To dream of converting here is wrong'

Luxor, March 1 1864. Dearest Mother. The glory of the climate now is beyond description, and I feel better every day. I go out early— at seven or eight o'clock—on my tiny black donkey, and come in to breakfast about ten, and go out again at four.

Senior has sent me a Sir Noman Lockhart whom he calls a 'distinguished young man', but who seemed to me more convinced of his own distinction than is quite pleasant—a sort of juvenile Pharisee he seems full of condescension. He came in while I was reading with Shaikh Yussuf and persisted in ignoring his existence in a manner which led me to draw odious comparisons.

I want to photograph Yussuf for you. The feelings and prejudices and ideas of a cultivated Arab, as I get at them little by little, are curious beyond compare. It won't do to generalize from one man, of course, but even one gives some very new ideas. The most striking thing is the sweetness and delicacy of feeling—the horror of hurting anyone (this must be individual, of course: it is too good to be general). I apologized to him two days ago for inadvertently answering the *Salaam aleykoum*, which he, of course, said to Omar on coming in.

Yesterday evening he walked in and startled me by a *Salaam aleykee* addressed to me; he had evidently been thinking it over whether he ought to say it to me, and come to the conclusion that it was not wrong. 'Surely it is well for all the creatures of God to speak peace (*Salaam*) to each other,' said he. Now, no uneducated Muslim would have arrived at such a conclusion. Omar would pray, work, lie, do anything for me—sacrifice money even; but I doubt whether he *could* utter *Salaam aleykoum* to any but a Muslim. I answered as I felt: 'Peace, oh my brother, and God bless thee!' It was almost as if a Catholic priest had felt impelled by charity to offer the communion to a heretic.

I observed that the story of the barber was new to him, and asked if he did not know the 'Thousand and One Nights'. No; he studied only things of religion, no light amusements were proper for an Alim (elder of religion); *we* Europeans did not know that, of course, as *our* religion was to enjoy ourselves; but *he* must not make merry with diversions, or music, or droll stories. (See the mutual ignorance of all ascetics!)

He has a little girl of six or seven, and teaches her to write and read; no one else, he believes, thinks of such a thing out of Cairo; there many of the daughters of the Alim learn—those who desire it. His wife died two years ago, and six months ago he married again a wife of twelve years old! (Shaikh Yussuf is thirty he tells me; he looks twenty-two or twenty-three.) What a stepmother and what a wife! He can repeat the whole Koran without a book, it takes twelve hours to do it. Has read the Towràt (old Testament) and the el-Aangeel (Gospels), of course, every Alim reads them. 'The words of Seyyidna Eesa[1] are the true faith, but Christians have altered and corrupted their meaning. So we Muslims believe. We are all the children of God'. I ask if Muslims call themselves so, or only the slaves of God. 'Tis all one, children or slaves. Does not a good man care for both tenderly alike?' Pray observe the Oriental feeling here. *Slave* is a term of affection, not contempt; and remember the Centurion's '*servant* (slave) whom he loved.' He had heard from Fadil Pasha how a cow was cured of the prevailing disease in Lower Egypt by water weighed against a *Mushaf* (copy of the Koran), and had no doubt it was true, Fadil Pasha had tried it. Yet he thinks the Arab doctors no use at all who use verses of the Koran.

Monsieur de Rougé, came here one evening; he speaks Arabic perfectly, and delighted Shaikh Yussuf, who was much interested in the translations of the hieroglyphics and anxious to know if he had found anything about *Moussa* (Moses) or *Yussuf* (Joseph). He looked pleased and grateful to be treated like a 'gentleman and scholar' by such an Alim as M. de Rougé and such a Shaikhah as myself. As he acts as clerk to Mustapha, our consular agent, and wears a shabby old brown shirt, or gown, and speaks no English, I dare say he not seldom encounters great slights (from sheer ignorance). He produced a bit of old Cufic MS. and consulted Monsieur de Rougé as to its meaning—a

[1] Jesus Christ.

pretty little bit of flattery in an Arab Alim to a Frenchman, to which the latter was not insensible, I saw.

In answer to the invariable questions about all my family I once told him my father had been a great Alim of the Law, and that my mother had got ready his written books and put some lectures in order to be printed. He was amazed—first that I had a mother, as he told me he thought I was fifty or sixty, and immensely delighted at the idea. 'God has favoured your family with understanding and knowledge; I wish I could kiss the *Shaikhah* your mother's hand. May God favour her!'

Maurice's portrait (as usual) he admired fervently, and said one saw his good qualities in his face—a compliment I could have fully returned, as he sat looking at the picture with affectionate eyes and praying, *sotto voce*, for *el gedda, el gemeel* (the youth, the beautiful), in the words of the *Fathah*, 'O give him guidance and let him not stray into the paths of the rejected!' Altogether, something in Shaikh Yussuf reminds me of Worsley: there is the same look of *Seelen reinheit*, with far less thought and intelligence; indeed little thought, of course, and an additional child-like innocence. I suppose some medieval monks may have had the same look, but no Catholic I have ever seen looks so peaceful or so unpretending. I see in him, like in all people who don't know what doubt means, that easy familiarity with religion. I hear him joke with Omar about Ramadán, and even about Omar's assiduous prayers, and he is a frequent and hearty laugher. I wonder whether this gives you any idea of a character new to you. It is so impossible to describe *manner*, which gives so much of the impression of novelty.

I was talking the other day with Shaikh Yussuf about people trying to make converts and I said that eternal bêtise, 'Oh they mean well'. 'True, oh Lady! perhaps they do mean well, but God says in the Noble Koran that he who injures or torments those Christians whose conduct is not evil, merely on account of religion, shall never smell the fragrance of the Garden (paradise). Now when men begin to want to make others change their faith it is extremely hard for them *not* to injure or torment them and therefore I think it better to abstain altogether and to wish rather to see a Christian a good Christian and a Muslim a good Muslim'.

A most pious old Scotsman told me that the truth which undeniably existed in the Mussulman faith was the work of Satan and the Ulema his *meenesters*. My dear saint of a Yussuf a *meenester* of Satan! I really think I *have* learnt some 'Muslim humility' in that I endured the harangue, and accepted a two-penny tract quite mildly and politely and didn't argue at all. As his friend 'Satan' would have it, the *Fikees* were reading the Koran in the hall at Omar's expense who gave a *Khatmeh* that day, and Omar came in and politely offered him some sweet prepared for the occasion.

I have been really amazed at several instances of English fanaticism this year. Why do people come to a Mussulman country with such bitter hatred 'in their stomachs' as I have seen three or four times. I feel quite hurt often at the way the people here thank me for what the poor at home would turn up their noses at.

If I go down to Cairo again I will get letters to some of the Alim there from Abd-el-Waris, the Imam here, and I shall see what no European but Lane has seen. I think things have altered since his day, and that men of that class would be less inaccessible than they were then; and then a woman who is old (Yussuf guessed me at sixty) and educated does not shock, and does interest them. All the Europeans here are traders, and only speak the vulgarest language, and don't care to know Arab gentlemen; if they see anything above their servants it is only Turks, or Arab merchants at times.

I wish you could see Shaikh Seleem, he is a sort of remnant of the Mameluke Beys—a Circassian—who has inherited his master's property up at Esneh, and married his master's daughter. The master was one of the Beys, also a slave inheriting from his master. Well, after being a terrible *Shaitan* (devil) after drink, women, etc. Seleem has repented and become a man of pilgrimage and prayer and perpetual fasting; but he has retained the exquisite grace and charm of manner which must have made him irresistible in his *shaitan* days, and also the beautifully delicate style of dress—a dove-coloured cloth *djibbeh* over a pale blue silk *kuftan*, a turban like a snow-drift, under which flowed the silky fair hair and beard, and the dainty white hands under the long muslin shirt sleeve made a picture; and such a smile, and such ready graceful talk. Shaikh Yussuf brought him to me as a sort of doctor, and also to try and convert me on one point.

Some Christians had made Yussuf quite miserable, by telling him of the doctrine that all unbaptized infants went to eternal fire; and as he knew that I had lost a child very young, it weighed on his mind that perhaps I fretted about this, and so he said he could not refrain from trying to convince me that God was not so cruel and unjust as the Nazarene priests represented Him, and that all infants whatsoever, as well as all ignorant persons, were to be saved. 'Would that I could take the cruel error out of the minds of all the hundreds and thousands of poor Christian mothers who must be tortured by it,' said he, 'and let them understand that their dead babies are with Him who sent and who took them'. I own I did not resent this interference with my orthodoxy, especially as it is the only one I ever knew Yussuf attempt.

My conclusion is the heretical one: that to dream of converting here is absurd, and, I will add, wrong. All that is wanted is general knowledge and education, and the religion will clear and develop itself. The elements are identical with those of Christianity, encumbered, as that has been, with asceticism and intolerance. On the other hand, the creed is simple and there are no priests, a decided advantage. I think the faith has remained wonderfully rational considering the extreme ignorance of those who hold it. I will add Sally's practical remark, that 'the prayers are a fine thing for lazy people; they must wash first, and the prayer is a capital drill'.

You would be amused to hear Sally when Omar does not wake in time to wash, pray, and eat before daybreak now in Ramadán. She knocks at his door and acts as Muezzin. 'Come, Omar, get up and pray and have your dinner' (the evening meal is 'breakfast,' the early morning one 'dinner'). Being a light sleeper she hears the Muezzin, which Omar often does not, and passes on the 'Prayers is better than sleep' in a prose version.

Ramadán is a dreadful business; everybody is cross and lazy—no wonder! The camel-men quarrelled all day under my window yesterday, and I asked what it was all about. 'All about nothing; it is Ramadán with them,' said Omar laughing. 'I want to quarrel with someone myself; it is hot today, and thirsty weather.' Moreover, I think it injures the health of numbers permanently, but of course it is the thing of most importance in the eyes of the people; there are many who never pray at ordinary times, but few fail to keep Ramadán. It answers to the Scotch Sabbath, a comparison also borrowed from Sally.

Friday.—My friend Seleem Effendi, (the Magistrate or Maōhn), has just been here talking about his own affairs and a good deal of theology. He is an immense talker, and I just put *eywas* (yes) and *là* (no) and *sahé* (very true), and learn manners and customs. He tells me he has just bought two black slave women, mother and daughter, from a Copt for about £35 the two. The mother is a good cook, and the daughter is 'for his bed,' as his wife does not like to leave Cairo and her boys at school there. He had to buy the mother too, as the girl refused to be sold without her. What would an [American] 'Southerner' say to a slave with such a will of her own?

It does give one a sort of start to hear a most respectable magistrate tell one such a domestic arrangement. He added that it would not interfere with the *Sitteh Kebeer* (the great lady), the black girl being only a slave, and these people never think they have children enough. Moreover, he said he could not get on with his small pay without women to keep house, which is quite true here, and women are not respectable in a man's house on other terms. Seleem was full of his purchase and told it over again to Omar, who remarked to me afterwards that it was 'rude' of him to talk to *men* so. To me it was quite proper.

Seleem has a high reputation, and is said not to 'eat the people.' He is a hot Mussulman, and held forth very much as a very superficial Unitarian might do, evidently feeling considerable contempt for the absurdities, as he thinks them, of the Copts (he was too civil to say Christians), but no hatred (and he is known to show no partiality), only he 'can't understand how people can believe such nonsense.' He is a good specimen of the good, honest, steady-going man-of-the-world Muslim, a strong contrast to the tender piety of dear Shaikh Yussuf, who has all the feelings which we call Christian charity in the highest degree, and whose face is like that of 'the beloved disciple,' but who has no inclination for doctrinal harangues like worthy Seleem.

There is a very general idea among the Arabs that Christians hate the Muslims; they attribute to us the old Crusading spirit. It is only lately that Omar has let us see him at prayer, for fear of being ridiculed, but now he is sure that is not so, I often find him praying in the room where Sally sits at work, which is a clean, quiet place. Yussuf went and joined him there yesterday evening, and prayed with him, and gave him some religious instruction quite undisturbed by Sally and her needlework, and I am continually complimented on *not hating* the Muslims.

Yussuf promises me letters to some Alim in Cairo when I go there again, that I may be shown the Azhar (the great college). Omar had told him that I refused to go with a janissary from the Consul for fear of giving offence to any very strict Muslims, which astonished him much. He says his friends shall dress me in their women's clothes and take me in. I asked whether as a concealment of my religion, and he said no, only there were 'thousands' of young men, and it would be 'more delicate' that they should not stare and talk about my face.

Seleem told me a very pretty grammatical quibble about 'son' and 'prophet' (apropos of Christ) on a verse in the Gospel, depending on the reduplicative sign ω (*sheddeh*) over one letter; he was just as put out when I reminded him that it was written in Greek, as our amateur theologians are if you say the Bible was not originally composed in English. However, I told him that many Christians in England, Germany, and America did not believe that Seyyidna Eesa [Jesus Christ] was God, but only the greatest of prophets and teachers, and I was myself of that opinion.

He at once declared that that was sufficient, that all such had 're-ceived guidance,' and were not 'among the rejected'; how could they be, since such Christians only believed the teaching of Eesa, which was true, and not the falsifications of the priests and bishops (the bishops always 'catch it,' as schoolboys say).

I was curious to hear whether on the strength of this he would let out any further intolerance against the Copts, but he said far less and far less bitterly than I have heard from Unitarians.

Monday March 7.—We have now settled into quite warm weather ways, no more going out at mid-day. It is now broiling, and I have been watching eight tall fine blacks swimming and capering about, their skins shining like otters' fur when wet. They belong to a *gelláab*— a slave-dealer's boat. The beautiful thing is to see the men and boys at work among the green corn, the men half naked and the boys wholly so; in the sun their brown skins look just like dark clouded amber— semi-transparent, so fine are they.

I rejoice to say that on Wednesday is Bairam, and tomorrow Ramadán 'dies'. Omar is very thin and yellow and headachy, and everyone is cross. How I wish I were going, instead of my letter, to see you all, but it is evident that this heat is the thing that does me good, if anything will.

I mount my donkey early and late, with little Ahmad trotting beside me. In the evenings comes my dear Shaikh Yussuf, and I blunder through an hour's dictation, and reading of the story of the Barber's fifth brother (he with the basket of glass). I presume that Yussuf likes me too, for I am constantly greeted with immense cordiality by grace-ful men in green turbans, belonging, like him, to the holy family of Shaikh Abu-'l-Hajjaj. They inquire tenderly after my health, and pray for me, and hope I am going to stay among them.

You would be much struck here with the resemblance to Spain, I think. '*Cosas de España*' is exactly the '*Shogl-el-Arab*,' and Don Fulano is the Arabic word *foolan* (such a one), as *Ojala* is *Inshallah* (please

God). The music and dancing here, too, are Spanish, only 'more so'.

March 10.—Yesterday was Bairam, and on Tuesday evening everybody who possessed a gun or a pistol banged away, every drum and taraboukeh was thumped, and all the children holloaed, *Ramadan Māt, Ramadan Māt* (Ramadan's dead) about the streets. At daybreak Omar went to the early prayer, a special ceremony of the day. There were crowds of people, so, as it was useless to pray and preach in the mosque, Shaikh Yussuf went out upon a hillock in the burying-ground, where they all prayed and he preached.

Omar reported the sermon to me, as follows (it is all extempore): First Yussuf pointed to the graves, 'Where are all those people?' and to the ancient temples, 'Where are those who built them? Do not strangers from a far country take away their very corpses to wonder at? What did their splendour avail them? etc., etc. What then, O Muslims, *will* avail that you may be happy when that comes which will come for all? Truly God is just and will defraud no man, and He will reward you if you do what is right; and that is, to wrong no man, neither in person, nor in his family, nor in his possessions. *Cease then to cheat one another, O men,* and to be greedy, and do not think that you can make amends by afterwards giving alms, or praying, or fasting, or giving gifts to the servants of the mosque. *Benefits come from God; it is enough for you if you do no injury to any man, and above all to any woman or little one.'*

Of course it was much longer, but this was the substance, Omar tells me, and pretty sound morality too, methinks, and might be preached with advantage to a meeting of philanthropists in Exeter Hall. There is no predestination in *Islam*, and every man will be judged upon his actions. 'Even unbelievers God will not defraud,' says the Koran. Of course, a belief in meritorious works leads to the same sort of superstition as among Catholics, the endeavour to 'make one's soul' by alms, fastings, endowments, etc.; therefore Yussuf's stress upon doing no evil seems to me very remarkable, and really profound. After the sermon, all the company assembled rushed on him to kiss his head, and his hands and his feet, and mobbed him so fearfully that he had to lay about him with the wooden sword which is carried by the officiating Alim. He came to wish me the customary good wishes soon after, and looked very hot and tumbled, and laughed heartily about the awful kissing he had undergone. All the men embrace on meeting on the festival of Bairam.

The kitchen is full of cakes (ring-shaped) which my friends have sent me, just such as we see offered to the gods in the temples and tombs. I went to call on the Maōhn in the evening, and found a lot of people all dressed in their best. Half were Copts, among them a very pleasing young priest who carried on a religious discussion with Seleem Effendi, strange to say, with perfect good-humour on both sides. A Copt came up with his farm labourer, who had been beaten and the field robbed. The Copt stated the case in ten words, and the Maōhn sent off his cavass with him to apprehend the accused persons, who were to be tried at sunrise and beaten, if found guilty, and forced to make good the damage.

General Hay called yesterday—a fine old, blue-eyed soldier. He found a lot of fellaheen sitting with me, enjoying coffee and pipes hugely, and they were much gratified at our pressing them not to move or disturb themselves, when they all started up in dismay at the entrance of such a grand-looking Englishman and got off the carpet. So we told them that in our country the business of a farmer was looked upon as very respectable, and that the General would ask his farmers to sit and drink wine with him. *'Mashallah, tayeb kateer'* (It is the will of God, and most excellent), said old Omar, my fellah friend, and kissed his hand to General Hay quite affectionately. We English are certainly liked here. Seleem said yesterday evening that he had often had to do business with them, and found them always *doghri* (straight), men of one word and of no circumlocutions, 'and so unlike all the other Europeans, and especially the French!' The fact is that few but decent English come here, I fancy our scamps go to the colonies, whereas Egypt is the sink for all the iniquity of the South of Europe.

A worthy Copt here, one Todorus, took 'a piece of paper' for £20 for antiquities sold to an Englishman, and after the Englishman was gone, brought it to me to ask what sort of paper it was, and how he could get it changed, or was he, perhaps, to keep it till the gentleman sent him the money? It was a circular note, which I had difficulty in explaining, but I offered to send it to Cairo to Brigg's and get it cashed; as to when he would get the money I could not say, as they must wait for a safe hand to send gold by. I told him to put his name on the back of the note, and Todorus thought I wanted it *as a receipt* for the money which was yet to come, and was going cheerfully to write me a receipt for the £20 he was entrusting to me. Now a Copt is not at all green where his pocket is concerned, but they will take anything from the English. I do hope no swindler will find it out.

XIX

'Concealing of evil is considered meritorious'

March 7 1864. While I was in England last year an Englishman to whom Omar acted as *laquais de place* went away owing him £7 for things bought. Omar had money enough to pay all the tradespeople, and kept it secret for fear any of the other Europeans should say, 'Shame for the English' and did not even tell his family. Luckily, the man sent the money by the next mail from Malta, and the Shaikh of the dragomans proclaimed it, and so Omar got it; but he would never have mentioned it else.

This 'concealing of evil' is considered very meritorious and, where women are concerned, positively a religious duty. *Le scandale est ce qui fait l'offense* is very much the notion in Egypt, and I believe that very forgiving husbands are commoner here than elsewhere. The whole idea is founded on the verse of the Koran, incessantly quoted, 'The woman is made for the man, but the man is made for the woman'; *ergo*, the obligations to chastity are equal; *ergo*, as the men find it difficult, they argue that the women do the same. I have never heard a woman's misconduct spoken of without a hundred excuses; perhaps her husband had slave girls, perhaps he was old or sick, or she didn't like him, or she couldn't help it. Violent love comes 'by the visitation of God,' as our juries say; the man or woman must satisfy it or die. A poor young fellow is now in the *muristan* (the madhouse) of Cairo owing to the beauty and sweet tongue of an English lady whose servant he was. How could he help it? God sent the calamity.

I often hear of Lady Ellenborough, who is married to the Shaikh-el-Arab of Palmyra, and lives at Damascus. The Arabs think it inhuman of English ladies to avoid her. Perhaps she has repented; at all events, she is married and lives with her husband.[1]

When my Omar was a small boy he travelled with an English couple, and the man visited the dancing girls at all the towns, and begged Omar not to tell the lady. Omar told him that he was not so accursed as to reveal secrets but wished he were big enough to do for the lady what her husband neglected, and got a thrashing for his impudence. Now Omar is very correct in his notions. I asked Omar if he would tell his brother if he saw his wife do anything wrong. (n.b. —He can't endure her.) 'Certainly not, I must cover her with my cloak.' He is a true *Akh-ul-Benât* (brother of girls), and truly chivalrous to hareem. How astonished Europeans would be to hear Omar's real opinion of their conduct to women. He mentioned some Englishman who had divorced his wife and made her frailty public. You should have seen him spit on the floor in abhorrence. Here it is quite black-guard not to forfeit the money and take all the blame in a divorce. 'What! Once he sleep in bed with her and after show her face black before the people, like Europeans! Never.'

I am told, also, that among the Arabs of the desert (the *real* Arabs), when a traveller, tired and way-worn, seeks their tents, it is the duty of his host, generally the Shaikh, to send him into the hareem, and leave him there three days, with full permission to do as he will after the women have bathed, and rubbed, and refreshed him. But then he must never speak of that hareem; they are to him as his own, to be reverenced. If he spoke, the husband would kill him; but the Arab would never do it for a European, 'because all Europeans are so hard upon women,' and do not fear God and conceal their offences.

If a dancing-girl repents, the most respectable man may and does

---

[1] Lady Ellenborough was born Jane Digby in 1807, the grand-daughter of Coke of Holkham who became the first Earl of Leicester and was a friend of the Taylor family of Norwich. Jane Digby was married, at the age of sixteen, to Edward Law who was later Governor-General of India and made Earl of Ellenborough. At the age of fifty she married her fourth husband Medjuel, Shaikh of the Mezrab tribe of Syria near Palmyra, and lived happily with him until her death twenty-five years later. Richard Burton knew her when he was Consul at Damascus and admired her knowledge of Arab ways, and his wife, Isabel, wrote estatically of her beauty and devotion to her husband: 'She was honoured and respected as queen of her tribe, wearing one blue garment, her beautiful hair in two long plaits down to the ground, milking the camels, serving her husband, preparing his food . . . and while he ate she stood and waited on him, and glorying in it'. But Isabel, in spite of her passion for the swarthy Richard Burton, who was far stranger than Shaikh Medjuel, could not accept the idea of Jane's marital relations—'the contact with that black skin I could not understand . . . that made me shudder'. Lady Ellenborough's adventurous life is described in *The Odyssey of a Loving Woman* by E. M. Oddie, New York 1936, and by Lesley Blanch in *The Wilder Shores of Love*, John Murray 1954.

marry her, and no one blames or laughs at him. I believe all this leads to a good deal of irregularity, but certainly the feeling is amiable. It is impossible to conceive how startling it is to a Christian to hear the rules of morality applied with perfect impartiality to both sexes, and to hear Arabs who know our manners talk of the English being 'jealous' and 'hard upon their women.' Any unchastity is wrong and *haram* (unlawful), but equally so in men and women. Seleem Effendi talked in this strain, and seemed to incline to greater indulgence to women on the score of their ignorance and weakness. Remember, I only speak of Arabs. I believe the Turkish ideas are different, as is their whole hareem system, and Egypt is not the rule for all Muslims.

Saturday, March 12. I dined last night with Mustapha, who again had the dancing-girls for some Englishmen to see. Seleem Effendi got the doctor, who was of the party, to prescribe for him, and asked me to translate to him all about his old stomach as coolly as possible. He, as usual, sat by me on the divan, and during the pause in the dancing called 'el Maghribeeyeh,' the best dancer, to come and talk. She kissed my hand, sat on her heels before us, and at once laid aside the professional *gaillardise* of manner, and talked very nicely in very good Arabic and with perfect propriety, more like a man than a woman; she seemed very intelligent. What a thing we should think it for a worshipful magistrate to call up a girl of that character to talk to a lady!

Yesterday we had a strange and unpleasant day's business. The evening before I had my pocket picked in Karnac by two men who hung about me, one to sell a bird, the other one of the regular 'loafers' who hang about the ruins to beg, and sell water or curiosities, and who are all a lazy, bad lot, of course. I went to Seleem, who wrote at once to the Shaikh-el-Beled of Karnac to say that we should go over next morning at eight o'clock to investigate the affair, and to desire him to apprehend the men.

Next morning Seleem fetched me, and Mustapha came to represent English interests, and as we rode out of Luxor the Shaikh-el-Ababdeh joined us, with four of his tribe with their long guns, and a lot more with lances. He was a volunteer, and furious at the idea of a lady and a stranger being robbed. It is the first time it has happened here, and the desire to beat was so strong that I went to act as counsel for the prisoner. Everyone was peculiarly savage that it should have happened to me, a person well known to be so friendly to *el Muslimeen.*

When we arrived we went into a square enclosure, with a sort of cloister on one side, spread with carpets where we sat, and the wretched fellows were brought in chains. To my horror, I found they had been beaten already. I remonstrated, 'What if you had beaten the wrong men?' '*Maleysh*! (Never mind!) we will beat the whole village until your purse is found.' I said to Mustapha, 'This won't do; you must stop this.' So Mustapha ordained, with the concurrence of the Maõhn, that the Shaikh-el-Beled and the *ghaffir* (the keeper of the ruins) should pay me the value of the purse. As the people of Karnac are very troublesome in begging and worrying, I thought this would be a good lesson to the said Shaikh to keep better order, and I consented to receive the money, promising to return it and to give a napoleon over if the purse comes back with its contents (3½ napoleons). The Shaikh-el-Ababdeh harangued the people on their ill-behaviour to hareemát, called them *harámee* (rascals), and was very high and mighty to the Shaikh-el-Beled.

Hereupon I went away to visit a Turkish lady in the village, leaving Mustapha to settle. After I was gone they beat eight or ten of the boys who had mobbed me, and begged with the two men. Mustapha, who does not like the stick, stayed to see that they were not hurt, and so far it will be a good lesson to them. He also had the two men sent over to the prison here, for fear the Shaikh-el-Beled should beat them again, and will keep them here for a time. So far so good, but my fear now is that innocent people will be squeezed to make up the money, if the men do not give up the purse.

I have told Shaikh Yussuf to keep watch how things go, and if the men persist in the theft and don't return the purse, I shall give the money to those whom the Shaikh-el-Beled will assuredly squeeze, or else to the mosque of Karnac. I cannot pocket it, though I thought it quite right to exact the fine as a warning to the Karnac *mauvais sujets*. As we went home the Shaikh-el-Ababdeh (such a fine fellow he looks) came up and rode beside me, and said, 'I know you are a person of kindness; do not tell this story in this country. If Effendina (Ismail Pasha) comes to hear, he may "take a broom and sweep away the village."' I exclaimed in horror, and Mustapha joined at once in the request, and said, 'Do not tell Mr Ross or anyone in Egypt. The Shaikh-el-Ababdeh is quite right; it might cost many lives.' I, of course, promised at once—so please do not allude to the affair in writing to Janet as I shall not mention it to any travellers.

The whole thing distressed me horribly. If I had not been there they would have beaten right and left, and if I had shown any desire to have anyone punished, evidently they would have half killed the two men. Mustapha behaved extremely well. He showed sense, decision, and more feelings of humanity than I at all expected of him. Pray do as I begged you, try to get him paid. Some of the Consuls in Cairo are barely civil, and old Mustapha has all the bother and work of the whole of the Nile boats (eighty-five this winter), and he is boundlessly kind and useful to the English, and a real protection against cheating, etc. When Mustapha was appointed there were five or six boats a year; now there always from 70 to 120, and he does not get a farthing and is really out of pocket.

March 16. It is already very hot, and the few remaining travellers' *dahabiehs* are now here on their way down the river; after that I shall not see a white face for many months, except Sally's.

Shaikh Yussuf laughed so heartily over a print in an illustrated paper, from a picture of Hilton's, of Rebekah at the well, with the old *Vakeel* of Sidi Ibraheem (Abraham's chief servant) *kneeling* before the girl he was sent to fetch like an old fool without his turban, and Rebekah and the other girls in queer fancy dresses, and the camels with snouts like pigs. 'If the painter could not go to Es-Sham (Syria) to see how the Beduin really look', said Shaikh Yussuf, 'why did he not paint a well in England with girls like English peasants? At least it would have looked natural to English people, and the *Vakeel* would not seem so like a madman if he had taken off a hat'. I cordially agreed with Yussuf's art criticism. Fancy pictures of Eastern things are hopelessly absurd, and fancy poems too. I have got hold of a stray copy of Victor Hugo's '*Orientales*', and I think I never laughed more in my life.

The corn is now full-sized here, but still green; in twenty days will be harvest, and I am to go to the harvest-home to a fellah friend of mine in a village a mile or two off. The crop is said to be unusually fine. Old Nile always pays back the damage he does when he rises so very high. The real disaster is the cattle disease, which still goes on, I hear, lower down. It has not at present spread above Minieh, but the destruction has been fearful.

I more and more feel the difficulty of quite understanding a people so unlike ourselves—the more I know them, I mean. One thing strikes me, that like children, they are not conscious of the great gulf which divides educated Europeans from themselves; at least, I believe it is so. We do not attempt to explain our ideas to them, but I cannot discover any such reticence in them. I wonder whether this has struck people who can talk fluently and know them better than I do? I find they appeal to my sympathy in trouble quite comfortably, and talk of religious and other feelings apparently as freely as to each other. In many respects they are more unprejudiced than we are, and very intelligent, and very good in many ways; and yet they seem so strangely childish, and I fancy I detect that impression even in Lane's book, though he does not say so.

I have extensive practice in the doctoring line; bad eyes, of course, abound. My love to Watts, and give greetings to any other of my friends. I grieve over Thackeray much, and more over his girls' lonely sort of position.

March 22. Dearest Alick. The whole of the European element has now departed from Thebes, save one lingering boat on the opposite shore, belonging to two young Englishmen—the same who lost their photographs and all their goods by the sinking of their boat in the cataract last year. They are an excellent sample of our countrymen, kind, well-bred and straightforward.

Lady Herbert's suite regretted Rome and their little profits there and hated this country. Poor Hajji Ali, her dragoman, had a sad time and left her at Cairo, though it was such a grand place for him. She 'made herself too big', as they say here, which is very expensive in the East and very troublesome, and she did not like to pay for it, as a Turk must do. Lord and Lady Spencer, who did not bring a retinue or make themselves out to be great Pasha, enjoyed their journey extremely. Italian couriers and French cooks are the very devil in Egypt. A good English servant of either sex gets along well here, and next best, a German. The Arabs like and respect them, but they despise the southern Europeans whose faults are an exaggeration of their own, and who are vulgar into the bargain. I speak from the Arab point of view entirely.

I am glad my letters amuse you. Sometimes I think they must breathe the unutterable dulness of Eastern life: not that it is dull to me, a curious spectator, but how the men with nothing to do can endure it is a wonder. I went yesterday to call on a Turk at Karnac; he is a gentlemanly man, the son of a former Mudir, who was murdered, I believe, for his cruelty and extortion. He has 1,000 feddans (acres, or a little more) of land, and lives in a mud house, larger but no better than any fellahs, with two wives and the brother of one of them. He leaves the farm to his fellaheen altogether, I fancy. There was one book, a Turkish one; I could not read the title-page, and he did not tell me what it was. In short, there was no means of killing time but the narghile, no horse, no gun, nothing, and yet they did not seem bored. The two women are always clamorous for my visits, and very noisy and school-girlish, but apparently excellent friends and very good-natured. The gentleman gave me a *kufyeh* (thick head kerchief for the sun), so I took the ladies a bit of silk I happened to have. You never heard anything like his raptures over Maurice's portrait, '*Mashallah, Mashallah, Wallahy ʒay el ward*' (It is the will of God, and by God he is like a rose). But I can't 'cotton to' the Turks. I always feel that they secretly dislike us European women, though they profess huge admiration and pay *personal* compliments, which an Arab very seldom attempts.

I heard Seleem Effendi and Omar discussing English ladies one day lately while I was inside the curtain with Seleem's slave girl, and they did not know I heard them. Omar described Janet, and was of the opinion that a man who was married to her could want nothing more. 'By my soul, she rides like a Beduin, she shoots with the gun and pistol, and rows the boat; she speaks many languages, works with the needle like an Efreet, and to see her hands run over the teeth of the music-box (keys of piano) amazes the mind, while her singing gladdens the soul. How then should her husband ever desire the coffee-shop? *Wallahy!* She can always amuse him at home. And as to my lady, there is nothing that she does not know. When I feel my stomach tightened, I go to the divan and say to her, 'Do you want anything, a pipe, or sherbet, or so and so?' and I talk till she lays down her book and talks to me, and I question her and amuse my mind, and, by God! if I were a rich man and could marry one English hareem like that I would stand before her and serve her like her mameluke. You see I am only this lady's servant, and I have not once sat in the coffee-shop because of the sweetness of her tongue. Is it not therefore true that the man who can marry such hareem is rich more than with money?'

Seleem seemed disposed to think a little more of looks, though he quite agreed with all Omar's enthusiasm, and asked if Janet were beautiful. Omar answered with decorous vagueness that she was a 'moon', but declined mentioning her hair, eyes, etc. (it is a liberty to describe a woman minutely). I nearly laughed out at hearing Omar relate his manoeuvres to make me 'amuse his mind'; it seems I am in no danger of being discharged for being dull. Compare this with Halim Pasha's detestation of all *femmes d'esprit* and he is a Frenchified Turk.

The weather has set in so hot that I have shifted my quarters out of my fine room to the south-west into one with only three sides looking over a lovely green view to the north-east, with a huge sort of solid veranda, as large as the room itself, on the open side; thus I live in the open air altogether. The bats and the swallows are quite sociable; I hope the serpents and scorpions will be more reserved. *El Khamseen* (the fifty) has begun, and the wind is enough to mix up heaven and earth, but it is not distressing like the Cape south-easter, and, though hot, not choking like the *Khamseen* in Cairo and Alexandria.

Mohammed brought me a handful of the new wheat just now. Think of harvest in March and April! These winds are as good for the crops here as a 'nice steady rain' is in England. It is not necessary to water so much when the wind blows strong.

As I rode through the green fields along the dyke, a little boy sang as he turned round on the musically-creaking Sakìah (the water-wheel turned by an ox) the one eternal Sakìah tune—the words are *ad libitum*, and my little friend chanted 'Turn oh Sakìah to the right and turn to the left—who will take care of me if my father dies? Turn oh Sakìah, etc., pour water for the figs and the grass and for the watermelons. Turn oh Sakìah!' Nothing is so pathetic as that Sakìah song.

I passed the house of the Shaikh-el-Ababdeh, who called out to me to take coffee. The moon was splendid and the scene was lovely. The handsome black-brown Shaikh in dark robes and white turban, Omar in a graceful white gown and red turban, and the wild Ababdeh in all manner of dingy white rags, and with every kind of uncouth weapon, spears, matchlocks, etc., in every kind of wild and graceful attitude, with their long black ringlets and bare heads, a few little black-brown children quite naked and shaped like Cupids. And there we sat and looked so romantic and talked quite like ladies and gentlemen about the merits of Sakna and Almás, the two great rival women-singers of Cairo. I think the Shaikh wished to display his experiences of fashionable life.

The Copts are now fasting and cross. They fast fifty-five days for Lent; no meat, fish, eggs, or milk, no exception for Sundays, no food till after twelve at noon, and no intercourse with the hareem. The only comfort is lots of arrak, and what a Copt can carry decently is an unknown quantity; one seldom sees them drunk, but they imbibe awful quantities. They offer me wine and arrak always, and can't think why I don't drink it. I believe they suspect my Christianity in consequence of my preference for Nile water. As to that, though, they scorn all heretics, *i.e.* all Christians but themselves and the Abyssinians, more than they do the Muslims, and dislike them more; the procession of the Holy Ghost question divides us with the Gulf of Jehannum.

The gardener of this house is a Copt, such a nice fellow, and he and Omar chaff one another about religion with the utmost good humour; indeed they are seldom touchy with the Moslems. There is a pretty little man called Michaïl, a Copt, vakeel to M. Mounier. I wish I could draw him to show a perfect specimen of the ancient Egyptian race; his blood must be quite unmixed. He came here yesterday to speak to Ali Bey, the Mudir of Keneh, who was visiting me (a splendid handsome Turk he is); so little Michaïl crept in to mention his business under my protection, and a few more followed, till Ali Bey got tired of holding a durbar in my divan and went away to his boat. You see the people think the *courbash* is not quite so handy with an English spectator.

The other day Mustapha Agha got Ali Bey (the Mudir of Keneh) to do a little job for him—to let the people in the Gezira (the island), which is Mustapha's property, work at a canal there instead of at the canal higher up for the Pasha. Very well, but down comes the Nazir (the Mudir's *sub.*), and courbashes the whole gezira, not Mustapha, of course, but the poor fellaheen who were doing his corvée instead of the Pasha's by the Mudir's order. I went to the Gezira and thought that Moses was at work again and had killed a firstborn in every house by the crying and wailing, when up came two fellows and showed me their bloody feet, which their wives were crying over like for a death, *Shoghl el Misr*—things for Egypt—like *Cosas de España*.

Wednesday. Last night I bored Shaikh Yussuf with Antara and Abu-Zeyd, maintaining the greater valour of Antara who slew 10,000 for the love of Ibla. Yussuf looks down on such profanities, and replied, 'What are Antara and Abu-Zeyd compared to the combats of our Lord Moses with Og and other infidels of might, and what is the love of Antara for Ibla compared to that of our Lord Solomon for Balkees (Queen of Sheba), or their beauty and attractiveness to that of our Lord Joseph?' And then he related the combat of *Seyyidna Mousa* with Og; and I thought, 'hear O ye Puritans, and give ear O ye Methodists, and learn how religion and romance are one to those whose manners and ideas are the manners and ideas of the Bible, and how Moses was not at all a crop-eared Puritan, but a gallant warrior!'

There is the Homeric element in the religion here, the Prophet is a hero like Achilles, and like him directed by God—Allah instead of Athene. He fights, prays, teaches, makes love, and is truly a *man*, not an abstraction; and as to wonderful events, instead of telling one to 'gulp them down without looking' (as children are told with a nasty dose, and as we are told about Genesis, etc.) they believe them and delight in them, and tell them to amuse people. Such a piece of deep-disguised scepticism as *credo quia impossibile* would find no favour here; 'What is impossible to God?' settles everything. In short, Mohammed has somehow left the stamp of romance on the religion, or else it is in the blood of the people, though the Koran is prosy and 'common-sensical' compared to the Old Testament. I used to think Arabs intensely prosaic till I could understand a little of their language, but now I can trace the genealogy of Don Quixote straight up to some Shaikh-el-Arab.

XX

'The Arabs are intensely impressionable'

Luxor, March 22 1864. A fine, handsome woman with a lovely baby came to me the other day. I played with the baby, and gave it a cotton handkerchief for its head. The woman came again yesterday to bring me a little milk and some salad as a present, and to tell my fortune with date stones. I laughed, and so she contented herself with telling Omar about his family, which he believed implicitly. She is a clever woman evidently, and a great sibyl here. No doubt she has faith in her own predictions. She told Mme Mounier (who is a Levantine) that she would never have a child, and was forbidden the house accordingly, and the prophecy has 'come true'. Superstition is wonderfully infectious here.

The fact is that the Arabs are so intensely impressionable, and so cowardly about inspiring any ill-will, that if a man looks askance at them it is enough to make them ill, and as calamities are not infrequent, there is always some mishap ready to be laid to the charge of somebody's 'eye'.

Omar would fain have had me say nothing about the theft of my purse, for fear the Karnac people should hate me and give me the eye. A part of the boasting about property, etc., is politeness, so that one may not be supposed to be envious of one's neighbours' nice things. My Sakka (water-carrier) admired my bracelet yesterday, as he was watering the verandah floor, and instantly told me of all the gold necklaces and ear-rings he had bought for his wife and daughters, that I might not be uneasy and fear his envious eye. He is such a good fellow. For two shillings a month he brings up eight or ten huge skins of water from the river a day, and never begs or complains, always merry and civil. I shall enlarge his backsheesh.

There are a lot of camels who sleep in the yard under my verandah; they are pretty and smell nice, but they growl and swear at night abominably. I wish I could draw you an Egyptian farmyard, men, women and cattle; but what no one can draw is the amber light, so brilliant and so soft, not like the Cape diamond sunshine at all, but equally beautiful, hotter and less dazzling. There is no glare in Egypt like in the South of France, and, I suppose, in Italy.

Thursday. I went yesterday afternoon to the island again to see the crops, and show Sally my friend farmer Omar's house and Mustapha's village. Of course we had to eat, and did not come home till the moon had long risen. Mustapha's brother Abdurrachman walked about with us, such a noble-looking man, tall, spare, dignified and active, grey-bearded and hard-featured, but as lithe and bright-eyed as a boy scorning any conveyance, but his own feet, and quite dry while we 'ran down'. He was like Boaz, the wealthy gentleman peasant—nothing except the Biblical characters give any idea of the rich fellah.

We sat and drank new milk in a 'lodge in a garden of cucumbers' (the 'lodge' is a neat hut of palm branches), and saw the moon rise over the mountains and light up everything like a softer sun. Here you see all colours as well by moonlight as by day; hence it does not look as brilliant as the Cape moon, or even as I have seen in Paris, where it throws sharp black shadows and white light. The night here is a tender, subdued, dreamy sort of enchanted-looking day.

As I sat with Abdurrachman on the threshing-floor and ate roasted corn, I felt quite puzzled as to whether I were really alive or only existing in imagination in the Book of Ruth. It is such a *kief* [pleasure] that one enjoys under the palm-trees, with such a scene. The harvest is magnificent here; I never saw such crops.

It is very hot now; what will it be in June? It is now 86° in my shady room at noon; it will be hotter at two or three. But the mornings and evenings are delicious. I am shedding my clothes by degrees; stockings are unbearable. Meanwhile my cough is almost gone, and the pain is quite gone. I feel much stronger too; the horrible feeling of exhaustion has left me; I suppose I must have salamander blood in my body to be made lively by such heat. Sally is quite well; she does not seem at all the worse at present.

Saturday. This will go tomorrow by some travellers, the last winter swallows. We went together yesterday to the Tombs of the Kings on the opposite bank. The mountains were red-hot, and the sun went down into Amenti all on fire. We met Mr Dümichen, the German, who is living in the temple of Der-el-Bahri, translating inscriptions, and went down Belzoni's tomb. Mr Dümichen translated a great many things for us which were very curious, and I think I was more struck with the beauty of the drawing of the figures than last year. The face of the Goddess of the Western shore, Amenti, Athor, or Hecate, is ravishing as she welcomes the King to her regions; death was never painted so lovely.[1]

The road is a long and most wild one—truly through the valley of the shadow of death—not an insect nor a bird. Our moonlight ride home was beyond belief beautiful. The Arabs who followed us were immensely amused at hearing me interpret between German and English, and at my speaking Arabic; they asked if I was dragoman of all the languages in the world.

One of them had droll theories about 'Amellica' (America), as they pronounce it always. Was the King very powerful that the country was called '*Al Melekeh*' (the Kings)? I said, 'No: all are Kings there: you would be a King like the rest'. My friend disapproved utterly: 'If all are Kings they must all be taking away every man the other's money'—a delightful idea of the kingly vocation.

When we landed on the opposite shore, I told little Ahmad to go back in the ferry-boat, in which he had brought me over with my donkey; a quarter of an hour after I saw him by my side. The guide asked why he had not gone as I told him. 'Who would take care of the lady?' The monkey is Rainie's size. Of course he got tired, and on the way home I told him to jump up behind me *en croupe* after the fellah fashion. I thought the Arabs would never have done laughing and saying *Wallah* and *Mashallah*.

Shaikh Yussuf talked about the excavations, and is shocked at the way the mummies are kicked about. One boy told him they were not Muslims as an excuse, and he rebuked him severely, and told him it was *haram* (accursed) to do so to the children of Adam. He says

---

[1] The temple of Der-el-Bahri is one of the most beautiful in Egypt and was built by Queen Hatshepset, probably the first woman to be Pharaoh, about 1500 B.C. Her architect, Senmut, also carried out many works at Karnak including a pair of granite obelisks which were nearly one hundred feet high.

The tomb known as Belzoni's was that of Seti I, the son of Rameses I, the founder of the nineteenth dynasty, and is a magnificent monument about 350 feet long hewn into the hill-side of the Valley of the Kings. Lucie must have found it very moving to be shown the tomb by an Egyptologist excited by the fact that he was still finding important new texts to translate, and also to see the Pharaoh's wonderful alabaster coffin *in situ* before its removal to the Sir John Soane Museum in Lincoln Inn Fields.

they have learned it very much of Mariette Bey, but I suspect it was always so with the fellaheen.

How I do long to see you and the children. Sometimes I feel rather down-hearted, but it is no good to say all that. And I am much better and stronger. I stood a long ride and some scrambling quite well last evening.

Last evening I went out to the threshing-floor to see the stately oxen treading out the corn, and supped there with Abdurrachman on roasted corn, sour cream, and eggs, and saw the reapers take their wages, each a bundle of wheat according to the work he had done— the most lovely sight. The graceful, half-naked, brown figures loaded with sheaves; some had earned so much that their mothers or wives had to help to carry it, and little fawn-like, stark-naked boys trudged off, so proud of their little bundles of wheat or of *hummuẓ* (a sort of vetch much eaten both green and roasted).

The *sakka* (water-carrier), who has brought water for the men, gets a handful from each, and drives home his donkey with empty water-skins and a heavy load of wheat, and the barber who has shaved all these brown heads on credit this year past gets his pay, and everyone is cheerful and happy in their gentle, quiet way; here is no beer to make men sweaty and noisy and vulgar; the harvest is the most exquisite pastoral you can conceive. The men work seven hours in the day (*i.e.*, eight, with half-hours to rest and eat), and seven more during the night; they go home at sunset to dinner, and sleep a bit and then to work again—these 'lazy Arabs'! The man who drives the oxen on the threshing-floor gets a measure and a half for his day and night's work, of threshed corn, I mean. As soon as the wheat, barley, *addas* (lentils) and *hummuẓ* are cut, we shall sow *dourrah* of two kinds, common maize and Egyptian, and plant sugar-cane, and later cotton. The people work very hard, but here they eat well, and being paid in corn they get the advantage of the high price of corn this year.

I told you how my purse had been stolen and the proceedings thereanent. Well, Mustapha asked me several times what I wished to be done with the thief, who spent twenty-one days here in irons. With my absurd English ideas of justice I refused to interfere at all, and Omar and I had quite a tiff because he wished me to say, 'Oh, poor man, let him go; I leave the affair to God'. I thought Omar absurd but it was I who was wrong.

The authorities concluded that it would oblige me very much if the poor devil were punished with a 'rigour beyond the law', and had not Shaikh Yussuf come and explained the nature of the proceedings, the man would have been sent up to the mines in Fazogli *for life*, out of civility to me, by the Mudir of Keneh, Ali Bey. There was no alternative between my 'forgiving him for the love of God' or sending him to a certain death by a climate insupportable to these people.

Mustapha and Co. tried hard to prevent Shaikh Yussuf from speaking to me, for fear I should be angry and complain at Cairo, if my vengeance were not wreaked on the thief, but he said he knew me better, and brought the *procès verbal* to show me. Fancy my dismay! I went to Seleem Effendi and to the Cadi with Shaikh Yussuf, and begged the man might be let go, and not sent to Keneh at all. Having settled this, I said that I thought it right that the people of Karnac should pay the money I had lost, as a fine for their bad conduct to strangers, but that I did not require it for the sake of the money, which I would accordingly give to the poor of Luxor in the mosque and in the church (great applause from the crowd).

Then the Cadi made me a fine speech, and said I had behaved like a great *Emeereh,* and one that feared God; and Shaikh Yussuf said he knew the English had mercy in their stomachs, and that I especially had Mussulman feelings (as we say, Christian charity).

Did you ever hear of such a state of administration of justice. Of course, sympathy here, as in Ireland, is mostly with the 'poor man' in prison—'in trouble,' as we say. I find that accordingly a vast number of disputes are settled by private arbitration, and Yussuf is constantly sent for to decide between contending parties, who abide by his decision rather than go to law; or else five or six respectable men are called upon to form a sort of amateur jury, and to settle the matter. In criminal cases, if the prosecutor is powerful, he has it all his own way; if the prisoner can bribe high, he is apt to get off. All the appealing to my compassion was quite *en règle.*

The other day we found all our water-jars empty and our house unsprinkled. On enquiry it turned out that the *sakkas* had all run away, carrying with them their families and goods, and were gone no one knew whither, in consequence of some 'person having authority'—a Turkish *cawass* (policeman), having forced them to fetch water for building purposes at so low a price that they could not bear it. My poor *sakka* is gone without a whole month's pay— two shillings!—the highest pay by far given in Luxor.

I am interested in another story. I hear that a plucky woman here has been to Keneh, and threatened the Mudir that she will go to Cairo and complain to Effendina himself of the unfair drafting for soldiers—her only son taken, while others have bribed off. She'll walk in this heat all the way, unless she succeeds in frightening the Mudir, which, as she is of the more spirited sex in this country, she may possibly do. You see these Saidis are a bit less patient than Lower Egyptians. The *sakkas* can strike, and a woman can face a Mudir.

You would be amused at the bazaar here. There is a barber, and on Tuesdays some beads, calico and tobacco are sold. The only artizan is—a jeweller! We spin and weave our own brown woollen garments, and have no other wants, but gold necklaces and nose- and ear-rings are indispensable. It is the safest way of hoarding, and happily combines saving with ostentation.

Can you imagine a house without beds, chairs, tables, cups, glasses, knives—in short, with nothing but an oven, a few pipkins and water-jars, and a couple of wooden spoons, and some mats to sleep on? And yet people are happy and quite civilized who live so. An Arab cook, with his fingers and one cooking-pot, will serve you an excellent dinner quite miraculously. The simplification of life possible in such a climate is not conceivable unless one has seen it.

The Turkish ladies whom I visit at Karnac have very little more. They are very fond of me, and always want me to stay and sleep, but how could I sleep in my clothes on a mat-divan, poor spoiled European that I am? But they pity and wonder far more at the absence of my 'master'. I made a bad slip of the tongue and said 'my husband' before Abdul Rafiah, the master of the house. The ladies laughed and blushed tremendously, and I felt awkward, but they turned the tables on me in a few minutes by some questions they asked quite coolly.

I hardly know what I shall have to do. If the heat does not turn out overpowering, I shall stay here; if I cannot bear it, I must go down the river. I asked Omar if he could bear a summer here, so dull for a young man fond of a little coffee-shop and gossip, for that, if he could not, he might go down for a time and join me again, as I could manage with some man here. He absolutely cried, kissed my hands, and declared he was never so happy as with me, and he could not rest if he thought I had not all I wanted. 'I am your mameluke not your servant—your mameluke'.

I wish you could see my teacher, Shaikh Yussuf. I never before saw a pious person amiable and good like him. He is intensely devout, and not at all bigoted—a difficult combination; and, moreover, he is lovely to behold, and has the prettiest and merriest laugh possible. It is quite curious to see the mixture of a sort of learning with utter ignorance and great superstition, and such perfect high-breeding and beauty of character. It is exactly like associating with St John. I gave him £4 (five napoleons) for three months' daily lessons and had quite a contest to force it on him.

I want dreadfully to be able to draw, or to photograph. The group at the Shaikh-el-Ababdeh's last night was ravishing, all but my ugly hat and self. The black ringlets and dirty white drapery and obsolete weapons—the graceful splendid Shaikh 'black but beautiful' like the Shulamite—I thought of Antar and Abu Zeyd.

Give my salaam to Mme Tastu and ask her whether I may stay on here, or if I go down stream during the heat whether I may return next winter, in which case I might leave some of my goods. Hekekian strongly advises me to remain here, and thinks the heat will be good. I will try; 88° seemed to agree with me wonderfully, my cough is much better.

XXI

Doctoring the people of Luxor

Luxor, April 14. Luckily I am very well for I am worked hard, as a strange epidemic has broken out, and I am the *hakeemeh* (doctress) of Luxor. The *hakeem* Pasha from Cairo came up and frightened the people, telling them it was catching, and Yussuf forgot his religion so far as to beg me not to be all day in the people's huts; but Omar and I despised the danger, I feeling sure it was not infectious, and Omar saying *Min Allah.*

The people get stoppage of the bowels and die in eight days unless they are physicked; all who have sent for me *in time* have recovered. Thank God that I can help the poor souls. It is harvest, and the hard work, and the spell of intense heat, and the green corn, beans, etc., which they eat, brings on the sickness. Then the Copts are fasting from all animal food, and full of green beans and salad, and green corn. The 'lavement machine' [enema] I brought was an inspiration.

Mustapha tried to persuade me not to give physick, for fear those who died should pass for being poisoned, but both Omar and I are sure it is only to excuse his own selfishness. Omar is an excellent assistant. The bishop tried to make money by hinting that if I forbade my patients to fast, I might pay for their indulgence.

One poor, peevish little man refused the chicken-broth, and told me that we Europeans had *our* heaven in *this* world; Omar let out *kelb* (dog), but I stopped him, and said, 'Oh, my brother, God has made the Christians of England unlike those of Egypt, and surely will condemn neither of us on that account; mayest thou find a better heaven hereafter than I now enjoy here'. Omar threw his arms round me and said, 'Oh, thou good one, surely our Lord will reward thee for acting thus with the meekness of a Muslimeh, and kissing the

155

hand of him who strikes thy face'. (See how each religion claims humility.) Suleyman was not pleased at his fellow-christian's display of charity. It does seem strange that the Copts of the lower class will not give us the blessing, or thank God for our health like the Muslimeen.

Most of my patients are Christians, and some are very nice people indeed. The people here have named me Sittee (Lady) *Noor-ala-Noor*. A poor woman whose only child, a young man, I was happy enough to cure when dreadfully ill, kissed my feet and asked by what name to pray for me. I told her my name meant *Noor* (light—*lux*), but as that was one of the names of God I could not use it. 'Thy name is *Noor-ala-Noor*', said a man who was in the room. That means something like 'God is upon thy mind', or 'light from the light', and *Noor-ala-Noor* it remains; a combination of one of the names of God is quite proper, like Abdallah, Abdurrachman, etc.

I begged some medicines from a Countess Braniscki, who went down the other day; when all is gone I don't know what I shall do. I am going to try to make castor oil; I don't know how, but I shall try, and Omar fancies he can manage it. The cattle disease has also broken out desperately up in Esneh, and we see the dead beasts float down all day. Of course we shall soon have it here.

Sunday, April 17. The epidemic seems to be over, but there is still a great deal of gastric fever, etc., about. The *hakeem* from Keneh has just been here—such a pleasing, clever young man, speaking Italian perfectly, and French extremely well. He is the son of some fellah of Lower Egypt, sent to study at Pisa, and has not lost the Arab gentility and elegance by a foreign education. We fraternized greatly, and the young *hakeem* was delighted at my love for his people, and my high opinion of their intelligence. He is now gone to inspect the sick, and is to see me again and give me directions. He was very unhappy that he could not supply me with medicines; none are to be bought above Cairo, except from the hospital doctors, who sell the medicines of the Government, as the Italian at Assiut did. But Ali Effendi is too honest for that.

The old bishop paid me a visit of three and a half hours yesterday, and *pour me tirer une carotte* he sent me a loaf of sugar, so I must send a present 'for the church' to be consumed in *arrak*. The old party was not very sober, and asked for wine. I cooly told him it was *haram* (forbidden) to us to drink during the day—only with our dinner. I never will give the Christians drink here, and now they have left off pressing me to drink spirits at their houses. The bishop offered to alter the hour of prayer for me, and to let me into the *Heykel* (where women must not go) on Good Friday, which will be eighteen days hence. All of which I refused, and said I would go on the roof of the church and look down through the window with the other *hareemat*. Omar kissed the bishop's hand, and I said: 'What! Do *you* kiss his hand like a Copt?' 'Oh yes, he is an old man, and a servant of my God, but dreadfully dirty,' added Omar; and it was too true. His presence diffused a fearful monastic odour of sanctity. A Bishop must be a monk, as priests are married.

Monday. Today Ali Effendi-*el-Hakeem* came to tell me how he had been to try to see my patients and failed; all the families declared they were well and would not let him in. Such is the deep distrust of everything to do with the Government. They all waited till he was gone away, and then came again to me with their ailments. I scolded, and they all said, '*Wallah, ya Sitt, ya Emeereh;* that is the *Hakeem* Pasha, and he would send us off to hospital at Keneh, and then they would poison us; by thy eyes do not be angry with us, or leave off from having compassion on us on this account'. I said, 'Ali Effendi is an Arab and a Muslim and an *Emeer* (gentleman), and he gave me good advice, and would have given more,' etc. No use at all. He is the Government doctor, and they had rather die, and will swallow anything from *el-Sittee Noor-ala-Noor*. Here is a pretty state of things.

Shaikh Yussuf had been about with Ali Effendi, but could not get the people to see him. The Copts, I find, *have* a religious prejudice against him, and, indeed, against all heretics. They consider themselves and the Abyssinians as the only true believers. If they acknowledge *us* as brethren, it is for money. I speak only of the low class, and of the priests; of course the educated merchants are very different. I had two priests and two deacons, and the mother of one, here today for physic for the woman. She was very pretty and pleasing; miserably reduced and weak from the long fast. I told her she must eat meat and drink a little wine, and take cold baths, and gave her quinine. She will take the wine and the quinine, but neither eat nor wash. The Bishop tells them they will die if they break the fast, and half the Christians are ill from it.

One of the priests spoke a little English; he fabricates false antiques very cleverly, and is tolerably sharp; but, Oh *mon Dieu*, it is enough to make one turn Muslim to compare these greasy rogues with such high-minded charitable *shurafa* (noblemen) as Abd-el-Waris and

Shaikh Yussuf. A sweet little Copt boy who is very ill will be killed by the stupid bigotry about the fast. My friend Suleyman is much put out, and backs my exhortations to the sick to break it. He is a capital fellow, and very intelligent, and he and Omar are like brothers; it is the priests who do all they can to keep alive religious prejudice— luckily they are only partially successful. Mohammed has just heard that seventy-five head of cattle are dead at El-Moutaneh. Here only a few have died as yet, and Ali Effendi thinks the disease less virulent than in Lower Egypt. I hope he is right; but dead beasts float down the river all day long.

To turn to something more amusing—but please don't tell it— such a joke against my grey hairs. I have had a proposal, or at least an attempt at one. A very handsome Shaikh-el-Arab (Beduin) was here for a bit, and asked Omar whether I were a widow or divorced, as in either case he would send a *dellaleh* (marriage brokeress) to me. Omar told him that would never do. I had a husband in England; besides, I was not young, had a married daughter, my hair was grey, etc. The Shaikh swore he didn't care; I could dye my hair and get a divorce; that I was not like stupid modern women, but like an ancient Arab *Emeereh*, and worthy of Antar or Abu Zeyd—a woman for whom men killed each other or themselves—and he would pay all he could afford as my dowry. Omar came in in fits of laughter at the idea, and the difficulty he had had in stopping the *dellaleh's* visit. He told the Shaikh I should certainly beat her I should be so offended. The disregard of differences of age here on marriage is very strange. My adorer was not more than thirty, I am sure. Don't tell people, my dear Alick; it is so very absurd; I should be 'ashamed before the people'.

Saturday, April 23. Thank goodness the sickness is going off. I have just heard Suleyman's report as follows: Hassan Abou-Ahmad kisses the Emeereh's feet, and the bullets have cleaned his stomach six times, and he has said the *Fathah* for the Lady. The two little girls who had diarrhoea are well. The Christian dyer has vomited his powder and wants another. The mother of the Christian cook who married the priest's sister has got dysentery. The hareem of Mustapha Abu-Abeyd has two children with bad eyes. The Bishop had a quarrel, and scolded and fell down, and cannot speak or move; I must go to him. The young deacon's jaundice is better. The slave girl of Kursheed Agha is sick, and Kursheed is sitting at her head in tears; the women say I must go to her, too. Kursheed is a fine young Turk, and very good to his *hareemat*. That is all; Suleyman has nothing on earth to do, and brings me a daily report; he likes the gossip and the importance.

The reis of a cargo-boat brought me up your Lafontaine, and some papers and books from Hekekian Bey. Shaikh Yussuf is going down to Cairo, to try to get back some of the lands which Mahommed Ali took away from the mosques and the Ulema without compensation. He asked me whether Ross would speak for him to Effendina! What are the Muslimeen coming to? As soon as I can read enough he offers to read in the Koran with me—a most unusual proceeding, as the 'noble Koran' is not generally put into the hands of heretics; but my 'charity to the people in sickness' is looked upon by Abd-el-Waris, the *Imám*, and by Yussuf, as a proof that I have 'received direction,' and am of those Christians of whom *Seyyidna* Mohammed (upon whose name be peace) has said 'that they have no pride, that they rival each other in good works, and that God will increase their reward'. There is no *arrière pensée* of conversion; that they think hopeless, but charity covers all sins with Muslimeen.

Next Friday is the *Djuma el-Kebeer* (Good Friday) with the Copts, and the prayers are in the daytime, so I shall go to the church. Next moon is the great Bairam, *el-Eed el-Kebeer* (the great festival), with the Muslimeen—the commemoration of the sacrifice of Isaac or Ishmael (commentators are uncertain which)—and Omar will kill a sheep for the poor for the benefit of his baby, according to custom.

Michaïl has just come down from El-Moutaneh, where he is *vakeel* to M. Mounier. He gives a fearful account of the sickness there among men and cattle—eight and ten deaths a day; here we have had only four a day, at the worst, in a population of (I guess) some 2,000. The Mouniers have put themselves in quarantine, and allow no one to approach their house, as Mustapha wanted me to do. One hundred and fifty head of cattle have died at El-Moutaneh; here only a few calves are dead, but as yet no full-grown beasts, and the people are healthy again. I really think I did some service by not showing any fear, and Omar behaved manfully. By-the-by, will you find out whether a *passaporto,* as they call it, a paper granting British protection, can be granted in England. It is the object of Omar's highest ambition to belong as much as possible to the English, and feel safe from being forced to serve a Turk. If it can be done by any coaxing and jobbing, pray do it, for Omar deserves any service I can render him in return for all his devotion and fidelity.

Someone tried to put it into his head that it was *haram* to be too fond of us heretics and be faithful, but he consulted Shaikh Yussuf, who promised him a reward hereafter for good conduct to me, and who told me of it as a good joke, adding that he was *raghil ameen*, the highest praise for fidelity, the sobriquet of the Prophet. Do not be surprised at my lack of conscience in desiring to benefit my own follower *in qualunque modo;* justice is not of Eastern growth, and *Europeo* is 'your only wear', and here it is only base not to stick by one's friends.

Omar kisses the hands of the *Sidi-el-Kebeer* (the great master), and desires his best salaam to the little master and the little lady, whose servant he is. He asks if I, too, do not kiss Iskender Bey's hand in my letter, as I ought to do as his hareem, or whether 'I make myself big before my master,' like some French ladies he has seen? I tell him I will do so if Iskender Bey will get him his *warak* (paper), where-upon he picks up the hem of my gown and kisses that, and I civilly expostulate on such condescension to a woman.

Yussuf is quite puzzled about European women, and a little shocked at the want of respect to their husbands they display. I told him that the outward respect shown to us by our men was *our veil*, and explained how superficial the difference was. He fancied that the law gave us the upper hand. Omar reports yesterday's sermon 'on toleration', it appears. Yussuf took the text of 'Thou shalt love thy brother as thyself, and never act towards him but as thou wouldest he should act towards thee'. I forget chapter and verse; but it seems he took the bull by the horns and declared *all men* to be brothers, not Muslimeen only, and desired his congregation to look at the good deeds of others and not at their erroneous faith, for God is all-knowing (*i.e.,* He only knows the heart), and if they saw aught amiss to remember that the best man need say *Astaghfir ul-Lah* (I beg pardon of God) seven times a day.

I wish the English could know how unpleasant and mischievous their manner of talking to their servants about religion is. Omar confided to me how bad it felt to be questioned, and then to see the Englishman laugh or put up his lip and say nothing. 'I don't want to talk about his religion at all, but if he talks about mine he ought to speak of his own, too. You, my Lady, say, when I tell you things, that is the same with us, or that is different, or good, or not good in your mind, and that is the proper way, not to look like thinking "all nonsense".'

Esneh, Saturday, April 30. On Tuesday evening as I was dreamily sitting on my divan, who should walk in but Arthur Taylor [her first cousin], on his way, all alone in a big *dahabieh,* to Edfu. So I offered to go too, whereupon he said he would go on to Aswan and see Philae as he had company, and we went off to Mustapha to make a bargain with his Reis for it; thus then here we are at Esneh. I embarked on Wednesday evening, and we have been two days *en route.* Yesterday we had the thermometer at 110; I was the only person awake all day in the boat. Omar, after cooking, lay panting at my feet on the deck. Arthur went fairly to bed in the cabin; ditto Sally. All the crew slept on the deck. Omar cooked amphibiously, bathing between every meal. The silence of noon with the *white heat* glowing on the river which flowed like liquid tin, and the silent Nubian rough boats floating down without a ripple, was magnificent and really awful. Not a breath of wind as we lay under the lofty bank. The Nile is not quite so low, and I see a very different scene from last year. People think us crazy to go up to Aswan in May, but I do enjoy it, and I really wanted to forget all the sickness and sorrow in which I have taken part.

When I went to Mustapha's he said Shaikh Yussuf was ill, and I said, 'Then I won't go'. But Yussuf came in with a sick headache only. Mustapha repeated my words to him, and never did I see such a lovely expression in a human face as that with which Yussuf said *Eh, ya Sitt!* Mustapha laughed, and told him to thank me, and Yussuf turned to me and said, in a low voice, 'My sister does not need thanks, save from God'. Fancy a Shereef, one of the Ulema, calling a foreigner 'sister'! His pretty little girl came in and played with me, and he offered her to me for Maurice. I cured Kursheed's Abyssinian slave-girl. You would have laughed to see him obeying my directions, and wiping his eyes on his gold-embroidered sleeve. And then the Coptic priest came for me for his wife who was ill. He was in a great quandary, because, if she died, he, as a priest, could never marry again, as he loudly lamented before her; but he was truly grieved, and I was very happy to leave her convalescent.

Verily we are sorely visited. The dead cattle float down by thousands. M. Mounier buried a thousand at El-Moutaneh alone, and lost forty men. I would not have left Luxor, but there were no new cases for four days before, and the worst had been over for full ten days. Two or three poor people brought me new bread and vegetables to the boat when they saw me going, and Yussuf came down and sat with us all the evening, and looked quite sad. Omar asked him why, and he said it made him think how it would seem when '*Inshalla* I should be well and should leave my place empty at Luxor and go back with the blessing of God to my own place and to my own people'. Whereupon Omar grew quite sentimental too, and nearly cried.

I don't know how Arthur would have managed without us, for he had come with two Frenchmen who had proper servants and who left the boat at Girgeh, and he has a wretched little dirty idiotic Coptic tailor as a servant, who can't even sew on a button. It is becoming quite a calamity about servants here. Arthur tells me that men, not fit to light Omar's pipe, asked him £10 a month in Cairo and would not take less, and he gives his Copt £4. I really feel as if I were cheating Omar to let him stay on for £3; but if I say anything he kisses my hand and tells me 'not to be cross'.

Everything is equally dear. The country people do not suffer but the town people must be dreadfully pinched and starved. Omar often looks grave when he thinks of what his wife must be paying now for her living in Alexandria. Sally desires me to say that you are to pay her wages to June—poor girl—now all her sisters are married she observes the fourth Commandment even more than Corporal Trim.

I have letters from Yussuf to people at Aswan. If I want anything I am to call on the Cadi. We have a very excellent boat and a good crew, and are very comfortable. When the Luxor folk heard the 'son of my uncle' was come, they thought it must be my husband. I was diverted at Omar's propriety. He pointed out to Mustapha and Yussuf how *he* was to sleep in the cabin between Arthur's and mine, which was considered quite satisfactory apparently, and it was looked upon as very proper of Omar to have arranged it so, as he had been sent to put the boat in order. Arthur has been all along the Suez Canal, and seen a great many curious things. The Delta must be very unlike Upper Egypt from all he tells me.

The little troop of pilgrims for Mecca left Luxor about ten days ago. It was a pretty and touching sight. Three camels, five donkeys, and about thirty men and women, several with babies on their shoulders, all uttering the *zaghareet* (cry of joy). They were to walk to Kosseir (eight days' journey with good camels), babies and all. It is the happiest day of their lives, they say, when they have scraped together money enough to make the *hajj*.

This minute a poor man is weeping beside our boat over a pretty heifer decked with many *hegabs* (amulets), which have not availed

17. 'The most beautiful object my eyes ever saw is the island of Philae
... I went and lay on the parapet of the Temple. What a night! What
a view! The stars gave as much light as the moon in Europe, and all
but the cataract was still as death and glowing hot'

18. (a) 'It is worth going to Nubia to see the girls. . . . Their very dress
and ornaments were the same as those
represented in the tombs'

18. (b) Dancing girls

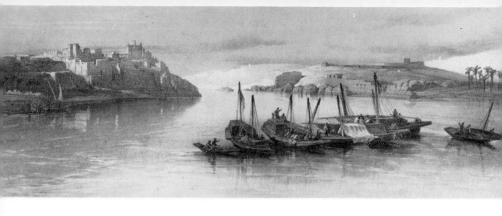

19. (a) Aswan. 'That most poetically melancholy spot, the granite quarry of old Egypt and burial place of Muslim martyrs'

19. (b) Abu Simbel, very much as it looked when Lucie visited it

20. Temple of Edfu

against the sickness. It is heart-rending to see the poor beasts and their unfortunate owners. Some dancing girls came to the boat just now for cigars which Arthur had promised them, and to ask after their friend el Maghribeeyeh, the good dancer at Luxor, whom they said was very ill. Omar did not know at all about her, and the girls seemed much distressed. They were both very pretty, one an Abyssinian.

XXII

Sleeping over the Temple of Philæ

April 1864. Dearest Alick. We spent two days and nights at Philæ and *Wallahy!* It was hot. The basalt rocks which enclose the river all round the island were burning. Sally and I slept in the Osiris chamber, on the roof of the temple, on our air-beds. Omar lay across the doorway to guard us, and Arthur and his Copt, with the well-bred sailor Ramadan, were sent to bivouac on the Pylon. Ramadan took the hareem under his special and most respectful charge, and waited on us devotedly, but never raised his eyes to our faces, or spoke till spoken to.

Philæ is six or seven miles from Aswan, and we went on donkeys through the beautiful Shellaleeh (the village of the cataract), and the noble place of tombs of Aswan. Great was the amazement of everyone at seeing Europeans so out of season; we were like swallows in January to them. I could not sleep for the heat in the room, and threw on an *abbayeh* (cloak) and went and lay on the parapet of the temple. What a night! What a lovely view! The stars gave as much light as the moon in Europe, and all but the cataract was still as death and glowing hot, and the palm-trees were more graceful and dreamy than ever. Then Omar woke, and came and sat at my feet, and rubbed them, and sang a song of a Turkish slave. I said, 'Do not rub my feet, oh brother—that is not fit for thee' (because it is below the dignity of a free Muslim altogether to touch shoes or feet), but he sang in his song, 'The slave of the Turk may be set free by money, but how shall one be ransomed who has been paid for by kind actions and sweet words?'

Then the day broke deep crimson, and I went down and bathed in the Nile, and saw the girls on the island opposite in their summer fashions, consisting of a leathern fringe round their slender hips—divinely graceful—bearing huge saucer-shaped baskets of corn on their stately young heads; and I went up and sat at the end of the colonnade looking up into Ethiopia, and dreamed dreams of 'Him who sleeps in Philæ', until the great Amun Ra kissed my northern face too hotly, and drove me into the temple to breakfast, and coffee, and pipes, and *kief*. And in the evening three little naked Nubians rowed us about for two or three hours on the glorious river in a boat made of thousands of bits of wood, each a foot long; and between whiles they jumped overboard and disappeared, and came up on the other side of the boat. Aswan was full of Turkish soldiers, who came and took away our donkeys, and stared at our faces most irreligiously.

We returned from Philæ to our boat the third morning and Sally fainted after we got back, from a combination of heat, fatigue and cucumber for supper. Omar came in and cried over Sally bitterly, frightened out of his senses at seeing a faint. She was all right again the next day. [Lucie was then ignorant of the fact that Sally had started to have a baby by Omar, and was probably suffering from 'morning sickness'.]

I did not go on shore at Kom Ombos or El Kab, only at Edfu, where we spent the day in the temple; and at Esneh, where we tried to buy sugar, tobacco, etc., and found nothing at all, though Esneh is a *chef-lieu*, with a Mudir. It is only in winter that anything is to be got for the travellers. We had to ask the Nazir in Edfu to *order* a man to sell us charcoal. People do without sugar, and smoke green tobacco, and eat beans, etc., etc. Soon we must do likewise, for our stores are nearly exhausted.

We stopped at El-Moutaneh, and had a good dinner in the Mouniers' handsome house, and they gave me a loaf of sugar. Mme. Mounier described Rachel's stay with them for three months at Luxor, in my house, where they then lived. She hated it so, that on embarking to leave she turned back and spat on the ground, and cursed the place inhabited by savages, where she had been *ennuyée a mort*. Mme. Mounier fully sympathized with her, and thought no *femme aimable* could live with Arabs, who are not at all *galants*. She is Levantine, and, I believe, half Arab herself, but hates the life here, and hates the Muslims.

There was one stupendous row at Aswan, however. The men had rigged out a sort of tent for me to bathe in over the side of the boat, and Ramadan caught the Copt trying to peep in, and half strangled him. Omar called him 'dog', and asked him if he was an infidel, and Macarius told him I was a Christian woman, and not *his* hareem. Omar lost his temper, and appealed to the old reis and all the sailors, 'O Muslims, ought not I to cut his throat if he had defiled the noble person of the lady with his pig's eyes? God forgive me for mentioning her in such a manner'. Then they all cursed him for a pig and an infidel, and threatened to put him ashore and leave him for his vile conduct towards noble hareem. Omar sobbed with passion, saying that I was to him like the 'back of his mother', and how 'dare Macarius take my name in his dirty mouth', etc. The Copt tried to complain of being beaten afterwards, but I signified to him that he had better hold his tongue, for that I understood Arabic, upon which he sneaked off.

Luxor, May 15. We had a good boat, and a capital crew; one man Mahommed, called Alatee (the singer), sang beautifully, to my great delight, and all were excellent fellows, quiet and obliging; only his [Arthur's] servant was a lazy beast, dirty and conceited—a Copt, spoiled by an Italian education and Greek associates, thinking himself very grand because he was a Christian. I wondered at the patience and good-nature with which Omar did all his work and endured all his insolence.

We returned to Luxor the evening before last just after dark. The salute which Omar fired with your old horse-pistols brought down a lot of people, and there was a chorus of *Alhamdullilah Salaameh ya Sitt*, and such a kissing of hands, and 'Welcome home to your place' and 'We have tasted your absence and found it bitter,' etc., etc. Mustapha came with letters for me, and Yussuf beaming with smiles, and Mahommed with new bread made of new wheat, and Suleyman with flowers, and little Ahmad rushing in wildly to kiss hands.

When the welcome had subsided, Yussuf, who stayed to tea, told me all the cattle were dead. Mustapha lost thirty-four, and has three left; and poor farmer Omar lost all—forty head. The distress in Upper Egypt will now be fearful. Within six weeks *all* our cattle are dead. They are threshing the corn with donkeys, and men are turning the sakiahs (water-wheels) and drawing the ploughs, and dying by scores of overwork and want of food in many places. The whole agriculture depended on the oxen, and they are all dead. At El-Moutaneh and the nine villages round Halim Pasha's estate 24,000 head have died; four beasts were left when we were there three days ago.

As I write this I glance at 'my brother' Yussuf, who is sleeping on a mat, quite overcome with the Simoom (which is blowing) and the fast which he is keeping today, as the eve of the *Eed-el-Kebir* (great festival).

This is the coolest place in the village. The glass is only $95\frac{1}{2}°$ now (eleven a.m.) in the darkened divan. The Cadi, and the Maōhn, and Yussuf came together to visit me, and when the others left he lay down to sleep. Omar is sleeping in the passage, and Sally in her room. I alone don't sleep—but the Simoom is terrible. Arthur runs about all day, sight-seeing and drawing, and does not suffer at all from the heat. I can't walk now, as the sand blisters my feet.

Tuesday, May 17. Yesterday the Simoom was awful, and last night I slept on the terrace, and was very hot. Today the north wind sprang up at noon and revived us, though it is still 102° in my divan. My old 'great-grandfather' has come in for a pipe and coffee; he was Belzoni's guide, and his eldest child was born seven days before the French under Bonaparte marched into Luxor.[1] He is superbly handsome and erect, and very talkative, but only remembers old times, and takes me for Mme. Belzoni. He is grandfather to Mahommed, the guard of this house, and great-grandfather to my little Ahmad. His grandsons have married him to a tidy old woman to take care of him; he calls me 'My lady grand-daughter', and Omar he calls 'Mustapha', and we salute him as 'grandfather'. I wish I could paint him; he is so grand to look at. Old Mustapha had a son born yesterday—his tenth child. I must go and wish him joy.

May 23. I went over to Mustapha's island to spend the day in the tent, or rather the hut, of dourrah-stalks and palm-branches, which he has erected there for the threshing and winnowing. He had invited me and 'his worship' the Maōhn to a picnic. Only imagine that it *rained!* all day, a gentle slight rain, but enough to wet all the desert. I laughed and said I had brought English weather, but the Maōhn shook his head and opined that we were suffering the anger of God. Rain in summer-time was quite a terror. However, we consoled ourselves, and Mustapha called a nice little boy to recite the 'noble Koran' for our amusement, and out of compliment to me he selected the chapter of the family of Amran (the history of Jesus), and recited it with marvellous readiness and accuracy. A very pleasant-mannered man of the Shourafa of Gurna came and joined us, and was delighted

[1] Bonaparte was still in Cairo but had sent General Desaix up the Nile in pursuit of the Mameluke leader, Murad Bey in 1798/9.

Giovanni Belzoni (1778–1823) was a remarkable Italian, see *The Great Belzoni*, by Stanley Mayes, Putnam 1959.

because I sent away a pipe which Abdurrachman brought me (it is highly improper to smoke while the Koran is being read or recited). He thanked me for the respect, and I told him I knew he would not smoke in a church, or while I prayed; why should I?

It rather annoys me to find that they always expect from us irreverence to their religion which they would on no account be guilty of to ours. The little boy was a fellah, the child of my friend Omar, who has lost all his cattle, but who came as pleasant and smiling as ever to kiss my hand and wait upon me.

After that the Maōhn read the second chapter, 'the Cow', in a rather nasal, quavering chant. I perceived that no one present understood any of it, except just a few words here and there—not much more than I could follow myself from having read the translation. I think it is not any nearer spoken Arabic than Latin is to Italian.

Then Mustapha, the Maōhn, Omar, Sally and I, sat down round the dinner-tray, and had a very good dinner of lamb, fowls and vegetables, such as *bahmias* and *melucheeah,* both of the mallow order, and both excellent cooked with meat; rice, stewed apricots (*mish-mish*), with nuts and raisins in it, and cucumbers and water-melons strewed the ground. One eats all *durcheinander*[1] with bread and fingers, and a spoon for the rice, and green limes to squeeze over one's own bits for sauce. We were very merry, if not very witty, and the Maōhn declared, '*Wallahi!* the English are fortunate in their customs, and in the enjoyment of the society of learned and excellent *hareemat;*' and Omar, lying on the rushes, said: 'This is the happiness of the Arab. Green trees, sweet water, and a kind face, make the "garden" ' (paradise)—an Arab saying. The Maōhn joked him as to how a 'child of Cairo' could endure fellah life.

I was looking at the heaps of wheat and thinking of Ruth, when I started to hear the soft Egyptian lips utter the very words which the Egyptian girl spake more than a thousand years ago: 'Behold my mother! where she stays I stay, and where she goes I will go; her family is my family, and if it pleaseth God, nothing but the Separator of friends (death) shall divide me from her'. I really could not speak, so I kissed the top of Omar's turban, Arab fashion, and the Maōhn blessed him quite solemnly, and said: 'God reward thee, my son; thou hast honoured thy lady greatly before thy people, and she has honoured thee, and ye are an example of masters and servants, and of kindness and fidelity'; and the brown labourers who were lounging

[1] Mixed up together.

about said: 'Verily, it is true, and God be praised for people of excellent conduct.'

I never expected to feel like Naomi, and possibly many English people might only think Omar's unconscious repetition of Ruth's words rather absurd, but to me they sounded in perfect harmony with the life and ways of this country and these people, who are so full of tender and affectionate feelings, when they have not been crushed out of them. It is not humbug; I have seen their actions. Because they use grand compliments, Europeans think they are never sincere, but the compliments are not meant to deceive, they only profess to be forms. Why do the English talk of the beautiful sentiment of the Bible and pretend to feel it so much, and when they come and see the same life before them they ridicule it.

Tuesday. We have a family quarrel going on. Mohammed's wife, a girl of eighteen or so, wanted to go home on Bairam day for her mother to wash her head and unplait her hair. Mohammed told her not to leave him on that day, and to send for a woman to do it for her; whereupon she cut off her hair, and Mohammed, in a passion, told her to 'cover her face' (that is equivalent to a divorce) and take her baby and go home to her father's house. Ever since he has been mooning about the yard and in and out of the kitchen very glum and silent.

This morning I went into the kitchen and found Omar cooking with a little baby in his arms, and giving it sugar. 'Why what is that?' say I. 'Oh don't say anything. I sent Ahmad to fetch Mohammed's baby, and when he comes here he will see it, and then in talking I can say so and so, and how the man must be good to the hareem, and what this poor, small girl do when she big enough to ask for her father.' In short, Omar wants to exercise his diplomacy in making up the quarrel.

After writing this I heard Mohammed's low, quiet voice, and Omar's boyish laugh, and then silence, and went to see the baby and its father. My kitchen was a pretty scene. Mohammed, in his ample brown robes and white turban, lay asleep on the floor with the baby's tiny pale face and little eyelids stained with kohl against his coffee-brown cheek, both fast asleep, baby in her father's arms. Omar leant against the *fournaise* in his house-dress, a white shirt open at the throat and white drawers reaching to the knees, with the red tarbush and red and yellow *kufyeh* (silk handkerchief) round it turban-wise, contemplating them with his great, soft eyes. The two young men made an excellent contrast between Upper and Lower Egypt.

169

Mohammed is the true Arab type—coffee-brown, thin, spare, sharp-featured, elegant hands and feet, bright glittering small eyes and angular jaw—not a handsome Arab, but *bien charactérisé*. Omar, the colour of new boxwood or old ivory, pale, with eyes like a cow, full lips, full chin and short nose, not the least negro, but perfectly Egyptian, the eyes wide apart—unlike the Arab—moustache like a woman's eyebrow, curly brown hair, bad hands and feet and not well made, but graceful in movement and still more in countenance, very inferior in beauty to the pure Arab blood which prevails here, but most sweet in expression.

Friday. We have had better weather again, easterly wind and pretty cool, and I am losing the cough and languor which the damp of the Simoom brought me. Shaikh Yussuf has just come back from Keneh, whither he and the Cadi went on their donkeys for some law business. He took our saddle bags at Omar's request, and brought us back a few pounds of sugar and some rice and tobacco (isn't it like Fielding's novels?). It is two days' journey, so they slept in the mosque at Koos half way.

XXIII

'Islam is ceasing to be a mere party flag'

May 23 1864. Dearest Mother. I told Yussuf how Suleyman's child had the smallpox and how Mohammed only said it was *'min Allah'* (from God) when I suggested that his baby should be vaccinated at once.

Yussuf called him in and said: 'Oh man, when thou wouldst build a house dost thou throw the bricks in a heap on the ground and say the building thereof is from God, or dost thou use the brains and hands which God has given thee, and then pray to Him to bless thy work? In all things do the best of thy understanding and means, and then say *min Allah*, for the end is with Him!' There is not a pin to choose in fatalism here between Muslim and Christian, the lazy, like Mohammed and Suleyman (one Arab the other Copt), say *min Allah* or any form of dawdle you please; but the true Muslim doctrine is just what Yussuf laid down—'do all you can and be resigned to whatever be the result'. *Fais ce que dois advienne qui pourra* is good doctrine.

In fact, I am very much puzzled to discover the slightest difference between Christian and Muslim morality or belief—if you exclude certain dogmas—and in fact, very little is felt here. No one attempts to apply different standards of morals or of piety to a Muslim and a Copt. East and West is the difference, not Muslim and Christian. As to that difference I could tell volumes. Are they worse? Are they better? Both and neither. I am, perhaps, not quite impartial, because I am *sympathique* to the Arabs and they to me, and I am inclined to be 'kind' to their virtues if not 'blind' to their faults, which are visible to the most inexperienced traveller.

You see all our own familiar 'bunkum' (excuse the vulgarity) falls so flat on their ears, bravado about 'honour', 'veracity', etc., etc.,

171

they look blank and bored at. The schoolboy morality as set forth by Maurice is current here among grown men. Of course we tell lies to Pashas and Beys, why shouldn't we? But shall I call in that ragged sailor and give him an order to bring me up £500 in cash from Cairo when he happens to come? It would not be an unusual proceeding. I sleep every night in a *makaab* (sort of verandah) open to all Luxor, and haven't a door that has a lock. They bother me for backsheesh; but oh how poor they are, and how rich must be a woman whose very servants drink sugar to their coffee! and who lives in the *Kasr* (palace) and is respectfully visited by Ali Bey—and, come to that, Ali Bey would like a present even better than the poor fellah, who also loves to give one.

When I know, as I now do thoroughly, all Omar's complete integrity—without any sort of mention of it—his self-denial in going ragged and shabby to save his money for his wife and child (a very great trial to a good-looking young Arab), and the equally unostentatious love he has shown to me, and the delicacy and real nobleness of feeling which come out so oddly in the midst of sayings which, to our ideas, seem very shabby and time-serving, very often I wonder if there be anything as good in the civilized West. And as Sally most justly says, 'All their goodness is quite their own. God knows there is no one to teach anything but harm!'

Please tell Dean Stanley[1] how his old dragoman Mahommed Gazowee cried with pleasure when he told me he had seen Shaikh Stanley's sister on her way to India, and the 'little lady' *knew his name* and shook hands with him, which evidently was worth far more than the backsheesh. I wondered who 'Shaikh' Stanley could be, and Mahommed (who is a darweesh and very pious) told me he was the *Gassis* (priest) who was *Imâm* (spiritual guide) to the son of our Queen, 'and in truth', said he, 'he is *really* a Shaikh and one who teaches the excellent things of religion, why he was kind even to his horse! and it is of the mercies of God to the English that such a one is the Imâm of your Queen and Prince'.

---

[1] Lucie appreciated the liberalism of Arthur Stanley, Dean of Westminster and Regius Professor of ecclesiastical history at Oxford. He was the centre of considerable theological controversy over such matters as his wish to make recital of the Athanasian creed optional in the Anglican Church and he considered that the first duty of a modern theologian was to study the Bible 'not for the sake of making or defending systems out of it, but for the sake of discovering what it actually contains'. He had visited Egypt in 1862, when Lucie was still in South Africa, accompanying the Prince of Wales on a tour of Egypt and Palestine at the request of Queen Victoria.

I said laughing, 'How dost thou, a darweesh among Muslims, talk thus of a Nazarene priest?' 'Truly oh Lady', he answered, 'one who loveth all the creatures of God, him God loveth also, there is no doubt of that'. Is any one bigot enough to deny that Stanley has done more for real religion in the mind of that Muslim darweesh than if he had baptised a hundred savages out of one fanatical faith into another?

There is no hope of a good understanding with Orientals until Western Christians can bring themselves to recognize the common faith contained in the two religions, the *real* difference consists in all the class of notions and feelings (very important ones, no doubt) which we derive—not from the Gospels at all—but from Greece and Rome, and which of course are altogether wanting here.

Tuesday. Two poor fellows have just come home from the Suez Canal work with gastric fever, I think. I hope it won't spread. The wife of one said to me yesterday, 'Are there more *Sittat* (ladies) like you in your village?' 'Wallah', said I, 'there are many better, and good doctors'. 'Thank goodness', said she, 'then the poor people don't want you so much, and by God you must stay here for *we* can't do without you, so write to your family to say so, and don't go away and leave us'.

Thursday, June 2. The epidemic here is all but over; but my medical fame has spread so, that the poor souls come twenty miles (from Koos) for physic. The constant phrase of 'Oh our sister, God hath sent thee to look to us!' is so sad. *Such* a little help is a wonder to my poor little fellaheen.

It is not so hot as it was I think, except at night, and I now sleep half the night outside the house. The cattle are all dead; perhaps five are left in all Luxor. 'God is merciful', said fellah Omar, 'I have one left from fifty-four'. The grain is unthreshed, and butter three shillings a pound! We get nothing here but by post; no papers, no nothing. I suppose the high Nile will bring up boats. Now the river is down at its lowest, and now I really know how Egyptians live.

I have had an abominable toothache, which quite floored me, and was aggravated by the Oriental custom, namely, that all the *beau monde* of Thebes *would* come and sit with me, and suggest remedies, and look into my mouth, and make quite a business of my tooth. Shaikh Yussuf laid two fingers on my cheek and recited verses from the Koran, I regret to say with no effect, except that while his fingers touched me the pain ceased. I find he is celebrated for soothing headaches and other nervous pains, and I daresay is an unconscious mesmerizer.

The other day our poor Maōhn was terrified by a communication from Ali Bey (Mudir of Keneh) to the effect that he had heard from Alexandria that someone had reported that the dead cattle had lain about the streets of Luxor and that the place was pestilential. The British mind at once suggested a counter-statement, to be signed by the most respectable inhabitants. So the Cadi drew it up, and came and read it to me, and took my deposition and witnessed my signature, and the Maōhn went his way rejoicing, in that 'the words of the Englishwoman' would utterly defeat Ali Bey. The truth was that the worthy Maōhn worked really hard, and superintended the horrible dead cattle business in person, which is some risk and very unpleasant. To dispose of three or four hundred dead oxen every day with a limited number of labourers is no trifle, and if a travelling Englishman smells one a mile off he calls us 'lazy Arabs'. The beasts could not be buried deep enough, but all were carried a mile off from the village. I wish some of the dilettanti who stop their noses at us in our trouble had to see or to do what I have seen and done.

June 17. We have had four or five days of such fearful heat with a Simoom that I have been quite knocked up, and literally could not write. Besides, I sit in the dark all day, and am now writing so—and at night go out and sit in the verandah, and can't have candles because of the insects. I sleep outside till about six a.m., and then go indoors till dark again. This fortnight is the hottest time. Today the drop falls into the Nile at its source, and it will now rise fast and cool the country. It has risen one cubit, and the water is green; next month it will be blood colour.

My cough has been a little troublesome again, I suppose from the Simoom. The tooth does not ache now. *Alhamdulillah!* for I rather dreaded the *muẓeyinn* (barber) with his *tongs,* who is the sole dentist here.

I was amused the other day by the entrance of my friend the Maōhn, attended by Osman Effendi and his cawass and pipe-bearer, and bearing a saucer in his hand, wearing the look, half sheepish, half cocky, with which elderly gentlemen in all countries announce what he did, *i.e.,* that his black slave-girl was three months with child and longed for olives; so the respectable magistrate had trotted all over the bazaar and to the Greek corn-dealers to buy some, but for no money were they to be had, so he hoped I might have some and forgive the request, as I, of course, knew that a man must beg or even steal for a woman under these circumstances. I called Omar and said, 'I trust there are olives for the honourable hareem of Seleem Effendi—they are needed there'. Omar instantly understood the case, and 'Praise be to God a few are left; I was about to stuff the pigeons for dinner with them; how lucky I had not done it'. And then we belaboured Seleem with compliments, 'Please God the child will be fortunate to thee,' say I. Omar says, 'Sweeten my mouth, oh Effendim, for did I not tell thee God would give thee good out of this affair when thou boughtest her?' While we were thus rejoicing over the possible little mulatto, I thought how shocked a white Christian gentleman of our Colonies would be at our conduct to make all this fuss about a black girl, and my heart warmed to the kind old Muslim as he took his saucer of olives and walked with them openly in his hand along the street.

Now the black girl is free, and can only leave Seleem's house by her own good will and probably after a time she will marry and he will pay the expenses. A man can't sell his slave after he has made known that she is with child by him, and it would be considered unmanly to detain her if she should wish to go. The child will be added to the other eight who fill the Maōhn's quiver in Cairo and will be exactly as well looked on and have equal rights if he is as black as a coal.

A most quaint little half-black boy a year and a half old has taken a fancy to me and comes and sits for hours gazing at me and then dances to amuse me. He is Mohammed our guard's son by a jet-black slave of his and is brown-black and very pretty. He wears a bit of iron wire in one ear and iron rings round his ankles, and that is all—and when he comes up little Ahmad, who is his uncle, 'makes him fit to be seen' by emptying a pitcher of water over his head to rinse off the dust in which of course he has been rolling—that is equivalent to a clean pinafore. You would want to buy little Said I know, he is so pretty and so jolly. He dances and sings and jabbers baby Arabic and then sits like a quaint little idol cross-legged quite still for hours.

I am now writing in the kitchen, which is the coolest place where there is any light at all. Omar is diligently spelling words of six letters, with the wooden spoon in his hand and a cigarette in his mouth, and Sally is lying on her back on the floor. I won't describe our costume. It is now two months since I have worn stockings, and I think you would wonder at the fellaha who 'owns you', so deep a brown are my face, hands and feet. One of the sailors in Arthur's boat said: 'See how the sun of the Arabs loves her; he has kissed her so hotly that she can't go home among English people'.

Poor Suleyman's little boy is dead of smallpox. Thank goodness it has not spread; the fact is that vaccination is far more general here than in Europe, very few neglect it.

Dearest Alick. Please answer me about money. I really don't know what to do at all or how to shape my plans till you fix how much I may spend. I do not think I can do at all with less than £400 a year—meat is one shilling a pound, butter three shillings and most things in proportion. I live really like the fellaheen and, of course, I have no expenses here. I have given no-one a sixpence, except five napoleons to Shaikh Yussuf for lessons and one napoleon as backsheesh to Mahommed and Suleyman at Bairam and to the boats' crew. I also paid the food in the boat as my share of the trip; but if I do go down to Cairo at all it costs a good bit and I owe Omar all his wages. Please give me a distinct answer or I will pack up and come home. I do not like the 'take what you want' system—the constant feeling that if I have a wish I must not indulge it, wearies me and you wrote as if you thought me extravagant.

June 18. I went last night to look at Karnac by moonlight. The giant columns were overpowering. I never saw anything so solemn. On our way back we met the Shaikh-el-Beled, who ordered me an escort of ten men home. Fancy me on my humble donkey, guarded most superfluously by ten tall fellows, with oh! such spears and venerable matchlocks.

At Mustapha's house we found a party seated before the door, and joined it. There was a tremendous Shaikh-el-Islam from Tunis, a Maghrabee, seated on a carpet in state receiving homage. I don't think he liked the heretical woman at all. Even the Maōhn did not dare to be as 'politeful' as usual to me, but took the seat above me, which I had respectfully left vacant next to the holy man. Mustapha was in a stew, afraid not to do the respectful to me, and fussing after the Shaikh. Then Yussuf came fresh from the river, where he had bathed and prayed, and then you saw the real gentleman. He salaamed the great Shaikh, who motioned to him to sit before him, but Yussuf quietly came round and sat *below* me on the mat, leaned his elbow on my cushion, and made more demonstration of regard for me than ever, and when I went, came and helped me on my donkey. The holy Shaikh went away to pray, and Mustapha hinted to Yussuf to go with him, but he only smiled, and did not stir; he had prayed an hour before down at the Nile. It was as if a poor curate had devoted himself to a rank papist under the eye of a scowling Shaftesbury Bishop.

Then came Osman Effendi, a young Turk, with a poor devil accused in a distant village of stealing a letter with money in it addressed to a Greek money-lender. The discussion was quite general, the man, of course, denying all. But the Nazir had sent word to beat him. Then Omar burst out, 'What a shame to beat a poor man on the mere word of a Greek money-lender who eats the people; the Nazir shouldn't help him'. There was a Greek present who scowled at Omar, and the Turk gaped at him in horror. Yussuf said, with his quiet smile, 'My brother, thou art talking English', with a glance at me; and we all laughed, and I said, 'Many thanks for the compliment'.

All the village is in good spirits; the Nile is rising fast, and a star of most fortunate character has made its appearance, so Yussuf tells me, and portends a good year and an end to our afflictions. I am much better today, and I think I too feel the rising Nile; it puts new life into all things. The last fortnight or three weeks have been very trying with the Simoom and intense heat. I suppose I look better for the people here are for ever praising God about my amended looks. I am too hot, and it is too dark to write more.

I fear Mustapha can't afford his journey to England; he has lost fifty-three head of cattle and his second son has turned out ill. He wants to know whether his boy Ahmad, a very nice boy of twelve, could be put to school and kept in England for £100 a year. Will you find out? Of course it must be a school where no conversion will be attempted. Mustapha is a strong Muslim. The boy is in Alexandria and is really a nice child; I had him with me a good deal.

June 26. I have just paid a singular visit to a political *detenu* or exile rather. Last night Mustapha came in with a man in great grief who said his boy was very ill on board a *cangia* just come from Cairo and going to Aswan. The watchman on the river-bank had told him that there was an English Sitt 'who would not turn her face from anyone in trouble' and advised him to come to me for medicine, so he went to Mustapha and begged him to bring him to me, and to beg the *cawass* (policeman) in charge of El-Bedrawee (who was being sent to Fazoghli in banishment) to wait a few hours. The *cawass* (may he not suffer for his humanity) consented.

He described his boy's symptoms and I gave him a dose of castor oil and said I would go to the boat in the morning. The poor fellow was a Cairo merchant but living at Khartum, he poured out his sorrow in true Eastern style. 'Oh my boy, and I have none but he, and how shall I come before his mother, a Habbesheeyeh,[1] oh Lady, and tell her "thy son is dead"?' So I comforted him and went this morning early to the boat.

It was a regular old Arab *cangia* lumbered up with corn, sacks of matting, a live sheep, etc., and there I found a sweet graceful boy of fifteen or so in a high fever. His father said he had visited a certain Pasha on the way and evidently meant that he had been poisoned or had the evil eye. I assured him it was only the epidemic and asked why he had not sent for the doctor at Keneh. The old story! He was afraid, 'God knows what a government doctor might do to the boy'.

Then Omar came in and stood before El-Bedrawee and said, 'Oh my master, why do we see thee thus? Mashallah, I once ate of thy bread when I was of the soldiers of Said Pasha, and I saw thy riches and thy greatness, and what has God decreed against thee?'

So El-Bedrawee who is (or was) one of the wealthiest men of Lower Egypt and lived at Tantah, related how Effendina (Ismail Pasha) sent for him to go to Cairo to the Citadel to transact some business, and how he rode his horse up to the Citadel and went in, and there the Pasha at once ordered a cawass to take him down to the Nile and on board a common cargo boat and to go with him and take him to Fazogli. Letters were given to the cawass to deliver to every Mudir on the way, and another despatched by hand to the Governor of Fazogli with orders concerning El-Bedrawee.

He begged leave to see his wife once more before starting, or any of his family. 'No, he must go at once and see no one.' But luckily a fellah, one of his relations had come after him to Cairo and had £700 in his girdle; he followed El-Bedrawee to the Citadel and saw him being walked off by the cawass and followed him to the river and on board the boat and gave him the £700 which he had in his girdle. The various Mudirs had been civil to him, and friends in various places had given him clothes and food. He had not got a chain round his neck or fetters, and was allowed to go ashore with the cawass, for he had just been to the tomb of Abu-l-Hajjaj and had told that dead Shaikh all his affliction and promised, if he came back safe, to come every year to his *moolid* (festival) and pay the whole expenses (*i.e.*, feed all comers).

Mustapha wanted him to dine with him and me, but the cawass

1 An Abyssinian.

21. 'As I rode through the green fields along the dyke, a little boy
sang as he turned round on the musically-creaking *sakiah* (the water-
wheel turned by an ox) the one eternal *sakiah* tune. . . "Turn Oh
sakiah to the right and turn to the left – who will take
care of me if my father dies?" '

22. (a) 'Mr Edward Lear has done a little drawing
of my house for you'

22. (b) Libyan hills as seen from the Temple of Luxor on which Lucie
had her house. 'I sit on my lofty balcony and drink the sweet
northerly breeze and look at the glorious
mountain opposite'

23. Entrance to the Temple of Luxor

24. 'I went to look at Karnac by moonlight. The giant columns were overpowering. I never saw anything so solemn'

could not allow it, so Mustapha sent him a fine sheep and some bread, fruit, etc. I made him a present of some quinine, rhubarb pills, and sulphate of zinc for eye lotion. Here you know we all go upon a more than English presumption and believe every prisoner to be innocent and a victim—as he gets no trial he *never* can be proved guilty— besides poor old El-Bedrawee declared he had not the faintest idea what he was accused of or how he had offended Effendina.

I listened to all this in extreme amazement, and he said, 'Ah! I know you English manage things very differently; I have heard all about your excellent justice'.

He was a stout, dignified-looking fair man, like a Turk, but talking broad Lower Egypt fellah talk, so that I could not understand him, and had to get Mustapha and Omar to repeat his words. His father was an Arab, and his mother a Circassian slave, which gave the fair skin and reddish beard. He must be over fifty, fat and not healthy; of course he is *meant* to die up in Fazogli, especially going at this season. He owns (or owned, for God knows who has it now) 12,000 feddans of fine land between Tantah and Samanhud, and was enormously rich. He consulted me a great deal about his health, and I gave him certainly very good advice. I cannot write in a letter which I know you will show what drugs a Turkish doctor had furnished him with to 'strengthen' him in the trying climate of Fazogli. I wonder was it intended to kill him or only given in ignorance of the laws of health equal to his own?

After a while the pretty boy became better and recovered consciousness, and his poor father, who had been helping me with trembling hands and swimming eyes, cried for joy, and said, 'By God the most high, if ever I find any of the English, poor or sick or afflicted up in Fazogli, I will make them know that I Abu-Mahommed never saw a face like the pale face of the English lady bent over my sick boy'. And then El-Bedrawee and his fellah kinsman, and all the crew blessed me and the Captain, and the cawass said it was time to sail. So I gave directions and medicine to Abu Mahommed, and kissed the pretty boy and went out.

El-Bedrawee followed me up the bank, and said he had a request to make—would I pray for him in his distress. I said, 'I am not of the Muslimeen', but both he and Mustapha said, *Maleysh* (never mind), for that it was quite certain I was not of the *Mushrikeen*, as they hate the Muslimeen and their deeds are evil—but blessed be God, many of the English begin to repent of their evil, and to love the Muslims

N

and abound in kind actions. So we parted in much kindness. It was a strange feeling to me to stand on the bank and see the queer savage-looking boat glide away up the stream, bound to such far more savage lands, and to be exchanging kind farewells quite in a homely manner with such utter 'aliens in blood and faith'. 'God keep thee Lady, God keep thee Mustapha.' Mustapha and I walked home very sad about poor El-Bedrawee.

Friday, July 7. It has been so 'awfully' hot that I have not had pluck to go on with my letter, or indeed to do anything but lie on a mat in the passage with a minimum of clothes quite indescribable in English. *Alhamdullilah!* laughs Omar, 'that I see the clever English people do just like the lazy Arabs'. The worst is not the positive heat, which has not been above 104° and as low as 96° at night, but the horrible storms of hot wind and dust which are apt to come on at night and prevent one's even lying down till twelve or one o'clock. Thebes is bad in the height of summer on account of its expanse of desert, and sand and dust.

The Nile is pouring down now gloriously, and *really* red as blood—more crimson than a Herefordshire lane—and in the distance the reflection of the pure blue sky makes it deep violet. It had risen five cubits a week ago; we shall soon have it all over the land here. It is a beautiful and inspiriting sight to see the noble old stream as young and vigorous as ever. No wonder the Egyptians worshipped the Nile: there is nothing like it. We have had all the plagues of Egypt this year, only the lice are commuted for bugs, and the frogs for mice; the former have eaten me and the latter have eaten my clothes. We are so ragged! Omar has one shirt left, and has to sleep without and wash it every night. The dust, the drenching perspiration, and the hard-fisted washing of Mahommed's slave-women destroys everything. Then I can't wear stockings or stays or petticoats. I go in my flannel shift and a loose dress and that is worn out.

Mustapha intends to give you a grand *fantasia* if you come, and to have the best dancing girls down from Esneh for you; but I am consternated to hear that you can't come till December. I hoped you would have arrived in Cairo early in November, and spent a month there with me, and come up the river in the middle of December when Cairo gets very cold.

I remain very well in general health, but my cough has been troublesome again. I do not feel at all like breathing cold damp air again. This depresses me very much as you may suppose. You will

have to divorce me, and I must marry some respectable Cadi. I have
been too 'lazy Arab', as Omar calls it, to go on with my Arabic
lessons, and Yussuf has been very busy with law business connected
with the land and the crops. Every harvest brings a fresh settling of
the land. Wheat is selling at £1 the ardeb (about 7½ bushels) here
on the threshing-floor, and barley at one hundred and sixteen piastres;
I saw some Nubians pay Mustapha that. He is in comic perplexity
about saying *Alhamdulillah* about such enormous gains—you see it
is rather awkward for a Muslim to thank God for dear bread—so he
compounds by very lavish almsgiving. He gave all his fellaheen
clothes the other day—forty calico shirts and drawers. Do you
remember my describing an Arab emancipated woman at Assiut?
Well, the other day I saw, as I thought, a nice-looking lad of sixteen
selling corn to my opposite neighbour, a Copt. It was a girl. Her
father had no son and is infirm, so she works in the field for him,
and dresses and does like a man. She looked very modest and was
quieter in her manner than the veiled women often are.

I am so glad to hear such good accounts of my Rainie and Maurice.
I can hardly bear to think of another year without seeing them.
However it is fortunate for me that 'my lines have fallen in pleasant
places', so long a time at the Cape or any Colony would have become
intolerable. Best love to Janet, I really can't write, it's too hot and
dusty. Omar desires his salaam to his great master and to that gazelle
Sittee Ross. Sally would like to go to Ellen in October for her sister's
lying in, but Omar will valet me perfectly during her absence.

August 13. Dearest Alick. For the last month we have had a
purgatory of hot wind and dust, such as I never saw—impossible to
stir out of the house. So in despair I have just engaged a return boat—
a *Gelegenheit* [a chance]—and am off to Cairo in a day or two, where
I shall stop till *Inshallah!* you come to me. Can't you get leave to
come at the beginning of November? Do try, that is the pleasant
time in Cairo. I have suffered horribly from prickly heat till I thought
it would end in erysipelis, but the Arabian doctor told me to do
nothing to it and to bear it patiently as he believed it would do my
lungs good, and I am sure he was right.

I had a pleasant visit lately from a great doctor from Mecca—a man
so learned that he can read the Koran in seven different ways, he is
also a physician of European *hekmeh* (learning). Fancy my wonder
when a great Alim in gorgeous Hejazi dress walked in and said:
'*Madame, tout ce qu'on m'a dit de vous fait tellement l'éloge de votre*

cœur et de votre esprit que je me suis arreté pour tâcher de me procurer le plaisir de votre connaissance !' A lot of Luxor people came in to pay their respects to the great man, and he said to me that he hoped I had not been molested on account of religion, and if I had I must forgive it, as the people here were so very ignorant, and *barbarians were bigots everywhere.*

'The people of Luxor are my brothers!' I said, and the Maōhn added, 'True, the fellaheen are like oxen, but not such swine as to insult the religion of a lady who has served God among them like this one. She risked her life every day.' 'And if she *had* died', said the great theologian, 'her place was made ready among the martyrs of God, because she showed more love to her brothers than to herself!'

Now if this was humbug it was said in Arabic before eight or ten people, by a man of great religious authority.

Omar was *aux anges* to hear his Sitt spoken of 'in such a grand way for the religion'. I believe that a great change is taking place among the Ulema, that Islam is ceasing to be a mere party flag, just as occurred with Christianity, and that all the moral part is being more and more dwelt on. My great Alim also said I had practised the precepts of the Koran, and then laughed and added, 'I suppose I ought to say the Gospel, but what matters it, *el Hakh* (the truth) is one, whether spoken by Our Lord Jesus or by Our Lord Mahommed!' He asked me to go with him to Mecca next winter for my health, as it was so hot and dry there. I found he had fallen in with El-Bedrawee and the Khartum merchant at Aswan. The little boy was well again, and I had been outrageously extolled by them. We are now sending off all the corn.

I sat the other evening on Mustapha's doorstep and saw the Greeks piously and zealously attending to the divine command to spoil the Egyptians. Eight months ago a Greek bought up corn at 60 piastres the ardeb (he follows the Coptic tax-gatherer like a vulture after a crow), now wheat is at 170 piastres the ardeb here, and the fellah has paid $3\frac{1}{2}$ *per cent a month* besides. Reckon the profit! Two men I know are quite ruined, and have sold all they had. The cattle disease forced them to borrow at these ruinous rates, and now alas, the Nile is sadly lingering in its rise, and people are very anxious. Poor Egypt! or rather, poor Egyptians! Of course, I need not say that there is great improvidence in those who can be fleeced as they are fleeced. Mustapha's household is a pattern of muddling hospitality, and Mustapha is generous and mean by turns; but what chance have people like these, so utterly uncivilized and so isolated, against Europeans of unscrupulous characters.

I can't write more in the wind and dust. You shall hear again from Cairo.

Cairo, October 21 1864. Dearest Mother. I never wrote about my leaving Luxor or my journey, for our voyage was quite tempestuous after the three first days and I fell ill as soon as I was in my house here. I hired the boat for six purses (£18) which had taken Greeks up to Aswan selling groceries and strong drinks, but the reis would not bring back their cargo of black slaves to dirty the boat and picked us up at Luxor. We sailed at daybreak having waited all one day because it was an unlucky day.

As I sat in the boat people kept coming to ask whether I was coming back very anxiously and bringing fresh bread, eggs and things as presents, and all the quality came to take leave and hope, *Inshallah*, I should soon 'come home to my village safe and bring the Master, please God, to see them', and then to say the *Fattah* for a safe journey and my health. In the morning the balconies of my house were filled with such a group to see us sail—a party of wild Abab'deh with their long Arab guns and flowing hair, a Turk elegantly dressed, Mohammed in his decorous brown robes and snow-white turban, and several fellaheen. As the boat moved off the Abab'deh blazed away with their guns and Osman Effendi with a sort of blunderbuss, and as we dropped down the river there was a general firing; even Todoros (Theodore), the Coptic Mallim, popped off his American revolver. Omar keeping up a return with Alick's old horse pistols which are much admired here on account of the excessive noise they make.

Poor old Ismain, who always thought I was Mme Belzoni and wanted to take me up to Abu Simbel to meet my husband, was in dire distress that he could not go with me to Cairo. He declared he was still *shedeed* (strong enough to take care of me and to fight). He is ninety-seven and only remembers fifty or sixty years ago and old wild times—a splendid old man, handsome and erect. I used to give him coffee and listen to his old stories which had won his heart. His grandson, the quiet, rather stately, Mohammed who is guard of the house I lived in, forgot all his Muslim dignity, broke down in the middle of his set speech and flung himself down and kissed and hugged my knees and cried. He had got some notion of impending ill-luck, I found, and was unhappy at our departure—and the backsheesh failed to console him. Shaikh Yussuf was to come with me, but a brother of his just wrote word that he was coming back from the Hejaz where he had been with the troops in which he is serving his time; I was very sorry to lose his company.

We had a lovely time on the river for three days, such moonlight nights, so soft and lovely; and we had a sailor who was as good as a professional singer, and who sang religious songs, which I observe excite people here far more than love songs. One which began 'Remove my sins from before thy sight Oh God' was really beautiful and touching, and I did not wonder at the tears which ran down Omar's face. A very pretty profane song was 'Keep the wind from me Oh Lord, I fear it will hurt me' (*wind* means *love*, which is like the Simoom) 'Alas! it has struck me and I am sick. Why do ye bring the physician? Oh physician put back thy medicine in the canister, for only he who has hurt can cure me.' The masculine pronoun is always used instead of *she* in poetry out of decorum—sometimes even in conversation.

Dearest Alick. If you do come will you pleased bring me four India gauze shirts (jerseys/largest size); those you bought me last summer have shrunk to nothing; also four of a commoner sort for Omar with short sleeves, about Maurice's size. Also the books in the enclosed list for a Yankee Egyptologist at Luxor, a friend of mine.

I don't make head or tail of your plans. If you don't come here till the middle of November I shall only see you for a week or two as (after being so ill especially) I must go up river again end of November or very early December. If you can go with me it will be delightful. I expected you this month and have this house until the last day of November. I will write all my other commissions to Janet as I know you don't like carrying goods.

When you are in Alexandria pray call on Madame Tastu and thank her and be civil about the house at Thebes. Smith [an American who used to visit Luxor], is gone to Alexandria en route home. Halim Pasha did not give him one farthing backsheesh, though I hear he delivered the houses in splendid condition. Smith was quite knocked up with anxiety and work.

Ellen has got a baby and Sally has gone this morning to stay with her a bit. Omar takes good care of me and is quite a competent lady's maid and sick nurse as far as I want one. The weather is bad here, so very damp. I stream with perspiration more than in June at Luxor, and I don't like civilization so very much. It keeps me awake at night in the grog shops and rings horrid bells and fights and quarrels in the street, and disturbs my Muslim nerves till I utter such epithets as *kelb* (dog) and *khanseer* (pig) against the Frangi, and wish I were in a 'beastly Arab' quarter.

October 23. Yesterday I met a Saidi—a friend of the brother of the Shaikh of the wild Abab'deh, and as we stood handshaking and kissing our fingers in the road, some of the Anglo-Indian travellers passed and gazed with fierce disgust; the handsome Hassan, being black, was such a flagrant case of a 'native'. It is heart-breaking to see what [types of men] we are sending to India now. They try their hands here on the Arabs in order to be in good training for insulting Hindus. The English tradesmen here complain as much as anyone, and I, who as the Cadi of Luxor said am 'not outside the family' (of Ishmael, I presume), hear what the Arabs really think. There are also crowds 'like lice' as one Mohammed said, of low Italians, French, etc., and I find my stalwart Hassan's broad shoulders no superfluous *porte-respect* in the Frangee quarter. Three times I have been followed and insolently stared at (*à mon age*) *! !* and once Hassan had to speak. Fancy how dreadful to Muslims! I hate the sight of a hat here now.

The dearness of all things is fearful here now, all is treble at least what it was in 1862-63, but wages have risen in proportion. A sailor who got 60 piastres a month now gets 300. Cairo is dearer than London, and Alexandria dearer still, I fancy, in rent at all events.

I can't write more now though I have much more to tell, but my eyes are very weak still.

*   *   *

On the Nile, Friday, December 23 1864. Dearest Mother. While Alick was with me I had as much to do as I was able and could not write for there was much to see and talk about. I think he was amused but I fear he felt the Eastern life to be very poor and comfortless. I have got so used to having nothing that I had quite forgotten how it would seem to a stranger.

I am quite sorry to find how many of my letters must have been lost from Luxor; in future I shall trust the Arab post which certainly is safer than English travellers. I send you my long plaits by Alick, for I had my hair cut short as it took to falling out by handfuls after my fever, and moreover it is more convenient Turkish hareem fashion.

Alick will tell you how curiously Omar illustrated the patriarchal feelings of the East by entirely dethroning me in favour of the 'Master'.

'That *our Master*, we all eat bread from his hand, and he work for *us*.'
Omar and I were equal before *our Seedee*. He can sit at his ease at my
feet, but when the Master comes in he must stand reverently, and
gave me to understand that I too must be respectful.

I have got the boat of the American Mission at an outrageous
price, £60, but I could get nothing under; the consolation is that the
sailors profit, poor fellows, and get treble wages. My crew are all
Nubians. Such a handsome reis and steersman—brothers—and there
is a black boy, of fourteen or so, with legs and feet so sweetly beautiful
as to be quite touching—at least I always feel those lovely round
young innocent forms to be somehow affecting. Our old boat of last
summer (Arthur Taylor's) is sailing in company with us, and stately
old reis Mubharak hails me every morning with the Blessing of God
and the Peace of the Prophet. Ali Kuptan, my steamboat captain
will announce our advent at Thebes; he passed us today. This boat
is a fine sailor, but iron built and therefore noisy, and not convenient.
The crew encourage her with 'Get along, father of three', because she
has three sails, whereas two is the usual number. They are active
good-humoured fellows—my men—but lack the Arab courtsey and
simpatico ways, and then I don't understand their language which is
pretty and sounds a little like Caffre, rather bird-like and sing-song,
instead of the clattering guttural Arabic.

I now speak pretty tolerably for a stranger, *i.e.* I can keep up a
conversation, and understand all that is said to me much better than
I can speak, and follow about half what people say to each other.
When I see you, *Inshallah,* next summer I shall be a good scholar, I
hope.

XXIV

Omar and Sally have a baby

Luxor from January to April 1865. I believe the letter in which I told you all the grievous history of Sally's misdemeanour has been lost. I can't write it all again, suffice to say that she behaved as badly and Omar as well as it is possible to conceive. I would not turn her out for old times' sake, but I will not keep her a day after I reach Cairo. I believe the end will be that she will go home to England and Omar will keep the child. He will pay her voyage back.

I must say, I think few Englishmen would have behaved as well as he has done in all save not being *quite* a Joseph—and he has been too much of that not to displease Sally most vehemently. I was amazed at the amount of grossness which these respectable English women can carry 'in their stomachs' as the Arabs say. Do not say anything of this for I don't want to injure her and she may keep herself straight at home.

I think I will not take another English maid, but bring only Omar to Europe and get a Syrian or a black woman when I return. I find that these disasters are wonderfully common here—is it the climate or the costume I wonder that makes the English maids ravish the Arab men so continually?

Fancy her concealing her state even from Omar and lying in four days after we sailed from Cairo. She said she knew he would not have let her come to lie in in the boat—of course not! *He* had some conscience about the misery of it to me. The poor boy has been really ill from remorse and shame.

The best plan is Omar's own arrangement. I cannot send her away now because she cannot speak Arabic and would be helpless at Cairo, but as soon as we get there he will put the baby out to nurse under

Hajji Hannah's care and will himself pay Sally's expenses to England. Meanwhile he has got the watchman and the boy Ahmad sleeping with him in the big hall outside my door, while she is *réleguée* to the other end of the house with her child, *sous prétexte* that its noise would disturb me, which is true, and he keeps Ahmad always with him.

I hope she will keep straight in England but I am sure she would not here. I must say that Omar has shown most gentlemanly feelings. He took the whole blame and tried all he could to screen her and married her before Shaikh Yussuf to legitimatize the child and, as far as possible, 'whiten her face'. But he afterwards told her he would never touch her again under my roof. In her anger at this she let out how entirely the whole thing was her own doing, and how he had resisted all along and, indeed, had declined any further intrigue after the first very few weeks because she refused to marry him and inform me.

As he said to me: 'I could not tell you *her* secret. She had been with you ten years and would not trust you, and she is a woman, you know I could not speak, but my stomach has burnt ever since.' She concealed her state from him as effectually as from us and from Dr Patterson who saw her before we sailed only a week before she lay in. She had no clothes or anything for the child. I never saw such a curious thing as her perfect coolness and Omar's utter despair. He wanted me to have him beaten and could not bear my saying a kind word without fresh tears. I never saw *real* repentance before. People usually are very sorry as long as the consequences of their sins pursue them and cheer up amazingly on being forgiven. But Omar has never left off and has worked really hard so as not to let me be put to inconvenience. You would think that he was the seduced girl and she a regular old roué by the way she took it. She is quite offended because her family don't approve of her, and really has not shown the least shame. I could not have believed it possible unless I had seen it.

I wish she were out of the house but the child is too young to give to Arab women yet unless Omar is there to make all arrangements about nursing it, and he, of course, is anxious to do the best for his child.

When Shaikh Yussuf was sent for and told the business and Omar asked him to marry them and keep the secret so that he might call her his hareem before the people here, I was struck indeed by the Shaikh's behaviour. He thanked me and even kissed my hand for my charity to the poor sinners and said I did quite right and then turned to Omar and said: 'My brother, thou hast blackened the faces of Muslims by thy conduct to women whom thou wast bound to defend and if this lady had thee heavily punished, she would not do amiss, though it is far more excellent to forgive. But remember this—that she has now covered thy fault and returned to thee good for evil, and that thou must never forget it nor cease to serve her with the utmost fidelity and to give thy blood for her if she need it, for God will indeed pardon the sins of the weak heart but the ungrateful and treacherous are hateful in his sight.'

When Sally was fetched Yussuf courteously handed her a chair— a thing an Arab does not do for a woman—and took the child in his arms. As he looked down at it I thought his face was just like what that of Christ must have been on similar occasions. Of course the marriage is nothing at all as far as Sally is concerned and I told her so, and told her that I should expect her 'to keep herself to herself' if I allowed her to remain here till we go down. The only use of it was to make it decent for her to remain and to account for the child to the Luxor people. But Omar does not look on it as a marriage either because it is not lawful for her. Hajji Ali was furious and told Omar never to enter his house or to mention his English wife to him.

I hope you will give Sally a character and enable her to make a fresh start, if she does go to England; but she has behaved so queerly that I should not be amazed if she were to perform some other strange antic. It seems quite incredible. It is no use lecturing a woman of thirty who evidently has no shame at all in her and I shall be glad to have done with her, and I hope the lesson will cure her. I must say I thought she might have spared me the task of being midwife and monthly nurse in a boat and frightened sick by it all. Of course it happened at midnight in a desolate place. However she was delivered without a twinge and did admirably and is very well and strong— all but her eyes which are bad now, so I am entirely 'done for' by Omar. Sally does not seem to perceive that I could have anything to complain of or find fault with. Enough.

I only hope I shall have done well in your eyes, and that you will agree with me that there is no cause for dismissing Omar. *He* at all events has had a lesson in sorrow and in money that he won't forget. You know Arab phraseology. He said when I told him it would be difficult to trust him with another maid, 'By God, if an English girl comes to me and pulls up her shirt before me again, with the permission of God, I will slap her face, though I am only an Arab and she English.'

Omar is very miserable about what you will think of him, and very anxious lest he should have to leave me. I told him it must all remain uncertain till I get to Cairo and see how he has behaved in the meanwhile and until I hear from you.

Dearest Janet. I hope Henry may have got my letter which was about this wretched business of Sally. Of course her marriage is simply *no marriage* at all according to our law and so I told her, but she persists and Omar, of course, is simply her slave. Anyhow she must leave me the day I reach Cairo—that I have distinctly told them both. As to Omar he is completely the victim in the business and I shall not dismiss him unless I see further cause.

I must tell you how well Hajji Ali behaved to me. He came here furious with Omar and would not see Sally at all. But to me he said that he felt his brother had injured me and that he would do all he could to atone it, and offered to come to me in Omar's place for £3 a month to cook and do everything as soon as the Prince and Princess of Augustenbourg were gone. He said: 'I would rather come for nothing but that would be to talk nonsense to a lady like you', but he offered to go with me to Europe or to Syria as sole servant.

Do not, if you please, say anything about Sally from *me* to Ellen, as I assured Sally I would leave her to tell her story her own way, and I have a regard of too long a standing for her not to wish to do all I can in her behalf, short of travelling about with her and her babies, present and future, in my train. It has been extremely painful to me the whole business, and if she could get anything to do in Cairo I should be quite relieved to ship her off from here at once. But in common humanity I cannot send her off alone and without money to seek employment.

She is in high health and certainly works extremely hard; her service is as good as ever and, indeed, better, in spite of the child. You are mistaken in thinking she has become like Ellen a Rayah. Ellen's is a lawful marriage by the English law, but the English law pronounces a marriage with a married man *impossible,* therefore Sally is simply an English subject living in open adultery, and her marriage is null and void from the beginning.

She can leave him and marry another man tomorrow. *He* is lawfully married according to the Sunni law, but *she* is not married at all. Omar knows this and is in great remorse. You can tell her family that much—I mean as to her legal position—if you please. Her child is before our law illegitimate and an English subject.

Dearest Alick. Sally begins to find that her marriage is not as pleasant as she expected, and says she intends to leave Omar altogether and do for herself here or in England. It will be much better and I think more respectable, as I have told her all along. Such a marriage is none at all, either in law or feeling with Europeans, and could only do on condition of living entirely among Arabs who have no contact with us.

Dearest Mother. Alick seems to think I am hard on Sally but I never was given to be a dragon of virtue and I have been perfectly kind to her, but I cannot keep her about me *es ware mir zunider* [it would be repugnant to me]. She is not half as ill off as most women in such a case. Omar bears all the trouble and expense and she will go back to England and may keep her own secret. She loses nothing but her place with me. She has desired Omar to divorce her when we go down, which I am glad of for his sake.

I did not like to oppose his marrying absolutely because the poor lad was so bent on doing every possible thing he could to make up for his fault, and that is a feeling I had not the heart to throw cold water on. But he has steadily refused to live with her or to divorce his other wife—a point on which I, too, was peremptory.

One of the dragomans here told an English lady of the marriage and added that Omar would divorce his first wife, and as soon as I heard it I sent for him and for two other respectable Alexandria dragomans and told Omar before them and before Sally that I would discharge him and disgrace her if such a cruel injustice were perpetrated on an innocent woman—that our English law recognized only the Sit Kebireh in Alexandria as Omar's lawful wife, and that if an Englishwoman chose to disregard her own laws, *she* must take the consequences herself. I desired them to tell Omar's brother what I said (that he might tell Mabrooka).

All the men kissed my hand and said I was the father and the mother of poor people, and that Mahmoud had eaten dirt in believing I could ever be pleased at an unjust act. But would you believe (only don't tell this lest the woman should recognize herself) that the pious English woman told me that the ways of Providence were inscrutable and that my maid's error (what would she call it under other circumstances?) might be the means of bringing my Mahommedan servant to divorce his *heathen* wife and found a Christian family.

(Faugh! Such bigotry stinks.) I fear I was rude, for I asked if Christian households were well established by trampling a few commandments under foot for a foundation—especially that great one about not doing to others what we would not have them do to us.

I was quite touched by the kind way Mabrooka spoke about Sally and how glad she would have been to serve her, if she would have consented to live with her. But nothing will satisfy English people short of the complete abolition of those who stand in the way of their selfish prejudices. Even education seems useless, as you see by Ross's and Janet's unrelenting virtuous indignation because a nice looking Arab lad dare to give way to the advances made him by a middle-aged British female.

Dearest Janet. If the new hotel will be finished next winter and if Henry would put Sally in that as housekeeper it would be an excellent thing for her. Otherwise she has made up her mind to go home to England. Omar takes the child, Abdallah, and pays her voyage back, and I myself think that much the best thing for both.

Her eyes are now bad and an English doctor here now says she must wean the child. I will see him again and ask if she can go on suckling it for two months more when she is to give it over to Omar and he will pay a woman to suckle it. If not, I suppose she must leave it here if a woman can be found to take it. In that way, if her family keep a quiet tongue, no one in England need ever know of her escapade here.

She has quite determined that she won't live in Omar's house Arab fashion and prefers to go to England and I think she is quite right and that it will be best in every way.

The child is, in my opinion, hideous, but I daresay the Arabs think it lovely as it has light hair and blue eyes and an extremely white skin—not a bit like Omar.

[Janet offered to take Sally into her household.] Many thanks for the arrangement, nothing could be better. Sally, of course, accepts your kind offer with much gratitude. I hope she will do well by you in all ways. She will put her child out to nurse in Cairo, or, rather, Omar will as soon as she arrives and will therefore need a week to prepare herself before going into your house. If the child continues to roar as much as now, I shall send her by the Kasneh steamer in three week's or a month's time, for I do hate a baby howling in a boat, there is no escape from it. If she goes with me in the *dahabieh*, of course, you can guess as well as I when she will reach Cairo.

Do you and Henry think it would be good for Maurice to spend next winter with me and to have an Effendi to teach him Turkish? If he is to be a diplomat it would be a good card, or is it a crotchet of mine merely. Folks living as I do grow crotchetty you know. I am not very well and my nerves were so shaken by Sally's lying in at midnight in the boat and my terror at having to do the mid-wife's business, which I don't understand, that I have never recovered my sleep and of course that aggravates my cough.

XXV

The welcome back to Luxor

In this chapter we return to January and the arrival at Luxor.

Considering Lucie's character and her affection for Sally she is, indeed, surprisingly vehement in defence of Omar; but the dying Lucie, who had been dependent upon the care and affection of Omar and Sally, suddenly had her domestic peace shattered, and she was afraid that Alexander might insist on Omar leaving her. There must certainly have been feelings of iealousy, nor, as George Meredith suggested, could she forgive anyone who deceived her. (Introduction p. 29.)

Lucie was right to defend Mabrooka's position and it did not seem likely that Sally would fit into an Arab household. She acted with justice but without her usual sympathy and understanding.

January 2 1865. Dearest Mother. My crew worked as I never saw men work, they were paid to get to Luxor, and for eighteen days they never rested or slept day or night, and all the time were merry and pleasant. It shows what power of endurance these 'lazy Arabs' have when there is good money at the end of a job, instead of the favourite panacea of 'stick'.

We arrived at midnight and next morning my boat had the air of being pillaged. A crowd of laughing, chattering fellows ran off to the house laden with loose articles snatched up at random, loaves of sugar, pots and pans, books, cushions, all helter-skelter. I feared breakages, but all was housed safe and sound. The small boys of an age licensed to penetrate into the cabin, went off with the oddest cargoes of dressing things and the like—of backsheesh not one word. *Alhamdulillah salaameh !* 'Thank God thou art in peace', and *Ya Sitt,*

194

Ya Emeereh, till my head went round. Old Ismain fairly hugged me and little Ahmad hung close to my side. I went up to Mustapha's house while the unpacking took place and breakfasted there, and found letters from all of you, from you to darling Rainie, Shaikh Yussuf was charmed with her big writing, and said he thought the news in that was the best of all.

The weather was intensely hot the first two days. Now it is heavenly, a fresh breeze and gorgeous sunshine. I brought two common Arab lanterns for the tomb of Abu-l-Hajjaj and his *moolid* is now going on. Omar took them and lighted them up and told me he found several people who called on the rest to say the *Fathah* for me.

I was sitting out yesterday with the people on the sand looking at the men doing *fantasia* on horseback for the Shaikh, and a clever dragoman of the party was relating about the death of a young English girl whom he had served, and so *de fil en aiguille* we talked about the strangers buried here and how the bishop had extorted £100. I said, '*Maleysh* (never mind) the people have been hospitable to me alive and they will not cease if I die, but give me a tomb among the Arabs'. One old man said, 'May I not see thy day, oh Lady, and indeed thou shouldest be buried as a daughter of the Arabs, but we should fear the anger of thy Consul and thy family, but thou knowest that wherever thou art buried thou wilt assuredly lie in a Muslim grave'.

'How so?' said I. 'Why, when a bad Muslim dies the angels take him out of his tomb and put in one of the good from among the Christians in his place'. This is the popular expression of the doctrine that the good are sure of salvation.

There are hardly any travellers this year, instead of a hundred and fifty or more boats, perhaps twenty. A son of one of the Rothschilds, a boy of fourteen, has just gone up like a royal prince in one of the Pasha's steamers—all his expenses paid and crowds of attendants. 'All that honour to the money of the Jew', said an old fellah to me with a tone of scorn which I could not but echo in my heart. He has turned out his dragoman—a respectable elderly man, very sick, and paid him his bare wages and the munificent sum of £5 to take him back to Cairo. On board there was a doctor and plenty of servants, and yet he abandons the man here on Mustapha's hands. I have brought Er-Rasheedee here (the sick man) as poor Mustapha is already overloaded with strangers. I am sorry the name of *Yahoodee* (Jew) should be made to stink yet more in the nostrils of the Arabs.

I am very well, indeed my cough is almost gone and I can walk quite briskly and enjoy it. I think, dear Mother, I am really better. I never felt the cold so little as this winter since my illness, the chilly mornings and nights don't seem to signify at all now, and the climate feels more delicious than ever.

Mr Herbert, the painter, went back to Cairo from Farshoot below Keneh; so I have no 'Frangee' society at all. But Shaikh Yussuf and Shaikh Ibrahim, the Cadi, drop into tea very often and as they are very agreeable men I am quite content with my company. So far as manners go, no company can possibly be better. Indeed, I must confess that since I have become accustomed to the respectful ways of well-bred Arabs to hareem, I feel quite astonished at the manners of Englishmen. And yet all the people here call me 'sister' and the poorest sit and talk quite freely and easily without any embarrassment or constraint.

I will tell you about the tenure of land in Egypt which people are always disputing about, as the Cadi laid it down for me. The *whole* land belongs to the Sultan of Turkey, the Pasha being his vakeel (representative), nominally of course as we know. Thus there are no owners, only tenants paying from one hundred piastres *tarif* (£1)[1] down to thirty piastres yearly per feddan (about an acre) according to the quality of the land, or the favour of the Pasha when granting it. This tenancy is hereditary to children only—not to collaterals or ascendants—and it may be sold, but in that case application must be made to the Government. If the owner or tenant dies childless the land reverts to the Sultan, *i.e.* to the Pasha [the Viceroy] and *if the Pasha chooses to have any man's land he can take it from him on payment—or without.* Don't let any one tell you that I exaggerate; I have known it happen: I mean the *without*, and the man received feddan for feddan of desert, in return for his good land which he had tilled and watered.

Tomorrow night is the great night of Shaikh Abu-l-Hajjaj's *moolid* and I am desired to go to the mosque for the benefit of my health, and that my friends may say a prayer for my children. The kind hearty welcome I found here has been a real pleasure, and every one was pleased because I was glad to come home to my *beled* (town), and they all thought it so nice of 'my master' to have come so far to

---

[1] An extra tax was imposed by establishing that money paid to the government should be in *tarif*, that is an artificially increased rate; so that whereas 1,000 piastres in current rate was worth about £6 5s. od., in *tarif* rate it was equivalent to a payment of £10.

see me because I was sick—all but one Turk, who clearly looked with
pitying contempt on so much trouble taken about a sick old woman.
[Lucie was then forty-three years old].

The festival of Abu-l-Hajjaj was quite a fine sight, not splendid
at all—*au contraire*—but spirit-stirring: the flags of the Shaikh borne
by his family chanting, and the men with their spears tearing about
on horseback in mimic fight.

My acquaintance of last year, Abd-el-Moutowil, the fanatical
Shaikh from Tunis was there. At first he scowled at me. Then someone
told him how Rothschild had left Er-Rasheedee, and he held forth
about the hatred of all the unbelievers to the Muslims, and ended by
asking where the sick man was. Shaikh Yussuf said demurely, 'Your
Honour must go and visit him at the house of the English Lady'. I
am bound to say that the Pharisee 'executed himself' handsomely,
for in a few minutes he came up to me and took my hand and even
hoped I would visit the tomb of Abu-l-Hajjaj with him!!

I received your letter here.[1] I did, indeed, feel with you; I have
never left off the habit of thinking how I shall tell my father this
and that, and how such things would interest him, and what he would
say. The thought comes and with it the sadness, more often than I
can tell.

I have left my letter for a long while. You will not wonder—for
after some ten days' fever, my poor guest Mohammed Er-Rasheedee
died today. Two Prussian doctors gave me help for the last four days,
but left last night. He sank to sleep quietly at noon with his hand in
mine, a good old Muslim sat at his head on one side and I on the
other. Omar stood at his head and his black boy Khayr at his feet.
We had laid his face to the Kibleh and I spoke to him to see if he knew
anything and when he nodded the three Muslims chanted the *Islamee
La Illáhá,* etc., etc., while I closed his eyes. The 'respectable men'
came in by degrees, took an inventory of his property which they
delivered to me, and washed the body, and within an hour and a half
we all went out to the burial place; I following among a troop of
women who joined us to wail for 'the brother who had died far from
his place'.

The scene as we turned in between the broken colossi and the
pylons of the temple to go to the mosque was over-powering. After
the prayer in the mosque we went out to the graveyard, Muslims and

[1] At Luxor Sarah Austin had written about her husband at the time of the anniversary
of his death on December 17 1859.

Copts helping to carry the dead, and my Frankish hat in the midst of the veiled and wailing women; all so familiar and yet so strange.

After the burial the Imám, Shaikh Abd-el-Waris, came and kissed me on the shoulders and the Shereef, a man of eighty, laid his hands on my shoulders and said, 'Fear not my daughter, neither all the days of thy life nor at the hour of thy death, for God is with thee'. I kissed the old man's hand and turned to go, but numberless men came and said, 'A thousand thanks, O our sister, for what thou hast done for one among us', and a great deal more.

Now the solemn chanting of the *Fikees*, and the clear voice of the boy reciting the Koran in the room where the man died are ringing through the house. They will pass the night in prayer, and tomorrow there will be the prayer of deliverance in the mosque. Poor Khayr has just crept in to have a quiet cry—poor boy. He is in the inventory and tomorrow I must deliver him up to *les autorités* to be forwarded to Cairo with the rest of the property. He is very ugly with his black face wet and swollen, but he kisses my hand and calls me his mother quite 'natural like'—you see colour is no barrier here.

The weather is glorious this year, and in spite of some fatigue I am extremely well and strong, and have hardly any cough at all. I am so sorry that the young Rothschild was so hard to Er-Rasheedee and that his French doctor refused to come and see the dying man. It makes bad blood naturally. However, the German doctors were most kind and helpful.

A young Englishman died at the house of the Austrian Consular agent. I was too ill to go to him, but a kind, dear young English-woman, a Mrs Walker, who was here with her family in a boat, sat up with him three nights and nursed him like a sister. A young American lay sick at the same time in the house, he is now gone down to Cairo, but I doubt whether he will reach it alive. The Englishman was buried on the first day of Ramadan where they bury strangers, on the site of a former Coptic church. Archdeacon Moore read the service; Omar and I spread my old flag over the bier, and Copts and Muslims helped to carry the poor stranger. It was a most impressive sight. The party of Europeans, all strangers to the dead but all deeply moved; the group of black-robed and turbaned Copts; the sailors from the boats; the gaily dressed dragomans; several brown-shirted fellaheen and the thick crowd of children—all the little Abab'deh stark naked and all behaving so well, the expression on their little faces touched me most of all. As Muslims, Omar and the boatmen laid him down in the grave, and while the English prayer was read the sun went down in a glorious flood of light over the distant bend of the Nile. 'Had he a mother, he was young?' said an Abab'deh woman to me with tears in her eyes and pressing my hand in sympathy for that far-off mother of such a different race.

Passenger steamboats come now every fortnight, but I have had no letter for a month. I have no almanack and have lost count of European time—today is the 3 of Ramadan, that is all I know. The poor black slave [Khayr] was sent back from Keneh, God knows why—because he had no money and the Mudir could not 'eat off him' as he could off the money and property—he believes. He is a capital fellow, and in order to compensate me for what he eats he proposed to wash for me, and you would be amused to see Khayr with his coal-black face and filed teeth doing laundrymaid out in the yard. He fears Er-Rasheedees' family will sell him and hopes he may fetch a good price—only on the other hand he would so like me to buy him—and so his mind is disturbed. Meanwhile the having all my clothes washed clean is a great luxury.

The steamer is come and I must finish in haste. I have corrected the proofs. There is not much to alter, and though I regret several lost letters I can't replace them. I tried, but it felt like a forgery. Do you cut out and correct, dearest Mother, you will do it much better than I.

I am very glad the people like the Cape Letters,[1] which I forget, but honestly I don't think the Egyptian good—not what I saw and felt and comprehended. You know I don't pretend if I think I have done something well and I was generally content with my trans-lations, but I feel it all to be poor and what Maurice calls dry, when I know how curious and interesting and poetical the country really is.

January 9. Dearest Mother. Ross's agent arrived yesterday and came to me for information as he had discovered that mine of last summer was quite correct. He is a Frenchman and seems intelligent and, like almost everyone that comes here and sees with his eyes, boiling with indignation at the state of things. In money calculations remember that one purse *tarif* is £5 and one purse current £3. The piastre current is three halfpence—more or less—a shilling passes in Cairo for eight piastres. When one mentions a sum it means current,

---

[1] *Letters from the Cape* by Lady Duff Gordon, were first published in 1864 in 'Vacation Tourists', 3rd series.

when one talks of *tarif* one adds *tarif.* All payments to and from the Government are made in tarif money, all others in current.

I told Alexander that Mustapha had advanced the money for the fellaheen at Gooneh who were literally starving six months ago and it is now ten months. Mustapha must lose as money fetches four per cent *per month* here. Ross's agents take that; the Greeks take seven per cent.

I gave Shaikh Yussuf your knife to cut his *kaleem* (reed pen) with, and to his little girl the coral waistband clasp you gave me *as from you.* He was much pleased. I also brought the Shereef the psalms in Arabic to his great delight. The old man called on all 'our family' to say a *fathah* for their sister, after making us all laugh by shouting out '*Alhamdulillah !* here is our darling safe back again'.

I find an exceedingly pleasant man here, an Abab'deh, a very great Shaikh from beyond Khartum, a man of fifty I suppose, with manners like an English nobleman, simple and polite and very intelligent. He wants to take me to Khartum for two months up and back, having a tent and a *takhterawan* (camel-litter) and to show me the Bishareen in the desert. We traced the route on my map which to my surprise he understood, and I found he had travelled into Zanzibar and knew of the existence of the Cape of Good Hope and the English colony there. He had also travelled in the Dinka and Shilluk country where the men are seven feet and over high (Alexander saw a Dinka girl at Cairo three inches taller than himself!).

XXVI

'The whole place is in desolation'

Luxor, January 9 1865. Dearest Mother. Today the sand in front of the house is thronged with all the poor people with their camels, of which the Government has made a new levy of eight camels to every thousand feddans. The poor beasts are sent off to transport troops in the Sudan, and not being used to the desert, they all die—at all events their owners never see one of them again. The discontent is growing stronger every day. Last week the people were cursing the Pasha in the streets of Aswan, and every one talks aloud of what they think.

January 11. The whole place is in desolation, the men are being beaten, one because his camel is not good enough, another because its saddle is old and shabby, and the rest because they have not money enough to pay two months' food and the wages of one man, to every four camels, to be paid for the use of the Government beforehand. The *courbash* has been going on my neighbours' backs and feet all the morning. It is a new sensation, too, when a friend turns up his sleeve and shows the marks of the wooden handcuffs and the gall of the chain on his throat.

The system of wholesale extortion and spoliation has reached a point beyond which it would be difficult to go. The story of Naboth's vineyard is repeated daily on the largest scale. I grieve for Abdallah-el-Habbashee and men of high position like him, sent to die by disease (or murder), in Fazogli, but I grieve still more over the daily anguish of the poor fellaheen, who are forced to take the bread from the mouths of their starving families and to eat it while toiling for the private profit of one man.

Egypt is one vast 'plantation' where the master works his slaves without even feeding them. From my window now I see men limping about among the poor camels that are waiting for the Pasha's boats to take them, and the great heaps of maize which they are forced to bring for their food. I can tell you the tears such a sight brings to one's eyes are hot and bitter. These are no sentimental grievances; hunger, and pain, and labour without hope and without reward, and the constant bitterness of impotent resentment.

To you all this must sound remote and almost fabulous. But try to imagine Farmer Smith's team driven off by the police and himself beaten till he delivered his hay, his oats and his farm-servant for the use of the Lord Lieutenant, and his two sons dragged in chains to work at railway embankments—and you will have some idea of my state of mind today.

I fancy from the number of troops going up to Aswan that there is another rising among the blacks. Some of the black regiments revolted up in the Sudan last summer, and now I hear Shaheen Pasha is to be here in a day or two on his way up, and the camels are being sent off by hundreds from all the villages every day.

Sunday. Every day new '*Plackerein*' ['vexations']. We are informed that the Viceroy is going to honour us with a visit—'to see the antiquities'—and the Shaikhs el Beled are called upon to furnish firewood, butter, eggs and poultry for his kitchen; if you knew the price of all these things and the quantity that will be eaten and wasted! But I am weary of telling you and you will sicken of hearing my constant lamentations.

Shaikh Hassan dropped in and dined with me yesterday and described his mother and her high-handed rule over him. It seems he had a 'jeunesse orageuse' and she defended him against his father's displeasure, but when the old Shaikh died she informed her son that if he ever again behaved in a manner unworthy of a Shaikh-el-Arab she would not live to see it. 'Now if my mother told me to jump into the river and drown I should say *hader* (ready), for I fear her exceedingly and love her above all people in the world, and have left everything in her hand'. He was good enough to tell me that I was the only woman he knew like his mother and that was why he loved me so much. I am to visit this Arab Deborah at the Abab'deh village two days' ride from the first Cataract. She will come and meet me at the boat. Hassan was splendid when he said how he *feared* his mother exceedingly.

To my amazement today in walked the tremendous Alim from Tunis, Shaikh Abd-el-Moutowil, who used to look so black at me.

He was very civil and pleasant and asked no end of questions about steam engines, and telegraphs and chemistry; especially whether it was true that the Europeans still fancied they could make gold. I said that no one had believed that for nearly two hundred years, and he said that the Arabs also knew it was 'a lie', and he wondered to hear that Europeans, who were so clever, believed it. He had just been across the Nile to see the tombs of the Kings and of course 'improved the occasion' and uttered a number of the usual fine sayings about the vanity of human things. He told me I was the only Frank he had ever spoken to. I observed he did not say a word about religion, or use the usual pious phrases. By the bye, Shaikh Yussuf filled up my inkstand for me the other evening and in pouring the ink said, 'In the name of God, the merciful, the compassionate'. I said, 'I like that custom, it is good to remind us that ink may be a cruel poison or a good medicine'.

I am better, and have hardly any cough. The people here think it is owing to the intercession of Abu-l-Hajjaj who specially protects me. I was obliged to be wrapped in the green silk cover of his tomb when it was taken off to be carried in procession, partly for my health and general welfare, and as a sort of adoption into the family. I made a feeble resistance on the score of being a Nazraneeyeh, but was told, 'Never fear, does not God know thee and the Shaikh also? no evil will come to thee on that account but good'. And I rather think that general goodwill and kindness is wholesome.

February 7. Dearest Alick. I am tolerably well, but I am growing very homesick or rather children-sick. As the time slips on I get more and more the feeling of all I am losing of my children. We have delicious weather here and have had all the time; there has been no cold at all this winter here.

M. Prévost Paradol[1] is here for a few days—a very pleasant man indeed, and a little good European talk is a very agreeable interlude to the Arab prosiness, or rather *enfantillage*, on the part of the women. He is intoxicated with Egypt, yet Egypt is not itself this year. All the land here, which last year glowed in emerald verdure, is now a dreary expanse of dry mud, brown and desolate! The Nile is lower already than it was at lowest Nile last July; it all ran away directly this year, so that in many places there will be no crops whatever.

---

[1] Prevost Paradol, 1829–70, French philosopher and journalist, became Editor-in-Chief of the *Journal des Débats* and came under attack for his liberal views by the republican party. He was sent to the United States as envoy to France; a little time later the Franco-Prussian war broke out and he shot himself in Washington dying on July 20 1870.

I have sought about for shells and a few have been brought me from the Cataract, but of snails I can learn no tidings nor have I ever seen one, neither can I discover that there are any shells in the Nile mud. At the first Cataract they are found sticking to the rocks. The people here are very stupid about natural objects that are of no use to them. As with the French small birds are all sparrows, and wild flowers there are none, and only about five varieties of trees in all Egypt.

This is a sad year—all the cattle are dead, the Nile is now as low as it was last July, and the song of the men watering with the *shadoofs* sounds sadly true, as they chant *Ana ga-ahn*, etc. 'I am hungry, I am hungry for a piece of dourrah bread', sings one, and the other chimes in, *Meskeen, meskeen*, 'Poor man, poor man'; or else they sing a song about 'Our master Job' and his patience. It is sadly appropriate now and rings on all sides as the *shadoofs* are greatly multiplied for lack of oxen to turn the *sakiahs* (waterwheels).

All is terribly dear, and many are sick from sheer weakness owing to poor food; and then I hear fifty thousand are to be taken to work at the canal from Giza to Assiut through the Fayoum. The only comfort is the enormous rise of wages, which however falls heavy on the rich. The sailors who got forty to fifty piastres five years ago now get three to five hundred piastres a month. So I fear I must give up my project of a *dahabieh*.

I am sorry Maurice is idle, but one can't have everything, and I do not insist on my son being a genius—a good, amiable man will satisfy me very well. If you thought it good I hope you will send him to Dresden.

I paid Fadil Pasha a visit on his boat, and it was just like the middle ages. In order to amuse me he called up a horrid little black boy of about four to do tricks like a dancing dog, which ended in a performance of the Mussulman prayer. The little beast was dressed in a Stamboulee dress of scarlet cloth.

All the Arab doctors come to see me now as they go up and down the river to give me help if I want it. Some are very pleasant men. Murad Effendi speaks German exactly like a German. The old Shaikh-el-Beled of Erment who visits me whenever he comes here, and has the sweetest voice I ever heard, complained of the climate of Cairo. 'There is no sun there at all, it is no brighter or warmer than the moon'. What do you think our sun must be now you know Cairo? We have had a glorious winter, like the finest summer weather at home only so much finer.

Janet wishes to go with me if I go to Soden; I must make enquiries about the climate. Ross fears it is too cold for an Egyptian like me. I should enjoy to have all the family *au grand complet*. I will leave Luxor in May and get to you towards the latter part of June, if that pleases you, *Inshallah!*

February 7. Dearest Janet. The black slave of the poor dragoman who died in my house is here still, and like a dog that has lost his master has devoted himself to me. It seems nobody's business to take him away—as the Cadi did the money and the goods—and so it looks as if I should quietly inherit poor ugly Khayr. He is of a degree of ugliness quite transcendent, with teeth filed sharp 'in order to eat people' as he says, but the most good-humoured creature and a very fair laundry-maid. It is evidently not my business to send him to be sold in Cairo, so I wait the event. If nobody ever claims him I shall keep him at whatever wages may seem fit, and he will subside into liberty. *Du reste,* the Maõhn here says he is legally entitled to his freedom.

If the new French Consul-General will let me stay on here I will leave my furniture and come down straight to your hospitable roof in Alexandria *en route* for Europe. I fear my plan of a *dahabieh* of my own would be too expensive.

It is quite a pleasure to see how the poor people instead of trying to sponge on one are anxious to make a return for kindness. I give nothing whatever but my physick. These country people are very good. A nice young Circassian *cawass* sat up with a stranger, a dying Englishman, all night, because I had doctored his wife. I have also a pupil, Mustapha's youngest boy, a sweet intelligent lad who is pining for an education. I wish he could go to England. He speaks English very well and reads and writes indifferently, but I never saw a boy so wild to learn. I wish Maurice had as much desire. I hope Alick will take him away from Eton.

March 1865. Now is Bairam, I rejoice to say, and I have lots of physic to make up for all the stomachs damaged by Ramadan. . . . Numbers of hareem came in their best clothes to wish me a happy year, and enjoyed themselves much with sweet cakes, coffee and pipes. Khursheed's wife (whom I cured completely) looked very handsome. Khursheed is a Circassian, a fine young fellow, much shot and hacked about, and with a Crimean medal. He is *cawass* here and a great friend of mine. He says, if ever I want a servant, he will go with me anywhere, and fight anybody, which I don't doubt in the least. He was a Turkish mameluke, and his condescension in wishing to serve a Christian woman is astonishing. His fair face and clear blue eyes and brisk, neat, soldier-like air, contrast curiously with the brown fellaheen. He is like an Englishman only fairer and, like Englishmen, too fond of the *courbash*. What would you say if I appeared attended by a mameluke with pistols, sword, dagger, carbine and *courbash*, and with a decided and imperious manner— the very reverse of the Arab softness? Such a Muslim too! Prayers five times a day and extra fasts besides Ramadan. 'I beat my wife', said Khursheed, 'she talks so much, and I am like the English, I don't like many words.'

XXVII

Revolt and massacre at Gau

Luxor, March 13 1865. Dearest Mother. I hope your mind has not been disturbed by any rumours of 'battle, murder and sudden death' up in our part of the world. A week ago we heard that a Prussian boat had been attacked, all on board murdered, and the boat burned; then that ten villages were in open revolt, and that Effendina (the Viceroy) himself had come up and 'taken a broom and swept them clean', *i.e.*— exterminated the inhabitants.

The truth now appears to be that a crazy darweesh has made a disturbance—but I will tell it as I heard it. He did as his father like-wise did thirty years ago, made himself *Ism* (name) by repeating one of the appellations of God, like *Ya Latif* three thousand times every night for three years which rendered him invulnerable. He made friends with a Jinn who taught him many more tricks—among others, that practised in England by the Davenports of slipping out of any bonds.

He then deluded the people of the desert by giving himself out as *El-Mahdi* (he who is to come with the Lord Jesus and to slay Anti-christ at the end of the world), and proclaimed a revolt against the Turks. Three villages below Keneh—Gau, Rayanaeh and Bedeh took part in the disturbance, and Fadil Pasha came up with steamboats, burnt the villages, shot about one hundred men and devastated the fields. (At first we heard one thousand were shot, now it is one hun-dred.) The women and children will be distributed among other villages. The darweesh some say is killed, others that he is gone off into the desert with a body of beduin and a few of the fellaheen from the three ravaged villages. Gau is a large place—as large, I think as Luxor. The darweesh is a native of Salamieh, a village close by here, and yesterday his brother, a very quiet man, and his father's father-in-law old Hajjee Sultan were carried off prisoners to Cairo, or Keneh, we don't know which. It seems that the boat robbed belonged to Greek traders, but no one was hurt, I believe, and no European boat has been molested.

Baron Kevenbrinck was here yesterday with his wife, and they saw all the sacking of the villages and said no resistance was offered by the people whom the soldiers shot down as they ran, and they saw the sheep, etc., being driven off by the soldiers.

You need be in no alarm about me. The darweesh and his followers could not pounce on us as we are eight good miles from the desert, *i.e.* the mountain, so we must have timely notice, and we have arranged that if they appear in the neighbourhood the women and children of the outlying huts should come into my house which is a regular fortress, and also any travellers in boats, and we muster little short of seven hundred men able to fight including Karnac, moreover Fadil Pasha and the troops are at Keneh only forty miles off.

I dined with Baron and Baroness Kevenbrinck; she is very lively and pleasant. I nearly died of laughing today when little Ahmad[1] came for his lesson. He pronounced that he was sick of love for her. He played at cards with her yesterday afternoon and it seems lost his heart (he is twelve and quite a boyish boy, though a very clever one) and he said he was wishing to play a game for a kiss as the stake. He had put on a turban today, on the strength of his passion, to look like a man, and had neglected his dress otherwise, as he said, young men do that when sick of love.

The fact is the Baroness was kind and amiable and tried to amuse him as she would have done to a white boy, hence Ahmad's susceptible heart was 'on fire for her'. He also asked me if I had any medicine to make him white, I suppose to look lovely in her eyes. He little knows how very pretty he is with his brown face. As he sat cross-legged on the carpet at my feet in his white turban and blue shirt, reading aloud, he was quite a picture. I have grown very fond of the little fellow, he is so eager to learn and to improve and so remarkably clever.

Ahmad is donkey-boy and general little slave, the smallest, slender-

---

[1] This was twelve-year-old Ahmad, the son of Mustapha Agha the British Consular representative, and is not the same as the Ahmad mentioned below,—'donkey-boy and general little slave'—who was an orphan.

est quietest little creature, and has implored me to take him with me to England. I wish Rainie could see him, she would be so 'arprized' at his dark brown little face, so *fein*, and with eyes like a dormouse. He is a true little Arab—can run all day in the heat, sleeps on the stones and eats anything—quick, gentle and noiseless and fiercely jealous. If I speak to any other boy he rushes at him and drives him away, and while black Khayr was in the house, he suffered martyrdom and the kitchen was a scene of incessant wrangle about the coffee. Khayr would bring me my coffee and Ahmad resented the usurpation of his functions—of course quite hopelessly, as Khayr was a great stout black of eighteen and poor little Ahmad not bigger than Rainie. I am really tempted to adopt the vigilant active little creature.

March 15. Shaikh Yussuf returned from a visit to Salamieh last night. He tells me the darweesh Ahmad et-Tayib is not dead, he believes that he is a mad fanatic and a communist. He wants to divide all property equally and to kill all the Ulema and destroy all theological teaching by learned men and to preach a sort of revelation or interpretation of the Koran of his own. 'He would break up your pretty clock', said Yussuf, 'and give every man a broken wheel out of it, and so with all things.'

One of the dragomans here had been urging me to go down but Yussuf laughed at any idea of danger, he says the people here have fought the Beduin before and will not be attacked by such a handful as are out in the mountain now; *du reste* the Abu-l-Hajjajieh (family of Abu-l-Hajjaj) will 'put their seal' to it that I am their sister and answer for me with a man's life. It would be foolish to go down into whatever disturbance there may be alone in a small country boat and where I am not known. The Pasha himself we hear is at Girgeh with steamboats and soldiers, and if the slightest fear should arise steamers will be sent up to fetch all the Europeans.

What I grieve over is the poor villagers whose little property is all confiscated, guilty and innocent alike, and many shot as they ran away. Hajjee Ali tells me privately that he believes the discontent against the Government is very deep and universal and that there will be an outbreak—but not yet. The Pasha's attempt to regulate the price of food by edicts has been very disastrous, and of course the present famine prices are laid to his charge—if a man will be omnipotent he must take the consequences when he fails.

I don't believe in an outbreak—I think the people are too thoroughly accustomed to suffer and to obey, besides they have no means of communication, and the steamboats can run up and down and destroy them *en détail* in a country which is eight hundred miles long by from one to eight wide, and thinly peopled. Only Cairo could do anything, and everything is done to please the Cairenes at the expense of the fellaheen.

The great heat has begun these last three days. My cough is better and I am grown fatter again. The Nile is so low that I fancy that six weeks or two months hence I shall have to go down in two little boats—even now the *dahabiehs* keep sticking fast continually. I have promised some neighbours to bring back a little seed corn for them, some of the best English wheat without beard. All the wheat here is bearded and they have an ambition for some of ours. I long to bring them wheelbarrows and spades and pickaxes. The great folks get steamploughs, but the labourers work with their bare hands and a rush basket *pour tout potage,* and it takes six to do the work of one who has got good tools.[1]

March 30. Dearest Alick. I dined three days running with the Kevenbrincks and one day after dinner we sent for a lot of Arab Shaikhs to come for coffee—the two Abab'deh and a relation of theirs from Khartum, the Shaikh of Karnac, one Mohammed a rich fellah, and we were joined by the A'gha of Halim Pasha's hareem, and an ugly beast he is. The little Baroness won all hearts. She is a regular *vif argent* or as we say *Efreeteh* and to see the dark faces glittering with merry smiles as they watched her was very droll. I never saw a human being so thoroughly amused as the black Shaikh from the Sudan.

Next day we dined at the Austrian agent's and the Baroness at last made the Maōhn dance a polka with her while the agent played the guitar. There were a lot of Copts about who nearly died of laughing and indeed so did I. Next day we had a capital dinner at Mustapha's, and the two Abab'deh Shaikhs, the Shaikh of Karnac, the Maōhn and Shaikh Yussuf dined with us. The Shaikh of Karnac gave a grand

---

[1] Lucie did not think that the fellaheen were so conservative that they would not use such tools. Janet Ross on her visit to the Canal with de Lesseps wrote in her letter to Lucie (March 1 1862): 'Eight miles still remain to be excavated between Lake Timsah and el-Gisr, and twenty thousand men were swarming up and down the steep banks chanting a sad, monotonous song as they carried the sand in small rush baskets from the bottom of the cutting to the top of the bank. As each basket only held about four spadeful, it seemed to me a vast amount of work with a very small result. But de Lesseps declared that the Arabs insisted on working in their own way, and showed me a lot of wheel-barrows he had imported. The barrows were lying bottom upwards and the men used them to sleep under.' Were wheel-barrows suitable, one wonders, to go 'up and down the sliding sand-banks'?

performance of eating like a Bedawee. I have heard you talk of *tripas elasticas* in Spain but *Wallahi!* anything like the performance of Shaikh Abdallah none but an eyewitness could believe. How he plucked off the lamb's head and handed it to me in token of the highest respect, and how the bones cracked beneath his fingers— how huge handfuls of everything were chucked right down his throat all scorching hot. I encouraged him of course, quoting the popular song about 'doing deeds that Antar did not' and we all grew quite uproarious. When Shaikh Abdallah asked for drink, I cried 'bring the *ballaree* (the big jar the women fetch water in) for the Shaikh', and Shaikh Yussuf compared him to Samson and to Og, while I more profanely told how Antar broke the bones and threw them about.

The little Baroness was delighted and only expressed herself hurt that no one had crammed anything into her mouth. I told the Maōhn her disappointment which caused more laughter as such a custom is unknown here, but he of course made no end of sweet speeches to her. After dinner she showed the Arabs how ladies curtsey to the Queen in England, and the Abab'deh acted the ceremonial of presentation at the court of Darfur, where you have to rub your nose in the dust at the King's feet.

Then we went out with lanterns and torches and the Abab'deh did the sword dance for us. Two men with round shields and great straight swords do it. One dances a *pas seul* of challenge and defiance with prodigious leaps and pirouettes and Hah! Hahs! Then the other comes and a grand fight ensues. When the handsome Shaikh Hassan (whom you saw in Cairo) bounded out it really was heroic. All his attitudes were alike grand and graceful. They all wanted Shaikh Yussuf to play *el-Neboot* (single stick) and said he was the best man here at it, but his sister was not long dead and he could not. Hassan looks forward to Maurice's coming here to teach him 'the fighting of the English'. How Maurice would pound him!

On the fourth night I went to tea in Lord Hopetoun's boat and their sailors gave a grand *fantasia* excessively like a Christmas pantomime. One danced like a woman, and there was a regular pantaloon only 'more so', and a sort of clown in sheepskin and a pink mask who was duly tumbled about, and who distributed *claques* freely with a huge wooden spoon. It was very good fun indeed, though it was quite as well that the ladies did not understand the dialogue, or that part of the dance which made the Maōhn roar with laughter.

The Hopetouns had two handsome boats and were living like in May Fair. I am so used now to our poor shabby life that it makes quite a strange impression on me to see all that splendour—splendour which a year or two ago I should not even have remarked—and thus out of 'my inward consciousness' (as Germans say), many of the peculiarities and faults of the people of Egypt are explained to me and accounted for.

I have just received your letter of March 3 with one from Janet, which shows of how little moment the extermination of four villages is in this country, for she does not allude to our revolt and evidently has not heard of it.

I can only send you the rumours which reach me. No doubt there is another version of this miserable story current at Cairo and Alexandria, and it may be that there are facts of which I have not heard. But I live among the oppressed race, and I cannot help it if the profound compassion inspired by their fate makes me lean to their side.

The truth, of course, we shall never know. But I do know that one Pasha said he had hanged five hundred, and another that he had sent three hundred to Fazogli (*comme qui dirait Cayenne*) and all for the robbery of one Greek boat in which only the steersman was killed. I cannot make out that anything was done by the 'insurgents' beyond going out into the desert to listen to the darweesh's nonsense, and 'see a reed shaken by the wind'; the party that robbed the boat was, I am told, about forty strong. But the most horrid stories are current among the people of the atrocities committed on the wretched villagers by the soldiers. Not many were shot, they say, and they attempted no resistance, but the women and girls were outraged and murdered and the men hanged and the steamers loaded with plunder.

The worst is that every one believes that the Europeans aid and abet, and all declare that the Copts were spared to please the *Frangees*. Mind I am not telling you *facts* only what the people are saying—in order to show you their feelings. One most respectable young man sat before me on the floor the other day and told me what he had heard from those who had come up the river. Horrible tales of the stench of the bodies which are left unburied by the Pasha's order—of women big with child ripped open, etc., etc.

'Thou knowest oh! our Lady, that we are people of peace in this place, and behold now if one madman should come and a few idle fellows go out to the mountain (desert) with him, Effendina will send his soldiers to destroy the place and spoil our poor little girls and hang us—is that right, oh Lady? ... Truly in all the world none are miserable like us Arabs. The Turks beat us, and the Europeans hate us and say *quite right*. By God, we had better lay down our heads in the dust (die) and let the strangers take our land and grow cotton for themselves. As for me I am tired of this miserable life and of fearing for my poor little girls.'

Mahommed [the man mentioned] was really eloquent, and when he threw his *melayeh* over his face and sobbed, I am not ashamed to say that I cried too. I know very well that Mahommed was not quite wrong in what he says of the Europeans. I know the cruel old platitudes about governing Orientals by fear which the English pick up like mocking birds from the Turks. I know all about 'the stick' and 'vigour' and all that—but—'I sit among the people' and I know too that Mohammed feels just as John Smith or Tom Brown would feel in his place, and that men who were very savage against the rioters in the beginning, are now almost in a humour to rise against the Turks themselves just exactly as free-born Britons might be. There are even men of the class who have something to lose who express their disgust very freely.

There was a talk among the three or four Europeans here at the beginning of the rumours of a revolt of organizing a defence among Christians only. Conceive what a silly and gratuitous provocation! There was no religion in the business at all and of course the proper person to organize defence was the Maōhn, and he and Mustapha and others had planned using my house as a castle and defending that in case of a visit from the rioters. I have no doubt the true cause of the row is the usual one—hunger—the high price of food. It was like our Swing, or bread riots, nothing more and a very feeble affair too.

It is curious to see the travellers' gay *dahabiehs* just as usual and the Europeans as far removed from all care or knowledge of the distresses as if they were at home. When I go and sit with the English I feel almost as if they were foreigners to me too, so completely am I now *Bint el-Beled* (daughter of the country).

Altogether, we are most miserable here—all we fellaheen. The country is a waste for want of water, the animals are skeletons, the people are hungry, the heat has set in like June, and there is some sickness, and, above all the massacres at Gau have embittered all hearts. There is no *zaghareet* to be heard and all faces are sad and gloomy. I shall not be surprised if there are more disturbances. At first everyone was furious against Ahmad et-Tayib and the insurgents; but since they have been so frightfully dealt with, of course we pity them and their poor women and children. These 'vigorous measures' will cause the evil they are meant to punish. You know I don't buy or sell or lend money, or even give it. So no one has any interest in concealing his true feelings from me, and the people talk to me wherever I go. I wish 'Effendina' [the Viceroy Ismail] could hear a little of what I hear. I have no doubt he is ignorant of much that is done in his name.

From Salamieh, two miles above Luxor, every man, woman and child in any degree kin to Ahmad et-Tayib has been taken in chains to Keneh and no one here expects to see one of them return alive. Some are remarkably good men, I hear, and I have heard men say 'if Hajjee Sultan is killed and all his family we will never do a good action any more, for we see it is of no use'.

I have just seen a man who was at Gau, and who tells me fourteen hundred men were decapitated, and a hundred were sent to Fazogli in the steamer. Ahmad et-Tayib has escaped. I think my informant is quite a truthful man. He says that all these cruelties were perpetrated by the local Pashas, and that the Viceroy ordered the massacre to be stopped as soon as he knew of it.

April 3 1865. I will go on with the stories about the riots. Here is a thing happening within a few weeks and within sixty miles, and already the events assume a legendary character. The affair began thus: A certain Copt had a Muslim slave-girl who could read the Koran and who served him. He wanted her to be his concubine and she refused and went to Ahmad et-Tayib who offered money for her to her master. He refused it and insisted on his rights, backed by the Government, and thereupon Ahmad proclaimed a revolt and the people, tired of taxes and oppressions, said 'we will go with thee'. But Ahmad et-Tayib is not dead, and where the bullets hit him he shows little marks like burns. He still sits in the island, invisible to the Turkish soldiers, who are still there. This is the only bit of religious legend connected with the business.

Now for a little fact. The man who told me fourteen hundred had been beheaded was Hassan, Shaikh of the Abab'deh, who went to Gau to bring up the prisoners. The boat stopped a mile above Luxor, and my Mohammed, a most quiet respectable man and not at all a romancer went up in her to El-Moutaneh. I rode with him along the Island.

When we came near the boat she went on as far as the point of the Island, and I turned back after only looking at her from the bank and smelling the smell of a slave-ship.

It never occurred to me, I own, that the Bey on board had fled before a solitary woman on a donkey, but so it was. He told the Abab'deh Shaikh on board not to speak to me or to let me on board, and told the Captain to go a mile or two further. Mohammed heard all this. He found on board 'one hundred prisoners less two'. Among them the Mudir of Sohag, a Turk, in chains and wooden handcuffs like the rest. Mohammed took him some coffee and was civil to him. He says the poor creatures are dreadfully ill-used by the Abab'deh and the Nubians (Berberi) who guard them.

It is more curious than you can conceive to hear all the people say. It is just like going back four or five centuries at least, but with the heterogeneous element of steamers, electric telegraphs and the Bey's dread of the English lady's pen—at least Mohammed attributed his flight to fear of that weapon. It was quite clear that European eyes were dreaded, as the boat stopped three miles above Luxor and its *dahabiehs*, and had all its things carried that distance.

Kursheed Agha came to take final leave being appointed to Kench. He had been at Gau and had seen Fadil Pasha sit and make the soldiers lay sixty men down on their backs by ten at a time and *chop* them to death with the pioneers' axes. He estimated the people killed—men, women and children at 1,600—but Mounier tells me it was over 2,000. Shaikh Hassan agreed exactly with Kursheed, only the Arab was full of horror and the Circassian full of exultation. His talk was exactly what we all once heard about '*Pandies*', and he looked and talked and laughed so like a fine young English soldier, that I was ashamed to call him the kelb (dog) which rose to my tongue, and I bestowed it on Fadil Pasha instead. I must also say in behalf of my own countrymen that they *had* provocation while here there was none.

Janet has written me the Cairo version of the affair cooked for the European taste—and monstrous it is. The Pasha accuses some Shaikh of the Arabs of having gone from Upper Egypt to India to stir up the Mutiny against us! *Pourquoi pas* to conspire in Paris or London? It is too childish to talk of a poor Saidi Arab going to a country of whose language and whereabouts he is totally ignorant, in order to conspire against people who never hurt him. You may suppose how Yussuf and I talk by ourselves of all these things.

Dearest Janet. Your version of our massacre is quite curious to us here . . . I have seen with my own eyes a second boat-load of prisoners. I wish fervently the Viceroy [Ismail Pasha] knew the deep exasperation which his subordinates are causing. I do not like to repeat all I hear. What must it be to force from all the most influential men and the most devout Muslims such a sentiment as this?—'We are Muslims but we would thank God to send Europeans to govern us.' The feeling is against the Turks and not against the Christians.

A Coptic friend of mine has lost all his uncle's family at Gau, all were shot down—Copt and Christian alike. As to Hajjee Sultan, who lies in chains at Keneh and his family up at Esneh, a better man never lived, nor one more liberal to Christians. Copts ate of his bread as freely as Muslims. He lies there because he is distantly related by marriage to Ahmad et-Tayib, the real reason is because he is wealthy and some enemy covets his goods.

All this could be confirmed to you by M. Mounier. Perhaps I know even more of the feelings of the people than he as I am almost adopted by the Abu-l-Hajjajiah, and sit every evening with some party or another of decent men and they speak freely before me.

Cairo is like Paris, things are kept sweet there, but up here—! Of course Effendina hears the 'smooth prophecies' of the tyrants whom he sends up river. When I wrote before I knew nothing certain but now I have eye-witnesses' testimony, and I say that the Pasha deceives or is deceived—I hope the latter. An order from him did stop the slaughter of women and children which Fadil Pasha was about to effect.

XXVIII

Letters to little Urania

Luxor. My Darling Rainie. I think you will like a letter from Mamma for yourself and I dare say Aunty Charley[1] will read it to you. I have written the name of the place where I am living in Arabic letters. It is very difficult to learn them, and I think the little Arab boys, who sit in the courtyard of the Mosque, as the Church is called, with their slates must have harder work with their A B C than you have: and only think, they read and write the other way from us—what we should call the wrong way, and begin their books from the end.

I went to a farmhouse near here a few days ago and I wished so you were there to play with the tiny calves and kids and lambs. They are all so very tame, the little kids jumped up on my lap for a bit of bread I was eating and they played so with the little children. And so many chickens and turkeys and such lots of pigeons and great camels who carry all the corn and sugar cane instead of waggons, and big ugly black buffaloes who give much better milk than even the very pretty cows. And the buffaloes go and swim about in the big river with only their noses out of the water for hours and come up all wet and slimy like otters. The chickens and turkeys and pigeons all live in sort of cupboards built up of mud which look like very big large jars, taller than Papa, and which stand in a row all round the yard. They run about in the day and go in at night to be safe from the foxes.

A Coptic boy brought me such a beautiful big lizard about a yard long. He lives in trees but he scratched so much and was so wild, that I let him go after a few days as he would not eat and I feared he might die; he was very handsome indeed. The house is full of little brown lizards who run on the ceilings and catch flies and chirrup very

[1] Miss Charlotte Austin, sister of John Austin.

loud indeed. They have curious feet with round tips to their toes, so as to stick tight to all the walls and ceilings and run quite fast in that topsy-turvy way.

I have got chickens and a great chestnut coloured turkey cock and hundreds of pigeons on top of my house and hawks come and fly about among them and never seem to hurt them. I wish I could send you my pretty white pigeons who say 'Allah Allah' (the Arabs say they are praying), and they are so kind that they take care of all the young pigeons which Omar buys in the market and feed them as if they were their own children. It is quite curious to see them with five or six young birds round them gaping for food. There are some funny little owls who live in the ruins under my house and who fly about and bark like little puppies and don't mind the brightest sunshine; but they look very angry at us, as if they thought we had no business in their home.

A little girl called Zeynab, comes to see me sometimes; her Papa is a very kind old gentleman with a black face and a white beard who lends me his horse to ride and is called Mustapha Agha. Little Zeynab is just as big as you, and if you were painted dark brown you would be very like her, so I enjoy to see her because she resembles my darling Rainie. I gave her a little dolly and some sugar plums and she made a feast on a little round plate like an Arab dinner which comes in on a big round tray.

I live in a very big house with hardly any furniture. The room outside my room is quite open on one side to the country and the swallows have begun to build their nests there and often fly in where I sit, for I have no doors, only Papa's old plaid hung up for a curtain. At night the funny little brown lizards run about on the ceiling and catch flies and chirrup very loud; and very little bats with white stomachs and brown backs fly about in the room sometimes.

I have just bought a little brown donkey and ridden him; he is very small but runs along so fast and does not seem to think me at all too heavy. The donkeys here are very good tempered and don't want a bridle, only to point with a little stick, first on one side of their heads and then on the other, to show them where to go, and they run along and scramble up and down banks so nicely . . .

I did not get your nice letter and the pretty bird till New Year's Day—for I had come up the great river Nile. So it came after me by the post which is carried all the 600 miles by men running from one place to another. I was so pleased to see your own writing and I have put my darling Rainie's first own letter in my box to keep it always.

A little Arab girl, Fatimeh (Shaikh Yussuf's daughter), was with me when it came, she is younger than you but can write a little which few little girls can in this country. Her father teaches her and she looked at your letter and thought it very nice though she could not read the writing and wondered at it as much as you would at hers. And she was so delighted at the robin, which she said was an English sparrow.

It is such beautiful warm weather here; while you had frost and snow, we had hot sun and warm air like the middle of summer. Perhaps when summer really comes I shall have a boat of my own and then I hope Papa will bring you to live in it with me all the winter and we will come up here. How nice it would be.

A poor man, a traveller, was very ill and died in my house, and his black slave, a boy bigger than Maurice, is here still. He is called Khayr, but his name in his own village far away in the middle of Africa was Faragella. He was stolen by Turkish soldiers and can only speak a little Arabic yet. When I heard you had been reading *Robinson Crusoe*, I wished to send him to you to be your Man Friday, when you play at Desert Islands. He is a very good boy and very merry and now is Man Friday to my other little boy Ahmad, who is very little and very brown and very clever and teaches big clumsy Khayr to clean knives and help cook and to wash the clothes and all sorts of things. Khayr is black as ink and very ugly and his teeth were filed to sharp points like a dog's when he was little in his own country, but he is a very good boy and I like him and shall be very sorry when he goes to his master who is a little boy of eight or nine and whom he means to take great care of and to work for, if his father has left him no money. But if his little master's family sell him he wants me to buy him very much.

Dear little Rainie I do long to see you so very much and I hope I shall next summer. Your picture hangs over my table where I write so I am looking at your face now. I wish I could kiss your real face.

Our gardener here, whose name is Suleyman and who is a Christian, has given me a pretty little very old silver cross for you, I will send it to Janet to take care of till she can send it with Suleyman's kind salaam—and Omar sends you his best love and kisses your hand, and Shaikh Yussuf, a very nice Arab gentleman who is teaching me to read and write, sends you his love and is very glad to hear you are learning to write.

I went yesterday evening and ate some supper with Abdurrachman, a gentleman who was seeing his wheat threshed. Here they thresh it out in the field with a sort of sledge with little iron sharp wheels, which cut up the straw all small for the cattle to eat. The sledge is drawn round and round by two great handsome bulls driven by a little boy, quite naked and very dark brown, who sings to the bulls, how they shall get some barley if they are good—and everybody is paid with corn, not money, and the little brown boys trot home quite pleased with their little bundles of wheat on their heads. It is very pretty to see.

I wish I could send you a jug of camel's milk every morning such as I drink; it is better than any other milk, with thick froth like whipped cream. The Arabs think it very good for sick people and a man called Shergeff brings his camel here every morning and milks her for me. Her baby camel is so funny; he looks all legs and big black eyes with soft fluffy buff coloured hair and so very little a body to such tall legs. You should see the camels have their dinner; they are the only people here who use a tablecloth. The camel driver spreads a cloth on the ground and pours a heap of maize (doura) upon it and then old Mrs and Mr Camel sit down at the top and bottom very gravely and the others all take their places in proper order and eat quite politely bowing their long necks up and down. Only one was sulky, and went and had his dinner by himself, like a naughty boy—and sometimes would not eat at all.

This year an American gentleman and lady came with two little boys and two little girls; the eldest eight, the youngest two. They were nice children and I was very glad to see them, and all the little Arabs ran after them and were so astonished at their white faces and fair hair—they had never seen white children before and admired them very much and wondered at their clothes.

Nothing amuses my Arab friends so much as the atlas I brought with me; Shaikh Hassan el-Ababdeh, the black Shaikh, especially sits on the carpet for hours looking at the maps and asking questions. He never saw any before but he understands them very well, and I found that he knew that the world was round like a ball.

I wish I had you to see all the strange things and to sail with me in the boat which is called the *Urania*, but the sailors call her *Arooset al Ghaliya* (the darling bride). All little girls are called brides here when people mean to be civil.

The river is very full now. You know each year it rises and waters all Egypt, and then the people sow their corn. It never rains, and when the earth gets dry, they water all the fields with wheels turned by oxen or with baskets lined with leather at the end of a long pole which goes up and down like a see-saw when the men work it, and the water runs in little gutters which are made all over the fields like the lines on a chess board, and the green of the fields is brighter than even in England.

XXIX

'Send Europeans to govern us'

Luxor, April 13 1865. Dearest Mother. My little Ahmad grows more pressing with me to take him. I will take him to Alexandria, I think, and leave him in Janet's house with Toderi and Ellen to learn more house service. He is a dear little boy and very useful. I don't suppose his brother will object and he has no parents. Ahmad ibn-Mustapha also coaxes me to take him with me to Alexandria, and to try again to persuade his father to send him to England to Mr Fowler. I wish most heartily I could. He is an uncommon child in every way, full of ardour to learn and do something, and yet childish and winning and full of fun. His pretty brown face is quite a pleasure to me. His remarks on the New Testament teach me as many things as I can teach him. The boy is pious and not at all ill taught; he is much pleased to find so little difference between the teaching of the Koran and the Gospels. He has been reading the gospels with me at his own desire. I refused till I had asked his father's consent, and Shaikh Yussuf who heard me begged me by all means to make him read it carefully so as to guard him against the heretical inventions he might be beset with among the English 'of the vulgar sort'. What a poser for a missionary!

Ahmad wanted me, in case Omar did not go with me, to take him to serve me. Here there is no idea of its being derogatory for a gentleman's son to wait on one who teaches him, it is positively incumbent. He does all 'menial offices' for his mother, hands coffee, waits at table or helps Omar in anything if I have company, nor will he eat or smoke before me, or sit till I tell him—it is like service in the middle ages.

Dearest Alick. I have persuaded Mr Fowler the engineer who was with Lord Dudley to take my dear little pupil Ahmad, son of Mustapha, to learn the business at Leeds instead of idling in his father's

house here. I will give the child a letter to you in case he should go
to London.

I sent down the poor black lad with Arakel Bey. He took leave of
me with his ugly face all blubbered like a sentimental hippopotamus.
He said 'for himself, he wished to stay with me, but then what would
his boy, his little master do—there was only a stepmother who would
take all the money, and who else would work for the boy?' Little
Ahmad was charmed to see Khayr go, of whom he chose to be horribly
jealous, and to be wroth at all he did for me. Now the Shaikh-el-Beled
of Baidyeh has carried off my watchman, and the Christian Shaikh-
el-Hara of our quarter of Luxor has taken the boy Yussuf for the
Canal. The former I successfully resisted and got back Mansoor, not
indeed *incolumes* for *he* had been handcuffed and bastinadoed to make
me pay 200 piastres, but he bore it like a man rather than ask me for
the money and was thereupon surrendered. But the Copt will be a
tougher business—he will want more money and be more resolved
to get it. *Veremus.* I must I suppose go to the Nazir at the Canal—a
Turk—and beg off my donkey boy.

I have heard from Janet that Ross has bought me a boat for £200
which is to take four of his agents to Aswan, and then come back for
me. So all my business is settled, and, *Inshallah!* I shall depart in
another three or four weeks.

The weather is quite cool and fresh again but the winds very violent
and the dust pours over us like water from the dried up land, as well
as from the Goomeh mountain. It is miserably uncomfortable, but
my health is much better again—spite of all. But there is a great deal
of sickness, chiefly dysentery and my 'practice' has become quite a
serious business. The doctoring business goes on at a rate; I have
four sick a day, sometimes a dozen.

A whole gipsy camp are great customers—the poor souls will
bring all manner of gifts it goes to my heart to eat, but they can't
bear to be refused. They are astounded to hear that people of their
blood live in England and that I knew many of their customs—which
are the same here.

I spent all day on Friday in the Abab'deh quarters where Shaikh
Hassan and his slave Rachmeh were both uncommonly ill. Both are
'all right' now. Rachmeh is the nicest negro I ever knew, and a very
great friend of mine. He is a most excellent, honest, sincere man, and
an Effendi (*i.e.* writes and reads) which is more than his master can
do. He has seen all the queer people in the interior of Africa.

I now know everybody in my village and the 'cunning women' have set up the theory that my eye is lucky; so I am asked to go and look at young brides, visit houses that are building, inspect cattle, etc., as a bringer of good luck—which gives me many a curious sight.

April 1865. Dearest Alick. How would it answer to send Maurice to spend next winter with me and learn Arabic and Turkish? Shaikh Yussuf would teach him one and Seleem Effendi the other. If Maurice seriously means [to go into] diplomacy, Eastern languages are a very good card in one's hand. Think of it. If he seems at all delicate in health, Egypt does wonders for young people that I really would advise it. I shall be so glad when the time comes to join you.

I gave Lord Dudley an Arab dinner on a grand scale to meet all the notabilities of Luxor. How vulgar the great English Pasha did seem compared with the fellaheen company of Luxor, and I saw that they thought so and were amazed at his haw-haw laughter and boisterous talk.

I saw Hassan Shaikh el-Ababdeh yesterday who was loud in praise of your good looks and gracious manners. We hear that Mr Colquhoun is going away and many vows are made that you might be Consul here. I wish I could persuade myself honestly to think it would suit you to live in dear old Cairo with me.

April 29. Dearest Mother. Shaikh Yussuf, urged me to try hard to get my husband here as Consul when Colquhoun leaves—assuming that he would feel as I do. I said that my master was not young and that to a just man the worry of such a place would be a martyrdom. 'Truly thou hast said it, but it is a martyr we Arabs want; shall not the reward of him who suffers daily vexation for his brethrens' sake be equal to that of him who dies in battle for the faith? If thou wert a man I would say: take thy labour and sorrow upon thee, and thine own heart would repay thee.'

He, too, said, like the old Shaikh, 'I only pray for Europeans to rule us—now the fellaheen are worse off than any slaves.'

I went a few days ago to the wedding of handsome Shaikh Hassan the Abab'deh, who married the butcher's pretty little daughter. The group of women and girls lighted by the lantern which little Ahmad carried up for me was the most striking thing I have seen. The bride—a lovely girl of ten or eleven all in scarlet, a tall dark slave of Hassan's blazing with gold and silver necklaces and bracelets, with long twisted locks of coal black hair and such glittering eyes and teeth, the wonderful wrinkled old women, and the pretty, wondering, yet fearless children were beyond description. The mother brought the bride up to me and unveiled her and asked me to let her kiss my hand, and to look at her, I said all the usual *Bismillah Mashallah's,* and after a time went to the men who were eating, all but Hassan who sat apart and who begged me to sit by him, and whispered anxious enquiries about his *aroosah's* looks. After a time he went to visit her and returned in half an hour very shy and covering his face and hand and kissed the hands of the chief guests. Then we all departed and the girl was taken to look at the Nile, and then to her husband's house. Last night he gave me a dinner—a very good dinner indeed, in his house which is equal to a very poor cattle shed at home. We were only five. Shaikh Yussuf, Omar, an elderly merchant and I. Hassan wanted to serve us but I made him sit.

A short time ago my poor friend the Maōhn had a terrible 'tile' fall on his head. His wife, two married daughters and nine miscellaneous children arrived on a sudden, and the poor man is now tasting the pleasures which Abraham once endured between Sarah and Hagar. I visited the ladies and found a very ancient Sarah and a daughter of wonderful beauty. A young man here—a Shereef—has asked me to open negotiations for a marriage for him with the Maōhn's grand-daughter a little girl of eight—so you see how completely I am 'one of the family'.

Poor Hajji Sultan lies in chains at Keneh. One of the best and kindest of men! I am to go and take secret messages to him, and money from certain men of religion to bribe the Mudir with. The Shurafa who have asked me to do this are from another place, as well as a few of the Abu-l-Hajjajieh.

A very great Shereef indeed from Lower Egypt, said to me the other day, 'Thou knowest if I am a Muslim or no. Well, I pray to the most Merciful to send us Europeans to govern us, and to deliver us from these wicked men.' We were all sitting after the funeral of one of the Shurafa and I was sitting between the Shereef of Luxor and the Imám—and this was said before thirty or forty men, all Shurafa. No one said 'No', and many assented aloud.

The Shereef asked me to lend him the New Testament, it was a pretty copy and when he admired it I said, 'From me to thee, oh my master the Shereef, write in it as we do in remembrance of a friend— the gift of a Nazraneeyeh who loves the Muslimeen.' The old man kissed the book and said, 'I will write moreover—to a Muslim who loves all such Christians'—and after this the old Shaikh of Abou Ali took me aside and asked me to go as messenger to Hajji Sultan for if one of them took the money it would be taken from them and the man get no good by it.

The Shaikh of the Bishareen—eight days' journey from Aswan has invited me and promises me all the meat and milk I can eat, they have nothing else. They live on a high mountain and are very fine handsome people. If only I were strong I could go to very odd places where Frangees are not.

Read a very stupid novel (as a story) called '*le Secret du Bonheur*' —it gives the truest impression of the manners of Arabs that I have read. The 'caressant' ways of Arabs are so well described. It is the same here. The people come and pat and stroke me with their hands, and one corner of my brown abbaieh is faded with much kissing. I am hailed as *Sitt Betaana* 'Our own Lady', and now the people are really enthusiastic because I refused the offer of some *cawasses* as a guard which a Bimbashee made me. As if I would have such fellows to help to bully my friends. The said Bimbashee (next in rank to a Bey) a coarse man like an Arnout, stopped here a day and night and played his little Turkish game, telling me to beware—for the Ulema hated all Franks and set the people against us—and telling the Arabs that Christian hakeems were all given to poison Muslims. So at night I dropped in at the Maõhn's with Shaikh Yussuf carrying my lantern—and was loudly hailed with a *Salaam Aleykee* from the old Shereef himself—who began praising the Gospel I had given him, and me at the same time. Yussuf had a little reed in his hand—the *kalem* for writing, about two feet long and of the size of a quill. I took it and showed it to the Bimbashee and said—'Behold the *neboot* wherewith we are all to be murdered by this Shaikh of the Religion'. The Bimbashee's bristly moustache bristled savagely, for he felt that the 'Arab dogs' and the Christian *khanzeereh* (feminine pig) were laughing at him together.

Soldiers are now to be quartered in the Said [Upper Egypt]—a new plague worse than all the rest. Do not the *cawasses* already rob the poor enough? They fix their own prices in the market and beat the water-carriers as sole payment. What will the soldiers do? The taxes are being illegally levied on lands which are *sheragi*, that is, totally unwatered by the last Nile and therefore exempt by law, and the people are driven to desperation. I feel sure that there will be more troubles as soon as there arises any other demagogue like Ahmad et Tayib to incite the people and now every Arab sympathizes with him.

I am sick of telling of the daily oppressions and robberies. If a man has a sheep, the Mudir comes and eats it, if a tree, it goes to the Nazir's kitchen. My poor sakka is beaten by the cawasses in sole payment of his skins of water—and then people wonder my poor friends tell lies and bury their money.

XXX

'Pity becomes a perfect passion'

April 29 1865. Another steamboat load of prisoners from Gau has just gone up. A little comfort is derived here from the news that, 'Praise be to God, Moussa Pasha (Governor of the Sudan) is dead and gone to Hell'. It must take no trifle to send him there judging by the quiet way in which Fadil Pasha is mentioned.

You will think me a complete rebel—but I may say to you what most people would think 'like my nonsense'—that one's pity becomes a perfect passion, when one *sits among the people*—as I do, and sees it all; least of all can I forgive those among Europeans and Christians who can help to 'break these bruised reeds'. However, in Cairo and more still in Alexandria, all is quite different. There, the same system which has been so successfully copied in France prevails. The capital is petted at the expense of the fellaheen. Prices are regulated in Cairo for meat and bread as they are or were in Paris, and the 'dangerous classes' enjoy all sorts of exemptions. Just like France! The Cairenes eat the bread and the fellaheen eat the stick.

The people here used to dislike Mounier who arrived poor and grew rich and powerful, but they all bless him now and say at El-Moutaneh a man eats his own meat and not the courbash of the Mudir—and Mounier has refused soldiers (as I refused them on my small account) and 'Please God', he will never repent it. Yussuf says 'What the Turkish Government fears is not for *your* safety, but lest we should learn to love you too well', and it is true. Here there is but one voice. 'Let the Franks come, let us have the laws of the Christians.'

In Cairo the Franks have dispelled this *douce illusion* and done the Turk's work as if they were paid for it. But here come only travellers who pay with money and not with stick—a degree of generosity not enough to be adored.

I perceive that I am a bore—but you will forgive my indignant sympathy with the kind people who treat me so well. Pray do publish something of what I tell but avoid names. God knows whether things may not be used in Cairo. Yussuf asked me to let the English papers know about the Gau business. An Alim ed Deen ul-Islam would fain call for help to the *Times!* Strange changes and signs of the times—these—are they not so?

I went to Church on Good Friday with the Copts. The scene was very striking—the priest dressed like a beautiful Crusader in white robes with crimson crosses. One thing has my hearty admiration. The few children who are taken to Church are allowed to play! Oh my poor little Protestant fellow Christians, can you conceive a religion so delightful as that which permits Peep-bo behind the curtain of the sanctuary! I saw little Butrus and Scendariah at it all church time—and the priest only patted their little heads as he carried the sacrament out to the hareem. Fancy the parson kindly patting a noisy boy's head, instead of the beadle whacking him! I am entirely reconciled to the Coptic rules.

On the Nile boat Urania, *May 1865.* Dearest Alick. I told you or Mother that I had sent off Sally and her child escorted by Ahmad ibn Mustapha. She was very much pulled by nursing and a great burden to me, so much so that I thought it better to pay for a boat than to wait for the arrival of the *dahabieh* which was quite uncertain. So little Ahmad is now acting ladies' maid and uncommonly happy in the function.

Happy as I was in the prospect of seeing you all and miserable as poor Upper Egypt has become, I could not leave Luxor without a pang. Our Bairam was not gay. There was horse riding for Shaikh Gibreel (the cousin of Abu'l Hajjaj) and the scene was prettier than ever I saw. My old friend Yunis the Shereef insisted on showing me that at eighty-five he could still handle a horse and throw a Gereed 'for Shaikh Gibreel and the Lady' as he said. Then arrived the Mufettish of Zenia with his gay attendants and filled the little square in front of the Cadi's castellated house where we were sitting. The young Shaikh of Salamieh rode beautifully and there was some excellent Neboot play (sort of very severe quarterstaff peculiar to the fellaheen).

Next day was the great dinner given by Mohammed and Mustapha outside Mohammed's house opposite Shaikh Gibreel's tomb—200 men ate at his gate. I went to see it and was of course asked to eat. 'Can one like thee eat the *Melocheea* of the fellaheen?' So I joined a party of five round a little wooden tray, tucked up my sleeve and ate —dipping the bread into the *Melocheea* which is like very sloppy spinach but much nicer. Then came the master and his servants to deal the pieces of meat out of a great basket—sodden meat—and like Benjamin my piece was the largest, so I tore off a bit and handed it to each of my companions, who said 'God take thee safe and happy to thy place and thy children and bring thee back to us in safety to eat the meat of the festival together once more'.

The moon rose clear and bright behind the one tall palm tree that overhangs the tomb of Shaikh Gibreel. He is a saint of homely tastes and will not have a dome over him or a cover for his tomb, which is only surrounded by a wall breast-high, enclosing a small square bit of ground with the rough tomb on one side. At each corner was set up a flag, and a few dim lanterns hung overhead. The 200 men eating were quite noiseless—and as they rose, one by one washed their hands and went, the crowd melted away like a vision. But before all were gone, came the Bulook, or sub-magistrate—a Turkish Jack-in-office with the manners of a Zouave turned parish beadle. He began to sneer at the *melocheea* of the fellaheen and swore he could not eat it if he sat before it 1,000 years. Omar [the farmer], began to 'chaff' him. 'Eat, oh Bulook Pasha and if it swells thy belly the Lady will give thee of the physick of the English to clean thy stomach upwards and downwards of all thou hast eaten of the food of the fellaheen.' The Bulook is notorious for his exactions—his 'eating the people'— so there was a great laugh. Poor Omar was very ill next day—and everyone thought the Bulook had given him the eye.

Then came the Mufettish in state to pay his *devoirs* to the Shaikh in the tomb. He came and talked to Mustapha and Yussuf and enumer- ated the people taken for the works, 200 from Luxor, 400 from Karnac, 310 from Zenia, 320 from Byadyeh, and 380 from Salamieh— a good deal more than half the adult men to go for sixty days leaving their fields uncultivated and their hareem and children hungry—for they have to take all the food for themselves.

I rose sick at heart from the Mufettish's harsh voice, and went down to listen to the *Moonsheeds* chanting at the tomb and the *Zikheers'* strange sobbing, Allah, Allah.

I leaned on the mud wall watching the slender figures swaying in the moonlight, when a tall, handsome fellah came up in his brown shirt, felt *libdeh* (skull cap), with his blue cotton *melaya* tied up and full of dried bread on his back. The type of the Egyptian. He stood close beside me and prayed for his wife and children, 'Ask our God to pity them, O Shaikh, and to feed them while I am away. Thou knowest how my wife worked all night to bake all the wheat for me and that there is none left for her and the children'. He then turned to me and took my hand and went on, 'Thou knowest this lady, oh Shaikh Gibreel, take her happy and well to her place and bring her back to us—*el Fathah, yah Beshoosheh!*'[1] and we said it together. I could have laid my head on Shaikh Gibreel's wall and howled. I thanked him as well as I could for caring about one like me while his own troubles were so heavy. I shall never forget that tall athletic figure and the gentle brown face, with the eleven days' moon of Zulheggeh, and the shadow of the palm tree. That was my farewell. 'The voice of the miserable is with thee, shall God not hear it?'

Next day Omar had a sharp attack of fever and was delirious—it lasted only two days but left him very weak—and the anxiety and trouble was great—for my helping hands were as awkward as they were willing.

The *Urania* is very nice indeed. A small saloon, two good berths— bath and cabinet, and very large *kasneh* (stern cabin). She is dirty, but will be extremely comfortable when cleaned and painted.

On May 15 we sailed. Shaikh Yussuf went with me to Keneh, Mustapha and Seyd going by land—and one of Hajji Sultan's disciples and several Luxor men were deck passengers. The Shereef gave me the bread and jars of butter for his grandsons in Gama'l Azhar, and came to see me off. We sat on the deck outside as there was a crowd to say good-bye and had a lot of hareem in the cabin. The old Shereef made me sit down on the carpet close to him and then said 'we sit here like two lovers'—at eighty-five *even* an Arab and a Shereef may be '*gaillard*'—so I cried, 'Oh Shereef, what if Omar tells my master the secret thou hast let out—it is not well of thee'. There was a great laugh which ended in the Shereef saying 'no doubt thy master is of the best of the people, let us say the *Fathah* for him', and he called on all the people '*El Fathah* for the master of the lady!' I hope it has benefited you to be prayed for at Luxor.

I had written so far and passed Minieh when I fell ill with pleurisy. If I had not loved Omar before, I must indeed now. He nursed me

---

[1] Lucie's nickname meaning 'one with a kindly face'.

as I never was nursed before, and was as handy and clever as he was tender. I believe he saved my life by cupping me Arab fashion with a tumbler and your old razor. I've arrived today after a tedious voyage of violent adverse winds.

Cairo, June 12. I've sent for the doctor and will let you know as soon as I can when I can go on. But as you wish me not to bring Omar, and Janet is gone, it will take some time before I dare travel alone.[1]

I've lots more to tell of my journey but am too weak after two weeks in bed (and unable to lie down from suffocation)—but I am *much* better now. A man from the Azhar is reading the Koran for me outside—while another is gone with candles to Seyeedele Zeyned.

Cairo, June 16. I have seen Dr Patterson two or three times and he says I have had inflammation of the whole left lung (the good one) so severe that it is now extensively hepatized. He says he can't conceive how I did not die and that but for Omar's cupping me I could not have fought through. I certainly never felt so near death. If I had not been left to Omar's care I was a 'gone coon'. I still cannot breathe well but am not in much pain. Dr P. says I cannot think of leaving Cairo for a fortnight. I wish you had seen little Ahmad doing sick nurse. Really Arab boys are wonderful—how clever and careful the little brown creature was; what would an English bumpkin boy be? And Ahmad is a 'savage'. I could not have been better nursed.

I will let you know when I can undertake the voyage but, of course, without a servant it will be longer as I now cannot rise from my bed or chair without help. I am much reduced by the frightful cold sweats of suffocation.

I will go down to Alexandria in the boat and Omar will work at her. She wants a great deal of repairing I find, and his superintendence will save much money—besides he will do one man's work as he is a much better carpenter than most here having learnt of the English workmen on the railroad—but the Reis says the boat must come out of the water as her bottom is unsound. She is a splendid sailer I hear and remarkably comfortable. The beds in the *kasneh* would do for Jacob Omnium. So when you 'honour our house' you will be happy. The saloon is small, and the berths as usual—there is a sort of closet

---

[1] It is likely that Alexander did not want Lucie to bring Omar because of the Sally affair, for he and the Rosses considered that Omar was to blame. The fact remained, however, that Lucie was dependent on Omar in her illness and it was not wise or kind to let her travel alone.

which holds my bath and the stern cabin is first rate. Also she is a very handsome shape—but she wants no end of repairs. So Omar is consoled at being left because he will 'save our money' a great deal by piecing sails, and cutting and contriving, and scraping and painting himself. Only he is afraid for me. However, *Allah Kereem*.

Sally wrote to want to come down and see Omar, and full of complaints and wanting money. Now I paid £17 for her journey, and as she is to get £30 a year and Omar pays everything for the child, I think she is unreasonable. She cannot see that she has done anything out of the way and quite resents being put to any inconvenience. I was too ill for Omar to leave me and, besides, as he has divorced her it is *haram* (forbidden) for him to see her face. I have advised him to go once and settle about the child and refuse to go again. He is afraid of being unkind as she is a stranger. But I will not see her. I am too ill to be worried and I cannot afford to give her more money.

Cairo is horribly dear, and by the time that I have paid Omar and my living here and the crew and my journey, there won't be too much left out of my £250 due in April and for the repairs of the boat which will be at least as much as her first cost I fear. However, I shall get my money back by letting her for the four winter months while I live at Luxor.

This illness is provoking, but the bad lung is very much better luckily, for I still can't use the other at all. I wanted to get a nurse but Omar resisted and said why spend ten shillings a day on a woman to do nothing. He had done all for a fortnight and would not be turned out now. Dr Patterson said the same and that the nurses are all bad and that none could do better than Omar, so he will go on to work double tides, and little Ahmad runs like a shot if I whistle in the night, so don't fancy I am the least neglected.

I have a very good Reis I think. The usual tight little black fellow from near Aswan—very neat and active and good tempered—the same cross steersman that we had up to Bedreshayn—but he knows his work well. We had contrary gales the whole way. My men worked all they possibly could, and pulled the rope all day and rowed all night, day after day—but we were twenty-eight days getting down.

June 18. I feel really better today. I send Dr Patterson's letter of two days ago, but I am better since then. I don't know what he says, but I have had a squeak for it. If I don't come round, I beg you won't ever forget Omar's truly filial care and affection for me.

233

XXXI

Return from England with a new maid

Sainte Marguerite, October 3 1865. Dearest Alexander. I arrived yesterday very tired having got up at 5.30 a.m. for the 7.30 train which never came to Lyons till 9.15. At Avignon they crammed in six filthy, garlicky peasants—male and female—who spat and scratched their heads in a very unpleasant way. It is hardly fair to pay first class and take third class company in the same carriage.

At Geneva I sat next to one Arnaud Bey at dinner. He has been twenty-seven years in Egypt and says, like Hekekian, that my letters are a photograph and he will endorse every opinion I have expressed. The Inn-keeper of the 'Couronné' at Geneva was most civil. He gave Marie [the new German maid] a capital luncheon packed up and half a bottle of good wine as a present for me on parting and sent a man to take tickets and see me off.

Marseilles, October 10. Dearest Mother. I have not been able to write the last four or five days having had so bad a cold that I was forced to keep to my bed. Today is fine and I hope soon to get well enough to go into town and settle my business and day of departure. I am so grieved to hear that your gout broke out again, it is very provoking. I do hope soon to hear a better account of you.

Alexandria, October 28. I arrived here on Thursday after a splendid passage and was very comfortable on board. I found M. Olagnier waiting for me, and Omar, of course, and am *installé* at Ross's till my boat gets done which I am told will be in six days. She will be remarkably comfortable. Omar had caused a sort of divan with a roof and back to be constructed just outside the cabin-door where I always sat every evening, which will be the most delightful little nest one can conceive. I shall sit like a Pasha there.

My cough is still very harassing, but my chest less tight and painful, and I feel less utterly knocked down. The weather is beautiful here just now—warm and not nearly so damp as usual.

Lord Edward St Maur was on board, he has much of his aunt's pleasantness. Also a very young Bombay Merchant—a Muslim who uttered not one syllable to anyone but to me. His talk was just like that of a well-bred and intelligent young Englishman. I am glad to say that his views of the state of India were very encouraging—he seemed convinced that the natives were gradually working their way up to more influence, and said 'We shall have to thank you for a better form of government by far than any native one ever would have been'—he added, 'We Muslims have this advantage over the Hindus—that our religion is no barrier at all, socially or politically—between us and you—as theirs is. I mean it ought not to be when both faiths are cleared of superstition and fanaticism'. He spoke very highly of Sir Bartle Frere but said 'I wish it were possible for more English *gentlemen* to come out to India'. He had been two years in England on mercantile business and was going back to his brother Ala-ed-deen much pleased with the English in England. It is one of the most comforting *Erscheinungen* [phenomenon] I have seen coming from India—if that sort of good sense is pretty common among the very young men they certainly will work their way up.

I think Marie seems very promising. She is truly attentive without being officious and in no way troublesome; she also seems very efficient and has good sense. I hope she will go on equally well. I sent her to the Sisters of Charity to 'make her soul' and they tried to persuade her to leave her heretical mistress and offered to get her 90 francs a month in Alexandria, but their pious exhortations were quite ineffectual. I think she is a very good girl and certainly a remarkably good servant. She and little Ahmad are on the most affectionate terms and keep up a continual giggling. She won his heart by blazing at Ellen who beat the child, whereat Marie's dander was up in good earnest.

Alexandria, November 2. The boat like all other things goes but slowly—however the weather here is unusually dry and fine.

I have just been to see my poor friend Sittee Zubeydeh, widow of Hassaneyn Effendi who died in England—and I am filled with admiration at her good sense and courage. She has determined to carry on her husband's business of letting boats herself, and to educate her children to the best of her power in habits of independence. I hope she will be successful, and receive the respect such rare conduct in a Turkish woman deserves from the English. I was much gratified to hear from her how kindly she had been treated in Glasgow. She said that nothing that could be done for her was left undone. She arrived this morning and I went to see her directly and was really astonished at all she said about her plans for herself and her children. Poor thing! it is a sad blow—for she and Hassaneyn were as thoroughly united as any Europeans could be.

I went afterwards to my boat, which I hope will be done in five or six days. I am extremely impatient to be off. She will be a most charming boat—both comfortable and pretty. The boom for the big sail is new—and I exclaimed, 'why you have broken the new boom and mended it with leather!' Omar had put on a *sham splice* to avert the evil eye from such a fine new piece of wood!

There is some cholera about again, I hear—ten deaths yesterday—so Olagnier tells me. I fancy the rush of Europeans back again, each bringing 'seven other devils worse than himself' is the cause of it.

I think I am beginning to improve a little; my cough has been terribly harassing especially at night—but the weather is very good, cool, and not damp.

Cairo, November 27. I had no heart to write any more from Alexandria where I was worried out of all courage and strength. At last after endless delays and vexations the *dahabieh* was *tant bien que mal* ready.

Talk of Arab dawdle! after what I went through—and now I have to wait here for fresh repairs, as we came up baling all the way and I fear cursing the Christian workmen who had bungled so shamefully.

However that is over, and I am much better as to my cough—indeed it is all but gone. Omar was very ill having had dysentery for two months, but he too is well again. He is very grateful for your kind mention of him and says, 'Send the Great Mother my best Salaam, and tell her her daughter's people are my people, and where she goes I will go too, and please God I will serve her rich or poor till "He who separates us" shall take me from her'.

The 'He who separated us' I must explain to you. It is one of the attributes of God, *The Separator of Religions* implies toleration and friendship by attributing the two religions alike to God—and is never used towards one whose religion is not to be respected.

I have got a levee of former reis's, sailors, etc. some sick—but most come to talk.

The climate changes quite suddenly as one leaves the Delta, and here I sit at eight in the evening with open doors and windows.

I am so glad to hear of the great success of my dear Father's book, and to think of your courage in working at it still.[1]

I suppose I shall be here a week longer as I have several jobs to do to my boat, and I shall try to get towed up so as to send back the boat as soon as possible in order to let her. Ali will give £80 a month for her if he gets a party of four to take up. I pay my Reis five napoleons a month while travelling and three while lying still. He is a good, active little fellow.

We were nearly smashed under the railway bridge by an iron barge—and *Wallah!* how the Reis of the bridge did whack the Reis of the barge. I thought it a sad loss of time, but Reis Ali and my Reis Mohammed seemed to look on the stick as the most effective way of extricating my anchor from the Pasha's rudder. My crew can't say 'Urania' so they sing 'go along, oh darling bride', *Arooset al-Ghaliya*, as the little Sitt's best description, and *Arooset al-Ghaliya* will be the *dahabieh's* exoteric name—as *'el Beshoosheeh'* ['The one with a kindly face'] is my popular name.

Cairo, December 5. Now I am at rest. I have got all the boat in order. My captain, Reis Mohammed, is very satisfactory, and today we sail as soon as Omar comes back with the meat, etc. from market.

Mohammed Gazowee begs to give his best Salaam to Shaikh Stanley whom he longs to see again. He says that all the people said he was not a Christian, for he was not proud ever towards them as Christians are, but a real Shaikh, and that the Bedaween still talk of Shaikh Stanley and of his piety. The old half-witted jester of Luxor has found me out—he has wandered down here to see his eldest son who is serving in the army. He had brought a little boy with him, but is 'afraid for him' here, I don't know why, and has begged me to take the child up to his mother. These licensed *possenreisser* are like our fools in old times—but less witty than we fancy them to have been—thanks to Shakespeare, I suppose. Each district has one who attends all *moolids* and other gatherings of the people, and picks up a living.

---

[1] In 1861 Sarah Austin had published a second edition of John Austin's *Province of Jurisprudence Determined*, made up of the early lectures he had delivered at University College; this was followed by two volumes of notes of other lectures that she edited and called *Lectures on Jurisprudence, or the Philosophy of Positive Law.* A review of this was written by J. S. Mill in the *Edinburgh Review* of October 1863 and republished in his *Dissertations and Discussions.* Other editions were in 1873, 1885, 1911 and 1954; Italian editions 1959 and 1962.

XXXII

'Pharaoh is laying intolerable burdens'

Cairo, December 5 1865. Dearest Mother. Of course I am anxious about my friends. All Haleem Pasha Oghdee's villages have been confiscated (those tributary to him for work) *sous prétexte* that he ill-used the people, *n.b.* he alone paid them—a bad example.[1] Pharaoh is indeed laying intolerable burdens—not on the Israelites—but on the fellaheen.

Omar said of the great dinner today, 'I think all the food will taste of blood, it is the blood of the poor, and more *haram* than any pork or wine or blood of beasts'. Of course such sentiments are not to be repeated—but they are general. The *meneggets* who picked and made ten mattresses and fourteen cushions for me in half a day, were laughing and saying, 'for the Pasha's boat we work also, at so much a day and we should have done it in four days'. 'And for me if I paid by the day instead of by the piece, how long?' 'One day instead of half, O Lady, for fear thou shouldest say to us, you have finished in half a day and half the wages is enough for you.' That is the way in which all the work is done for Effendina—no wonder his steamers don't pay.

Luxor, December 25 to January 3. Dearest Alick. We left Cairo on the 5th December. I was not well. No wind as usual, and we were a week getting to Benisuef, where the Stambuli Greek lady who was so kind to me last summer in my illness came on board with a very well-bred Arab lady. I was in bed, and only stayed a few hours.

On to Minieh another five or six days—walked about and saw the preparations for the Pasha's arrival. Nothing so flat as these affairs here. Not a creature went near the landing-place but his own servants,

---

[1] Ismail was doing his utmost to disgrace Abdul Haleem Pasha, son of Mohammed Ali, as he was next in succession according to Ottoman law, and Ismail wanted his own son, Tewfik, to follow him as ruler. (See last para n. p. 263.)

soldiers, and officials. I thought of the arrival of the smallest of German princes, which makes ten times the noise. Next on to Assiut. Ill again, and did not land or see anyone. On to Girgeh, where we only stayed long enough to deliver money and presents which I had been begged to take for some old sailors of mine to their mothers and wives there.

Between Assiut and Girgeh an Abyssinian slave lad came and wanted me to steal him; he said his master was a Copt and ill-used him, and the lady beat him. But Omar sagely observed to the sailors, who were very anxious to take him, that a bad master did not give his slave such good clothes and even a pair of shoes—*quel luxe!*—and that he made too much of his master being a Copt; no doubt he was a lazy fellow, and perhaps had run away with other property besides himself.

Soon after I was sitting on the pointed prow of the boat with the Reis, who was sounding with his painted pole (*vide* antique scultures and paintings), and the men towing, when suddenly something rose to the surface close to us: the men cried out *Beni Adam!* and the Reis prayed for the dead. It was a woman: the silver bracelets glittered on the arms raised and stiffened in the agony of death, the knees up and the beautiful Egyptian breasts floated above the water. I shall never forget the horrid sight. 'God have mercy on her', prayed my men, and the Reis added to me, 'let us also pray for her father, poor man: you see, no robber has done this (on account of the bracelets). We are in the Said now, and most likely she has blackened her father's face, and he has been forced to strangle her, poor man'. I said 'Alas!' and the Reis continued, 'ah, yes, it is a heavy thing, but a man must whiten his face, poor man, poor man. God have mercy on him'. Such is Saidi *point d'honneur*. However, it turned out she was drowned bathing.

Above Girgeh we stopped awhile at Dishné, a large village. I strolled up alone, *les mains dans les poches*, '*sicut meus est mos*': and was soon accosted with an invitation to coffee and pipes in the strangers' place, a sort of room open on one side with a column in the middle, like two arches of a cloister, and which in all the villages is close to the mosque: two or three cloaks were pulled off and spread on the ground for me to sit on, and the milk which I asked for, instead of the village coffee, brought.

In a minute a dozen men came and sat round, and asked as usual, 'Whence comest thou, and whither goest thou?' and my gloves, watch, rings, etc. were handed round and examined; the gloves always call forth many *mashallah's*. I said, 'I come from the Frank country, and am going to my place near Abu'l Hajjaj'. Hereupon everyone touched my hand and said, 'Praise be to God that we have seen thee. Don't go on: stay here and take 100 feddans of land and remain here'.

I laughed and asked, 'Should I wear the *zaboot* (brown shirt) and the *libdeh*, and work in the field, seeing there is no man with me?' There was much laughing, and then several stories of women who had farmed large properties well and successfully. Such undertakings on the part of women seem quite as common here as in Europe, and more common than in England.

The last night before reaching Keneh, the town forty miles north of Luxor, my men held a grand fantasia on the bank. There was no wind, and we found a lot of old maize stalks; so there was a bonfire, and no end of drumming, singing and dancing. Even Omar relaxed his dignity so far as to dance the dance of the Alexandria young men; and very funny it all was. I laughed consumedly; especially at the modest airs and graces of a great lubberly fellow—one Hezayin, who acted the bride—in a representation of a Nubian wedding festivity. The new song of this year is very pretty—a declaration of love to a young Mohammed, sung to a very pretty tune. There is another, rather like the air of 'Di Provenza al mar' in the 'Traviata', with extremely pretty words. As in England, every year has its new song, which all the boys sing about the streets.

I took leave of my new friends who had given me the first welcome home to the Said, and we went on to Keneh, which we reached early in the morning, and I found my well-known donkey-boys putting my saddle on. The father of one, and the two brothers of the other, were gone to work on the railway for sixty days' forced labour, taking their own bread, and the poor little fellows were left alone to take care of the hareem.

As soon as we reached the town, a couple of tall young soldiers in the Nizam uniform rushed after me, and greeted me in English; they were Luxor lads serving their time. Of course they attached themselves to us for the rest of the day. We then bought water jars (the *specialité* of Keneh); *gullehs* and *zees*—and I went on to the Cadi's house to leave a little string of beads, just to show that I had not forgotten the worthy Cadi's courtesy in bringing his little daughter to sit beside me at dinner when I went down the river last summer.

I saw the Cadi giving audience to several people, so I sent in the beads and my salaam; but the jolly Cadi sallied forth into the street, and 'fell upon my neck' with such ardour that my Frankish hat was sent rolling by contact with the turban of Islam.

The Cadi of Keneh is the real original Cadi of our early days; sleek, rubicund, polite—a puisne judge and a dean rolled into one, combining the amenities of the law and the church—with an orthodox stomach and an orthodox turban, both round and stately. I was taken into the hareem, welcomed and regaled, and invited to the festival of Seyd Abd er-Racheem, the great saint of Keneh. I hesitated, and said there were great crowds, and some might be offended at my presence; but the Cadi declared 'by Him who separated us' that if any such ignorant persons were present it was high time they learnt better, and said that it was by no means unlawful for virtuous Christians, and such as neither hated nor scorned the Muslimeen, to profit by, or share in their prayers, and that I should sit before the Shaikh's tomb with him and the Mufti; and that *du reste*, they wished to give thanks for my safe arrival.

Such a demonstration of tolerance was not to be resisted. So after going back to rest, and dine in the boat, I returned at nightfall into the town and went to the burial-place. The whole way was lighted up and thronged with the most motley crowd, and the usual mixture of holy and profane, which we know at the Catholic *fêtes* also; but more *prononcé* here. Dancing girls, glittering with gold brocade and coins, swaggered about among the brown-shirted fellaheen, and the profane singing of the *Alateeyeh* mingled with the songs in honour of the Arab prophet chanted by the *Moonsheeds* and the deep tones of the 'Allah, Allah' of the *Zikeers*. Rockets whizzed about and made the women screech, and a merry-go-round was in full swing.

And now fancy me clinging to the skirts of the Cadi ul Islam (who did not wear a spencer, as the Methodist parson threatened his congregation he would do at the Day of Judgement) and pushing into the tomb of the Seyd Abd er-Racheem, through such a throng. No one seemed offended or even surprised. I suppose my face is so well known at Keneh. When my party had said a *Fattah* for me and another for my family, we retired to another *kubbeh*, where there was no tomb, and where we found the Mufti, and sat there all the evening over coffee and pipes and talk. I was questioned about English administration of justice, and made to describe the process of trial by jury. The Mufti is a very dignified gentlemanly man, and extremely kind and civil. The Cadi pressed me to stay next day and dine with him and the Mufti, but I said I had a lantern for Luxor, and I wanted to arrive before the *moolid* was over, and only three days remained. So the Cadi accompanied me back to the boat, looked at my maps, which pleased him very much, traced out the line of the railway as he had heard it, and had tea.

Next morning we had the first good wind, and bowled up to Luxor in one day, arriving just after sunset. Instantly the boat was filled. Of course Omar and the Reis at once organized a procession to take me and my lantern to the tomb of Abu-l-Hajjaj—it was the last night but one of his *moolid*. The lantern was borne on a pole between two of my sailors, and the rest, reinforced by men from a steamer which was there with a Prussian prince, sung and thumped the tarabookeh, and we all marched up after I had undergone every variety of salutation, from Shaikh Yussuf's embrace to the little boys' kissing of hands.

The first thing I heard was the hearty voice of the old Shereef, who praised God that 'our darling' was safe back again, and then we all sat down for a talk; then more *Fattahs* were said for me, and for you, and for the children; and I went back to bed in my own boat. I found the guard of the French house had been taken off to Keneh to the works, after lying eight days in chains and wooden handcuffs for resisting, and claiming his rights as a French *protégé*. So we waited for his return, and for the keys which he had taken with him, in hopes that the Keneh authorities would not care to keep me out of the house. I wrote to the French Consular agent at Keneh, and to the Consul at Alexandria, and got him back the third day.

What would you think in Europe to see me welcome with enthusiasm a servant just out of chains and handcuffs? At the very moment, too, that Mohammed and I were talking, a boat passed up the river with musick and singing on board. It was a Shaikh-el-Beled, of a place above Esneh, who had lain in prison three years in Cairo, and whose friends were making all the fantasia they could to celebrate the end of his misfortune; of disgrace, *il n'en est pas question*; and why should it? So many honest men go to prison that it is no presumption at all against a man.

The day after my arrival was the great and last day. The crowd was but little and not lively—times are too hard. But the riding was beautiful.

I dined with the Maōhn, whose wife cooked me the best dinner I ever ate in this country, or almost anywhere. Marie, who was invited, rejoiced the kind old lady's heart by her German appreciation of the excellent cookery. 'Eat, my daughter, eat', and even I managed to give satisfaction. Such *bakloweh* I never tasted.

One Shaikh Alee—a very agreeable man from beyond Khartum, offers to take me up to Khartum and back with a *takherawan* (camel litter) in company with Mustapha Agha, Shaikh Yussuf and a troop of his own Abab'deh. It is a terrible temptation—but it would cost £50—so I refused. Shaikh Alee is so clever and well-bred that I should enjoy it much, and the climate at this season is delightful. He has been in the Dinka country where the men are a cubit taller than Shaikh Hassan whom you know, and who enquires tenderly after you.

Now let me describe the state of things. From the mudiriat of Keneh only, 25,000 men are taken to work for sixty days without food or pay; each man must take his own basket, and each third man a hoe, not a basket. If you want to pay a substitute for a beloved or delicate son, it costs 1,000 piastres—600 at the lowest; and about 300 to 400 for his food. From Luxor alone, 220 men are gone; of whom a third will very likely die of exposure to the cold and misery (the weather is unusually cold). That is to say that this little village, of at most 2,000 souls male and female (we don't usually count women, from decorum), will pay in labour at least £1,320 in sixty days. We have also already had eleven camels seized to go up to the Sudan; a camel is worth from £18 to £40.

Last year Mariette Bey made excavations at Gurna forcing the people to work but promising payment at the rate of—— Well, when he was gone the four Shaikhs of the village at Gurna came to Mustapha and begged him to advance the money due from Government, for the people were starving. Mustapha agrees and gives above 300 purses—about £1,000 in *current* piastres on the understanding that he is to get the money from Government in *tarif*—and to keep the difference as his profit. If he cannot get it at all the fellaheen are to pay him back without interest. Of course at the rate at which money is here, his profit would be but small interest on the money unless he could get the money directly, and he has now waited six months in vain.

Abdallah the son of el-Habbeshee of Damanhoor went up the river in chains to Fazogli a fortnight ago and Osman Bey ditto last week—El-Bedrawi is dead there, of course.

Shall I tell you what became of the hundred prisoners who were sent away after the Gau business? As they marched through the desert the Greek mameluke looked at his list each morning, and said, 'Hoseyn,

Ahmad, Foolan [like the Spanish Don Fulano, Mr so and so], you are free; take off his chains'. Well, the three or four men drop behind, where some arnouts strangle them out of sight. This is banishment to Fazogli. Do you remember *le citoyen est élargi* of the September massacres of Paris? Curious coincidence, is it not? Everyone is exasperated—the very hareem talk of the government. It is in the air. I had not been five minutes in Keneh before I knew all this and much more. Of the end of Hajji Sultan I will not speak till I have absolute certainty, but, I believe the proceeding was as I have described—set free in the desert and murdered by the way. I wish you to publish these facts; it is no secret to any but to those Europeans whose interests keep their eyes tightly shut, and they will soon have them opened. The blind rapacity of the present ruler will make him astonish the Franks some day, I think.

Wheat is now 400 piastres the ardeb up here; the little loaf, not quite so big as our penny roll, costs a piastre—about three-half-pence—and all in proportion. I need not say what the misery is. Remember that this is the second levy of 220 men within six months, each for sixty days, as well as the second seizure of camels; besides the conscription, which serves the same purpose, as the soldiers work on the Pasha's works. But in Cairo they are paid—and well paid.

It is curious how news travels here. The Luxor people knew the day I left Alexandria, and the day I left Cairo, long before I came. They say here that Abu-l-Hajjaj gave me his hand from Keneh, because he would not finish his moolid without me. I am supposed to be specially protected by him, as is proved by my health being so far better here than anywhere else.

By the bye, Shaikh Ali Abab'deh told me that all the villages *close* on the Nile escaped the cholera almost completely, whilst those who were half or a quarter of a mile inland were ravaged. At Keneh 250 a day died; at Luxor one child was supposed to have died of it, but I know he had diseased liver for a year or more. In the desert the Bishareen and Abab'deh suffered more than the people at Cairo, and you know the desert is usually the place of perfect health; but fresh Nile water seems to be *the* antidote. Shaikh Yussuf laid the mortality at Keneh to the canal water, which the poor people drink there. I believe the fact is as Shaikh Alee told me.

Now I will say good-bye, for I am tired. I was very poorly till I got above Assiut, and then gradually mended—constant blood spitting and great weakness and I am very thin, but by the protection of Abu-l-Hajjaj I suppose I am already much better and begin to eat again. I have not been out yet since the first day, having much to do in the house to get to rights. I felt very dreary on Christmas-day away from you all, and Omar's plum-pudding did not cheer me at all, as he hoped it would. He begs me to kiss your hand for him, and everyone sends you salaam, and all lament that you are not the new Consul at Cairo.

Kiss my chicks, and love to you all. Janet, I hope is in Egypt ere this.

January 3 1866. Darling Maurice. I was delighted to get your note, which arrived on New Year's day in the midst of the hubbub of the great festival in honour of the Saint of Luxor. I wish you could have seen two young Arabs (real Arabs from the Hedjaz, in Arabia) ride and play with spears and lances. I never saw anything like it—a man who played the tom-fool stood in the middle, and they galloped round and round him, with their spears crossed and the points resting on the ground, in so small a circle that his clothes whisked round with the wind of the horses' legs. Then they threw jereeds and caught them as they galloped: the beautiful thing was the perfect mastery of the horses: they were 'like water in their hands', as Shaikh Hassan remarked. I perceived that I had never seen *real* horsemanship in my life before.

I am now in the 'palace' at Luxor with my *dahabieh, Arooset al-Ghaliya* (the Darling Bride), under my windows; quite like a Pasha.

January 15. Dearest Alick. Two great Shaikhs of Bishareen and Abab'deh came here and picked me up out walking alone. We went and sat in a field, and they begged me to communicate to the Queen of England that they would join her troops if she would invade Egypt. One laid my hand on his hand and said 'Thou hast 3,000 men in thy hand'. The other rules 10,000. They say there are 30,000 Arabs (Beduin) ready to join the English, for they fear that the Viceroy will try to work and rob them like the fellaheen, and if so they will fight to the last, or else go off into Syria. I was rather frightened—for them, I mean, and told them that our Queen could do nothing till 600 Shaikhs and 400 Emirs had talked in public—all whose talk was printed and read at Stambool and Cairo, and that they must not think of such a thing from our Queen, but if things became bad, it would be better for them to go off into Syria. I urged great caution upon them, and I need not repeat that to you, as the lives of thousands may be endangered. Above all, do not mention a word to Ross or Janet, and take care whom you trust in England, if anyone. It might be interesting to be known in high places and in profound secret, as one of the indications of what is coming here. Do not answer about this as the post is not to be relied on and the espionage is now, I am told, very well done.[1]

If the saddle comes, as I hope, I may very likely go up to Aswan, and leave the boat and servants, and go into the desert for a few days to see the place of the Bishareen. They won't take anyone else: but you may be quite easy about me 'in the face' of a Shaikh-el-Arab. Handsome Shaikh Hassan, whom you saw at Cairo, will go with me. But if my saddle does not appear, I fear I should be too tired with riding a camel.

The little district of Koos, including Luxor, has been mulcted of camels, food for them and drivers, to the amount of 6,000 purses— last week—£18,000, in fact. I cast up the account, and it tallied with what I got from a sub *employé*, nor is the discontent any longer whispered. Everyone talks aloud—and well they may.

[1] When the British did invade Egypt in 1882 they failed to gain support among the Beduin or the Egyptians as a whole, since they made the mistake of supporting the oppressive and vacillating Khedive Tewfik, son of the exiled Ismail. They fought against the nationalist movement of Ahmed Arabi and others, described later by Lord Cromer as 'a genuine revolt against misgovernment'. (See Introduction pp. 5 and 7.)

XXXIII

On marriage, fatalism and medicine

Luxor, February 11 1866. Dearest Mother. I have just received your letter of Christmas Day and am glad to answer it with a really amended report of myself. Omar was so terrified by the attack I had at Cairo that he hardly lets me out of his sight, and sleeps on a mat outside my door to be ready to come to me when he hears me cough. He is vexed that I did not bring cupping glasses to put on my back in case of a fit of haemorrhage and has learnt all the medicines by heart. He was so ill with chronic dysentery that I took it upon myself to forbid him to fast at Ramadan this year, whereby I incur the pains and penalties of his omission, if omission it be. I sent for one of the Arab doctors of the Azizeeyeh steamer to see Omar, and myself also, and he was very attentive, and took a note of medicines to send me from Cairo by a *confrère:* and when I offered a fee he said, 'God forbid—it is only our duty to do anything in the world for you'. Likewise a very nice Dr Ingram saw some of my worst cases for me, and gave me good advice and help; but I want better books—Kesteven is very useful, as far as it goes, but I want something more *ausführlich* [detailed] and scientific.

Ramadan is a great trouble to me, though Shaikh Yussuf tells the people not to fast, if I forbid it: but many are ill from having begun it, and one fine old man of about fifty-five died of apoplexy on the fourth night. My Christian patient is obstinate, and fasts, in spite of me, and will, I think, seal his fate; he was so much better after the blistering and Dr Ingram's mixture. I wish you could have seen a lad of eighteen or so, who came here today for medicine. I think I never saw such sweet frank, engaging manners, or ever heard anyone express himself better: quite *une nature distinguée,* not the least

247

handsome, but the most charming countenance and way of speaking.

My good friend the Maōhn spent the evening with me, and told me all the story of his marriage, though quite 'unfit to meet the virtuous eyes of British propriety—' as I read the other day in some paper apropos of I forget what—it will give you an idea of the feelings of a Muslim *honnête homme,* which Seleem is through and through.

He knew his wife before he married her, she being twenty-five or twenty-six, and he a boy; she fell in love with him, and at seventeen he married her, and they have had ten children, all alive but two, and a splendid race they are. He told me how she courted him with glasses of sherbet and trays of sweatmeats, and how her mother proposed the marriage, and how she hesitated on account of the difference of age, but, of course, at last consented: all with the naïvest vanity in his own youthful attractions, and great extolling of her personal charms, and of her many virtues. When he was sent up here she would not, or could not, leave her children.

Seleem related how, being a very healthy man and not old (46) he was assailed by such fearful temptations that he was constantly forced to ask pardon of God for his wicked thoughts at sight of a woman, and how, from terror lest he should commit some offence quite unpardonable in a religious man, he bought the black slave girl who was the only woman he had ever known in his life besides the Sitt, his wife.

On his wife's arrival his slave girl was arrogant, and refused to kiss her hand, and spoke saucily of her age, whereupon Seleem gave her in marriage to a black man and pays for her support, as long as she likes to suckle the child he (Seleem) had by her, which child will in due time return to his house.

In short, the fundamental idea in it all, in the mind of an upright man, is, that if a man 'takes up' with a woman at all, he must make himself responsible for her before the world, and above all for the fate of any child he may have by her. (You see the Prophet of the Arabs did not contemplate ladies *qui savent nager* so well in the troubled waters of life as we are now blessed with. I don't mean to say that many men are as scrupulous as my excellent friend Seleem, either here or even in our own moral society.) All this was told with expressions quite incompatible with our manners, though not at all *leste*—and he expatiated on his wife's personal charms in a very quaint way; the good lady is now hard upon sixty and looks it fully; but he evidently is as fond of her as ever. As a curious trait of primitive manners, he told me of her piety and boundless hospitality; how when some friends came late one evening, unexpectedly, and there was only a bit of meat, she killed a sheep and cooked it for them with her own hands. And this is a Cairene lady, and quite a lady too, in manners and appearance.

The day I dined there she was dressed in very ragged, old cotton clothes, but spotlessly clean; and she waited on me with a kind, motherly pleasure, that quite took away the awkwardness I felt at sitting down while she stood. In a few days she and her husband are to dine with me, a thing which no Arab couple ever did before (I mean dine out together), and the old lady was immensely amused at the idea. Omar will cook and all male visitors will be sent to the kitchen. Now that I understand all that is said to me, and a great deal of the general conversation, it is much more amusing. Seleem Effendi jokes me a great deal about my blunders, especially my lack of *politikeh,* the Greek word for what we should call flummery; and my saying *laẕim* (you must, or rather *il faut*), instead of humble entreaties. I told him to teach me better, but he laughed heartily, and said, 'No, no, when you say *laẕim,* it is *laẕim,* and nobody wants the stick to force him to say *hadr* (ready) O Shaikh-el-Arab, O Emeereh'.

Fancy my surprise the other day, just when I was dictating letters to Shaikh Yussuf (letters of introduction for Ross's inspecting agent) with three or four other people here, in walked Miss Marianne North[1] whom I have not seen since she was a child. She and her father were going up the second cataract. She has done some sketches which, though rather unskilful, were absolutely true in colour and effect, and are the very first that I have seen that are so. I shall see something of them on their return. She seemed very pleasant. Mr North looked rather horrified at the turbaned society in which he found himself. I suppose it did look odd to English eyes.

We have had three days of the south wind, which the *Saturday Review* says I am not to call Samoom; and I was poorly, and kept in bed two days with a cold.

We have just had a scene, rather startling to notions about fatalism,

[1] Miss Marianne North, 1830–90, had had a great admiration for Lucie when as a girl Lucie used to come to stay with her parents; (Introduction p. 15–16.) Miss North had developed into a talented naturalist and it was her knowledge and observation which made her paintings of flowers so valuable. On her father's death in 1869 she decided to travel widely to paint the flora of South America, Australia, New Zealand, Japan, Borneo, Ceylon, India, South Africa and of other places. Her magnificent collection of paintings are in the gallery at Kew which was opened in 1882.

etc. Owing to the importation of a good deal of cattle from the Sudan, there is an expectation of the prevalence of small-pox, and the village barbers are busy vaccinating in all directions to prevent the infection brought, either by the cattle or, more likely, by their drivers. Now, my maid had told me she had never been vaccinated, and I sent for Hajji Mahmood to cut my hair and vaccinate her. To my utter amazement the girl, who had never shown any religious bigotry and does not fast, or make any demonstrations, refused peremptorily.

It appears that the priests and sisters appointed by the enlightened administration of Prussia instil into their pupils and penitents that vaccination is a 'tempting of God'. *Oh oui*, she said, *je sais bien que chez nous mes parents pouvaient recevoir un procès verbal, mais il vaut mieux cela que d'aller contre la volonté de Dieu. Si Dieu le veut, j'aurai la petite-vérole, et s'il ne veut pas, je ne l'aurai pas.* I scolded her pretty sharply, and said it was not only stupid, but selfish.

'But what can one do?' as Hajji Mahmood said, with a pitying shake of his head; 'these Christians are so ignorant!' He blushed, and apologized to me, and said, 'It is not their fault; all this want of sense is from the priests who talk folly to them for money, and to keep them afraid before themselves. Poor things, *they* don't know the Word of God.—"Help thyself, oh my servant, and I will help thee".' This is the second contest I have had on this subject. Last year it was with a Copt, who was all *Allah kereem* and so on about his baby, with his child of four dying of small-pox. 'Oh, man' said Shaikh Yussuf, 'if the wall against which I am now sitting were to shake above my head, should I fold my feet under me and say *Allah kereem*, or should I use the legs God has given me to escape from it?'

I had a visit the other day from a lady who, as I was informed, had been a harlot in Assiut. She has repented, and married a converted Copt. They are a droll pair of penitents, so very smart in their dress and manner. But no one *se scandalise* at their antecedents—neither is it proper to repent in sackcloth and ashes, or to confess sins, except to God alone. You are not to *indulge* in telling them to others; it is an offence. Repent inwardly, and be ashamed to show it before the people—ask pardon of God only. A little of this would do no harm in Europe.

February 15. I await a saddle I can use for a horse to visit the Ababdeh up the river, whose Chief is a lady; her son takes me.

A young French gentleman has arrived with letters from the French Consul. He turns out to be a Monsieur Brune *grand prix de*

Rome, an architect, and is a very nice fellow indeed, and a thorough gentleman. At first his manner was awkward at finding himself quartered on a stranger, and a woman; but we have made great friends, and I have made him quite happy by telling him that he shall pay his share of the food. He was going to hurry off from shyness though he had begun a work here by which I fancy he hopes to get kudos. I see he is poor and very properly proud. He goes out to the temple at sunrise, and returns to dinner at dark, and works well, and his drawings are very clever. In short, I am as much obliged to the French Consul for sending me such an intelligent man as I was vexed at first. An *homme sérieux* with an absorbing pursuit is always good company in the long run. Moreover M. Brune behaves like a perfect gentleman in every way. So *tout est pour le mieux.*

XXXIV

The problem of having European maids

Luxor, February 15 1866. Dearest Mother. I am sorry to say that Marie has become so excessively bored, dissatisfied, and, she says, ill, that I am going to send her back rather than be worried so—and *damit hats eine ende* [and that's the end] of European maids. Of course an ignorant girl *must* be bored to death here—a land of no amusements and no flirtation *is* unbearable.

I shall borrow a slave of a friend here, an old black woman who is quite able and more than willing to serve me, and when I go down to Cairo I will get either a *ci-devant* slave or an elderly Arab woman. Dr Patterson strongly advised me to do so last year. He has one who has been thirteen years his housekeeper, an old Beduin, I believe, and as I now am no longer looked upon as a foreigner, I shall be able to get a respectable Arab woman, a widow or a divorced woman of a certain age who will be too happy to have 'a good home', as our maids say. I shall be taken good care of if I fall ill, much better than I should get from a European in a sulky frame of mind.

Hajji Ali has very kindly offered to take Marie down to Cairo and start her off to Alexandria whence Ross's people can send her home. If she wants to stay in Alexandria and get placed by the nuns who piously exhorted her to extort ninety francs a month from me, so much the better for me. Ali refuses to take a penny from me for her journey—besides bringing me potatoes and all sorts of things: and if I remonstrate he says he and all his family and all they have is mine, in consequence of my treatment of his brother.

February 22. Dearest Janet. In case Marie arrives with this letter please pay her hotel bill for me and let her have the money to travel home to Frankfurt second class per rail right through. Should she want to stay with you, I advise you to decline, and also don't be so foolishly good-natured and hospitable and take her into your house. She will turn the head of your new German maid. Also don't send your German maid, if a Catholic, to confess at the Church of the Sisters of Charity.

Marie's idea of happiness is a rollicking hotel life such as, I fancy, she had at Spa. If I had known she had been servant in an hotel at a German watering place, I would not have taken her. She is thoroughly cunning and boundlessly wasteful and greedy. I only say this for your information in case you should think of taking her. You know I hate rows and allow her to say that she leaves me of her own accord, which is, indeed, true. She is mad with impatience to be gone.

Luxor. A certain Baron Clary, who came here in a steamer lent him by the Khedive, has taken Marie down to Cairo and very possibly will take her on further as maid to the ladies of his party. I did not see them and they asked me no questions, so I did not feel bound to volunteer information as to her conduct, so if she keeps herself decent for a few weeks, I shall save the expense of her journey home. At all events she gets to Cairo for nothing. I have not yet got any woman.

That donkey Abdurrachman Effendi offered to sell me an Abyssinian cheap because she would not sleep with him, but I don't care for a girl out of a regular dirty Turkish house, all mess and confusion. Little Ahmad has grown very clever and Omar has developed a talent for ironing of which I was unaware, and we do very well indeed. You need be under no fear for my health, for while Marie was with me, the care of me in illness always devolved upon Omar, so in that respect I am no worse off.

A letter came for Marie directed to me only, and consequently I opened it and had read enough, before I found who it was meant for, to edify me sufficiently. It was from her mother reproaching her with owing money to people at home for two years and never paying a sou—(Marie told me she had sent home all the money I gave her and nearly all her wages), and desiring her to send something towards the support of her child, whom she seemed to have quite forgotten while she was '*à s'amuser et à fricasser ses florins et ses francs à l'étranger*'. Marie was a regular prostitute, and your maid much the same I suppose.

It is something curious to see the sort of terror that Marie's kind of badness inspired here; that she should plunder and drink, *passe encore*, and that she should be loose in her morals; but the European style of abusing me and making faces behind my back, and trying to set my household against me—in short, the vulgar servant view of the master as a natural enemy—struck absolute dismay among my hangers-on, paid and unpaid. 'That is a daughter of the devil', and God was praised at her departure throughout the place. She had inspired a sort of terror in everyone except my Reis who, being half a Nubian, is not afraid of Europeans and simply called her a *sharmuta*, literally *torchon*, and with the same second meaning that the French word conveys.

I have come to the unpleasant conclusion that we don't know the lives of our servant maids at home. Ali, one of the steadiest dragoman of Egypt has for some years utterly refused all engagements with ladies, 'because where there are ladies there is a maid, and I fall in it somehow. If I refuse her she tells lies of me all the way, and if I do as she likes, there is some mischief'. Ali is rather young and very handsome and his experience comes to that.

These are not women 'corrupted by a long stay in the East', but 'maids' who come for three months. The American missionaries' wives have ended, like me, in having only men and boys after no end of distress from European maids.

You will be amused and pleased to hear how Shaikh Yussuf was utterly puzzled and bewildered by the civilities he received from the travellers this year, till an American told Mustapha I had written a book which had made him (the American) wish well to the poor people of this country, and desire to behave more kindly to them than would have been the case before.

Tomorrow is the smaller Bairam, and I shall have all the hareem here to visit me.

Two such nice Englishmen called the other day and told me they lived in Hertford Street opposite Lady Duff Gordon's and saw Alexander go in and out, and met Maurice in the gardens. It gave me a terrible twinge of *Heimweh* [home-sickness], but I thought it so kind and pretty and *herzlich* [touching] of them to come and tell me how Alexander and Maurice looked as they went along the street.

February 22. Dearest Alick. There have not been above twenty or thirty boats up this year—mostly Americans. There are some here now, very nice people. The weather here is just beginning to get warm, and I of course to get better. There has been a good deal of nervous headache here this Ramadan. I had to attend the Cadi, and several more. My Turkish neighbour at Karnac has got a *shaitan* (devil), *i.e.* epileptic fits, and I was sent for to exorcise him, which I am endeavouring to do with nitrate of silver, etc.; but I fear imagination will kill him, so I advise him to go to Cairo, and leave the devil-haunted house. I have this minute killed the first snake of this year—a sign of summer.

I hope you will get this as old fat Hassan will take it to the office in Cairo himself, for the post is very insecure indeed. I have written very often; if you don't get my letters, I suppose they interest the court of Pharaoh.

March 17. I went a few days ago out to Medamoot, and lunched in Mustapha's tent, among his bean harvest. I was immensely amused by the man who went with me on to Medamoot, one Sheriff, formerly an illustrious robber, now a watchman and very honest man. He rode a donkey, about the size of Stirling's wee pony, and I laughed, and said, 'The man should carry the ass'. No sooner said than done, Sheriff dismounted, or rather let his beast down from between his legs, shouldered the donkey, and ran on.

His way of keeping awake is original; the nights are still cold, so he takes off all his clothes, rolls them up and lays them under his head, and the cold keeps him quite lively. I never saw so powerful, active and healthy an animal. He was full of stories how he had had 1,000 stripes of the courbash on his feet and 500 on his loins at one go. 'Why?' I asked. 'Why, I stuck a knife into a *cawass* who ordered me to carry water-melons; I said I was not his donkey; he called me worse: my blood got up, and so!—and the Pasha to whom the *cawass* belonged beat me. Oh, it was all right, and I did not say "ach" once, did I?' (addressing another). He clearly bore no malice, as he felt no shame. He has a grand romance about a city two days' journey from here, in the desert, which no one finds but by chance, after losing his way; and where the ground is strewed with valuable *anteekehs* (antiquities). I laughed, and said, 'Your father would have seen gold and jewels'. 'True', said he, 'when I was young, men spat on a statue or the like, when they turned it up in digging, and now it is a fortune to find one'.

March 31. As for me I am much better again; the cough has subsided, I really think the Arab specific, camel's milk, has done me great good. I have mended ever since I took it.

Yesterday I was much amused when I went for my afternoon's drink, to find Sheriff in a great taking at having been robbed by a woman, under his very nose. He saw her gathering hummuz from a field under his charge, and went to order her off, whereupon she coolly dropped the end of her *boordeh* which covered her head and shoulders, effectually preventing him from going near her; made up her bundle and walked off. His respect for the hareem did not, however, induce him to refrain from strong language.

Mr Brune has made very pretty drawings of the mosque here, both outside and in; it is a very good specimen of modern Arab architecture; and he won't believe it could be built without ground plan, elevations, etc., which amuses the people here, who build without any such inventions.

The harvest here is splendid this year, such beans and wheat, and prices have fallen considerably in both: but meat, butter, etc., remain very dear.

My fame as a doctor has become far too great, and on market-days I have to shut up shop. Yesterday a very handsome woman came for medicine to make her beautiful, as her husband had married another who teased her, and he rather neglected her. And a man offered me a camel load of wheat if I would read something over him and his wife to make them have children. I don't try to explain to them how very irrational they are but use the more intelligible argument that all such practices savour of the *Ebu er Rukkeh* (equivalent to black art), and are *haram* to the greatest extent; besides, I add, being 'all lies' into the bargain. The applicants for child-making and charm-reading are Copts or Muslims, quite in equal numbers, and appear alike indifferent as to what 'Book': but all but one have been women; the men are generally perfectly rational about medicine and diet.

I find there is a good deal of discontent among the Copts with regard to their priests and many of their old customs. Several young men have let out to me at a great rate about the folly of their fasts, and the badness and ignorance of their priests. I believe many turn Muslim from a real conviction that it is a better religion than their own, and not as I at first thought merely from interest; indeed, they seldom gain much by it, and often suffer tremendous persecution from their families; even they do not escape the rationalizing tendencies now abroad in Christendom. Then their early and indissoluble marriages are felt to be a hardship: a boy is married at eight years old, perhaps to his cousin aged seventeen (I know one here in that case), and when he grows up he wishes it had been let alone.

A clever lad of seventeen propounded to me his dissatisfaction, and seemed to lean to Islam. I gave him an Arabic New Testament, and told him to read that first, and judge for himself whether he could not still conform to the Church of his own people, and inwardly believe and try to follow the Gospels. I told him it was what most Christians had to do, as every man could not make a sect for himself, while few could believe everything in any Church. I suppose I ought to have offered him the Thirty-nine Articles, and thus have made a Muslim of him out of hand. He pushed me a little hard about several matters, which he says he does *not* find in 'the Book': but on the whole he is well satisfied with my advice.

Coptic Palm Sunday, April 1. We hear that Fadil Pasha received orders at Aswan to go up to Khartum in Giaffar Pasha's place: it is a civil way of killing a fat old Turk, if it is true. He was here a week or two ago. My informant is one of my old crew who was in Fadil Pasha's boat.

My medical reputation has become far too great, and all my common drugs—Epsom salts, senna, aloes, rhubarb, quassia—run short. Especially do all the poor, tiresome, ugly old women adore me, and bore me with their aches and pains. They are always the doctor's greatest plague. To one old body I gave a powder wrapped up in a fragment of a *Saturday Review*. She came again and declared *mash-allah!* the *hegab* (charm) was a powerful one, for though she had not been able to wash off all the fine writing from the paper, even that little had done her a deal of good. I regret that I am unable to inform you what was the subject of the article in the *Saturday* which had so drastic an effect.

The mark of confidence is that they now bring the sick children, which was never known before, I believe, in these parts. I am sure it would pay a European doctor to set up here; the people would pay him a little, and there would be good profit from the boats in the winter. I got turkeys when they were worth six or eight shillings apiece in the market, and they were forced upon me by the fellaheen.

Bairam, April. Dearest Mother. I write this to go down by Mr Palgrave. He has been with Mustapha Bey conducting an enquiry into Mustapha Agha's business. Mariette Bey struck Mustapha, and I and some Americans took it ill and wrote a very strong complaint to our respective Consuls. Mariette denied the blow and the words 'liar, and son of a dog'—so the American and English Consuls sent up Palgrave as commissioner to enquire into the affair, and the Pasha sent Mustapha Bey with him. Palgrave is very amusing of course, and his knowledge of languages is wonderful. Shaikh Yussuf says few *Ulema* know as much of the literature and niceties of grammar and composition. Mustapha Bey is a darling; he knew several friends of mine, Hassan Effendi, Mustapha Bey Soubky, and others, so we were friends directly.

I have not yet got a woman-servant, but I don't miss one at all; little Ahmad is very handy, Mahommed's slave girl washes, and Omar irons and cleans the house and does housemaid, and I have kept on the meek cook, Abd el-Kader, whom I took while the Frenchman was here. I had not the heart to send him away; he is such a *meskeen*. He was a smart travelling waiter, but his brother died, leaving a termagant widow with four children, and poor Abd el-Kader felt it his duty to bend his neck to the yoke, married her, and has two more children. He is a most worthy, sickly, terrified creature.

I have heard that a decent Copt here wants to sell a black woman owing to reverses of fortune, and that she might suit me. Shaikh Yussuf is to negotiate the affair and to see if the woman herself likes me for a mistress, and I am to have her on trial for a time, and if I like her and she me, Shaikh Yussuf will buy her with my money in his name. I own I have very little scruple about the matter, as I should consider her price as an advance of two or three years' wages and tear the paper of sale as soon as she had worked her price out, which I think would be a fair bargain. But I must see first whether Feltass (the Copt) really wants to sell her or only to get a larger price than is fair, in which case I will wait till I go to Cairo. Anything is better than importing a European who at once thinks one is at her mercy on account of the expense of the journey back.

Dearest Janet. You have never told me your plans for this year or whether I shall find you when I go down. The last three days the great heat has begun and I am accordingly feeling better. I have just come home from the Bairam early prayer out in the burial-place, at which Palgrave also assisted. He is unwell, and tells me he leaves Luxor tomorrow morning. I shall stay on till I am too hot here, as evidently the summer suits me.

Many thanks for Miss Berry and for the wine, which makes a very pleasant change from the rather bad claret I have got. Palgrave's book I have read through hard, as he wished to take it back for you. It is very amusing.[1]

---

[1] William Gifford Palgrave (1826–1888) served in the East India Company as a soldier after a brilliant scholastic career at Oxford. He left the army to become a Roman Catholic

If you come here next winter Mustapha hopes you will bring a saddle, and ride 'all his horses'. I think I could get you a very good horse from a certain Shaikh Abdallah here.

May 10. Dearest Alick. The real summer heat—the *Shems el-Kebeer* (big sun) has fairly set in, and of course I am all the better. You would give my camel a good backsheesh if you saw how prodigiously fat I have grown on her milk; it beats codliver-oil hollow. You can drink a gallon without feeling it, it is so easy of digestion.

I have lent the *dahabieh* to Mustapha and to one or two more, to go to Keneh on business, and when she returns (which will be today) I shall make ready to depart too, and drop down stream. Omar wants me to go down to Damietta, to 'amuse my mind and dilate my stomach' a little; and I think of doing so.

Palgrave was here about a fortnight ago, on Mustapha's and Mariette's business. 'By God! this English way is wonderful,' said a witness, 'that English Bey questioned me till my stomach came out.' *Entre nous*, I did not much like Palgrave. I loved Mustapha Bey, who was with him; such a nice, kind, gentle creature, and very intelligent and full of good sense. I rejoice to hear that he returns my liking, and has declared himself 'one of my darweeshes'. Talking of darweeshes reminds me of the Festival of Shaikh Gibriel this year. I had forgotten the day, but in the evening some people came for me to go and eat some of the meat of the Shaikh, who is also a good patron of mine, they say; being a poor man's saint, and of a humble spirit, it is said he favours me. There was plenty of meat and *melocheea* and bread; and then *zikrs* of different kinds, and a *Gama el Fokara* (assembly of the poor). *Gama* is the true word for Mosque—*i.e.*, Meeting, which consists in a great circle of men seated thick on the ground, with two poets facing each other, who improvise religious verses.

On this occasion the rule of the game was to end each stanza with a word having the sound of *wahed* (one), or *el had* (the first). Thus one sung: 'Let a man take heed how he walks', etc., etc.; and 'pray to God not to let him fall', which sound like *had*. And so they went on, each chanting a verse alternately. One gesticulated almost as much as an Italian and pronounced beautifully; the other was quiet, but had a nice voice, and altogether it was very pretty. At the end of

---

priest and served in India, Syria and Arabia as a Jesuit missionary. In 1865 he published *A Narrative of a Year's Journey through Central and Eastern Arabia*, the book that he lent Lucie to read. When he came to Egypt he was in the employment of the British Foreign Office.

each verse the people made a sort of chorus, which was sadly like the braying of asses. The *zikr* of the Edfu men was very curious. Our people did it quietly, and the *moonsheed* sang very sweetly—indeed 'the song of the *moonsheed* is the sugar in the sherbet to the *Zikkeer*', said a man who came up when it was over, streaming with perspiration and radiant with smiles. Some day I will write to you the whole *'grund Idee'* of a *zikr*, which is, in fact, an attempt to make present 'the communion of saints', dead or living. As I write arrives the *Arooset al-Galiya,* and my crew furl her big sail quite 'Bristol fashion'. My men have come together again, some from Nubia and some from the Delta; and I shall go down with my old lot.

Omar and Ahmad have implored me not to take another maid at all; they say they live like Pashas now they have only the lady to please; that it will be a pleasure to 'lick my shoes clean', whereas the boots of the *cameriera* were intolerable. The feeling of the Arab servants towards European colleagues is a little like that of 'niggers' about 'mean whites'—mixed hatred, fear, and scorn.

The two have done so well to make me comfortable that I have no possible reason for insisting on encumbering myself with 'an old man of the sea', in the shape of a maid; and the difference in cost is immense. The one dish of my dinner is ample relish to their bread and beans, while the cooking for a maid, and her beer and wine, cost a great deal. Omar irons my clothes very tidily, and little Ahmad cleans the house as nicely as possible. I own I am quite as much relieved by the absence of the 'civilized element' as my retainers are.

I went the other day to the old church six or eight miles off, where they buried the poor old Bishop who died a week ago. Abu Khom, a Christian *shaheed* (martyr), is buried there. He appeared to Mustapha's father when lost in the desert, and took him safe home. On that occasion he was well mounted, and robed all in white, with a *litham* over his face. No one dares to steal anything near his tomb, not one ear of corn. He revealed himself long ago to one of the descendants of Abu-l-Hajjaj, and to this day every Copt who marries in Luxor gives a pair of fowls to the family of that Muslim in remembrance of Abu Khom.

I shall leave Luxor in five or six days—and write now to stop all letters in Cairo.

I don't know what to do with my sick; they come from forty miles off, and sometimes twenty or thirty people sleep outside the house.

XXXV

'The Khedive is nearly bankrupt'

Cairo, June and July 1866. Dearest Mother. The heat, when I left Luxor, was prodigious. I was detained three days by the death of Shaikh Yussuf's poor little wife and baby (in childbirth) so I was forced to stay and eat the funeral feast, and be present at the *Khatmeh* (reading of the Koran on the third night), or it would not have seemed kind. The Cadi gave me a very curious prayer-book, the Guide of the Faithful, written in Darfur! in beautiful characters, and with very singular decorations, and in splendid binding. It contains the names of all the prophets and of the hundred appellations of Mohammed, and is therefore a powerful *hegab* or talisman. He requested me never to give it away and always to keep it with me. Such books cannot be bought with money at all. I also bought a most beautiful *hegab* of cornelian set in enamel, the verse of the throne splendidly engraved, and dated 250 years ago. I sent over by Palgrave to Alick, M. Brune's lovely drawings of Luxor and Karnac.

It was so hot that I could not face the ride up to Keneh, when all my friends there came to fetch me, nor could I go to Assiut. I never felt such heat. At Benisuef I went to see our Maōhn's daughter married to another Maōhn there; it was a pleasant visit. The master of the house was out, and his mother and wife received me like one of the family; such a pretty woman and such darling children!—a pale, little slight girl of five, a sturdy boy of four, and a baby of one year old. The eager hospitality of the little creatures was quite touching. The little girl asked to have on her best frock, and then she stood before me and fanned me seriously and diligently, and asked every now and then, 'Shall I make thee a sherbet?' 'Shall I bring thee a coffee?' and then questions about grandpapa and grandmamma, and Abd el-

Hameed and Abd el-Fattah; while the boy sat on his heels before me and asked questions about my family in his baby talk, and assured me it was a good day to him, and wanted me to stay three days, and to sleep with them.

Their father came in and gave each an ashara (10 foddahs, ½ piastre) which, after consulting together, they tied in the corner of my hand-kerchief, 'to spend on my journey'. The little girl took such care of my hat and gloves and shoes, all very strange garments to her, but politeness was stronger than curiosity with the little things. I break-fasted with them all next day, and found much cookery going on for me. I took a doll for my little friend Ayoosheh, and some sugar-plums for Mohammed, but they laid them aside in order to devote themselves to the stranger, and all quietly, and with no sort of show-off or obtrusiveness. Even the baby seemed to have the instinct of hospitality, and was full of smiles.

It was all of a piece with the good old lady, their grandmother at Luxor, who wanted to wash my clothes for me herself, because I said the black slave of Mohammed washed badly. Remember that to do 'menial offices' for a guest is an honour and pleasure, and not dero-gatory at all here. The ladies cook for you, and say, 'I will cook my best for thee'. The worst is that they stuff one so. Little Ayoosheh asked after my children, and said, 'May God preserve them for thee! Tell thy little girl that Mohammed and I love her from afar off'. Whereupon Mohammed declared that in a few years, please God, when he should be *balal* (marriageable) he would marry her and live with me. When I went back to the boat the Effendi was ill with asthma, and I would not let him go with me in the heat (a polite man accom-panies an honoured guest back to his house or boat, or tent). So the little boy volunteered, and we rode off on the Effendi's donkey, which I had to bestride, with Mohammed on the hump of the saddle before me. He was delighted with the boat, of course, and romped and played about till we sailed, when his slave took him home. Those children gave me quite a happy day with their earnest, gracious hospitality.

I am very comfortable here, anchored off Boulaq, with my Reis and one sailor who cleans and washes my clothes which Omar irons, as at Luxor, as he found the washerwomen here charged five francs a dozen for all small things and more for dresses. A bad *hashash* boy turned Ahmad's head, who ran away for two days and spent a dollar

in riotous living; he returned penitent, and got no fatted calf, but dry
bread and a confiscation of his new clothes.

Off Boulaq, Cairo, July 10 1866. I have been shamefully lazy of
late: what with feeling unwell and what with finding such an alarming
state of things as to Ross's affairs when I arrived, that I was quite
knocked down and really could not screw up courage to write at all.
I hope now the worst is over and that Ross will tide over these terrible
difficulties. Is it not a strange thing that so many intelligent Europeans
should have been led by the nose by a 'Turkish mule' all this time,
and have gone on extolling the 'administrative talents' of a rapacious
tyrant until the day when they felt his claws? No-one is paid now; all
pensions and salaries are three months in arrears; the soldiers and
workmen unpaid; a forced loan of £3,000 each on five hundred
villages—in short universal ruin and distress. The poor Shaikh el-
Howara, the last Arab Grand Seigneur at Girga, is, I hear, to go to
Fazogli and all his lands seized. The Pasha is nearly bankrupt; even
pensions of sixty piastres a month (seven shillings) to poor old female
slaves of Mahommed Ali are stopped.[1]

I have got a very fine lion's head of granite which I will send to
Alexandria in a cargo boat; whenever there is a chance you can have
it over. I have also a lovely broken face, but I can't part with it, I
love it so; likewise a little god in black touch-stone, and some very
good scarabaei—all presents from my patients at Luxor.

Dearest Maurice. I send you a [gold] Roman coin which a man gave

---

[1] The Egyptian Commercial and Trading Company was hit very hard by the crisis.
One of the company's directors in London wrote on May 24 1866, 'the evil from which
we are suffering . . . comes down to this, that our manager in Alexandria has taken on too
many affairs'. On 'Black Friday', May 11, when several banks closed, creditors were
besieging the doors in London of the Egyptian Commercial and Trading Company.
Henry Ross was seriously ill and Janet went to London to see what help she could give.
She found, according to her account, the London board of the company at a loss to know
what to do, and she obtained their authority to take what action she could. Thereupon
she went to see her friend Henry Layard, who was then Under-Secretary for Foreign
Affairs, and persuaded him to telegraph to the British Consul-General in Egypt; 'the
result was that part of the money owing by the Egyptian Government was sent over by
the next mail'. (*The Fourth Generation.*)
It was the beginning of the end for the Egyptian Commercial and Trading Company
which had started with such high hopes. Henry and Janet Ross returned to Egypt for a
time and then settled in Italy.
In spite of the fact that the Viceroy Ismail was besieged by creditors and the country
was near bankruptcy, he visited Constantinople in April and May 1866 and obtained from
the Sultan, at a very high cost, the right to pass the succession to his son thus breaking
the Turkish custom that the succession passed to the eldest relative. In the next year the
Sultan granted him the title of Khedive instead of Wali or Viceroy, also a great expense.

me as a fee for medical attendance. I hope you will like it for your watch-chain. I made our Coptic goldsmith bore a hole in it.

Why don't you write to me, you young rascal? I am now living in my boat, and I often wish for you here to donkey ride about with me. I can't write you a proper letter now as Omar is waiting to take this up to Mr Palgrave with the drawings for your father. Omar desires his best salaam to you and to Rainie, and is very much disappointed that you are not coming out in the winter to go up to Luxor. We had a hurricane coming down the Nile, and a boat behind us sank. We only lost an anchor, and had to wait and have it fished up by the fishermen of a neighbouring village. In places the water was so shallow that the men had to push the boat over by main force, and all went into the river. The captain and I shouted out, *Islam el Islam*, equivalent to, 'Heave away, boys'. There are splendid illuminations about to take place here, because the Pasha has got leave to make his youngest boy his successor, and people are ordered to rejoice, which they do with much grumbling—it will cost something enormous.

July 14. Dearest Alick. I have had the boat topsy-turvy, with a carpenter and a *menegget* (cushion-stuffer), and had not a corner even to write in. I am, however, much better, and have quite got over the nervous depression which made me feel unable and ashamed to write.

My young carpenter—a Christian—half Syrian, half Copt, of the Greek rite, and altogether a Cairene—would have pleased you. He would not work on Sunday, but instead, came mounted on a splendid tall black donkey, and handsomely dressed, to pay me a visit, and go out with me for a ride. So he, I, and Omar went up to the Sittee (Lady) Zeyneb's mosque, to inquire for Mustapha Bey Soubky, the Hakeem Pasha, whom I had known at Luxor. I was told by the porter of the mosque to seek him at the shop of a certain grocer, his particular friend, where he sits every evening. On going there we found the shop with its lid shut down (a shop is like a box laid on its side with the lid pulled up when open and dropped when shut; as big as a cobbler's stall in Europe). The young grocer was being married, and Mustapha Bey was ill. So I went to his house in the quarter—such narrow streets!—and was shown up by a young eunuch into the hareem, and found my old friend very poorly, but spent a pleasant evening with him, his young wife—a Georgian slave whom he had married—his daughter by a former wife—whom he had married when he was fourteen, and the female dwarf buffoon of the Valideh Pasha (Ismail's mother), whose heart I won by rising to her, because she was so old and deformed. The other women laughed, but the little old dwarf liked it. She was a Circassian, and seemed clever. You see how the 'Thousand and One Nights' are quite true and real; how great Beys sit with grocers, and carpenters have no hesitation in offering civility to *naas omra* (noble people). This is what makes Arab society quite unintelligible and impossible to most Europeans.

My carpenter's boy was the son of a *moonsheed* (singer in the Mosque), and at night he used to sit and warble to us, with his little baby-voice, and little round, innocent face, the most violent love-songs. He was about eight years old, and sang with wonderful finish and precision, but no expression, until I asked him for a sacred song, which begins, 'I cannot sleep for longing for thee, O Full Moon' (the Prophet), and then the little chap warmed to his work, and the feeling came out.

Palgrave has left Egypt and I am to inherit his little black servant Mabrook, whom he left ill at Luxor in Mustapha's house. The child told me he was a *nyan-nyan* (cannibal), but he did not look ogreish. I have written to Mustapha to send him me by the first opportunity. Ahmad has quite recovered his temper, and I do so much better without a maid that I shall remain so. The difference in expense is enormous, and the peace and quiet a still greater gain; no more grumbling and 'exigencies' and worry; Omar irons very fairly, and the sailor washes well enough, and I don't want toilette—anyhow, I would rather wear a sack than try the experiment again. An uneducated, coarse-minded European is too disturbing an element in the family life of Easterns; the sort of filial relation, at once familiar and reverential of servants to a master they like, is odious to English and still more to French servants. If I fall in with an Arab or Abyssinian woman to suit me I will take her; but of course it is rare; a raw slave can do nothing, nor can a fellaha, and a Cairo woman is bored to death up in the Said. As to care and attention, I want for nothing. Omar does everything well and with pride and pleasure, and is delighted at the saving of expense in wine, beer, meat, etc. etc. One feeds six or eight Arabs well with the money for one European.

While the carpenter, his boy, and two *meneggets* were here, a very moderate dish of vegetables, stewed with a pound of meat, was put before me, followed by a chicken or a pigeon for me alone. The stew was then set on the ground to all the men, and two loaves of a piastre each, to everyone, a jar of water, and, *Alhamdulillah,* four men and two boys had dined handsomely. At breakfast a water-melon and another loaf a-piece, and a cup of coffee all round; and I pass for a true Arab in hospitality. Of course no European can live so, and they despise the Arabs for doing it, while the Arab servant is not flattered at seeing the European get all sorts of costly luxuries which he thinks unnecessary; besides he has to stand on the defensive, in order not to be made a drudge by his European fellow-servant, and despised for being one; and so he leaves undone all sorts of things which he does with alacrity when it is for 'the master' only. What Omar does now seems wonderful, but he says he feels like the Sultan now he has only me to please.

July 15. Last night came the two *meneggets* to pay a friendly visit, and sat and told stories; so I ordered coffee, and one took his sugar out of his pocket to put in his cup, which made me laugh inwardly. He told a fisherman, who stopped his boat alongside for a little conversation, the story of two fishermen, the one a Jew, the other a Muslim, who were partners in the time of the Arab Prophet (upon whom be blessing and peace!). The Jew, when he flung his nets, called on the Prophet of the Jews, and hauled it up full of fish every time; then the Muslim called on our Master Mohammed, etc., etc., and hauled up each time only stones, until the Jew said, 'Depart, O man, thou bringest us misfortune; shall I continue to take half thy stones, and give thee half my fish? Not so'. So the Muslim went to our Master Mohammed, and said, 'Behold, I mention thy name when I cast my net, and I catch only stones and calamity. How is this?' But the blessed Prophet said to him, 'Because thy stomach is black inwardly, and thou thoughtest to sell thy fish at an unfair price, and to defraud thy partner and the people, while the Jew's heart was clean towards thee and the people, and therefore God listened to him rather than to thee'. I hope our fisherman was edified by this fine moral.

I also had good stories from the chief diver of Cairo, who came to examine the bottom of my boat, and told me, in a whisper, a long tale of his grandfather's descent below the waters of the Nile, into the land of the people who lived there, and keep tame crocodiles to hunt fish for them. They gave him a sleeve-full of fishes' scales, and told him never to return, and not to tell about them: and when he got home the scales had turned to money. But most wonderful of all was Hajji Hanna's story of her own life, and the journey of Omar's mother carrying her old mother in a basket on her head from Damietta to Alexandria, and dragging Omar then a very little boy, by the hand. The energy of many women here is amazing.

The Nile is rising fast, and the *Bisheer* is come (the messenger who precedes the Hajj, and brings letters). *Bisheer* is 'good tidinger', to coin a word. Many hearts are lightened and many half-broken today. I shall go up to the Abassia to meet the Mahmal and see the Hajjis arrive.

Next Friday I must take my boat out of the water, or at least heel her over, to repair the bad places made at Alexandria. It seems I once cured a Reis of the Pasha's of dysentery at Minieh, and he has not forgotten it, though I had; so Reis Awad will give me a good place on the Pasha's bank, and lend ropes and levers which will save a deal of expense and trouble. I shall move out all the things and myself into a boat of Zubeydeh's for four or five days, and stay alongside to superintend my caulkers.

Miss Berry *is* dull no doubt, but few books seem dull to me now, I can tell you, and I was much delighted with such a *pièce de résistance*. Miss Eden I don't wish for—that sort of theatre burlesque view of the customs of a strange country is inexpressibly tedious to one who is familiar with one akin to it.[1] There is plenty of real fun to be had here, but *that* sort is only funny to cockneys. I want to read Baker's book very much.[2] I am much pleased with Abd el-Kader's book which Dozon sent me, and want the original dreadfully for Shaikh Yussuf, to show him that he and I are supported by such an authority as the great Emir in our notions about the real unity of the Faith. The book is a curious mixture of good sense and credulity—quite 'Arab of the Arabs'. I will write a paper on the popular beliefs of Egypt; it will be curious, I think.[3]

By the way, I see in the papers and reviews speculations as to some imaginary Mohammedan conspiracy, because of the very great number of pilgrims last year from all parts to Mecca. *C'est chercher midi à*

[1] Lucie had been sent the three volumes published in 1866 of the journals and correspondence of Miss Mary Berry (1763–1852), the close friend of Horace Walpole whose works she had edited in five volumes and published in 1798.

Hon. Emily Eden (1797–1869) went to India with her brother, Lord Auckland, appointed Governor-General in 1835; she published *Up the Country* in 1866.

[2] Sir Samuel Baker, 1821–1893, published in 1866 *The Albert N'yanza, Great Basin of the Nile, and exploration of the Nile sources.* He had started on his first exploration of the sources of the Nile with his wife in March 1861 and proved that the fertilizing properties carried down by the Nile came from Abyssinia. In December 1862 he left Khartum to follow up the course of the White Nile and at Gondokoro met Speke and Grant who had discovered the source in Lake Victoria Nyanza, and were proceeding home down the Nile. Baker went on to discover Lake Albert Nyanza through which the Nile flowed.

[3] Abdel Kader wrote a philosophical treatise, a translation of which was published in France in 1858 with the title *Rappel à l'intelligent. Avis à l'indifférent.*

quatorze heures. Last year the day of Abraham's sacrifice—and therefore *the* day of the pilgrimage—(the sermon on Mount Arafat) fell on a Friday, and when that happens there is always a rush, owing to the popular notion that the *Hajj el-Gumma* (pilgrimage of the Friday) is seven times blessed, or even equivalent to making it seven times in ordinary years. As any beggar in the street could tell a man this, it may give you some notion of how absurdly people make theories out of nothing for want of a little commonsense.

The *Moolid en-Nebbee* (Festival of the Prophet) has just begun. I am to have a place in the great Dervish's tent to see the *Dóseh*.

The Nile is rising fast; we shall kill the poor little Luxor black lamb on the day of the opening of the canal, and have a *fantasia* at night; only I grieve for my little white pussy, who sleeps every night on Ablook's (the lamb's) woolly neck, and loves him dearly. Pussy ('Bish' is Arabic for puss) was the gift of a Coptic boy at Luxor, and is wondrous funny, and as much more active and lissom than a European cat as an Arab is than an Englishman. She and Ahmad and Ablook have fine games of romps. Omar has set his heart on an English signet ring with an oval stone to engrave his name on; here you know they sign papers with a signet, not with a pen. It must be *solid* to stand hard work. Considering how hard he works for me, and how atrociously he was tormented by that devil Marie, I should like to give him a present he would like.

Well, I must finish this endless letter. Here comes *such* a bouquet from the Khedive's garden (somebody's sister's son is servant to the chief eunuch and brings it to me), a great round of scarlet, surrounded with white and green and with tall reeds, on which are threaded single tube-rose flowers, rising out of it so as to figure a huge flower with white pistils. Arab gardeners beat French flower-girls in bouquets.

Cairo, July 17. Dearest Alick. I am perfectly comfortable now with my aquatic *ménage*. The Reis is very well behaved and steady and careful, and the sort of Caliban of a sailor is a very worthy savage. Omar of course is hardworked—what with going to market, cooking, cleaning, ironing, and generally keeping everything in nice order but he won't hear of a maid of any sort. No wonder!

A clever old Reis has just come and overhauled the bottom of the boat, and says he can mend her without taking her out of the water. We shall see; it will be great luck if he can. As I am the river doctor, all the sailoring men are glad to do me a civility.

We have had the hottest of summers; it is now 98 in the cabin. I have felt very unwell, but my blue devils are quite gone, and I am altogether better. What a miserable war it is in Europe! I am most anxious for the next papers.[1] Here it is money misery; the Pasha is something like bankrupt, and no one has had a day's pay these three months.

August 4. The heat is and has been something fearful: we are all panting and puffing. I can't think what Palgrave meant about my being tired of poor old Egypt; I am very happy and comfortable, only I felt rather weak and poorly this year, and sometimes, I suppose, rather *wacham*, as the Arabs say, after you and the children. The heat, too, has made me lazy—it is 110 in the cabin, and 96 at night.

I saw the *Moolid en-Nebbee* (Festival of the Prophet), and the wonderful *Dóseh* [treading]; it is an awful sight; so many men drunk with religious ardour.[2] I also went to a Turkish hareem, where my dervish friends sent me; it is just like a tea-party at Hampton Court, only handsomer, not as to the ladies, but the clothes, furniture and jewels, and not a bit like the description in Mrs Lott's most extra-ordinary book.[3] Nothing is so clean as a Turkish hareem, the furniture is Dutch as to cleanliness, and their persons only like themselves— but oh! how dull and *triste* it all seemed. One nice lady said to me, 'If I had a husband and children like thee, I would die a hundred times rather than leave them for an hour', another envied me the power of going into the street, and seeing the *Dóseh*. She had never seen it, and never would.

Tomorrow Olagnier will dine and spend the night here, to see the cutting of the canal, and the 'Bride of the Nile' on Monday morning. We shall sail up to old Cairo in the evening with the Bride's boat; also Hajji Hanna is coming for the *fantasia;* after the high Nile we shall take the boat out and caulk her and then, if the excessive heat continues, I rather think of a month's jaunt to Beirut just to freshen

---

[1] This was the Austro-Prussian war of 1866 which resulted in the triumph of Prussia under Bismarck and the establishment of the North German Confederation under Prussia's leadership. It also weakened the position of France under Napoleon III.

[2] The *Dóseh* was a religious ceremony carried out by the Saadiya Dervishes. The climax took place in the Ezbekyia square in Cairo when as many sometimes as a hundred dervishes lay tightly packed together on the ground on their stomachs while the Shaikh rode over them on his horse.   -

[3] *The English Governess in Egypt, Harem Life in Egypt and Constantinople*, by Emmeline Lott, formerly Governess of His Highness the Grand Pasha, Ibrahim, son of Hi Highness Ismail Pasha, Viceroy of Egypt; two volumes, London 1866. Miss Emmeline Lott later published *Nights in the Harem*, two volumes, 1867 and *The Grand Pasha's Cruise on the Nile in the Viceroy of Egypt's Yacht*, also two volumes, 1869.

me up. Hajji Ali is there, with all his travelling materials and tents, so I need only take Omar and a bath and carpetbag. If the weather gets cool I shall stay in my boat. The heat is far more oppressive here than it was at Luxor two years ago; it is not so dry.

The Viceroy is afraid of cholera, and worried the poor Hajjis this year with most useless quarantine. The *Mahmal* was smuggled into Cairo before sunrise, without the usual honours, and all sightseers and holiday makers disappointed, and all good Muslims deeply offended. The idea that the Pasha has turned Christian or even Jew is spreading fast; I hear it on all sides. The new firman illegitimatizing so many of his children is of course just as agreeable to a sincere Moslem as a law sanctioning polygamy for our royal family would be with us.

Off Boulaq, August 20. Since I wrote I have had a bad bilious attack, which has of course aggravated my cough. Everyone has had the same, and most far worse than I, but I was very wretched and most shamefully cross. Omar said, 'That is not you but the sickness', when I found fault with everything, and it was very true. I am still seedy. Also I am beyond measure exasperated about my boat. I went up to the *Ata el-Khalig* (cutting of the canal), to see the great sight of the 'Bride of the Nile', a lovely spectacle; and on returning we all but sank.[1] I got out into a boat of Zebeydeh's with all my goods, and we hauled up my boat, and found her bottom rotten from stem to stern. So here I am in the midst of wood merchants, sawyers, etc., etc., rebuilding her bottom. My Reis said he had 'carried her on his head all this time' but 'what could such a one as he say against the word of a gentleman, like Mr Watson, Ross's storekeeper?' When the English cheat each other there remains nothing but to seek refuge with God. I saw that Mr Watson had cheated me in the repairs last year, but I did not know how colossal a swindle it had been.

Omar buys the wood and superintends, together with the Reis, and the builders seem good workmen and fair-dealing. I pay day by

[1] The mound of earth which blocked the water in the Cairo canal from reaching the city was called the 'Bride of the Nile' because the early dynasties of the Ancient Egyptians were stated to have sacrificed a virgin, who was conveyed to her funeral in a gaily decked boat, to ensure a plentiful Nile to flood the fields throughout the country. The decorated boat continued to be retained in this important ceremony which took place in Cairo when the river had risen about twenty feet. A gun on board the boat was fired every quarter of an hour and when the Governor of Cairo, accompanied by the Cadi and other dignitaries, gave the order for the cutting of the canal or Khalig, rockets and fire-works went up; there was great rejoicing and a procession of boats ascended the canal into the city.

day, and have a scribe to keep the accounts. If I get out of it for £150 I shall think Omar has done wonders, for every atom has to be new. I never saw anything so rotten afloat. If I had gone up the Cataract I should never have come down alive. It is a marvel we did not sink long ago.

Mabrook, Palgrave's boy, has arrived, and turns out well. He is a stout lubberly boy, with infinite good humour, and not at all stupid, and laughs a good real nigger yahyah, which brings the fresh breezes and lilac mountains of the Cape before me when I hear it. When I tell him to do anything he does it with strenuous care, and then asks, *tayib?* (is it well?) and if I say 'Yes' he goes off, as Omar says, 'like a cannon in Ladyship's face', in a guffaw of satisfaction. Ahmad, who is half his size, orders him about and teaches him, with an air of extreme dignity and says pityingly to me, 'You see, oh Lady, he is quite new, quite green'. Ahmad, who had never seen a garment or any article of European life two years ago, is now a smart valet, with very distinct ideas of waiting at table, arranging my things, etc., and cooks quite cleverly. Arab boys are amazing. I have promoted him to wages—one napoleon a month—so now he will keep his family. He is about a head taller than Rainie.

I intend to write a paper on the various festivals and customs of Copts and Muslims; but I must wait to see Abu Seyfeyn, near Luxor, the great Christian Saint, where all go to be cured of possession—all mad people. The Viceroy wages steady war against all festivals and customs. The *Mahmal* was burked this year, and the fair at Tantah forbidden. Then the Europeans spoil all; the Arabs no longer go to the *Ata el-Khalig,* and at the *Dóseh,* the Frangee carriages were like the Derby day. It is only up country that the real thing remains.

Tomorrow my poor black sheep will be killed over the new prow of the boat; his blood 'straked' upon her, and his flesh sodden and eaten by all the workmen, to keep off the evil eye; and on the day she goes into the water, some *Fikees* will read the Koran in the cabin, and again there will be boiled mutton and bread. The Christian *Ma-allimeen* (skilled workmen) hold to the ceremony of the sheep quite as much as the others, and always do it over a new house, boat, mill, waterwheel, etc.

Did I tell you Omar has another girl—about two months ago? His wife and babies are to come up from Alexandria to see him, for he will not leave me for a day, on account of my constantly being so ailing and weak. I hope if I die away from you all, you will do something for Omar for my sake, I cannot conceive what I should do without his faithful and loving care. I don't know why he is so devotedly fond of me, but he certainly does love me as he says 'like his mother', and moreover as a very affectionate son loves his mother.

How pleasant it would be if you could come—but please don't run any risks of fatigue or exposure to cold on your return. If you cannot come I shall go to Luxor early in October and send back the boat to let. I hear from Luxor that the people are all running away from the land, unable to pay triple taxes and eat bread: the ruin is universal. The poor Shaikhs el-Beled, who had the honour of dining with the Viceroy at Minieh have each had a squeeze politely administered. One poor devil I know had to 'make a present' of 50 purses.

How is my darling Rainie? I do so long for her earnest eyes at times, and wonder if I shall ever be able to get back to you all again. I fear that break-down at Soden sent me down a great terrace. I have never lost the pain and the cough for a day since. I have not been out for an age, or seen anyone. Would you know the wife of your bosom in a pair of pink trousers and a Turkish *tob?* Such is my costume as I write. The woman who came to sew could not make a gown, so she made me a pair of trousers instead. Farewell, dearest, I dare hardly say how your hint of possibly coming has made me wish it, and yet I dread to persuade you. The great heat is quite over with the high Nile, and the air on the river fresh and cool—cold at night even.

XXXVI

Preparing the 'Urania' for sailing

Off Boulaq, August 27 1866. Dearest Alick. The last two or three days we have been in great tribulation about the boat. On Saturday all her ribs were finished, and the planking and caulking ready to be put on, when in the night up came the old Nile with a rush, and threatened to carry her off; but by the favour of Abu-l-Hajjaj and Shaikh el-Bostawee she was saved in this wise.

You remember the tall old steersman who went with us to Bedree-shayn, and whom we thought so ill-conditioned; well, he was in charge of a *dahabieh* close by, and he called up all the Reises and steermen to help. 'Oh men of el-Bostawee, this is *our* boat (*i.e.* we are the servants of her owner) and she is in our faces'; and then he set the example, stripped and carried dust and hammered in piles all night, and by the morning she was surrounded by a dyke breast-high. The 'long-shore' men of Boulaq were not a little surprised to see dignified Reises working for nothing, like fellaheen. Meanwhile my three *Ma-allimeen*, the chief builder, caulker and foreman, had also stayed all night with Omar and my Reis, who worked like the rest, and the Shaikh of all the boat-builders went to visit one of my *Ma-allimeen*, who is his nephew, and hearing the case came down too, at one in the morning and stayed till dawn. Then as the workmen passed, going to their respective jobs, he called them, and said, 'Come and finish this boat; it must be done by tomorrow night'. Some men who objected and said they were going to the Pasha's dockyard, got a beating *pro forma* and the end of it was that I found forty-six men under my boat working 'like Afreets and Shaitans', when I went to see how all was going in the morning.

The old Shaikh marked out a piece to each four men, and then said,

'If that is not done tonight, Oh dogs! tomorrow I'll put on the hat'—
i.e. 'Today I have beaten moderately, like an Arab, but tomorrow,
please God, I'll beat like a Frank, and be mad with the stick'. *Kurz
und gut* [in short], the boat which yesterday morning was a skeleton,
is now, at four p.m. today, finished, caulked, pitched and all capitally
done; so if the Nile carries off the dyke, she will float safe. The shore
is covered with *débris* of other people's half-finished boats. I believe
I owe the ardour of the *Ma-allimeen* and of the Shaikh of the builders
to one of my absurd pieces of Arab civility. On the day when Omar
killed poor Ablook, my black sheep, over the bows and 'straked' his
blood upon them, the three *Ma-allimeen* came on board this boat to
eat their dish, and I followed the old Arab fashion and ate out of
the wooden dish with them and the Reis 'for luck', or rather 'for a
blessing' as we say here; and it seems that this gave immense satisfaction.

My Reis wept at the death of the black sheep, which used to follow
him to the coffee-shop and the market, and 'was to him a son', he
said, but he ate of him nevertheless. Omar surreptitiously picked out
the best pieces for my dinner for three days, with his usual eye to
economy; then lighted a fire of old wood, borrowed a cauldron of
some darweeshes, cut up the sheep, added water and salt, onions and
herbs, and boiled the sheep. Then the big washing copper (a large
round flat tray, like a sponging bath) was filled with bread broken in
pieces, over which the broth was slowly poured till the bread was
soaked. Next came a layer of boiled rice, on the top of that the pieces
of boiled meat, and over all was poured butter, vinegar and garlic
boiled together. This is called a *Fettah*, and is the orthodox dish of
darweeshes and given at all *Khatmehs* and other semi-religious
semi-festive, semi-charitable festivities. It is excellent and not expensive. I asked how many had eaten and was told one hundred and
thirty men had 'blessed my hand'. I expended 160 piastres on bread,
butter and vinegar, etc., and the sheep was worth two napoleons;
three napoleons in all, or less—for I ate for two days of the mutton.

The three *Ma-allimeen* came on board this boat, as I said and ate;
and it was fine to hear us—how polite we were. 'A bit more, oh
Ma-allim?' 'Praise be to God, we have eaten well—we will return
to our work'; 'By the Prophet, coffee and a pipe'. 'Truly thou art of
the most noble people'. 'Oh *Ma-allim*, ye have honoured us and
rejoiced us', 'Verily this is a day white among days', etc. A very
clever Egyptian engineer, a pupil of Whitworth's, who is living in a

boat alongside mine, was much amused, and said, 'Ah you know how to manage 'em'.

I have learnt the story of the two dead bodies that hitched in my anchor-chain some time ago. They were not Europeans as I thought, but Circassians—a young man and his mother. The mother used to take him to visit an officer's wife who had been brought up in the hareem of the Pasha's mother. The husband caught them, killed them, tied them together and flung them into the Nile near Rhoda, and gave himself into the hands of the police. All was of course hushed up. He goes to Fazogli; and I don't know what becomes of the slave-girl, his wife. These sort of things happen every day (as the bodies testify) among the Turks; but the Europeans never hear it. I heard it by a curious chance.

September 3. My boat will soon be finished, and now will be as good as new. Omar has worked like a good one from daybreak till night, overlooking, buying all the materials, selling all the wood and iron, etc., and has done capitally. I shall take a paper from my *Ma-allimeen* who are all first-class men, to certify what they have done and that the boat is as good as new. I have a neighbour now, Goodah Effendi, an engineer, who studied and married in England. His wife is gone there with the children, and he is living in a boat close by; so he comes over of an evening very often, and I am glad of his company: he is a right good fellow and very intelligent.

He has kindly looked at the boat several times for me and highly approves the work done. I never saw men do a better day's work than those at the boat. It is pretty to see the carpenter holding the wood with one hand and one foot while he saws it, sitting on the ground—just like the old frescoes. Do you remember the picture of boat-building in the tomb at Sakkara? Well, it is just the same; all done with the adze; but it is stout work they put into it, I can tell you.

If you do not come (and I do not like to press you, I fear the fatigue for you and the return to the cold winter) I shall go to Luxor in a month or so and send back the boat to let.

My best love to all at home. I've got a log from the cedars of Lebanon, my Moslem carpenter who smoothed the broken end, swallowed the sawdust, because he believed 'Our Lady Mary' had sat under the tree with 'Our Lord Jesus'.

September 21. I am better again now and go on very comfortably with my two little boys. Omar is from dawn till night at work at my boat, so I have only Mabrook and Ahmad, and you would wonder to see how well I am served. Ahmad cooks a very good dinner, serves it and orders Mabrook about. Sometimes I whistle and hear *hader* (ready) from the water, and in tumbles Ahmad, with the water running 'down his innocent nose' and looking just like a little bronze triton of a Renaissance fountain, with a blue shirt and white skull-cap added. Mabrook is a big lubberly lad of the laugh-and-grow-fat breed, clumsy, but not stupid, and very good and docile. You would delight in his guffaws, and the merry games and hearty laughter of my *ménage* is very pleasant to me. Another boy swims over from Goodah's boat (his Ahmad), and then there are games at piracy, and much stealing of red pots from the potter's boats. The joke is to snatch one under the owner's very nose, and swim off brandishing it, whereupon the boatman uses eloquent language, and the boys out-hector him, and everybody is much amused.

I only hope Palgrave won't come back from Sookum Kaleh to fetch Mabrook just as he has got clever—not at stealing jars, but in his work. He already washes my clothes very nicely indeed; his stout black arms are made for a washer-boy.

Ahmad looked forward with great eagerness to your coming. He is mad to go to England, and in his heart planned to ingratiate himself with you, and go as a 'general servant'. He is very little, if at all bigger than a child of seven, but an Arab boy *'ne doute de rien'* and does serve admirably. What would an English respectable cook say to seeing 'two dishes and a sweet' cooked over a little old wood on a few bricks, by a baby in a blue shirt? and very well cooked too, and followed by incomparable coffee.

Can't you save up your holidays and come for four months next winter with my Maurice? However, perhaps you would be bored on the Nile. I don't know. People either enjoy it rapturously or are bored, I believe. I suppose this year we shall have troops of Yankees. They are always civil and inoffensive, I find, though hardly ever agreeable. I am glad to hear from Janet that you are well. I am much better. The carpenter will finish in the boat today, then the painter begins and in a week, Inshallah, I shall get back into her.

Dearest Mother. I am a good deal better again; the weather is delightful, and the Nile in full flood, which makes the river scenery from the boat very beautiful. Alick made my mouth water with his descriptions of his rides with Janet about the dear old Surrey country, having her with him seems to have quite set him up. I have seen nothing and nobody but my 'next boat' neighbour, Goodah Effendi, as Omar has been at work all day in the boat, and I felt lazy and disinclined to go out alone. Big Hassan of the donkeys has grown too lazy to go about and I don't care to go alone with a small boy here. However I am out in the best of air all day and am very well off. My two little boys are very diverting and serve me very well.

The news from Europe is to my ignorant ideas *désolant,* a *dégringolade* back into military despotism, which would have excited indignation with us in our fathers' days, I think. I get lots of newspapers from Ross, which afterwards go to an Arab grocer, who reads *The Times* and the *Saturday Review* in his shop in the bazaar! what next? The cargo of books which Alick and you sent will be most acceptable for winter consumption.

If I were a painter I would take up the Moslem traditions of Joseph and Mary. He was not a white-bearded old gentleman at all you must know, but young, lovely and pure as Our Lady herself. They were cousins, brought up together; and she avoided the light conversation of other girls, and used to go to the well with her jar, hand in hand with Joseph carrying his. After the angel Gabriel had announced to her the will of God, and blown into her sleeve, whereby she conceived 'the Spirit of God', Joseph saw her state with dismay, and resolved to kill her, as was his duty as her nearest male relation. He followed her, knife in hand, meaning always to kill her at the next tree, and each time his heart failed him, until they reached the well and the tree under which the Divine messenger stood once more and said, 'Fear not oh Joseph, the daughter of thy uncle bears within her Eesa, the Messiah, the Spirit of God'. Joseph married his cousin without fear. Is it not pretty? The two types of youthful purity and piety, standing hand in hand before the angel. I think a painter might make something out of the soft-eyed Syrian boy with his jar on his shoulder (hers on the head), and the grave, modest maiden who shrank from all profane company.

A letter from aunt Charley all about her own and Rainie's country life, school feasts etc., made me quite cry, and brought before me— oh, how vividly—the difference between East and West, not quite *all* to the advantage of home however, though mostly. What is pleasant here is the primitive ways. Three times since I have been here lads of most respectable families of Luxor have come to ask hospitality, which consists in a place on the deck of the boat, and liberty to dip their bread in the common dish with my slave boy and Ahmad. The bread they brought with them, 'bread and shelter' were not asked, as they slept *sub dio*. In England I must have refused the hospitality, on account of *gêne* and expense.

The chief object to the lads was the respectability of being under my eye while away from their fathers, as a satisfaction to their families; and while they ate and slept like beggars, as we should say, they read their books and chatted with me, when I was out on the deck, on perfectly equal terms, only paying the respect proper to my age. I thought of the 'orphanages and institutions' and all the countless difficulties of that sort, and wondered whether something was not to be said for this absence of civilization in knives, forks, beds, beer, and first and second tables above all. Of course, climate has a good deal to do with the facility with which widows and orphans are absorbed here.

Goodbye dearest Mother: today is post day, and Reis Mohammed is about to trudge into town in such a dazzling white turban and such a grand black robe. His first wife, whom he was going to divorce for want of children, has brought him a son, so there was an end of the divorce; with us it would be *raison de plus*, as by her reckoning she must be eleven months gone. But my worthy Reis is apparently not given to making calculations, and was mighty attentive to her when she came here to visit him for a few days. The curious thing is that Omar and Husain have made the calculation in question, and mentioned it to me, but nothing would induce them to say anything to the husband. It is impious to speak anything to injure a woman.

Cairo, October 15. Dearest Alick. I have been back in my own boat four days, and most comfortable she is. I enlarged the saloon, and made a good writing table, and low easy divans instead of benches, and added a sort of pantry and sleeping cabin in front; so that Omar has not to come through the saloon to sleep; and I have all the hareem part to myself. Inside there is a good large stern cabin, excellent w.c. and wash-closet and two small cabins, with beds long enough even for you. Inshallah, you and Maurice will come next winter and go up the Nile and enjoy it with me. I intend to sail in ten days and to send back the *Urania* to seek work for the winter. We had a very narrow escape of being flooded this year. I fear a deal of damage has been done to the dourrah and cotton crops. It was sad to see the villagers close by here trying to pull up a little green dourrah as the Nile slowly swallowed up the fields.

I was forced to flog Mabrook yesterday for smoking on the sly, a grave offence here on the part of a boy not yet nubile (*ballagh*); it is considered disrespectful; so he was ordered, with much parade, to lie down, and Omar gave him two cuts with a rope's end, an apology for a flogging which would have made an Eton boy stare. The stick here is quite nominal, except in official hands. I can't say Mabrook seemed at all impressed, for he was laughing heartily with Omar in less than ten minutes; but the affair was conducted with as much solemnity as an execution.

'Shaikh' Stanley's friend, Gazowee, has married his negro slave to his own sister, on the plea that he was the best young man he knew. What would a Christian family say to such an arrangement?

I have had a long business of entreating the French Consul to pay their guard Mohammed arrears of two years of wages and also to increase them a little. The result of the enquiry is that Monsieur Mounier has been eating half (fifteen francs monthly) for seven years, and the whole for two. Really the Europeans are too rascally! Poor Zubeydeh can't get a farthing of the pension to which she is entitled, and I can't think what is to become of her and her four young children. Ross has kindly spoken to Hafiz Pasha about it, but God knows if it is any use.

Maurice wrote me such a good letter about his Scotch visit. I hope he will learn French and German; why has he suddenly taken a fancy to the Foreign Office? I fear that he will never qualify for the examination.

You are quite right not to come; the quarantine would be too great a nuisance and cut short your holiday so much.

My boat is beautifully buoyant now, and has come up by the bows in fine style. I have not sailed her yet, but have no doubt she will 'walk well' as the Arabs say. Omar got £10 by the sale of old wood and nails, and also gave me 2,000 piastres, nearly £12, which the workmen had given him as a sort of backsheesh. They all pay one, two or three piastres daily to any *wakeel* (agent) who superintends; that is his profit, and it is enormous at that rate. I said, 'Why did you not refuse it?' But Omar replied they had pay enough after that reduction, which is always made from them, and that in his opinion therefore, it came out of the master's pocket, and was 'cheatery'.

Baker's effusion is a very poor business. There may be blacks like tigers (and whites too in London for that matter). I myself have seen at least five sorts of blacks (negroes, not Arabs), more unlike each other than Swedes are unlike Spaniards; and many are just like ourselves. Of course they want governing with a strong hand, like all ignorant, childish creatures. But I am fully convinced that custom and education are the only real differences between one set of men and another, their inner nature is the same all the world over.[1]

My Reis spoke such a pretty parable the other day that I must needs write it. A coptic Reis stole some of my wood, which we got back by force and there was some reviling of the Nazarenes in consequence from Hoseyn and Ali; but Reis Mohammed said: 'Not so; Girgis is a thief, it is true, but many Christians are honest; and behold, all the people in the world are like soldiers, some wear red and some blue; some serve on foot, others on horseback, and some in ships; but all serve one Sultan, and each fights in the regiment in which the Sultan has placed him, and he who does his duty best is the best man, be his coat red or blue or black.' I said, 'Excellent words, oh Reis, and fit to be spoken from the best of pulpits.'

It is surprising what happy sayings the people here hit upon; they cultivate talk for want of reading, and the consequence is great facility of narration and illustration. Everybody enforces his ideas, like Christ, in parables. Hajji Hannah told me two excellent fairy tales, which I will write for Rainie with some Bowdlerizing, and several laughable stories, which I will leave unrecorded, as savouring too much of Boccaccio's manner, or that of the Queen of Navarre.

I told Ahmad to sweep the floor after dinner just now. He hesitated, and I called again: 'What manner is this, not to sweep when I bid thee?' 'By the most high God', said the boy, 'my hand shall not sweep in thy boat after sunset, oh Lady; I would rather have it cut off than sweep thee out of thy property.' I found that you must not sweep at night, nor for three days after the departure of a guest whose return you desire, or of the master of the house.

'Thinkest thou that my brother would sweep away the dust of thy feet from the floors at Luxor,' continued Ahmad, 'he would fear never to see thy fortunate face again.' If you don't want to see your visitor again you break a *gulleh* (water-jar) behind him as he leaves the house, and sweep away his footsteps.

---

[1] Lucie had been reading Samuel Baker's *Albert N'Yanza Great Basin of the Nile* in which he stated: 'I wish the black sympathisers in England could see Africa's inmost heart as I do, much of their sympathy would subside. Human nature viewed in its crude state as pictured amongst African savages is quite on the level with that of the brute, and not to be compared with the noble character of the dog. There is neither gratitude, pity, love, nor self-denial; no idea of duty; no religion; but covetousness, ingratitude, selfishness and cruelty.' (Last paragraph of chapter 5.)

What a canard your papers have in Europe about a constitution here. I won't write any politics, it is all too dreary; and Cairo gossip is odious, as you may judge by the productions of Mesdames Odouard and Lott. Only remember this, there is no law nor justice but the will, or rather the caprice, of one man.[1] It is nearly impossible for any European to conceive such a state of things as really exists; and between ourselves Ross, for instance, has not yet understood it and will make mistakes in consequence.

Nothing but perfect familiarity with the governed, that is oppressed class, will teach it. I am à *l'index*, and none of the people I know here dare come to see me—Arabs I mean. It was whispered in my ear in the street by a friend I met. I would not let in Osman Bey because I know him to be a spy and he is always at Ross's heels; however, Ross knows it too. Ismail Pasha's chief pleasure is gossip, and a certain number of persons, chiefly Europeans, furnish him with it daily, true or false. If the farce of the Constitution ever should be acted here it will be superb. Something like old Colquhoun [the British Consul-General] going in his cocked hat to ask the fellaheen what wages they got! I could tell you a little of the value of consular information, but what is the use? Europe is enchanted with the enlightened Pasha who has ruined this poor country.

I long to see you and Rainie! I don't like to hope too much, but God willing, next year I shall see you all.

October 19. Dearest Janet. I have just received your letter from Venice. I own that I am much of your mind about the Italians, and perhaps you won't object to my including the Greeks in my antipathies. At the same time, as I know neither Greece nor Italy I feel that my attitude is of the nature of an unfounded prejudice. I am making ready to start; but if you should come I will stop a little in order to have a sight of your 'fortunate face', my darling.

The hat turns out to be an extinguisher on me for lack of 'back hair'. If you can use it, pray do, also two pair of gloves which are too small for my claws. If you ever want a court dress and like my gold Indian one, take it. I wish you were coming up; my boat is lovely now and I could make you and your maid quite comfortable.

[1] Shaikh Mohammed Abdu, 1849–1905, the Egyptian religious and educational reformer, wrote: 'Although Ismail set up a Consultative Assembly in 1866 whose task it was supposed to be to convince the people that they had a voice in the affairs of their country, nevertheless no one, not even the members of the Consultative Assembly itself, believed that they really possessed those rights'. *The Arabs* by Arnold Hottinger, p 185, London, 1963.

Dearest Alick. Last night was a great Shaikh fête, such drumming and singing, and ferrying across the river. The Nile is running down unusually fast, and I think I had better go soon, as the mud of Cairo is not so sweet as the mud of the upper land.

I shall soon sail up the river. Yesterday Sayed Mustapha arrived, who says that the Greeks are all gone, and the poor Austrian at Thebes is dead, so I shall represent Europe in my single person from Assiut to, I suppose, Khartum.

You would delight in Mabrook; a man asked him the other day after his flogging, if he would not run away, to see what he would say, as he alleged; I suspect he meant to steal and sell him. 'I run away, to eat lentils like you? when *my* Effendi gives me meat and bread every day, and *I eat such a lot.*' Is not that a delicious practical view of liberty? The creature's enjoyment of life is quite a pleasure to witness, and he really works very well and with great alacrity. If Palgrave claims him I think I must buy him.

I hear sad accounts from the Said: the new taxes and the new levies of soldiers are driving the people to despair, and many are running away from the land, which will no longer feed them after paying all exactions, to join the Beduin in the desert, which is just as if our peasantry turned gipsies.

A Sheikh el-Beled of a village, Dishne, some fifty miles distant from Luxor, has been with me wanting me to buy land there and offering on the part of his fellaheen a voluntary *corvée* of two days a month each man on my land to see my 'fortunate face' among them. What a queer people these are! It is a very large, rich place, or *was* rich I suppose. That you must take care *not* to print anywhere or my poor friends would get into trouble. The espionage is becoming more and more close and jealous and I have been warned to be very careful.

Omar's wife, Mabrookah, came here yesterday, a nice young woman, and the babies are fine children and very sweet-tempered. She told me that the lion's head, which I sent down to Alexandria to go to you, was in her room when a neighbour of hers, who had never had a child, saw it, and at once conceived. The old image worship survives in the belief, which is all over Egypt, that the 'Anteeks' can cure barrenness. Mabrookah was of course very smartly dressed, and the reckless way in which Eastern women treat their fine clothes gives them a grand air, which no Parisian Duchess could hope to imitate—not that I think it a virtue mind you, but some vices are genteel.

October 25. Dearest Mother. I have got all ready, and shall sail on Saturday. My men have baked the bread, and received their wages to go to Luxor and bring the boat back to let. It is turning cold, but I feel none the worse for it, though I shall be glad to go. I have had a dreary, worrying time here, and am tired of hearing of all the meannesses and wickedness which constitute the *on dits* here. Not that I hear much, but there is nothing else. I shall be best at Luxor now the winter has set in so early. You would laugh at such winter when one sits out all day under an awning in English summer clothes, and wants only two blankets at night; but all is comparative *ici bas,* and I call it cold, and Mabrook ceases to consider his clothes such a grievance as they were to him at first, and takes kindly to a rough *capote* for the night.

I have just been interrupted by my Reis and one of my men, who came in to display the gorgeous printed calico they have bought; one for his Luxor wife and the other for his betrothed up near Aswan. (The latter is about eight years old, and Hosein has dressed her and paid her expenses these five years, as is the custom up in that district.) The Reis has bought a silk head-kerchief for nine shillings, but that was in the marriage contract. So I must see, admire and wish good luck to the finery, and to the girls who are to wear it. Then we had a little talk about the prospects of letting the boat, and, *Inshallah,* making some money for *el gamma, i.e.,* 'all our company', or 'all of us together'. The Reis hopes that the *Howagat* [the foreign Gentlemen] will not be too outrageous in their ways or given to use the stick, as the solution of every difficulty.

The young Shurafa of Abu-l-Hajjaj came from Gama'l Azhar today to bid me goodbye and bring their letters for Luxor. I asked them about the rumours that the Ulema are preaching against the Franks (which is always being said), but they had heard nothing of the sort, and said they had not heard of anything the Franks had done lately which would signify to the Muslims at all. It is not the Franks who press so many soldiers, or levy such heavy taxes three months in advance! I will soon write again. I feel rather like the wandering Jew and long for home and rest, without being dissatisfied with what I have and enjoy, God knows. If I *could* get better and come home next summer.

XXXVII

An Indian walee and twin brothers become cats

Luxor, November 21 1866. Dearest Alick. I arrived here on the morning of the 11th. I am a beast not to have written, but I caught cold after four days, and have really not been well, so forgive me, and I will narrate and not apologize. We came up best pace, as the boat is a flyer now, only fourteen days to Thebes, and to Keneh only eleven. Then we had bad winds, and my men pulled away at the rope, and sang about the *Reis el-Arousa* (bridegroom) going to his bride, and even Omar went and pulled the rope.

On arriving at Luxor I heard a *charivari* of voices, and knew I was 'at home,' by the shrill pipe of the little children, *el Sitt, el Sitt.* Visitors all day of course, at night comes up another *dahabieh*, great commotion, as it had been telegraphed from Cairo (which I knew before I left, and was to be stopped). So I coolly said, 'Oh Mustapha, the Indian saint (Walee) is in thine eye, seeing that an Indian is all as one with an Englishman'. 'How did I know there was an Indian and a Walee?' etc.

Meanwhile the Walee, Sayyed Abdurrachman, had a bad thumb, and someone told his slave that there was a wonderful English doctress, so in the morning he sent for me, and I went inside the hareem. He was very friendly, and made me sit close beside him, told me he was fourth in descent from Abd el-Kader Gylamee of Bagdad, but his father settled at Hyderabad, where he has great estates. He said he was a Walee or saint, and would have it that I was in the path of the darweeshes; gave me pills for my cough; asked me many questions, and finally gave me five dollars and asked if I wanted more? I thanked him heartily, kissed the money politely, and told him I was not poor enough to want it, and would give it in his name to the poor of Luxor, but that I would never forget that the Indian Shaikh had behaved like a brother to an English woman in a strange land.

He then spoke in great praise of the 'laws of the English', and said many more kind things to me, adding again, 'I tell thee thou art a darweesh, and do not thou forget me'.

He huffs Pashas and Mudirs ruthlessly and gives away immense charity to the poor. The Government intends to murder him in the Sudan, I hear, though I can't conceive why. He was perfectly outside all that could affect Egyptian politics as his estates are at Hyderabad, but he is watched at every place and after Aswan he will be dogged by Arnouts. I am sorry for he was a right good straightforward fellow, whether saint or magician. Some urge me to take the pills he gave me and others tell me on no account to take them but to throw them into the Nile, lest they should turn me into a mare or a donkey. I shall keep them until I find a chemist to analyse them.

I hope Sayyed Abdurrachman will come down safe again, but no one knows what the Government wants of him or why he is so watched. It is the first time I ever saw an Oriental travelling for pleasure He had about ten or twelve in the hareem, among them his three little girls, and perhaps twenty men outside, Indians, and Arabs from Syria, I fancy.

Next day I moved into the old house, and found one end in ruins, owing to the high Nile and want of repair. However there is plenty more safe and comfortable. I settled all accounts with my men, and made an inventory in Arabic, which Shaikh Yussuf wrote for me, which we laughed over hugely. How to express a sauce-boat, a pie-dish, etc. in Arabic, was a poser. A genteel Effendi, who sat by, at last burst out in uncontrollable amazement; 'There is no God but God: is it possible that four or five Franks can use all these things to eat, drink and sleep on a journey?' (n.b. I fear the Franks will think the stock very scanty.) Whereupon master Ahmad, with the swagger of one who has seen cities and men, held forth. 'Oh Effendim, that is nothing: Our Lady is almost like the children of the Arabs. One dish or two, a piece of bread, a few dates, and Peace (as we say, there is an end of it). But thou shouldst see the merchants of Alexandria, three tablecloths, forty dishes, to each soul seven plates of all sorts, seven knives and seven forks and seven spoons, large and small, and seven different glasses for wine and beer and water'. 'It is the will of God', replied the Effendi, rather put down: 'but', he added, 'it must be a dreadful fatigue to them to eat their dinner'.

Everything is cheaper than last year, but there is no money to buy with, and the taxes have grown beyond bearing, as a fellah said, 'a man can't (we will express it "blow his nose", if you please; the real phrase was less parliamentary, and expressive of something at once *ventose* and valueless) without a *cawass* behind him to levy a tax on it'. The ha'porth of onions we buy in the market is taxed on the spot, and the fish which the man catches under my window. I paid a tax on buying charcoal, and another on having it weighed. People are terribly beaten to get next year's taxes out of them, which they have not the money to pay.

The Nubian M.P.s passed the other day in three boats, towed by a steamer, very frightened and sullen. I fell in with some Egyptians on my way, and tried the European style of talk. 'Now you will help to govern the country, what a fine thing for you', etc. I got such a look of rueful reproach. 'Laugh not thou at our beards O Effendim! God's mercy, what words are these? and who is there on the banks of the Nile who can say anything but *hader* (ready), with both hands on the head, and a salaam to the ground even to a Mudir; and thou talkest of speaking before Effendina! Art thou mad, Effendim?'

Of all the vexations none are more trying than the distinctions which have been inflicted on the unlucky Shaikhs el-Beled. In fear and trembling they ate their Effendina's banquet and sadly paid the bill: and those who have had the *Nishan* (the order of the Mejeedee) have had to disburse fees whereat the Lord Chamberlain's staff's mouths might water, and now the wretched delegates to the Egyptian Chamber (God save the mark) are going down with their hearts in their shoes. The Nubians say that the Divan is to be held in the Citadel and that the road by which the mameluke Beys left is not stopped up, though perhaps it goes underground nowadays.[1]

I am glad you liked the old lion. I stole him for you from a temple where he served as footstool for people to mount their donkeys. A man has stolen a very nice silver antique ring for me out of the last excavations—don't tell Mariette. See how we get demoralized. My fellah friend said 'better thou have it than Mariette sell it to the French

[1] It was a road out of the Citadel in Cairo that the mameluke leaders tried to follow in 1811 after being invited to a huge banquet by Mohammed Ali Pasha, the Viceroy, who had arranged to have them massacred on the way out.

and pocket the money; if I didn't steal it, he would'—so I received the stolen property calmly.

Luxor, November 23. Dearest Mother. Your letter of October 30 has this moment reached me, and so I take up my pen to reply at once, though I shall wait for the steamer to send my letters as I rather distrust the post. I was told that I had the honour of a special spy in Cairo, so I prefer sending by men who are sure, and I have one in the steamer and one in the transit who will post for me in Alexandria.

I am truly grateful to you, dearest Mother, for doing for me what I should wish for my good Omar. The only safe thing in this country is to leave him the money down. He is scraping and saving in order to buy a house, that is, one floor in a house which is the best thing here. It is dismal to say, but no Europeans can be trusted in their dealings with 'natives'. Fancy that my poor guard Mohammed has been swindled these seven years of half his pay. I have exploded the roguery at the French Consulate, but I fear redress is hopeless. In future he will have his rightful wages (30 francs per month) instead of fifteen.

It is not possible for you who live at home to conceive the pettiness of the cheatery executed by the Europeans here, as well as its amount. Thus, if you are kindly minded to leave Omar £100, the best is to order Coutts to have it paid to him. Omar's full name and style is Omar Abu Halaweh, Dragoman of Alexandria. He has now £50 of his wages in my hands, and I let him dress as shabbily as he likes in order to save for the purchase of a house which he and his nice wife, Mabrooka, have set their minds on.

I wanted to invest it in Cairo, but Omar begged me to keep it. 'I know you and my master (Alexander), and I don't like anyone else to know about my money; besides I am a Muslim and interest is not good for me.' The fact is that the Arabs are fast being convinced that the old savings bank (the wife's bracelets) it the only safe thing. Who can wonder after the state of trade they have lately seen and suffered by? Mabrooka has a *safa* of gold coins which she will sell whenever Omar can add enough to buy a house. It is her fortune, about £75, from her Mother. She told me her intention; she is a truly good woman.

I have given Omar a signed paper stating that, if I die, he is to take all my things down to Alexandria and wait for orders. If the Consulate gets hold of them, the boat will be sold to a friend for nothing and everything spoiled. I will give him a list of what he is to send home and what to keep and what to sell.

I am better but very weak. I find the Darfur woman's rubbing does me much good; her soft, strong hands warm me all over.

November 27. The first steamer full of travellers has just arrived, and with it the bother of the ladies all wanting my saddle. I forbade Mustapha to send for it, but they intimidate the poor old fellow, and he comes and kisses my hand not to get him into trouble with one old woman who says she is the relation of a Consul and a great lady in her own country. I am what Mrs Grote called 'cake' enough to concede to Mustapha's fears what I had sworn to refuse henceforth. Last year five women on one steamer all sent for my saddle, besides other things—campstools, umbrellas, beer, etc., etc. This year I'll bolt the doors when I see a steamer coming.

I hear the big people are angry with the Indian saint because he treated them like dirt everywhere. One great man went with a Mudir to see him, and asked him to sell him a mameluke (a young slave boy). The Indian, who had not spoken or saluted, burst forth, 'Be silent, thou wicked one! dost thou dare to ask me to sell thee a soul to take it with thee to hell?' Fancy the surprise of the 'distinguished' Turk. Never had he heard such language. The story has travelled all up the river and is of course much enjoyed.

Last night Shaikh Yussuf gave an entertainment, killed a sheep, and had a reading of the Koran—the Chapter on the Prophet. It was the night of the Prophet's great vision, and is a great night in Islam. I was sorry not to be well enough to go. Now that there is no Cadi here, Shaikh Yussuf has lots of business to settle; and he came to me and said, 'Expound to me the laws of marriage and inheritance of the Christians, that I may do no wrong in the affairs of the Copts, for they won't go and be settled by the priest out of the Gospels, and I can't find any laws, except about marriage in the Gospels.' I set him up with the text of the tribute money, and told him to judge according to his own laws, for that Christians had no laws other than those of the country they lived in. Poor Yussuf was sore perplexed about a divorce case. I refused to 'expound', and told him all the learned in the law in England had not yet settled which text to follow.

A few evenings ago. I was sitting here quietly drinking tea, and four or five men were present, when a cat came to the door. I called 'biss, biss', and offered milk, but pussy, after looking at us, ran away. 'Well dost thou, oh Lady', said a quiet, sensible man, a merchant here, 'to be kind to the cat, for I dare say he gets little enough at home; *his* father, poor man, cannot cook for his children every day.' And then in an explanatory tone to the company, 'That is Alee Nasseeree's boy Yussuf—it must be Yussuf, because his fellow twin Ismaeen is with his mule at Negadeh.' I shivered, I confess, not but what I have heard things almost as absurd from gentlemen and ladies in Europe; but an 'extravagance' in a *kuftan* has quite a different effect from one in a tail coat. 'What! My butcher's boy who brings the meat— a cat?' I gasped. 'To be sure, and he knows well where to look for a bit of good cookery, you see. All twins go out as cats at night if they go to sleep hungry; and their own bodies lie at home like dead meanwhile, but no one must touch them, or they would die. When they grow up to ten or twelve they leave it off. Why your boy Ahmad does it. Oh Ahmad! do you go out as a cat at night?' 'No,' said Ahmad tranquilly, 'I am not a twin—my sister's sons do.' I inquired if people were not afraid of such cats. 'No, there is no fear, they only eat a little of the cookery, but if you beat them they will tell their parents next day, "So-and-so beat me in his house last night", and show their bruises. No, they are not Afreets, they are *beni Adami* (sons of Adam), only twins do it, and if you give them a sort of onion broth and camel's milk the first thing when they are born, they don't do it at all.' Omar professed never to have heard of it, but I am sure he had, only he dreads being laughed at.

One of the American missionaries told me something like it as belonging to the Copts, but it is entirely Egyptian, and common to both religions. I asked several Copts who assured me it was true, and told it just the same. Is it a remnant of the doctrine of transmigration? However the notion fully accounts for the horror the people feel at the idea of killing a cat.

A poor pilgrim from the black country was taken ill yesterday at a village six miles from here, he could speak only a few words of Arabic and begged to be carried to the Abab'deh. So the Shaikh el-Beled put him on a donkey and sent him and his little boy, and laid him in Shaikh Hassan's house. He called for Hassan and begged him to take care of the child, and to send him to an uncle somewhere in Cairo. Hassan said, 'Oh you will get well, *Inshallah,* etc., and take the boy with you.' 'I cannot take him into the grave with me,' said the black pilgrim.

In the night he died and the boy went to Hassan's mat and said, 'Oh Hassan, my father is dead'. So the two Shaikhs and several men got up and went and sat with the boy till dawn, because he refused to lie down or to leave his father's corpse. At daybreak he said, 'Take me now and sell me, and buy new cloth to dress my father for the tomb'. All the Abab'deh cried when they heard it, and Hassan went and bought the cloth, and some sweet stuff for the boy who remains with him.

Such is death on the road in Egypt. I tell it as Hassan's slave told it to me, and somehow we all cried again at the poor little boy rising from his dead father's side to say, 'Come now sell me to dress my father for the tomb'. These strange black pilgrims always interest me. Many take four years to Mecca and home, and have children born to them on the road, and learn a few words of Arabic.

XXXVIII

'Like Don Quixote but quite in his senses'

Luxor, December 5 1866. Dearest Janet. I fancy I should be quite of your mind about Italy and Germany. I hate the return of Europe to 'the good old rule and ancient plan, that he should take who has the power, and he should keep who can'. Nor can I be bullied into looking on 'might' as 'right'.

Many thanks for the papers; I am anxious to hear about the Candia[1] business. All my neighbours who have sons growing up are sick at heart. The hatred against the Viceroy is quite openly expressed everywhere and the poor wretches here are miserable indeed.

An idiot of a woman has written to me to get her a place as governess in an 'European or Arabian family in the neighbourhood of Thebes!' Considering she has been six years in Egypt as she says, she must be well fitted to teach. She had better learn to make *gilleh* and spin wool. The young Americans whom Mr Hale sent were very nice. The Yankees are always the best bred and best educated travellers that I see here.

December 31. Dearest Alick. Dr Osman Ibraheem (a friend of mine, an elderly man who studied in Paris in Mohammed Ali's time) wants me to spend the summer up here and take sand baths, *i.e.* bury myself up to the chin in the hot sand, and to get a Dongola slave to rub me. A most fascinating dervish from Esneh gave me the same advice; he wanted me to go and live near him at Esneh, and let him treat me.

Dr Osman is a lecturer in the Cairo school of medicine, a Shereef, and eminently a gentleman. He came up in the passenger steamer and

[1] In 1866 the Cretans revolted against the Sultan of Turkey who had refused the reforms they had demanded, and fellaheen had been conscripted in Egypt to fight alongside the Turks in Crete (Candia).

called and spent all his spare time with me. He was amazed and delighted at what he heard here about me. '*Ah Madame, on vous aime comme une soeur, et on vous respecte comme une reine cela rejouit le coeur des honnêtes gens de voir tous les préjugés oubliés et détruits à ce point*'. We had no end of talk. Osman is the only Arab I know who has read a good deal of European literature and history and is able to draw comparisons. He said, '*Vous seule dans toute l'Egypte connaissez le peuple et comprenez ce qui se passe, tous les autres Européens ne savent absolument rien que les dehors; il n'y a que vous qui ayez inspiré la confiance qu'il faut pour connaître la vérité*'. Of course this is between ourselves, I tell you, but I don't want to boast of the kind thoughts people have of me, simply because I am decently civil to them.

My heart warmed to him directly, because like most high-bred Arabs, he is so like Don Quixote—only Don Quixote quite in his senses. The sort of innocent sententiousness, and perfectly natural love of fine language and fine sentiments is unattainable to any European, except, I suppose, a Spaniard. It is quite unlike Italian fustian or French *sentiment*. I suppose to most Europeans it is ridiculous, but I used to cry when the carriers beat the most noble of all knights, when I was a little girl and read Don Quixote; and now I felt as it were like Sancho, when I listened to Osman reciting bits of heroic poetry, or uttering 'wise saws' and 'modern instances', with the peculiar mixture of strong sense of 'exultation' which stamps the great Don.

I may not repeat all I heard from him of the state of things here, and the insults he had to endure—a Shereef and an educated man—from coarse Turkish Pashas; it was the carriers over again. He told me he had often cried like a woman, at night in his own room, at the miseries he was forced to witness and could do nothing to relieve; all the men I have particularly liked I find are more or less pupils of the Shaikh el-Bagooree now dead, who seems to have had a gift of inspiring honourable feeling. Our good Maōhn is one; he is no conjuror, but the honesty and goodness are heroic which lead a man to starve on £15 a month, when he is expected to grow rich on plunder.

In Egypt we are eaten up with taxes; there is not a penny left to anyone. The taxes for the whole year *eight months in advance* have been levied, as far as they can be beaten out of the miserable people. I saw one of the poor dancing girls the other day (there are three in

Luxor) and she told me how cruel the new tax on them is. It is left to the discretion of the official who farms it to make each woman pay according to her presumed gains, *i.e.* her good looks, and thus the poor women are exposed to all the caprices and extortions of the police. This last new tax has excited more disgust than any. 'We now know the name of our ruler,' said a fellah who had just heard of it, 'he is *Mawas* Pasha'—literally it is 'pimp'. It is a terrible epithet when uttered in a tone which gives it the true meaning, though in a general way the commonest word of abuse to a donkey, or a boy, or any other cattle. The wages of prostitution are unclean, and this tax renders all Government salaries unlawful according to strict law. The capitation tax too, which was remitted for three years on the Pashas' accession to the people of Cairo, Alexandria, Damietta and Rascheed, is now called for. Omar will have to pay about £8 back tax, which he had fondly imagined himself excused from. You may conceive the distress this must cause among artisans, etc., who have spent their money and forgotten it, and feel cheated out of the blessings they then bestowed on the Pasha—as to that they will take out the change in curses.

There was a meeting here the other day of the Cadi, Shaikh el-Beled, and other notables to fix the amount of tax each man was to pay towards the increased police tax; and the old Shereef at the end spoke up, and said he had heard that one man had asked me to lend him money, and that he hoped such a thing would not happen again. Everyone knew I had had heavy expenses this year, and most likely had not much money; that my heart was soft, and that as everyone was in distress it would be 'breaking my head', and in short that he should think it unmanly if anyone tried to trouble a lone woman with his troubles. I did offer one man £2 that he might not be forced to run away to the desert, but he refused it and said, 'I had better go at once and rob out there, and not turn rogue towards thee—never could I repay it'. The people are running away in all directions.

At the Moolid of the Shaikh the whole family of Abu-l-Hajjaj could only raise six hundred and twenty piastres among them to buy the buffalo cow, which by custom—strong as the laws of the Medes and Persians—must be killed for the strangers who come; and a buffalo cow is worth one thousand piastres. So the stout old Shereef (aged 87) took his staff and the six hundred and twenty piastres, and sallied forth to walk to Erment and see what God would send them; and a charitable woman in Erment did give a buffalo cow for the six hundred and twenty piastres, and he drove her home the twenty miles rejoicing.

There has been a burglary over at Gurna, an unheard-of event Some men broke into the house of the Coptic *gabit* (tax-gatherer) and stole the money-box containing about sixty purses—over £150. The *gabit* came to me sick with the fright which gave him jaundice, and about eight men are gone in chains to Keneh on suspicion. Hajji Baba too, a Turkish *cawass,* is awfully bilious; he says he is 'sick from beating men, and it's no use, you can't coin money on their backs and feet when they haven't a para in the world'. Altogether everyone is gloomy, and many desperate. I never saw the aspect of a population so changed.

Well now, for my own affairs. My boat is let for three months at £80 per month and £2 per day for any overtime if they keep her beyond the three months. I suppose the men's wages, cataract money, etc., will take half and that I shall make £120 clear by it; that is the usual profit, half for the crew and expenses, and half for the owner. So I have done very well. I shall have to pay the crew another month here or perhaps two. But I am wroth with my Reis who took seventeen days to go down and unless he can prove quite clearly what he was about I shall dismiss him. Food is cheap here: that is, meat and poultry, because everyone is forced to sell in order to pay the new taxes, and the market is glutted with turkeys; Omar bought nine fine ones for one pound sterling.

January 1 1867. God Bless you dearest Alick, and grant you many good years more. I must finish this to go tomorrow by the steamer. I would give a great deal to see you again, but when will that be.

January 12. Only two days ago I received letters from you of the 17 September and the 19 November. I wonder how many get lost and where? Janet gives me hopes of a visit of a few days in March and promises me a little terrier dog, whereat Omar is in raptures. I have made no plans at all, never having felt well enough to hope to be able to travel. The weather has changed for the better, and it is not at all cold now; we shall see what the warmth does for me.

I do hope, dear Alick, that if Maurice does not go on well at Brussels you will send him to Dresden or some quieter place. I look upon Brussels as the *most* dangerous place possible with all the French and English vices and the idleness and *kleinstädlerei* [narrow mentality] of a provincial town. I would much rather have him in Paris or in a

French provincial town. You make my bowels yearn with your account of Rainie. If only we had Prince Ahmad's carpet, and you could all come here for a few months.

We were greatly excited here last week; a boy was shot out in the sugar-cane field: he was with four Copts, and at first it looked ugly for the Copts. But the Maōhn tells me he is convinced they are innocent, and that they only prevaricated from fear—it was robbers shot the poor child. What struck and surprised me in the affair was the excessive horror and consternation it produced; the Maōhn had not had a murder in his district at all in eight years. The market-place was thronged with wailing women, Omar was sick all day, and the Maōhn pale and wretched. The horror of killing seems greater here than ever I saw it.

Palgrave says the same of the Arabian Arabs in his book: it is not one's notion of Oriental feeling, but a murder in England is taken quite as a joke compared with the scene here. I fear there will be robberies, owing to the distress, and the numbers who are running away from the land unable to pay their taxes. Don't fear for me, for I have two watchmen in the house every night—the regular guard and an amateur, a man whose boy I took down to Cairo to study in Gama el Azhar.

Palgrave has written to Ross wanting Mabrook back. I am very sorry, the more so as Mabrook is recalcitrant. 'I want to stay with thee, I don't want to go back to the Nazarene.' A boy who heard him said, 'but the Lady is a Nazarene too'; whereupon Mabrook slapped his face with great vigour. He will be troublesome if he does turn restive, and he is one who can only be managed by kindness. He is as good and quiet as possible with us, but the stubborn will is there and he is too ignorant to be reasoned with. I fear Palgrave will thrash him and arouse the bulldog spirit. Ghefieh is teaching him to pray and I promised him a shilling when he could say the *Fathah* to me without a fault. I hope Palgrave won't have him forcibly baptized, for he is as stout a Muslim as ignorant persons usually are.

January 14. We have had a very cold winter and I have been constantly ailing, luckily the cough has transferred itself from the night to the day, and I get some good sleep. The last two days have been much warmer and I hope matters will mend. I am beginning to take cod-liver oil, as we can't find a milch camel anywhere.

My boat has been well let in Cairo and is expected here every day. The gentlemen shoot, and tell the crew not to row, and in short take it easy, and give them £2 in every place. Imagine what luxury for my crew. I shall have to dismiss the lot, they will be so spoilt. The English Consul-General came up in a steamer with Dr Patterson and Mr Francis. I dined with them one day; I wish you could have seen me carried in my armchair high up on the shoulders of four men, like a successful candidate, or more like one of the Pharaohs in an ancient bas-relief, preceded by torch bearers and other attendants and followers, my procession was quite regal.

Poor Mustapha has been very unwell and I stopped his Ramadan, gave him some physic and ordered him not to fast, for which I think he is rather grateful. The Imaam and Mufti always endorse my prohibitions of fasting to my patients.

Old Ismaeen is dead, aged over a hundred; he served Belzoni, and when he grew doting was always wanting me to go with him to join Belzoni at Abu Simbel. He was not at all ill—he only went out like a candle. His grandson brought me a bit of the meat cooked at his funeral, and begged me to eat it, that I might live to be very old, according to the superstition here. When they killed the buffalo for the Shaikh Abu-l-Hajjaj, the man who had a right to the feet kindly gave them to Omar, who wanted to make calves' foot jelly for me. I had a sort of profane feeling, as if I were eating a descendant of the bull Apis.

I am reading Mme du Deffand's letters.[1] What a repulsive picture of a woman. I don't know which I dislike most, Horace Walpole or herself: the conflict of selfishness, vanity and *ennui* disguised as sentiment is quite hateful: to her Turgot was *un sot animal*—so much for her great gifts.

---

[1] The letters to Horace Walpole were published in 1810 edited by Miss Mary Berry— *Letters of the Marquise du Deffand to the Hon. Horace Walpole, afterwards Earl of Orford, from the year 1766 to the year 1780*, four volumes. Lucie may have obtained the 1865 edition of Marquise du Deffand's letters edited by Monsieur de Lescure.

Marquise du Deffand, 1697–1780, was a friend of Voltaire's and was famous for her Paris salon, her intelligence and cynical turn of mind.

XXXIX

'Arab versus Turk'

January 22 1867. Dearest Alick. Mr Edward Lear[1] has been here the last few days, and is just going up to the second cataract; he has done a little drawing of my house for you—a new view of it. He is a pleasant man and I was glad to see him.

Americans swarm in the steamboats, and a good many in *dahabiehs*.

Such a queer fellow came here the other day—a tall stalwart Holsteiner, I should think a man of fifty, who has been four years up in the Sudan and Sennaar, and being penniless, had walked all through Nubia begging his way. He was not the least 'down upon his luck' and spoke with enthusiasm of the hospitality and kindness of Sir Samuel Baker's 'tigers'. '*Ja, das sind die rechten kerls; das its das glückliche leben*' ['Those are the right sort of fellows. It's a glorious life'], he said.

His account is that if you go with an armed party, the blacks naturally show fight, as men with guns, in their eyes, are always slave hunters; but if you go alone and poor, they kill an ox for you, unless you prefer a sheep, give you a hut, and generally anything they have to offer, *merissey* (beer) to make you as drunk as a lord, and young ladies to pour it out for you—and—you need not wear any clothes. If you had heard him you would have started for the interior at once. I gave him a dinner and a bottle of common wine, which he emptied, and a few shillings, and away he trudged merrily towards Cairo. I wonder what the Nubians thought of a *howagah* begging. He said

[1] Edward Lear, 1812–88, visited Egypt and other Middle East countries in 1848–9 and returned to winter on the Nile in 1854–5 adding to his *Illustrated Journals of a Landscape Painter*. His first *Book of Nonsense* was written when he was employed by the Stanley family to draw the Knowsley menagerie and was for the amusement of Edward, the 15th earl.

they were all kind, and that he was sure he often ate what they pinched themselves to give—dourrah bread and dates.

January 23. Your letters of the 19th and 26th December came yesterday. I did write Maurice a 'jobation' setting forth that if you were to die he was at present very unfit to have the care of me and Rainie which it behoved him to consider. Don't mention it to him unless he tells you, as young people don't always like to think their faults are being 'talked over' by the old fogies. What a pity he is not more like Rainie. How different she is from both her seniors.

The weather has been lovely, for the last week, and I am therefore somewhat better. My boat arrived today, with all the men in high good-humour, and Omar tells me all is in good order, only the people in Cairo gave her the evil eye, and broke the iron part of the rudder which had to be repaired at Benisuef.

I am uneasy about the Egyptian Trading Company which I still think will go to the dogs. You know I thought badly of it long before anyone else did.

A certain Sir Drummond Stewart—I fancy an old soldier—and a Mr Trevelyan came to see me. They are furious with Ross who told them they might have confidence in Watson his storekeeper 'being an Englishman', and they accordingly hired a miserable little boat off him for £80 a month, which he told them was the regular price; he also told them it would take them four months to get to Aswan and back and persuaded them to sign a contract for that time. He sent them out with so bad a Reis that they have had to turn back from Esneh and, of course, finding that they have paid nearly double for a very bad article they are very savage and intend to write to *The Times* and to have an explanation with Ross. It is quite beyond belief how Ross perseveres in letting himself and others be cheated. I should have thought Watson had done enough in the way that he had swindled me. It is true the Englishmen were very green, but they say their Arab dragoman has not cheated them, and they thought that Ross's word sufficient to vouch for his storekeeper's honesty.

January 24. I am a good deal better since the weather got warmer, but I fear that I ought to stay here. The risk of the journey to Europe would be very great. I wish you could take November to February here with Maurice and go up the Nile. There is the boat so nice and only the crew to pay. Do think of it; are you too possessed with the idea that the Nile is a bore? Ask Mr Lear who was here the other day. He was in raptures.

The French Consul has sent up a man with a letter of introduction desiring me to receive him; he is going to open a drinking shop here—a sort of low *commis voyageur*. The man is gone to Esneh and I have written to the Consul to resign the house. Either it is a gross affront or a piece of carelessness. Luckily all Mustapha's hareem are away, except dear old black Mahboobeh, and I shall go and live with her and be very comfortable. My Arab friends are rabid at the notion of a low Frangee—a seller of arrak—being quartered on their Sitt.

January 26. Dearest Mother. Shaikh Yussuf's nice new wife was eager to have me with her; but the house is small and has no windows, and it is not yet warm enough for me to sleep *al fresco*. I must betray dear Yussuf's confidence and tell you his love story.

A young fellow ran away with a girl he loved a short time ago, she having told him that her parents wanted to marry her to another, and that she would go to such a spot for water, and he must come on a horse, beat her and carry her off (the beating saves the maiden's blushes). Well, the lad did it, and carried her to Salamieh where they were married, and then they went to Shaikh Yussuf to get him to conciliate the family, which he did. He told me the affair, and I saw he sympathized much with the runaways. 'Ah', he said 'Lady, it is love, and that is terrible, I can tell thee love is dreadful indeed to bear.'

Then he hesitated and blushed, and went on, 'I felt it once, Lady, it was the will of God that I should love her who is now my wife. Thirteen years ago I loved her and wished to marry her, but my father, and her grandfather my uncle the Shereef, had quarrelled, and they took her and married her to another man. I never told anyone of it, but my liver was burning and my heart ready to burst for three years; but when I met her I fixed my eyes on the ground for fear she should see my love, and I said to myself, Oh Yussuf, God has afflicted thee, praise be unto Him, do thou remember thy blood (Shereef) and let thy conduct be that of the Beni Azra who when they are thus afflicted die rather than sin, for they have the strongest passion of love and the greatest honour.

'And I did not die but went to Cairo to the Gama el-Azhar and studied, and afterwards I married twice, as thou knowest, but I never loved any but that one, and when my last wife died the husband of this one had just divorced her to take a younger and prettier one and my father desired me then to take her, but I was half afraid not knowing whether she would love me; but, Praise be to God I consented, and behold, poor thing, she also had loved me in like manner.'

I thought when I went to see her that she was unusually radiant with new-married happiness, and she talked of 'el-Shaikh' with singular pride and delight, and embraced me and called me 'mother' most affectionately. Is it not a pretty piece of regular Arab romance like Ghanem?

My boat has gone up today with two very nice Englishmen in her. Their young Maltese dragoman, aged twenty-four, told me his father often talked of my father and George Lewis, 'the Commissioners', and all they had done, and how things were changed in the island for the better.

Here we have the other side of the misery of the Candian business; in Europe, of course, the obvious thing is the sufferings of the Cretans, but really I am more sorry for the poor fellah lads who are dragged away to fight in a quarrel they had no hand in raising, and with which they have no sympathy.

The war in Crete saddens many a household here. Shaikh Yussuf's brother, Shaikh Yooris, is serving there, and many more. People are actually beginning to say 'We hope the English and French won't fight for the Sultan if the Moscovites want to eat him—there will be no good for us till the Turks are driven out'. All the old religious devotion to the Sultan seems quite gone.[1]

The Times suggests that the Sultan should relinquish the island, and that has been said in many an Egyptian hut long before. The Sultan is worn out, and the Muslims here know it, and say it would be the best day for the Arabs if he were driven out; that after all a Turk never was the true *Ameer el-Moomeneen* (Commander of the Faithful). Only in Europe people talk and write as if it were all Muslim *versus* Christian, and the Christians were all oppressed, and the Muslims all oppressors. I wish they could see the domineering of the Greeks and Maltese as Christians.

The Englishman domineers as a free man and a Briton, which is different, and that is the reason why the Arabs wish for English rule, and would dread that of Eastern Christians. Well they may; for if ever

[1] When Greece was declared independent of Turkey in 1830 it was decided by Britain, France and Russia that Crete should not be included in the new kingdom, but Mahmud II, Sultan of Turkey, was persuaded to cede it to Mohammed Ali Pasha, Viceroy of Egypt. Mustapha Pasha, an Albanian, was made Governor and carried out a more enlightened policy than any previous Turkish Governor. In 1840, when Mohammed Ali revolted against his suzerain, the Sultan, the Turks once more took control, though they left Mustapha Pasha as Governor until 1852. The Cretans became discontented and started a revolt in 1866 which lasted nearly three years before being suppressed by the Turkish Government, but some measure of autonomy was granted.

the Greeks do reign in Stamboul the sufferings of the Muslims will satisfy the most eager fanatic that ever cursed Mahound.

I know nothing of Turkey, but I have seen and heard enough to know that there are plenty of other divisions besides that of Christian and Muslim. Here in Egypt it is clear enough: it is Arab *versus* Turk and the Copt siding with the stronger for his interest, while he rather sympathizes with his brother fellah. At all events the Copt doesn't want other Christians to get power; he would far rather have a Muslim than a heretic ruler, above all the hated Greek. The Englishman he looks on as a variety of Muslim—a man who washes, has no pictures in his church, who has married bishops, and above all, who does not fast from all that has life for half the year, and this heresy is so extreme as not to give offence, unless he tries to convert.

The Pasha's sons have just been up the river; they ordered a reading of the Koran at the tomb of Abu-l-Hajjaj and gave every Alim sixpence. We have not left off chaffing (as Maurice would say) Shaikh Allah-ud-deen, the Muezzin, and sundry others on this superb backsheesh, and one old Fikee never knows whether to laugh, to cry, or to scold, when I ask to see the shawl and tarboosh he has bought with the presents of Pashas. Yussuf and the Cadi too had been called on to contribute baskets of bread to the steamer so that their sixpences were particularly absurd.

The little boy whose father died is still with the Abab'deh, who will not let him travel to Cairo till the weather is warmer and they find a safe person to be kind to him. Rachmeh says 'Please God, he will go with the Sitt, perhaps'. Hassan has consoled him with sugar-cane and indulgence, and if I lose Mabrook, and the little boy takes to me, he may fall into my hands as Ahmad has done. I hear he is a good boy but a perfect savage; that however, I find makes no difference—in fact, I think they learn faster than those who have ways of their own.

February 3. Dearest Alick. I cannot describe to you the misery here now, indeed it is wearisome even to think of: every day some new tax. Now every beast; camel, cow, sheep, donkey, horse, is made to pay. The fellaheen can no longer eat bread, they are living on barley meal, mixed with water and new green stuff, vetches, etc., which to people used to good food is terrible, and I see all my acquaintances growing seedy and ragged and anxious. Yussuf is clear of debt, his religion having kept him from borrowing, but he wants to sell his little slave girl, and has sold his donkey, and he is the best off. The taxation makes life almost impossible—100 piastres per feddan, a tax on every crop, on every annual fruit, and again when it is sold in the market; on every man, on charcoal, on butter, on salt, on the dancing girls. I wonder I am not tormented for money—not above three people have tried to beg or borrow.

The French Consul has written me a very civil letter, and one to turn out the grog shop man when he comes and assures me I shall not be disturbed. He also promises to get Mohammed's wages paid him about which I have written six or seven letters. I was forced to lend him ten napoleons as it seemed a scandal that the French servant should be beaten for taxes for lack of wages. I also hope the Prussian consul will appoint my Coptic friend Todoros agent here. He has done the work for eight years for another man who abjured his allegiance to the Franks the other day before the Mudir, whereupon Todoros was ordered to haul down his flag. The poor fellow is in an agony of dread lest his son (a charming lad of sixteen) should be taken as a soldier. So I wrote to Janet to get her to beg the Consul to appoint the man real agent and he says he will. I am a great fool not to make people backsheesh me. I daresay Hoseyn Bey, the Mudir of Keneh, thinks I do.

XL

Uncle Omar and the little 'slaves'

February 3 1867. Thanks for the Westminster epilogue; it always amuses me much. So Terence was a nigger. There is no trace of the negro 'boy' in his Davus. My nigger boy Mabrook has grown huge, and has developed a voice of thunder. He is of the elephantine rather than the tiger species, a very mild young savage. I shall be sorry when Palgrave takes him. I am tempted to buy Yussuf's nice little Dinka girl to replace him, only a girl is such an impossibility where there is no regular hareem.

I have just had Mabrook vaccinated. He is a very good boy, only he can't keep his clothes clean, never having been subject to that annoyance before. He has begun to be affectionate ever since I did not have him beaten for breaking my only looking-glass. I wish an absurd respect for public opinion did not compel the poor lad to wear a blue shirt and a tarbush (his suit); I see it is a misery to him. He has also got to be circumcised when the cold weather is over, as he declared positively he is a Muslim and of Muslim family, and he is rather big for the operation.

In the boat Ahmad is enough under Omar; but in this large dusty house, and with errands to run, and comers and goers to look after, pipes and coffee and the like, it takes two boys to be comfortable. Mabrook too washes very well.

It is surprising how fast the boys learn, and how well they do their work. Ahmad, who is quite little, would be a perfectly sufficient servant for a man alone; he can cook, wash, clean the rooms, make the beds, do all the table service, knife and plate cleaning, all fairly well, and I believe now he would get along even without Omar's orders.

Mabrook is slower, but he has the same merit our poor Hassan had,[1] he never forgets what he has been once told to do, and he is clean in his work, though hopelessly dirty as to his clothes. He cannot get used to them, and takes a roll in the dust, or leans against a dirty wall, oblivious of his clean-washed blue shirt. Ahmad is quicker and more careless, but they both are good boys and very fond of Omar. 'Uncle Omar' is the form of address, though he scolds them pretty severely if they misbehave; and I observe that the high jinks take place chiefly when only I am in the way, and Omar gone to market or to the mosque. The little rogues have found out that their laughing does not 'affect my nerves', and I am often treated to a share in the joke.

How I wish Rainie could see the children: they would amuse her. Yussuf's girl, *Meer en Nezzil*, is a charming child, and very clever; her emphatic way of explaining everything to me, and her gestures, would delight you. Her cousin and future husband, age five (she is six), broke the doll which I have given her, and her description of it was the most dramatic, ending with a wheedling glance at the cupboard and 'of course there are no more dolls there; oh no, no more'. She is a fine little creature, far more Arab than fellaha; quite a *Shaitan*, her father says. She came in full of making cakes for Bairam, and offered her services; 'Oh my aunt, if thou wantest anything I can work,' said she, tucking up her sleeves.

Luxor, February 18. I am in great anxiety having heard that the soldiers of Omar's old regiment are being called out, and he is in an agony of terror at the idea of going away from me into that miserable life again. I have written to the English Consul to grant him a passport or a nominal appointment in the Transit Office or Post Office or anything. I wonder whether it would be possible to get a *hemaya*, a Foreign Office passport or protection for him. I need not tell you what a sword of Damocles it is to think of being left without his care among people, who, kind as they are, know as much of sickness or of our habits as their own camels. If you get at Lord Stanley and get him to give a passport or anything indicating that he is under English protection, it would be an immense comfort.

P.S. Omar's name *has* been called in Cairo, but one of the dragomans managed to get it put aside for the present. You can't think what the war in Crete is to the people here. They, who take no sort of pleasure in killing Christians and only hate leaving their families— and the cold and the misery. Omar was illegally kidnapped in the

[1] See Introduction p. 18-20.

beginning, not being a fellah but a townsman and served his three years under the Viceroy Said Pasha.

February 19. Dearest Janet. My boat is up safe but not yet down the cataract, with three others in company. Should she get to Cairo before you leave you might tow her up; I daresay the beds would be better than the steamer's.

I continue very poorly and weak. I am not ill exactly, but I think I am getting near the end of the lease; my blood seems to go slower.

I have a good story. The Imam spoke of the snares of spiritual pride and said: 'Once an old Shaikh of religion deplored the difficulty he found in fixing his attention entirely on his prayer. A young Shaikh declared *he* had no difficulty, *he* was always totally absorbed. 'Well', said the elder holy man, 'it is now the *Asr*, pray, Oh man, and if thou canst keep thy thoughts fixed on God alone without wandering one moment I will give thee my cloak.' The younger stood up, said the 'Intention' and bowed to the earth; in the first *rekaa* '*Allahu Akbar*', said his lips, but inwardly it crossed his mind as he rose, 'will he give me the old black cloak or the new green one?'

March 6. Dearest Mother. I am going to write to Palgrave and ask him to let me send another boy or the money for Mabrook, who can't endure the notion of leaving me. Ahmad, who was always hankering after the fleshpots of Alexandria, got some people belonging to the boats to promise to take him, and came home and picked a quarrel and departed. Poor little chap; the Shaikh el-Beled 'put a spoke in his wheel' by informing him he would be wanted for the Pasha's works and must stay in his own place. Since he went Mabrook has come out wonderfully, and does his own work and Ahmad's with the greatest satisfaction. He tells me he likes it best so; he likes to be quiet. He just suits me and I him, it is humiliating to find how much more I am to the taste of savages than of the 'polite circles'.

I must tell you a black standard of respectability (it is quite equal to the English one of the gig, or the ham for breakfast). I was taking counsel with my friend Rachmeh, a negro, about Mabrook, and he urged me to buy him off Palgrave, because he saw that the lad really loved me. 'Moreover', he said, 'the boy is of a respectable family, for he told me his mother wore a cow's tail down to her heels (that and a girdle to which the tail is fastened, and a tiny leathern apron in front, constituted her whole wardrobe), and that she beat him well when he told lies or stole his neighbour's eggs.' Poor woman; I wish this abominable slave trade had spared her and her boy. What folly it is to stop the Circassian slave trade, if it is stopped, and to leave this. The Circassians take their own children to market, as a way of providing for them handsomely, and both boys and girls like being sold to the rich Turks; but the blacks and Abyssinians fight hard for their own liberty and that of their cubs.

Mabrook swears that there were two Europeans in the party which attacked his village and killed he knew not how many, and carried him and others off. He was not stolen by Arabs, or by Barrabia, like Hassan, but taken in war from his home by the seaside, a place called Bookee, and carried in a ship to Jedda, and thence back to Kosseir and Keneh, where Palgrave bought him.

I must say that once here the slaves are happy and well off, but the waste of life and the misery caused by the trade must be immense. The slaves are coming down the river by hundreds every week, and are very cheap—twelve to twenty pounds for a fine boy, and nine pounds and upwards for a girl. I heard that the last *gellab* offered a woman and baby for anything anyone would give for them, on account of the trouble of the baby. By-the-bye, Mabrook displays the negro talent for babies. Now that Ahmad is gone, who scolded them and drove them out, Mohammed's children, quite babies, are for ever trotting after 'Maboo', as they pronounce his name, and he talks incessantly to them. It reminds me so of Janet and poor Hassan,[1] but Mabrook is not like Hassan, he is one of the sons of Anak, and already as big and strong as a man, with the most prodigious chest and limbs.

If Palgrave will accept a replacement for Mabrook, perhaps I'll buy him a wife some day. It would be an eminently respectable and pious transaction and he could keep her in order.

I am drinking camel's milk again. Every morning the *naga* (she-camel) comes with her son and gives a huge jug of warm foaming milk, better than of any beast I know.

Don't be at all uneasy about me as to care. Omar knows exactly what to do as he showed the other day when I was taken with the blood-spitting. I had shown him the medicines and given him instructions so I had not even to speak, and if I were to be ill enough to want more help, Yussuf would always sit up alternate nights; but it is not necessary. Arabs make no grievance about broken rest; they don't 'go to bed properly', but lie down half dressed, and have a happy faculty of sleeping at odd times and anyhow, which enables

[1] See illustration 4.

25. The famous colossi of 'Memnon' in the Theban plain passed by
Lucie on the way back to Luxor from the Valley of the Kings – 'our
moonlight ride home was beyond belief beautiful'

26. Lucie's daughter Urania who died in 1878
at the age of twenty

them to wait on one day and night without distressing themselves as it distresses us. Omar sleeps in the room next mine, and in the hall beyond him the two Mohammeds, our guard and his cousin and Mabrook; so if Omar does not hear my whistle Mohammed does and calls him. I never had to wait one half minute, so be quite easy on that score. Omar continues to protest against any more servants.

March 6. Yussuf is so sorry I have not health nor he money enough, to go together to India. When I told him I had been invited, he said he should like to go with me, and we could visit the Ulema and hear all about everything. There would be a chance of hearing something instructive. A Mufti from the el Azhar University in Cairo and a Shereef to boot, is revered in the whole Muslim world, and with that guarantee would one hear all sorts of things. I question whether Yussuf would be as eager to see the English rule in Egypt as he is now. I fear not.

An American whom I saw tells me that there is a very handsome illustrated edition of my letters published in America. I wish they'd pay one for it. I saw in a catalogue of Williams and Norgate, to be sold cheap, a good edition of the *Arabian Nights* in Arabic. I should much like to have it, and also to give Yussuf Lane's Arabic Dictionary. Is it published yet? I can't read the *Arabian Nights,* but it is a favourite amusement to make one of the party read aloud. A stray copy of *Kamar-es-Zeman* and *Sitt Boodoora* went all round Luxor, and was much coveted for the village soirées. But its owner departed and left us to mourn over the loss of his MSS.

The warm weather has set in, and I am already as much the better for it as usual. I had a slight attack, not nearly so bad as that at Soden, but it lingered and I kept my bed as a measure of precaution. Dear Yussuf was with me the evening I was attacked, and sat up all night to give me my medicine every hour. At the prayer of dawn, an hour and a half before sunrise, I heard his supplications for my life and health, and for you and all my family; and I thought of what I had lately read, how the Greeks massacred their own patriots because the Turks had shown them mercy—a display of temper which I hope will enlighten Western Christendom as to what the Muslims have to expect, if they (the Western Christians) help the Eastern Christians to get the upper hand.

Yussuf was asking about Lady Herbert the other day who has turned Catholic. 'Poor thing', said he, 'the priests have drawn out her brains through her ears, no doubt: but never fear, her heart is good and her charity is great, and God will not deal hardly with those who serve Him with their hearts, though it is sad she should bow down before images. But look at thy slave Mabrook, can he understand one hundredth part of the thoughts of thy mind? Nevertheless he loves thee, and obeys thee with pleasure and alacrity; and wilt thou punish him because he knows not all thy ways? And shall God, who is so much higher above us as thou art above thy slave, be less just than thou?' I pinned him at once, and insisted on knowing the orthodox belief; but he quoted the Koran and the decisions of the Ulema to show that he stretched no point as far as Jews and Christians are concerned, and even that idolaters are not to be condemned by man.

Yussuf wants me to write a short account of the faith from his dictation. Would anyone publish it? It annoys him terribly to hear the Muslims constantly accused of intolerance, and he is right—it is not true. They show their conviction that their faith is the best in the world with the same sort of naïveté that I have seen in very innocent and ignorant English women; in fact, display a sort of religious conceit; but it is not often bitter or *haineux*, however much they are in earnest.

March 7. Dearest Alick. The heat has set in, and, of course with it my health has mended, but I am a little shaky and afraid to tire myself. Moreover I want to nurse up and be stronger by next Thursday when Janet and Ross are expected.

A dragoman gave me an old broken travelling armchair, and Yussuf sat in an armchair for the first time in his life. 'May the soul of the man who made it find a seat in Paradise', was his exclamation, which strikes me as singularly appropriate on sitting in a very comfortable armchair. Yussuf was thankful for small mercies in this case.

The state of business here is curious. The last regulations have stopped all money lending, and the prisons are full of Shaikh el-Beled whose villages can't pay the taxes. Most respectable men have offered me to go partners with them now in their wheat, which will be cut in six weeks, if only I would pay their present taxes, I to take half the crop and half the taxes, with interest out of their half—some such trifle as 30 per cent per month.

Our prison is full of men, and we send them their dinner *à tour de rôle*. The other day a woman went with a big wooden bowl on her head, full of what she had cooked for them, accompanied by her husband. One Khaleel Effendi, a new vakeel here, was there, and said, 'What dost thou ask here thou harlot?' Her husband answered, 'That

is no harlot, oh Effendim, but my wife'. Whereupon he was beaten till
he fainted, and then there was a lamentation; they carried him down
past my house, with a crowd of women all shrieking like mad creatures,
especially his wife, who yelled and beat her head and threw dust over
it, *more majorum*, as you see in the tombs. The humours of tax-
gathering in this country are quite *impayable* you perceive—and
ought to be set forth on the escutcheon of the new Knight of the Bath
whom the Queen hath delighted to honour. *Cawass* battant, fellah
rampant, and fellaha pleurant would be the proper blazon.[1]

Distress in England is terrible, but, at least, it is not the result of
extortion, as it is here, where everything from nature is so abundant
and glorious, and yet mankind so miserable. It is not a little hunger,
it is the cruel oppression which maddens the people now. They never
complained before, but now whole villages are deserted.

---

[1] The new Knight was Robert Colquhoun, after his retirement as British Consul.

XLI

Henry and Janet Ross visit Lucie in Luxor

Luxor, March 7 1867. I enclose a note from a Copt boy, which will amuse you. He is 'sapping' at English, and I teach him whenever I am able. I am a special favourite with all the young lads; they must not talk much before grown men, so they come and sit on the floor round my feet, and ask questions and advice, and enjoy themselves amazingly. Hobble-de-hoy-hood is very different here from what it is with us; they care earlier for the affairs of the grown-up world, and are more curious and more polished, but lack the fine animal gaiety of our boys. The girls are much more *gamin* than the boys, and more romping and joyous.

A telegram has just come announcing that Janet will leave Cairo tomorrow in a steamer, and therefore be here, *Inshallah*, this day week.

It is very warm now. I fear Janet will sigh terribly over the heat. They have left their voyage too late for such as do not love the Shems el-Kebeer (the big sun), which has just begun. I who worship Ammun Ra, love to feel him in his glory. I am afraid Janet may be bored by all the people's civility; they will insist on making great dinners and fantasias for her I am sure. I hope they will go on to Aswan and take me with them; the change will do me good, and I should like to see as much of her as I can before she leaves Egypt for good.

*   *   *

Luxor, March 11 1867. [Janet Ross to her father Alexander]. Here we are enjoying Mamma's wonderful talk, all we wish for is that you were here too. We got here at eight in the morning of the 9th and the heat was tremendous. You'll hardly believe that when my small black-and-tan-terrier Bob, which I am going to leave with Mamma, ran ashore before me, he immediately began to howl; I found his poor tiny feet had been blistered by the hot sand. However, my mother enjoys it and declares this burning sun does her good. I can't say she looks well, and I find her a good deal aged.

You have no idea what a power she is in the land. Henry, who knows the East, is astonished. At first when we stopped to coal or to try and buy food, we found the village deserted. Only a few tiny children or very old women were to be seen, who said they had nothing, no sheep, no chicken, no milk, no bread. Our Mohammed grasped the situation. A Government steamer meant no piastres and *courbash* into the bargain, so he tumbled over the side of the boat, swam ashore, and cut across the fields, where the river made a great bend to the village where we were to anchor for the night. There he proclaimed aloud that the daughter of the Sitt-el-Kebir (the Great Lady) was on board, who, like her mother, loved the Arabs. The effect was magical. No more difficulties about food. Milk, fowls, lambs, etc., suddenly appeared at absurdly low prices, some were even brought as gifts and we had to insist on the people taking money for them. It is extraordinary how fast news travels here. As we got nearer to Luxor, we found people waiting at the landing places with presents of bread, milk, fowls, etc. One man had been doctored by *Sittee Noor-ala-Noor*, to another she had given a lift in her boat, and a man to whose child she had been kind rode all the way from Keneh to Luxor to announce our arrival. Mohammedan intolerance was shown by the *Ulema* bringing the religious flags to decorate Mamma's house in honour of our visit.

[This was not Lucie's view.] When I got up on the morning Janet was expected, I found the house decked with palm branches and lemon blossoms, and the holy flags of Abu-l-Hajjaj waving over my balcony. The mosque people had brought them, saying all the people were happy today, because it was a fortunate day for me. I suppose if I had had a mind to *testify*, I ought to have indignantly torn down the banners which bore the declaration, 'There is no God but God, and Mohammed is His Prophet'. But it appeared to me that if Imams and Muezzins could send their banners to decorate a Christian house, the Christian might manage to endure the kindness. Then there was *fantasia* on horseback, and all the notables to meet the boat, and general welcome and jubilation.

In the evening [continued Janet Ross], we dined with Seleem Effendi, the *Maōhn*, or magistrate of Luxor, a pleasant, jovial man with a dear old wife who insisted on waiting on us at table, in spite of Henry's presence. Our procession to dinner was quite Biblical. Mamma on her donkey, which I led, while Henry walked by her side. Two boys in front had lanterns, and Omar in his best clothes walked behind carrying some sweet dish for which he is famous, followed by more lantern bearers. As we went through the little village the people came out of their mud huts and called on Allah to bless us, the men throwing down their poor cloaks for my mother to ride over and the women kissing the hem of her dress. The dinner was an elaborate one of many courses, during which we made no end of pretty speeches to each other, and then we had pipes and coffee, and the *Maōhn's* wife actually came and sat with us. Henry belonged to the Sitt-el-Kebir—that was enough. Yesterday we went to the ruins of Karnac close by, which are magnificent.

I long to tunnel under this house [the *Maison de France*]. It is built on the top of a big temple, and our floor is composed of the huge slabs of the roof. Where there are cracks one looks down into seemingly bottomless darkness. I don't think part of it is quite safe, indeed three or four rooms fell in last year, but not where Mamma lives. That side looks all right. Her balcony, looking over the river, is enchanting, and the sunsets are glorious. Tomorrow we go up to Aswan as Mamma thinks a change will do her good, and thus we shall see Philæ.

March 17. We stopped at Esneh for the night and then went on to Aswan, a small dirty village in a beautiful situation. Mamma is ever so much better, I think having a good talk has done her good. And how she talks! There is no one like her. At Aswan we crossed the river in our small boat and went to the island of Elephantine, where there are a few remains of ruins. I longed to dig. We slept on the steamer, of course, and next morning Mamma and Henry hired a little boat and were towed up the cataracts to Philæ. I do hope that some day you will see all this, only I fear the intense heat would knock you up. Both Henry and I have bad eyes from the reflection of the sun off the sand, and the whole land shimmers and quivers with the heat. We hoped to find Mamma's *dahabieh* here, as she would like to go down to Keneh with us and then sail back, but we have just heard that Mr Baird and Mr Eaton, who hired the boat, will not be coming down the Nile for some weeks. We were lamenting over this when a Nubian trader, who had heard in the mysterious way people do hear things in Egypt, that the *Sitt-el-Kebir* wanted a boat, sent up to ask for an audience. With many salaams he came in and said he had taken all his goods out of his and cleaned her well, and that now she belonged to the *Sittee* who had saved his nephew's life when ill of cholera last year at Luxor. Mamma refused to take the boat unless the man let her pay for it, saying she could not detain him on his journey and perhaps spoil the sale of his goods without in some way making it up to him. The Nubian answered in an eloquent speech: 'My boat is, I know, not worthy of sheltering so great an Emeereh, but I hoped she would have accepted so small a thing.' Then Omar stepped forward and spoke for the Nubian, and the end was that she [the boat] was accepted and Omar promised to make the man take a present.

March 21. Our departure from Luxor was very touching. The inhabitants came to say good-bye and bring us presents.[1]

* * *

April 12. Dearest Mother. You will hear from Janet about her excursion. What I liked best was shooting the Cataract in a small boat; it was fine *fantasia*.

Janet has left me her little black-and-tan terrier, a very nice little dog, but I can't hope to rival Omar in his affections. He sleeps in Omar's bosom, and Omar spoils and pets him all day, and boasts to the people how the dog drinks tea and coffee and eats dainty food, and the people say Mashallah! whereas I should have expected them to curse the dog's father.

The other day a scrupulous person drew back with an air of alarm from Bob's approach, whereupon the dog stared at him, and forthwith plunged into Shaikh Yussuf's lap, from which stronghold he 'yapped' defiance at whoever should object to him. I never laughed more heartily, and Yussuf went into a *fou rire*. The mouth of the dog only is unclean, and Yussuf declares he is a very well-educated dog, and does not attempt to lick; he pets him accordingly, and gives him tea in his own saucer, only *not* in the cup.

I am to inherit another little blackie from Ross's agency at Keneh: the funniest little chap. I cannot think why I go on expecting so-called savages to be different from other people. Mabrook's simple talk about his village, and the animals and the victuals; and how the men

[1] *Fourth Generation*, by Janet Ross, p. 164–9.

of a neighbouring village stole him in order to sell him for a gun (the price of a gun is a boy), but were prevented by a razzia of Turks, etc., who killed the first aggressors and took all the children—all this he tells just as an English boy might tell of bird-nesting—delights me. He has the same general notion of right and wrong; and yet his tribe know neither bread nor any sort of clothes, nor cheese nor butter, nor even drink milk, nor the African beer; and it always rains there, and is always deadly cold at night, so that without a fire they would die. They have two products of civilization—guns and tobacco, for which they pay in boys and girls, whom they steal. I wonder where the country is, it is called Sowaghli [Sawahil or East coast of Africa], and the next people are Mueseh [possibly Masai], on the sea-coast, and it is not so hot as Egypt.

The new *négrillon* is from Darfur. Won't Maurice be amused by his attendants; the Darfur boy will trot after him, as he can shoot and clean guns, tiny as he is. Maurice seems to wish to come and I hope Alexander will let him spend the winter here, and I will take him up to the second Cataract; I really think he would enjoy it.

Mabrook quarrelled with a boy belonging to the quarter close to us about a bird, and both boys ran away. The Arab boy is missing still I suppose, but Mabrook was brought back by force, swelling with passion, and with his clothes most scripturally 'rent'. He had regularly 'run amuck'.

Shaikh Yussuf lectured him on his insolence to the people of the quarter, and I wound up by saying, 'Oh my son! whither dost thou wish to go? I cannot let thee wander about like a beggar, with torn clothes and no money, that the police may take thee and put thee in the army; but say where thou desirest to go, and we will talk about it with discretion'. It was at once borne in upon him that he did not want to go anywhere, and he said, 'I repent; I am but an ox, bring the courbash, beat me, and let me go to finish cooking the Sitt's dinner'. I remitted the beating, with a threat that if he bullied the neighbours again he would get it at the police, and not from Omar's very inefficient arm. In half an hour he was as merry as ever. It was a curious display of negro temper, and all about nothing at all. As he stood before me, he looked quite grandly tragic; and swore he only wanted to run outside and die; that was all.

April 12. Dearest Mother. I have just received your letters including the one for Omar which I read to him, and which he kissed and said he would keep as a talisman. I have given him an order on Coutts' correspondent for the money, in case I die. Omar proposes to wait until we get to Cairo and then to buy a floor in a house (in Alexandria) in which he will settle his wife and children. I am to keep all the money until the house is found. In this way he will be delivered from the rapacity of his brothers, with one or other of whom his wife has had to live hitherto, and he will be in no way tempted to do anything foolish with it. I hope you approve.

Many thanks, too, for the trouble you have taken to get a 'protection'. I don't think the notion of buying him off at all advisable. If you offer backsheesh (and it would be illegal) the Turks think you are afraid and keep on asking for more. Of course, if Colonel Stanton chooses to get him a discharge he can and I doubt not he will after the letters he has received.

The post here is dreadful, I would not mind their reading one's letters if they would only send them on. Omar begs me to say that he and his children will pray for you all his life, please God, not for the money only but still more for the good words and the trusting him. But he says, 'I can't say much *politikeh*, Please God she shall see, only I kiss her hand now.'

So Victor Cousin[1] is gone! Well, he had rather outlived himself in some respects. It is well he had not time to make a scandal with priests and 'sacraments', which I believe he would have done. I hope it is true that he has provided for St Hilaire;[2] that will be better for him than all the prayers in Christendom. I must leave off now and write a few lines to Janet.

[1] Victor Cousin, 1792–1867, the French philosopher and educationist, was a close friend of the family. Janet Ross wrote in *The Fourth Generation*: 'My grandmother Austin, then in the height of her beauty, met him at Bonn in 1828, just before he returned to France. They became intimate friends, fraternized on the subject of popular education, and four years later she translated his report on the state of education in Prussia and Holland. In 1840 Monsieur Thiers appointed him Minister of Public Instruction, but twelve years later he retired from public life, as he refused to take the oath or to serve under the Prince President [Louis Napoleon]. No words can describe the charm and brilliancy of his talk.'

[2] Barthelmy St Hilaire, 1805–96, first became a friend of the Austin family when Sarah used to have a salon in Paris where eminent men of different countries used to come to drink tea in her humble apartment where, he wrote, 'l'intelligence seule faisait tous les frais'. St Hilaire was a close friend of Victor Cousin and they were both strongly opposed to Louis Napoleon's rise to power as a semi-dictator and Emperor. With the return of the Republic he took service with Monsieur Thiers. St Hilare was a poor and kind man who used to get up at 4.30 in the morning to save his *bonne* the trouble of lighting his fire while he was working on his translation of Aristotle.

XLII

'The dignified manner of men of learning'

Luxor, April 19. Dearest Alick. I have been much amused lately by a new acquaintance, who, in romances of the last century, would be called an 'Arabian sage'. Shaikh Abdurrachman lives in a village half a day's journey off, and came over to visit me and to doctor me according to the science of Galen and Avicenna.

Fancy a tall, thin, graceful man, with a grey beard and liquid eyes, absorbed in studies of the obsolete kind, a doctor of theology, law, medicine and astronomy. We spent three days in arguing and questioning; I consented to swallow a potion or two which he made up before me, of very innocent materials. My friend is neither a quack nor superstitious, and two hundred years ago would have been a better physician than most in Europe. Indeed I would rather swallow his physic now than that of many a M.D.

I found him like all the learned theologians I have known, extremely liberal and tolerant. You can conceive nothing more interesting and curious than the conversation of a man learned and intelligent, and utterly ignorant of all our modern Western science. If I was pleased with him, he was enchanted with me, and swore by God that I was a Mufti indeed, and that a man could nowhere spend time so delightfully as in conversation with me. He said he had been acquainted with two or three Englishmen who had pleased him much, but that if all Englishwomen were like me the power must necessarily be in our hands, for that my intellect was far above that of the men he had known.

He objected to our medicine that it seemed to consist in palliatives, which he rather scorned, and aimed always at a radical cure. I told him that if he had studied anatomy he would know that radical cures were difficult of performance, and he ended by lamenting his ignorance of English or some European language, and that he had not learned our *Ilm* (science) also.

Then we plunged into sympathies, mystic numbers, and the occult virtues of stones, etc., and I swallowed my mixture (consisting of liquorice, cummin and soda) just as the sun entered a particular house, and the moon was in some favourable aspect. He praised to me his friend, a learned Jew of Cairo. I could have fancied myself listening to Abu Suleyman of Cordova, in the days when we were the barbarians and the Arabs were the learned race.

There is something very winning in the gentle, dignified manners of all the men of learning I have seen here, and their homely dress and habits make it still more striking. I longed to photograph my Shaikh as he sat on the divan pulling MSS out of his bosom to read me the words of *El-Hakeem Lokman*, or to overwhelm me with the authority of some physician whose very name I had never heard.

Abdurrachman was wroth at my want of faith in physic generally, as well as in particular, and said I talked like an infidel, for had not God said, 'I have made a medicine for every disease?' I said, 'Yes, but He does not say that He has told the doctors which it is; and meanwhile I say, *hekmet Allah* (God will cure), which can't be called an infidel sentiment'. Then we got into alchemy, astrology, magic and the rest; and Yussuf vexed his friend by telling gravely stories palpably absurd. Abdurrachman intimated that he was laughing at *El-Ilm el-Muslimeen* (the science of the Muslims), but Yussuf said, 'What is the *Ilm el-Muslimeen?* God has revealed religion through His prophets, and we can learn nothing new on that point; but all other learning He has left to the intelligence of men, and the Prophet Mohammed said, "All learning is from God, even the learning of idolaters". Why then should we Muslims shut out the light, and want to remain ever like children? The learning of the Franks is as lawful as any other.' Abdurrachman was too sensible a man to be able to dispute this, but it vexed him.

The hand of the Government is awfully heavy upon us. All this week the people have been working night and day cutting their unripe corn, because three hundred and ten men are to go tomorrow to work on the railroad below Assiut. This green corn is, of course, valueless to sell and unwholesome to eat; so the magnificent harvest of this year is turned to bitterness at the last moment. From a neighbouring village all the men are gone, and seven more are wanted to make up the *corvée*. The population of Luxor is 1,000 males of all ages, so you can guess how many strong men are left after three hundred and ten are taken. Omar begs me to tell you how deeply he feels your kindness in saying you would have him bought off. I hear the affair is settled, though I don't know in what way.

I don't like to think too much about seeing you and Maurice next winter for fear I should be disappointed. If I am too sick and wretched I can hardly wish you to come, because I know what a nuisance it is to be with one always coughing and panting, and unable to do like other people. But if I pick up tolerably this summer I shall indeed be glad to see you and him once more.

This house is falling sadly to decay, which produces snakes and scorpions. I sent for the *hawee* (snake-charmer) who caught a snake, but who can't conjure the scorpions out of their holes. One of my fat turkeys has just fallen a victim, and I am in constant fear for little Bob, only he is always in Omar's arms. A real calamity is the loss of our good Maōhn, Seleem Effendi. The Mudir hailed him from his steamer to go to Keneh directly, with no further notice. We hoped some good luck for him, and so it would have been to a Turk. He is made overseer over the poor people at the railway work, and only gets two pounds five shillings per month additional, he has to keep a horse and a donkey, and to buy them and to hire a sais, and he does *not* know how to squeeze the fellaheen.

It is true 'however close you skin an onion, a clever man can always peel it again', which means that even the poorest devils at the works can be beaten into giving a little more; but our dear Seleem, God bless him, will be ruined and made miserable by his promotion. I had a very woeful letter from him yesterday.

I can't write more, a rat having *eaten* a piece of my thumb in the night.

May 15. I am tired of telling all the *plackerein* of our poor people, how three hundred and ten men were dragged off on Easter Monday with their bread and tools, how in four days they were all sent back from Keneh, because there were no orders about them, and made to *pay their boat hire*. Then in five days they were sent for again. Meanwhile the harvest was cut green, and the wheat is lying out unthreshed to be devoured by birds and rats, and the men's bread was wasted and spoiled with the hauling in and out of boats. I am obliged to send camels twenty miles for charcoal, because the Abab'deh won't bring it to market any more, the tax is too heavy. Butter too we have to buy secretly, none comes into the market.

When I remember the lovely smiling landscape which I first beheld from my windows, swarming with beasts and men, and look at the dreary waste now, I feel the 'foot of the Turk' heavy indeed. Where there were fifty donkeys there is but one; camels, horses, all are gone; not only the horned cattle, even the dogs are more than decimated, and the hawks and vultures seem to me fewer; mankind has no food to spare for hangers-on. The donkeys are sold, the camels confiscated, and the dogs dead (the one sole advantage). Meat is cheap, as everyone must sell to pay taxes and no one has money to buy. I am implored to take sheep and poultry for what I will give.

We had a fright about Bob who walked up to a large Arab dog and, quite unprovoked, bit his leg. The dog returned the compliment in his shoulder. Omar was in such a state! He wanted to kill the dog and wept over Bob; however, the latter is none the worse. He goes about in a neat white waistcoat to keep off the flies and to prevent him from scratching the sore place. Omar is quite besotted with Bob and spoils him worse than any fine lady, and Bob gives himself airs in consequence but is well and happy.

XLIII

The Coptic Patriarch is insulting

Luxor, May 15 1867. Dearest Alick. All the Christendom of Upper Egypt is in a state of excitement, owing to the arrival of the Patriarch of Cairo, who is now in Luxor. My neighbour, Michaïl, entertains him, and Omar has been busily decorating his house and arranging the illumination of his garden, and today is gone to cook the confectionery, he being looked upon as the person best acquainted with the customs of the great.

Last night the Patriarch sent for me, and I went to kiss his hand, but I won't go again. It was a very droll caricature of the thunders of the Vatican.

Poor Michaïl had planned that I was to dine with the Patriarch, and had borrowed my silver spoons, etc., etc., in that belief. But the representative of St Mark is furious against the American missionaries who have converted some twenty Copts at Koos, and he could not bring himself to be decently civil to a Protestant.

I found a coarse-looking man seated on a raised divan smoking his chibouk, on his right were some priests on a low divan; I went up and kissed his hand and was about to sit by the priests, but he roughly ordered a *cawass* to put a wooden chair *off the carpet* to his left, at a distance from him, and told me to sit there. I looked round to see whether any of my neighbours were present, and I saw the consternation in their faces so, not wishing to annoy them, I did as if I did not perceive the affront, and sat down and talked for half an hour to the priests, and then took leave.

I was informed that the Catholics were *naas meskeen* (poor inoffensive people), and that the Muslims at least were of an old religion, but that the Protestants ate meat all the year round, 'like dogs'— 'or

Muslims', put in Omar, who stood behind my chair and did not relish the mention of dogs and the 'English religion' in one sentence.

As I went the Patriarch called for dinner, it seems he had told Michaïl he would not eat with me. It is evidently 'a judgment' of a most signal nature that I should be snubbed for the offences of missionaries, but it has caused some ill blood; the Cadi and Shaikh Yussuf, and the rest, who all intended to do the civil to the Patriarch, now won't go near him on account of his rudeness to me. He has come up in a steamer, at the Pasha's expense, with a guard of *cawasses*, and, of course, is loud in praise of the Government, though he failed in getting the Mudir to send all the Protestants of Koos to the public works, or the army.

Saturday. Yesterday I heard a little whispered grumbling about the money demanded by the 'Father'. One of my Copt neighbours was forced to sell me his whole provision of cooking butter to pay his quota. This a little damps the exultation caused by seeing him so honoured by the Effendina. Keneh gave him 200 purses (£600). I do not know what Luxor has given yet, but it falls heavy on the top of all the other taxes. One man who had heard that he had called the American missionaries 'beggars,' grumbled to me, 'Ah yes, beggars, beggars, they didn't beg of me for money'. I really do think that there must be something in this dread of the Protestant movement.

Evidently the Pasha is backing up the Patriarch who keeps his church well apart from all other Christians, and well under the thumb of the Turks. It was pretty to hear the priests talk so politely of Islam, and curse the Protestants so bitterly. We were very nearly having a row about a woman, who formerly turned Muslimeh to get rid of an old blind Copt husband who had been forced upon her, and was permitted to recant, I suppose in order to get rid of the Muslim husband in his turn. However he said, 'I don't care, she is the mother of my two children, and whether she is Muslim or Christian she is my wife, and I won't divorce her, but I'll send her to church as much as she likes'. Thereupon the priests of course dropped the wrangle, much to the relief of Shaikh Yussuf, in whose house she had taken up her quarters after leaving the church, and who was afraid of being drawn into a dispute.

The Patriarch has made a blunder with his progress. He has come ostentatiously as the *protegé* and *pronem* of the Pasha, and he has 'eaten' and beaten the fellaheen. The Copts of Luxor have had to pay fifty pounds for the honour of his presence, besides no end of sheep, poultry, butter, etc. If I were of a proselytizing mind I could make converts of several whose pockets and backs are smarting, and the Amercian missionaries will do it. Of course the Muslims sympathize with the converts to a religion which has no 'idols', and no monks, and whose priests marry like other folk, so they are the less afraid. I hear there are now fifty Protestants at Koos, and the Patriarch was furious because he could not beat them. Omar cooked a grand dinner for him last night for our neighbour Michaïl, and the eating was not over till two in the morning.

From what he said before me about the Abyssinians, and still more, from what he said to others about the English prisoners up there, I am convinced that the place to put the screw on is the *Batrarchane* (Patriarch's palace) at Cairo, and that the priests are at the bottom of that affair. The Patriarch answered me sharply when I asked about the state of religion in Abyssinia that, 'they were lovers of the faith, and his obedient children'. Whenever there is mischief among the Copts, the priests are at the bottom of it. If the Patriarch chose those people would be let go; and so it would be but he hates all Europeans bitterly.[1]

I wonder when Europe will drop the absurd delusion about

[1] The Coptic Patriarch was and is in control of the Copts throughout Egypt, where they numbered then about two to three hundred thousand, and of the Copts throughout Abyssinia where they were the majority of the population and the rulers were of the Coptic faith.

The Emperor Theodore was a particularly zealous Copt but it was not for that reason that he had imprisoned fifteen Europeans including Captain C. D. Cameron, the British Consul, the Rev. Henry Stern, Agent for the London Society for Promoting Christianity among the Jews, and a number of German Protestants.

At the beginning of 1862 Captain Cameron had presented the Emperor with various presents from the British Government and with a letter from Queen Victoria to which the Emperor replied with a letter which required an answer. This reached the Foreign Office in February 1863 but it was mislaid and no answer was sent which angered the proud Emperor. He was also infuriated by a visit paid by Cameron to Kassala on the frontier with the Egyptians and Turks with whom Theodore considered he was at war. In revenge for what he considered were insults he imprisoned the Europeans. Henry Layard, who was Under-Secretary of State for Foreign Affairs, tried every method he could think of to have the prisoners released and received many suggestions from Samuel Baker, Gifford Palgrave, Dr Charles Beke and others.

The British Government belatedly sent Hormuzd Rassam from Aden with presents and a letter from Queen Victoria. But the Emperor Theodore, who had taken to drinking heavily, continued to be suspicious and it was not until January 1866 that Rassam's party was able to enter Abyssinia and contact the prisoners. They were released but then imprisoned again and sent to Magdala where they were put in chains. Lord Russell, the Prime Minister, and Layard were under strong attack for their failure to release the prisoners. 'How miserable, shabby, paltry our whole conduct,' wrote Sir Henry Bulwer to Layard. 'A housemaid of the defunct Britannia would have been ashamed of it.'

27. (a) Lucie's son Maurice, 1849–96, 4th baronet
and 6th Laird of Fyvie

27. (b) Fyvie Castle near Aberdeen

28. Lucie's grand-daughter, Lina Duff Gordon (Mrs Aubrey Waterfield), 1874-1962, only daughter of Sir Maurice Duff Gordon,
painted by G. F. Watts in a dress which originally
belonged to Lucie Duff Gordon

Christians being persecuted by Muslims. It is absolutely the other way
—here at all events. The Christians know that they will always get
backed by some Consul or other, and it is the Muslims who go to
the wall invariably. The brute of a Patriarch is resolved to continue
his persecution of the converts, and I was urged the other day by a
Shaikh to go to the Shaikh ul-Islam himself and ask him to demand
equal rights for all religions, which is the law, on behalf of these
Coptic Protestants. Everywhere the Ulema have done what they
could to protect them, even at Assiut, where the American missionaries
had caused them (the Ulemas) a good deal of annoyance on a former
occasion. No one in Europe can conceive how much the Copts have
the upper hand in the villages. They are backed by the Government,
and they know that the Europeans will always side with them.

The Abab'deh have just been here and propose to take me, two
months hence, to the Moolid of Shaikh Abu-l-Hassan el-Shadlee (the
coffee saint) in the desert three days' journey from Edfu. No English
have ever been there they think, and all the wild Abab'deh and Bishareen go with their women and their camels. It is very tempting for
I sleep very ill and my cough is harassing and perhaps a change like
that might do me good.

Yussuf and his uncle want to take me next year to Mecca, the good
folks in Mecca would hardly look for a heretical face under the green
veil of a *Shereefateh* of Abu-l-Hajjaj. The Hajjis (pilgrims) have just
started from here to Kossier with camels and donkeys, but most
are on foot. They are in great numbers this year. The women chanted
and drummed all night on the river bank, and it was fine to see fifty
or sixty men in a line praying after their Imám with the red glow of
the sunset behind them. The prayer in common is quite a drill and
very stately to see. There are always quite as many women as men;
one wonders how they stand the march and the hardships.

It is so dreadfully hot and dusty that I shall rather hasten my departure if I can. The winds seem to have begun, and as all the land
which last year was green is now desert and dry the dust is four
times as bad. If I hear that Ross has bought and sent up a *dahabieh*
I will wait for that, if not I will go in three weeks if I can.

Luxor, May 23. Dearest Mother. The boat arrived all right on
Tuesday and I have made £150 by her. She brought the tin box.
Many thanks for all the things, above all for the spectacles which
made me shake to see and touch them. I saw the dear white head

shining at the little side window, and the gesture of taking them off and laying them on the table, like a vision; also your gown brought back a picture to me. The books and toys are very welcome. The latter threw little Darfur into ecstasies, and he got into disgrace for 'playing with the Sitt' instead of minding some business on hand. I fear I shall spoil him, he is so extremely engaging and such a baby. He is still changing his teeth, so cannot be more than eight; at first I did not like him, and feared he was sullen, but it was the usual *khoss* (fear), the word that is always in one's ears, and now that is gone, he is always coming hopping in to play with me. He is extremely intelligent, and has a pretty baby nigger face.

The Darfur people are, as you know, an independent and brave people, and by no means 'savages'. I can't help thinking how pleased Rainie would be with the child. He asked me to give him the picture of the English Sultaneh out of the *Illustrated London News,* and has pasted it inside the lid of his box. [Lucie described him in a letter to Urania:]

One boy is no bigger than you; he comes from Darfur, a country far away to the south, where they have a king of their own, and all the people learn to read and write so they are not savages, though quite black and with thick lips and woolly hair. When a little boy has learnt to read and write quite well, his master carries him on his shoulders to his father's house who makes a feast for him and all his school-fellows. At least so my little boy tells me, only he was stolen when he was too little to know his letters. [Lucie's letter to her mother continued:]

I am better as usual, since the hot weather has begun, the last six days. I shall leave this in a week, I think, and Mustapha and Yussuf will go with me to Cairo. Yussuf was quite enchanted with your note to him; his eyes glistened, and he took an envelope to keep it carefully. Omar said such a letter is like a *hegab* (amulet) and Yussuf said, 'Truly it is, and I could never have one with more *baraka* (blessing) or more like the virtue which went out of Jesus, if ever I wore one at all; I will never part with it.'

We had a very pretty festival for the Shaikh, whose tomb you have a photograph of, and I spent a very pleasant evening with Shaikh Abd el-Moutowil, who used to scowl at me, but now we are 'like brothers'. I found him very clever, and better informed than any Arab I have met, who is quite apart from all Franks. I was astonished to find that he *abondait dans mon sens* [entirely agreed with me] in my dispute with Shaikh Abdurrachman, and said that it was the duty of Muslims to learn what they could from us, and not to stick to the old routine.

I should like to have the *Revue des Deux Mondes* of all things, but I don't know how it is to come here, or what the postage would cost. They send nothing but letters above Cairo by post, as all goes on men's backs. 'Inshallah! I am the bearer of good news', cries the postman, as he flings the letter over the wall. I am so glad of the chance of getting news to you quick by Giafar Pasha, who came here like a gentleman, alone, without a retinue; he is on his way from two years in the Sudan, where he was absolute Pasha. He is very much liked and respected, and seems a very sensible and agreeable man, quite unlike any Turkish big-wig I have seen. Great potentate as he is, he made Yussuf, Mustapha and Abdallah sit down, and was extremely civil and simple in his manners. I believe he is a real Turk and not a mameluke like the rest.

A queer little Indian from Delhi who had been converted to Islam, and spent four years at Mecca acting as dragoman to his own countrymen, is now settled at Karnac. I sent for him, and he came shaking in his shoes. I asked why he was afraid? 'Oh, perhaps I was angry about something, and he was my *rayah*, and I might have him beaten.' I cried out at him, 'Ask pardon of God, O man. How could I beat thee any more than thou couldst beat me? Have we not laws? and art thou not my brother, and the *rayah* of our Queen, as I am and no more?' '*Mashallah!*' exclaimed the six or eight fellaheen who were waiting for physic, in prodigious admiration and wonder; 'and did we not tell thee that the face of the Sitt brings good fortune and not calamity and stick?' I found the little Indian had been a hospital servant in Calcutta, and was practising a little physic on his own account. So I gave him a few drugs especially for bad eyes, which he knew a good deal about, and we became very good friends; he was miserable when I left and would have liked me to have taken him as a volunteer servant.

I have come to a curious honour. *Ich bin beim lebendigem Leibe besungen* [I am praised to my face]. Several parties of real Arabs came with their sick on camels from the desert above Edfu. I asked at last what brought them, and they told me that a *Shaer* (bard or poet) had gone about singing my praises, as how the daughter of the English was a flower on the heads of the Arabs, and those who were sick should go and smell the perfume of the flower and rejoice in the brightness of the light (*nooreen*)—my name. Rather a highflown way of mentioning the 'exhibition' of a black dose. But we don't feel that a man makes a fool of himself here when he is romantic in his talk even about an old woman.

Benisuef, June 30. Dearest Alick. I write on the chance that this may go safe by post so that you may not think me lost. I left Luxor on May 31, got to Assiut (half-way) in a week, and have ever since been battling with an unceasing furious north and north-east wind. I feel like the much travelled Odysseus, and have seen 'villages and men', unlike him, however 'my companions' have neither grumbled nor deserted, though it is a bad business for them, having received their money at the rate of about twenty days' pay, for which they must take me to Cairo. They have eaten all, and are now obliged to stop and make bread here, but they are as good-humoured as if all were well.

My fleet consisted of my *dahabieh*, flag ship; tender, a *kyasseh* (cargo boat) for my horse and sais, wherein were packed two extremely poor shrivelled old widows, going to Cairo to see their sons, now in garrison there; lots of hard bread, wheat, flour, jars of butter, onions and lentils for all the lads of 'my family' studying at Gama el-Azhar, besides in my box queer little stores of long hoarded money for those *megowareen* (students of Gama el-Azhar). Don't you wish you could provide for Maurice with a sack of bread, a basket of onions and one pound sixteen shillings?

The handsome brown Shaikh el-Arab, Hassan, wanted me to take him, but I knew him to be a 'fast' man, and asked Yussuf how I could avoid it without breaking the laws of hospitality, so my 'father', the old Shereef, told Hassan that he did not choose his daughter to travel with a wine-bibber and a frequenter of loose company. Under my convoy sailed two or three little boats with family parties. One of these was very pretty, whose steersman was a charming little fat girl of five years old. All these hoped to escape being caught and worried by the way, by belonging to me, and they dropped off at their several villages. I am tolerably well, better than when I started, in spite of the wind.

Poor Reis Mohammed had a very bad attack of ophthalmia, and sat all of a heap, groaning all day and night, and protesting 'I am a Muslim', equivalent to 'God's will be done'. At one place I was known, and had a lot of sick to see, and a civil man killed a sheep and regaled us all with meat and *fateereh*. The part of the river in which we were kept by the high wind is made cheerful by the custom of the hareem being just as free to mix with men as Europeans, and I quite enjoyed the pretty girls' faces, and the gossip with the women who came to fill their water-jars and peep in at the cabin windows, which, by the way, they always ask leave to do. The Shaikh el-Hawarra gave me two sheep which are in the cargo-boat with four others—all presents —which Omar intends you to eat at Cairo. The Shaikh is very anxious to give you an entertainment at his palace, if you come up the river, with horse-riding, feasting and dancing girls. In fact I am charged with many messages to *el-Kebir* (the great master).

[In a letter to Urania Lucie describes her quarters on the boat:]

My boat is quite a nice little house; there is first a bedroom and a pantry for Omar, then a little drawing-room with divans and a writing table in one corner and your picture and Janet's and Maurice's on the walls; then two little bedrooms, then a bath place, etc., and quite at the end under the steersman is my bedroom which is very comfortable. All the sailors and the boys sleep outside on the decks; they have no beds at all, but they are used to it and sleep quite soundly on the boards. When we travel there are eight or ten men, the Reis, a steersman and a boy. Up the river we sail with such a big sail, and if there is no wind, the men tow the boat with a rope, which is hard work against the stream. When we come down the river the great great big sail is taken down and we float down or the men row singing very prettily all the while. They cannot pronounce Urania, so they sing:

'Sail fast and safe on our darling bride.'

XLIV

'Romance and curiosity seem dead and gone'

Cairo, July 8 1867. Dearest Alick. I arrived today, after thirty-eight days' voyage, one month of ceaseless furious wind. My poor men had a hard pull down against it. However I am feeling better than when I left Luxor.

Omar has just brought a whole cargo of your letters, the last of the 26 June. Let me know your plans. If you can go up the river I might send the boat beforehand to Minieh, so far there is a railway now, which would break the neck of the tedious part of the voyage for you if you are pressed for time. I must send this off at once to catch early post tomorrow. Excuse haste, I write in all the bustle of arrival.

Boulaq, July 28. Dearest Mother. I know I can write nothing more sure to please you than that I am a good deal better. It has been intensely hot, and the wind very worrying, but my cough has greatly abated and I do not feel so weak as I did.

I am anchored here in the river at my old quarters, and have not yet been ashore owing to the hot wind and the dust, which of course are far less troublesome here on the river. I have seen but very few people and have but one neighbour, in a boat anchored near mine, a very bewitching Circassian, the former slave of a rich Pasha, now married to a respectable dragoman, and staying in his boat for a week or two. She is young and pretty, and very amiable, and we visit each other often and get on very well indeed. She is a very religious little lady, and was much relieved when I assured her it was not part of my daily devotions to curse the Prophet, and revile the noble Koran.

Alexander seems to doubt whether he will come and to fear that Maurice will be bored. Was I different to other children and young people or has the race changed? When I was of Maurice's age I should have thought anyone mad who talked of a Nile voyage as possibly a bore, and would have embarked in a washing tub if anyone would have offered to take me, and that with rapture. All romance and all curiosity, too, seem dead and gone. Even old and sick and not very happily placed I still cannot understand the idea of not being amused and interested.

Janet says she thinks her father very unwell. I wish I knew what to wish about it all. Of course, I fancy the voyage must do him good, but one man's meat is another man's poison, and the dread of ennui is really an illness in itself to Alexander and to Janet.

It is no use to talk of the state of things here; all classes are suffering terribly under the fearful taxation, the total ruin of the fellaheen, and the destruction of trade brought about by this much extolled Pasha. The universal prayer now is, 'may he not return in safety, may he die in France and be buried in the graves of unbelievers'.[1] My grocer is half ruined by the 'improvements' made *a l'instar de Paris*—long military straight roads cut through the heart of Cairo. The owners are expropriated, and there is an end of it. Only those who have half a house left are to be pitied, because they are forced to build a new front to the street on a Frankish model, which renders it uninhabitable to them and unsaleable.

The river men are excited about the crews gone to Paris, for fear they should be forcibly detained by the *Sultaneh Franzaweeh*; I assured them that they will all come home safe and happy, with a good backsheesh. Many of them think it a sort of degradation to be taken for the Parisians to stare at like an *anteeka*, a word which here means what our people call a 'curiosity'.

I go on very well with my two boys. Mabrook washes very well and acts as *marmiton*. Darfur is housemaid and waiter in his very tiny way. He is only troublesome as being given to dirty his clothes in an incredibly short time. His account of the school system of Darfur is curious . . . I suppose you will be surprised to hear that the Darfur

---

[1] Ismail had accompanied the Sultan of Turkey on a visit to France for the great Paris Exhibition of 1867. Napoleon III made much of the first Sultan ever to visit Europe, except as a conqueror, but Abdel Aziz hated it all.

'niggers' can nearly all read and write. Poor little Darfur apologized to me for his ignorance, he was stolen he said, when he had only just begun to go to school. I wish an English or French servant could hear the instructions given by an Alim here to serving men. How he would resent them! 'When thou hast tired out thy back do not put thy hand behind it (do not shirk the burden). Remember that thou art not only to obey, but to please thy master, whose bread thou eatest'; and much more of the like. In short, a standard of religious obedience and fidelity fit for the highest Catholic idea of the 'religious life'. Upon the few who seek instruction it does have an effect (I am sure that Omar looks on his service as a religious duty), but of course they are few; and those who don't seek it themselves get none. It is curious how all children here are left utterly without any religious instruction. I don't know whether it is in consequence of this that they grow up so very devout.

Boulaq, July 29. Dearest Alick. Your letter has arrived to my great relief—only I fear you are not at all well. Pray go with the Rosses to Hamburg or anywhere to do you good and never mind about me. I am better. About Maurice. If he wishes to see the Nile let him come, but if he is only to be sent because of me, let it alone. I know I am oppressive company now, and am apt, like Mr Wodehouse in 'Emma', to say, 'Let us all have some gruel', and so I am best alone. Moreover, billiards and *lorettes* [courtesans] do not exist in the Said.

We know nothing here of a prohibition of gunpowder, at this moment some Europeans are popping away incessantly at Embabeh just opposite. Evidently the Pasha wants to establish a right of search on the Nile. That absurd speech about slaves he made in Paris shows that. With 3,000 in his hareem, several slave regiments, and lots of gangs on all his sugar plantations, his impudence is wonderful. He is himself the greatest living slave trader as well as owner. My lads are afraid to go out alone for fear of being snapped up by *cawasses* and taken to the army or the sugar works.

You will be sorry to hear that your stalwart friend Hassan has had fifty blows on each foot-sole, and had to pay six pounds. He was taking two donkeys to Shepheard's hotel before sunrise for a French lady and gentleman to go to the pyramids, when a *cawass* met him, seized the donkeys, and on Hassan's refusal to give them up, spat on the side-saddle and reviled Hassan's own hareem and began to beat him with his courbash. Hassan got impatient, took the *cawass* up in his arms and threw him on the ground, and went on. Presently four

330

cawasses came after him, seized him and took him to the Zaptieh (police office), where they all swore he had beaten them, torn their clothes, and robbed one of an imaginary gold watch—all valued at twenty-four pounds. After the beating he was carried to prison in chains, and there sentenced to be a soldier. A friend however interfered and settled the matter for six pounds. Hassan sends you his best salaam.

To me nothing is more depressing than the Sheffield enquiry. How dare we talk of *savages* forsooth and abuse the Aybssinians after that. If such is the result of freedom and Christian civilization, I begin to be reconciled to the Turkish rule. It is less dreadful to see men suffer oppression than to see them so deeply degraded, and to see educated men tacitly approving such corruption.[1]

Last night was very pretty—all the boats starting for the *moolid* of Sayyed el-Bedawee at Tanta. Every boat had a sort of pyramid of lanterns, and the darweeshes chanted, and the worldly folks had profane music and singing, and I sat and looked and listened, and thought how many thousand years ago just the same thing was going on in honour of Bubastis.

There is to be a great illumination and the Cairenes are ordered to show their joy at their master's return home.

July 30. I am glad the English have given a hearty welcome to the Sultan. An Alim of Cairo visited me last night and expressed immense approbation of the English people and their 'friendship towards the Muslims' as displayed by the Sultan's reception. It will have an excellent effect among all Muslims.[2]

[1] The British Government set up the Sheffield Commission of Enquiry in 1867 to investigate the condition of Trades Unions as a result of a series of intimidations, including murder, which had been perpetrated in Sheffield and Manchester by some Unions on a number of workmen who were not obeying the orders of their unions.

Political reformers, such as John Stuart Mill, had realized that the outrages were due to a great extent to the very unjust way in which Trade Unions were treated by the Law—they were considered illegal and a combination of workmen to organize a strike was regarded as a conspiracy; the Press and public opinion were against them and it was considered that Trade Union action on behalf of workers was not only immoral but contrary to the recognized principles of good national economy. 'For centuries our legislation had acted on the principle that the working man was a serf of society, bound to work for the sake of the employer and on the employers' terms.' (Chapter 54, *A History of Our Own Times*, by Justin McCarthy M.P., London, 1880.)

Lucie was attacking the educated men of England who had allowed such a situation to arise and was on the side of John Stuart Mill and the working man.

[2] The good reception to the Sultan Abdel Aziz and to Ismail, Viceroy of Egypt, was given on the insistence of the British Government; it did not wish to be outdone by the magnificent hospitality given in Paris by Louis Napoleon, Emperor of the French, to the

Little Alick's style [Janet's son] is quite oriental. 'Oh my poor Grandmamma' is his way of addressing me. I hope that he will grow up with more sense than Maurice seems to be gifted with. I fear he is a trouble to his father, but, Oh! why would he send him to such a sink of iniquity as Brussels? I shall be infinitely relieved when Maurice leaves it.

August 8. Two of my sailors were in Paris and have just come home. I hear they are dreadfully shocked by the dancing, and by the French women of the lower class generally. They sit in the coffee-shops like *shaers* (poets), and tell of the wonders of Paris to admiring crowds. They are enthusiastic about the courtesy of the French police, who actually did not beat them when they got into a quarrel, but scolded the Frankish man instead, and accompanied them back to the boat quite politely. The novelty and triumph of not being beaten was quite intoxicating. When I see them I expect I shall have some fun out of their account of their journey. Poor Adam's father died of grief at his son's going, nothing would persuade him that Adam would come back safe, and having a heart complaint, he died. And now the lad is back, well and with fine clothes, but is much cut up, I hear, by his father's death.

Please send me a tremendous whistle; mine is not loud enough to wake Omar at the other end of the cabin; a boatswain's whistle or something in the line of the 'last trump' is needed to wake sleeping Arabs.

My pretty neighbour has gone back into the town. She was a nice little woman, and amused me a good deal. I see that a good respectable

---

Sultan on his way to London. Queen Victoria did not wish to receive the Sultan at Windsor since it meant delaying her departure for Osborne. 'If the Sultan *knew* how inconvenient it was to the Queen . . . Still whatever the poor Queen *can* do she will.'

Besides having expressed a strong wish to be received by the Queen at Windsor, the Sultan had also stated that he wished to receive the Garter, as his predecessor had done; but again the Queen objected, thinking that it was unsuitable for a monarch who was not a Christian, but the Sultan received the Garter during a review of the British fleet off Osborne in very gusty weather. The Queen noted in her diary that the Sultan 'feels very uncomfortable at sea . . . he was continually retiring below and can have seen very little'.

Ismail was 'shy and subdued in the presence of the Sultan. I sat outside the deck saloon with the Sultan, all the others beyond; and he made the Viceroy sit opposite to us and interpret, which he did, sitting at the edge of his chair, his short legs hardly reaching the ground'.

The Sultan received the Order of the Garter on board the ship, *Victoria and Albert*, at a little ceremony just inside the entrance to the saloon and the Sultan was very pleased, describing it as a public mark of friendship and as a personal souvenir. Ismail had already received the G.C.B.

Turkish hareem is an excellent school of useful accomplishments—needlework, cookery, etc. But it must be rather a bore to have to educate little girls for her husband's use, as my friend's 'lady' did. I observed that she did not care a bit for the Pasha, by whom she had a child, but was extremely fond of 'her lady', as she politely called her, also that like every Circassian I ever knew, she regarded being sold as quite a desirable fate, and did not seem sorry for her parents, as the negroes always are.

The heat has been prodigious, but I am a good deal better. Yesterday the Nile had risen above ten cubits, and the cutting of the Kalig took place. The river is pretty full now, but they say it will go down fast this year. I don't know why. It looks very beautiful, blood-red and tossed into waves by the north wind fighting the rapid stream.

There is such a curious sight of a crowd of men carrying huge blocks of stone up out of a boat. One sees exactly how the stones were carried in ancient times; they sway their bodies all together like one great lithe animal with many legs, and hum a low chant to keep time. It is quite unlike any carrying heavy weights in Europe.

It is getting dusk and too windy for candles, so I must say goodnight and eat the dinner which Darfur has pressed upon me two or three times, he is a pleasant little creature, so lively and so gentle. It is washing day. I wish you could see Mabrook squatting out there, lathering away at the clothes with his superb black arms. He is a capital washer and a fair cook, but an utter savage.[1]

---

[1] This last letter, written to her mother, reached England the day after Sarah Austin's death.

XLV

Death of Sarah Austin

Boulaq, August 19 1867. Dearest Alick. Your letter came this morning and of course gave me a shock. I had felt convinced from what Dr Patterson had explained to me that my poor mother would not live many months, but somehow I did not expect the end so soon. Thank goodness she did not linger—for her own sake—and far more, dearest Alick for yours. I have felt very miserable about the heavy burden you had to bear for me, and I thank you most heartily for your kindness to her. She wrote to me after her former illness: 'your excellent husband has been a true son to me', so she was not insensible to your patience and kindness whatever her infirmities of temper may have made her seem.

My kind love to your mother and kiss my Maurice boy for me. I wish he would work; it is a great heaviness of heart to me to know that he is so idle and unsatisfactory. I can't write any more today for this post as I have got a bad sick headache, quite a new ailment to me. I think it is because I can't cry like other people. I thank you a hundred thousand time for your kindness to poor Mother.

August 28. Poor Mother weighs on my mind. There is something inexpressibly painful to me in the very sense of relief which I cannot but feel. Thank God she did not outlive me, for her own sake and, above all for yours. I can only feel as the people here say for an affliction *Alhamdulillah* and yet that very feeling is somehow distressing. You can understand, I fancy, what I mean though it sounds unreasonable.

Omar takes especial comfort in the reflection that the Koran was said in the boat for my mother on the day she died, beginning at 3 p.m. on Thursday and ending a little before daybreak on Friday.

The notice of Mother is very nice;[1] poor woman she had many great and good qualities, but yet one cannot regret that her life was not prolonged.

You do not say whether you and Maurice have decided to come here or not. If you do not, I shall go up in six weeks from now so as to send back the boat in good time for letting. If you *do* come pray bring a good folding armchair; my back is broken at times for want of one. My old one which Mrs Grote gave us twenty years ago is worn out in the cane work and no one here can mend it.

There is great excitement here now; all government employees are cut down one-fifth of their pay and half are to be dismissed. Every artisan is to pay twenty-five tariff piastres for leave to pursue his trade, and the hated poll-tax is to be reimposed and, they say, to be extended to women and children. No one has had a farthing from government for nine months. The poorer employees are in rags and really starving, and the Jews will not lend on the hopes of their arrears being paid up.

September 7. It was Mother's object to leave all she could to Maurice, but in spite of that, I think you are right and that he is 'advantaged' quite enough. I asked her to leave the £4,000 to you unconditionally, but I unluckily added: 'in case you married again it was but fair' etc., and I excited her vehement indignation. To whom has she left the copyright of my father's book? She promised it to me, and then she talked of leaving it to Maurice; it has brought her always a good sum every year.

If you cannot keep on at Weybridge, I hope you will consider my plan of your taking a house now that you have Mother's furniture and an increased income. I don't like your having no home of your own and, if ever I am able to travel, I would rather come home to you in England than elsewhere. I only wish I were not the expense and trouble I am to you. Do just as you like and think best, dearest, and I shall be pleased.

There is such a group all stitching away at the big new sail; Omar, the Reis, two or three volunteers, some old sailors of mine, and little

---

[1] Sarah Austin died at Weybridge on August 8 and on August 12 *The Times* wrote: 'To the attractions of great personal beauty in early life, and of a grace of manner undiminished by years, Mrs Austin added a masculine intellect and a large heart ... The power she exercised in society was due to the sterling qualities of her judgement, her knowledge, her literary style—which was one of great purity and excellence—and, above all, to her cordial readiness to promote all good objects, to maintain high principles of action and to confer benefits on all who claimed her aid ...'

Darfur. If I die I think you must have that tiny nigger over; he is such a merry little soul, I am sure you would love him, he is quite a civilized being and has a charming temper, and he seems very small to be left alone in the world.

I hope Maurice is not of the faction of the *ennuyés* of this generation. I am more and more of Omar's opinion, who said, with a pleased sigh, as we sat on the deck under some lovely palm-trees in the bright moonlight, moored far from all human dwellings, 'how sweet are the quiet places of the world'.

September 10. Dearest Janet. I hope that when Alick leaves Weybridge he will take a house for himself. I am very anxious he should do this and not go on always on the plan of anything being good enough for himself and picking himself bare like a poor old pelican.

I am sorry you are wroth with my grandson [Alick Ross]. I fancy you hardly know what children are and how they all do make a 'horrid row'.

I hear nothing more of your father and Maurice coming here so I shall go up in a month and send back the *Urania* to let.

September 18. Dearest Alick. You may imagine how glad I was yesterday to receive your last letter of 31st August, from which I conclude that Maurice is coming here, though you say nothing about yourself. So to business. If really Maurice and M. Soubre [his Belgian tutor] do come, please let me know by what boat that I may send Omar to meet them, for I well remember the horrid desolation of being landed in Alexandria without any help whatever. [There follows a list of groceries needed.] Do try to attend to this. I never know whether you get my letters as you never answer my questions, or acknowledge them.

My notion is for Maurice to see all Cairo well first and then to start (up the Nile) for four or five months, so as to go to Wadi Halfa (the second cataract) and not come down too soon for me, when, if I am able, I would go to England with Maurice; but, of course, I shall do just what he and you wish, and if he wants to leave sooner I can be left at Luxor.

Omar is crazy with delight at the idea of Maurice's arrival, and Reis Mohammed is planning what men to take who can make fantasia. I think Maurice will be diverted with small Darfur. Mabrook now really cooks very fairly under Omar's orders, but he is beyond belief uncouth, and utters the wildest howls now that his voice is grown big and strong like himself. Moreover he 'won't be spoken to', as our servants say; but he is honest, clean, and careful. I should not have thought any human creature could remain so completely a savage in a civilized community. I rather respect his savage *hauteur*, especially as it is combined with truth and honesty.

September 23. I hereby acknowledge that I have received £200 paid to Omar in Alexandria about one month ago and that I have signed a bill for £100. I have told you all this several times. I at the same time advanced to Omar £60—one year's wages, that is till August 30 1868. I have not taken any receipt from him as it is not the custom among real Arabs and, moreover, it is now of no use, as you can't enforce a debt here. But if I die he will pay you the difference back I have no doubt. In that case I should advise you not to sell my boat as no property is worth a 'cuss' in Egypt now, but to let Omar work her for you on fair terms. I know people who have done so and found it answer very well.

I am anxious that if I die, Rainie should remain with Charlotte. I have a great objection to her being with Janet or with your sisters—at all events until she is old enough not to be influenced by the one or ruled by the other.

XLVI

Preparing the Nile-boat for Maurice

Boat Marie Louise *off Boulaq, October 17 1867.* The other day Omar
met in the market an 'agreeable merchant', an Abyssinian fresh from
his own country, which he had left because of the tyranny of Kassa,
alias Theodore, the Sultan. The merchant had brought his wife and
concubines to live here. His account is that the mass of the people
are delighted to hear that the English are coming to conquer them, as
they hope, and that everyone hates the King except two or three
hundred scamps who form his bodyguard.[1]

He had seen the English prisoners, who, he says, are not ill-treated,
but certainly in danger, as the King is with difficulty restrained from
killing them by the said scamps, who fear the revenge of the English;
also that there is one woman imprisoned with the native female
prisoners. Hassan the donkeyboy, when he was a *marmitoon* in
Cairo, knew the Sultan Theodore—the only man who could be
found to interpret between the then King of Abyssinia and Mohammed Ali Pasha, whom Theodore had come to visit.

The merchant also expressed a great contempt for the Patriarch,
and for their *Matraam* or Metropolitan, whom the English papers
call the *Abuna. Abuna* is Arabic for 'our father'. The man is a Cairene

---

[1] The Emperor Theodore was educated, intelligent, with a natural talent for administration, and regarded as the best shot, runner and horseman in Abyssinia. In his younger
days he was generous and merciful, but he always suffered from violent bursts of anger.
His character seems to have changed after the death of his first wife, who was a good and
wise counsellor, and after embarking on exhausting campaigns against the Wollo Gallas
which led to heavy taxes on his people and revolts in various parts of the country. He
lost, too, in 1860 the good advice of his great friend the British Consul, Plowden, who
was killed by rebels on his journey to Massawa, for which the Emperor took terrible
revenge, killing and mutilating two thousand of the rebels held responsible for the deaths
of Plowden and the engineer Bell, Theodore's 'Grand Chamberlain'.

Copt and was a hanger-on of two English missionaries (they were really Germans) here, and he is more than commonly a rascal and a hypocrite. I know a respectable Jew whom he had robbed of all his merchandise, only Ras Alee forced the *Matraam* to disgorge. Pray what was all that nonsense about the Armenian Patriarch of Jerusalem writing to Theodore? what could he have to do with it? The Coptic Patriarch, whose place is Cairo, could do it if he were forced.

You must not be wroth with me because I have not written for a long time—I have been ill, but am much better. Omar will go down to Alexandria to meet Maurice on Monday.

My boat is being painted, but is nearly finished; as soon as it is done I shall move back into her. I got out into a little *cangia* but it swarmed with bugs and wasps, and was too dirty, so I moved yesterday into a good boat belonging to a dragoman, and hope to be back in my own by Sunday. But Oh Lord! I got hold of the Barber[1] himself turned painter; and as the little *cangia* was moored alongside the *Urania* in order to hold all the mattresses, carpets, etc., I was his victim. First, it was a request for 'three pounds to buy paint'. 'None but the best of paint is fitting for a noble person like thee, and that thou knowest is costly, and I am thy servant and would do thee honour'. 'Very well', say I, 'take the money, and see, oh man, that the paint is of the best, or thy backsheesh will be bad also'. Well, he begins and then rushes in to say: 'Come oh Bey, oh Pasha! and behold the brilliancy of the white paint, like milk, like glass, like the full moon'. I go and say, 'Mashallah! but now be so good as to work fast, for my son will be here in a few days, and nothing is ready'. Fatal remark. 'Mashallah! Bismillah! may the Lord spare him, may God prolong thy days, let me advise thee how to keep the eye from him, for doubtless thy son is beautiful as a mameluke of 1,000 purses. Remember to spit in his face when he comes on board, and revile him aloud that all the people may hear thee, and compel him to wear torn and dirty clothes when he goes out:—and how many children hast thou, and our master, thy master, and is he well?' etc., etc. '*Shukr Allah!* all is well with us', say I: 'but, by the Prophet, paint, oh *Ma-alim* (exactly the German *Meister*) and do not break my head any more'. But I was forced to take refuge at a distance from Hajj' Alee's tongue. Read the story of the Barber, and you will know exactly what Ma-alim Hajj' Alee is.

Also just as I got out of my boat and he had begun, the painter

[1] i.e., the Barber of *The Arabian Nights*.

whom I had last year and with whom I was dissatisfied, went to the Shaikh of the painters and persuaded him to put my man in prison for working too cheap—that was at daybreak. So I sent up my Reis to the Shaikh to inform him that if my man did not return by next day at daybreak, I would send for an European painter and force the Shaikh to pay the bill. Of course my man came.

My steersman Hassan, and a good man, Hoseyn, who can wash and is generally nice and pleasant, arrived from el-Bastowee a few days ago, and are waiting here till I want them. Poor little ugly black Hassan has had his house burnt down in his village, and lost all the clothes which he had bought with his wages; they were very good clothes, some of them, and a heavy loss. He is my Reis's brother, and a good man, clean and careful and quiet, better than my Reis even— they are a respectable family. Big stout Hazazin owes me 200 piastres which he is to work out, so I have still five men and a boy to get. I hope a nice boy, called Hederbee (the lizard), will come.

The crew don't take pay till the day before we sail, except the Reis and Abdul Sadig, who are permanent. But Hassan and Hoseyn are working away as merrily as if they were paid. People growl at the backsheesh, but they should also remember what a quantity of service one gets for nothing here, and for which, oddly enough, no one dreams of asking backsheesh. Once a week we shift the anchors, for fear of their silting over, and six or eight men work for an hour; then the mast is lowered—twelve or fourteen men work at this—and nobody gets a farthing.

At last my boat is finished, so tomorrow Omar will clean the windows, and on Saturday move in the cushions, etc., and me, and on Sunday go to Alexandria. I hear the dreadful voice of Hajj' Alee, the painter, outside, and will retire before he gets to the cabin door, for fear he should want to bore me again. I do hope Maurice will enjoy his journey; everyone is anxious to please him. The Shaikh of the Hawara sent his brother to remind me to stop at his 'palace' near Girgeh, that he might make a fantasia for my son. So Maurice will see real Arab riding, and jereed, and sheep roasted whole and all the rest of it. The Shaikh is the last of the great Arab chieftains of Egypt, and has thousands of fellaheen and a large income. He did it for Lord Spencer and for the Duke of Rutland and I shall get as good a fantasia, I have no doubt. Perhaps at Keneh Maurice had better not see the dancing for Zeyneb and Latefeeh are terribly fascinating; they are such pleasant jolly girls as well as pretty and graceful, but old Oum ez-Zeyn (mother of beauty), so-called on account of his hideousness, will want us to eat his good dinner. [He was the magistrate of Keneh.]

Urania, Boulaq, October 21. So many thanks for the boxes and their contents. My slaves are enchanted with all that the 'great master' has sent. Darfur hugged the horsecloth in ecstasy that he should never again be cold at night. The waistcoats of printed stuff, and the red flannel shirts are gone to be made up, so my boys will be like Pashas this winter, as they told the Reis. He is awfully perturbed about the evil eye. 'Thy boat, *Mashallah*, is such as to cause envy from all beholders; and now when they see a son with thee, *Bismillah! Mashallah!* like a flower, verily I fear, I fear greatly from the eye of the people.' We have brought a tambourine and a *tarabouka*, and are on the look-out for a man who can sing well, so as to have fantasia on board.

October 22. I hear today that the Pasha sent a telegram *höchst eigenhändig*[1] to Koos, in consequence whereof one Stefanos, an old Copt of high character, many years in Government employ, was put in chains and hurried off within twenty minutes to Fazogli with two of his friends, for no other crime than having turned Presbyterian. This is quite a new idea in Egypt, and we all wonder why the Pasha is so anxious to 'brush the coat' of the Copt Patriarch. We also hear that the people up in the Said are running away by wholesale, utterly unable to pay the new taxes and to do the work exacted. Even here the beating is fearful. My Reis has had to send all his month's wages to save his aunt and his sister-in-law, both widows, from the courbash. He did not think so much of the blows, but of the shame; 'those are women, lone women, from whence can they get the money?'

[1] which was highly personal.

XLVIII

'If I were to buy Maurice a slave girl you'd be shocked'

Boulaq, November 3 1867. Dearest Janet. Maurice arrived on Friday week and is as happy as can be and has grown fat. He says he never felt so well and never had such good snipe-shooting.

Omar had already frightened him so much about the syrens here that he won't go with M. Soubre who has made friends with young Bedel and all the French set at the 'Cercle' here. 'I shall hold the child by his neck', says Omar, 'and not let him go near the bad women. Indeed I would rather do (continued Omar), what I never did, and get him a clean fellahah [girl] if I cannot keep him from it entirely; but what a pity we can't buy him a nice Abyssinian like respectable people'.

How was it, my dearest Alick, that you thought fit to have him with a tutor whose wife was like that? Do you think that you need such instruction so much? I own I do not understand your *strict* European morals. If I were to buy him a slave girl you would be shocked, but I think it a sight worse to deliver a lad over to such an instructress.

What an amiable boy Maurice is; he is as considerate and kind as it is possible to conceive. I wish he had a little more turn for something besides shooting, but he is very good. Of course Maurice wants money and my expenses are increased; he arrived with £8 in his pocket and I can get none of what Alexander told me was ready for me. Tomorrow Omar must go and try to borrow £300. I wish Coutts had a correspondent here; it is so disagreeable to be always in such difficulties about getting money.

Little Darfur's amusement at Maurice is boundless; he grins at him all the time he waits at table, he marvels at his dirty boots, at his bathing, at his much walking out shooting, at his knowing no Arabic.

The dyke burst the other day up at Bahr Yussuf, and we were nearly all swept away by the furious rush of water. My little boat was upset while three men in her were securing the anchor, and two of them were nearly drowned, though they swim like fish; all the *dahabiehs* were rattled and pounded awfully; and in the middle of the *fracas*, at noonday, a steamer ran into us quite deliberately. I was rather frightened when the steamer bumped us, and carried away the iron supports of the awning; and they cursed our fathers into the bargain, which I thought needless. The English have fallen into such contempt here that one no longer gets decent civility from anything in the *Miri* (Government).

Olagnier has lent us a lovely little skiff, and I have had her repaired and painted, so Maurice is set up for shooting and boating. Darfur calls him the 'son of a crocodile' because he loves the water, and generally delights in him hugely, and all my men are enchanted with him.

November 19. Dearest Alick. Here we are still at Cairo. Maurice is, I am glad to say, nearly cured, but he has had a narrow escape of a serious ailment. It seems that he had been ill for four months and had doctored himself which had made him much worse. Dr Patterson says we may go at the end of the week. I tell you this that if such a thing should happen again you may send him to a doctor in time.

Maurice is otherwise extremely well and very happy and I am sure so am I. I feel it like a new life to me to have the dear boy with me, and to find him such a good and affectionate son to me; he is so kind and thoughtful.

If we can get no answer from Ross about the money, I must go to Todd and Rathbone and see what arrangement I can make to get money. I fear I must have £400. I have had to pay Maurice's doctoring, powder, shot, shoes, trousers, etc. Also Monsieur Soubre is so greedy that I have had to lay in stores of sweetstuffs, etc., for him, all of which costs money. I must also ask you what your agreement with him amounted to. I expected a tutor, but Monsieur Soubre does nothing but amuse himself with the acquaintances he has made in Cairo and comes back to eat, sleep and ride roughshod over us. His manners are a heavy trial to our tempers, and if Maurice does 'kick his bottom' as he fears he must, I shall not wonder.

343

I never was ordered about by a man of his years before and Maurice does not like to hear it. If you sent him merely to be 'company' we had rather pay him and let him go, for I think he dislikes us (certainly Maurice) as much as we dislike him. I will do what I can in reading with Maurice whenever my lungs will let me, but we could do that much better without a man sneering at us and contradicting us every minute. I tell you this now because I fear that when we are up the river and more together, it will be still harder to bear. In the beginning Maurice refused to go with him to dine at *table d'hôtes* where the *café chantant* women dine and to the 'Cercle' which is a gambling place, and Soubre has been insolent ever since; he evidently counted on Maurice paying for the two.

Yesterday I told him he must take a donkey up to the Abbassieh to see a review since my horse was for sale, and a long day without food and water would not improve his price. Omar and Maurice went up to Dr Patterson's and then Omar was to take the horse to show, but Monsieur Soubre coolly mounted it at Dr Patterson's door, rode off and left it with some Nubian on the racecourse where Omar found it and brought it home. Whereupon Monsieur Soubre came back, called my groom names and made a row with all the people. I was ill in bed so I could not interfere, but it made me very nervous.

In short, he is a thorough 'brave Belge' and my Reis summed him up the other day while talking to the steersman over my head: 'I call him a monkey for he is shameless, greedy and ill-tempered after the manner of monkeys'. I suppose he must have been wonderfully on his good behaviour with you or you never would have sent him.

Do not omit to send me a copy of your contract with Monsieur Soubre in case he drives us to utter desperation, that I may know what it would cost to effect my emancipation. I could stand anything if he were the least use, but as he never opens a book but a novel of Dumas and never is here except to come in and order some meal for himself like in an hotel, I see no compensation whatever for the expense and vexation.

Young Mr Coope has come and has taken Mohammed Gazowee at my recommendation and seems well pleased with him. We hope to sail together but he, too, has a credit on the Egyptian Trading Company and can get no money. He is on board his boat and will start soon. Maurice is chiefly with him now as he cannot stand Monsieur Soubre's presence and Coope and his friend won't endure him either.

I will do my best but it is hard lines to find such a vulgar, illiterate young beast in authority over one. Little Dr Patterson wants to kick him out so wrath is he. Dr Patterson is very anxious I should remain for a long spell up in Nubia as he thinks it would do me much good. But I fear Monsieur Soubre will not tolerate the dull life up there and that we shall be forced to hurry back to Cairo. I have borrowed French books from Hekekian Bey and will begin reading and dictating with Maurice today. I will do my best as far as my bad breathing and coughing will let me.

Luxor, December 20. We arrived here all safe three days ago. The 'blow up', which I dreaded, came the day after our arrival. Monsieur Soubre had been very troublesome and insolent all the way, but we had all knocked under perfectly. He, however, chose to go over to Mr Coope's boat and to seat himself at breakfast and inform the four gentlemen that he was going with them to Gooneh. I don't know what he said or did, as I have never seen young Coope's three friends, but the consequence was that they sent Coope over to desire me or Maurice to tell Soubre that they would not receive him.

I was ill in bed having been worried into a haemorrhage ten days before below Assiut by Monsieur Soubre leaving Maurice alone on the further side of the shore at nightfall, while he went off in the little boat to scrape acquaintance with some Yankees who, after all, would not let him into the cabin. Meanwhile we were all in a horrid stew, knowing it to be a bad neighbourhood, and sent six men in different directions while Monsieur Soubre ate his dinner . . . Well, to return to my story. Maurice told him that Coope's friends did not want him or Soubre, whereupon Soubre cried and stamped in his monkeyish way and Maurice came into my cabin to take breath.

I really could not stand it any longer and having heard Monsieur Soubre say he would rather go, I gave Maurice 1,500 francs to take to him and to tell him that I would pay for him at the hotel till he could go. Next day he wrote to me a pert note asking for a testimonial that he had never given me offence. I wrote to him that I was sorry I had not been able to show him as much attention as I had hoped, but that he had from the first reduced me to the position of an hotel-keeper by the tone of command and rudeness he had taken towards me, and that I could not prevent gentlemen I never saw from forbidding him their presence.

He stayed four days at the hotel and is gone today (December 22) in a boat belonging to a Belgian which is on its way to Cairo to be let. So he will have £60 to travel home from Cairo; therefore, if he tries to get any more out of you, don't be weak enough to give it. Mr Tolfrey, Coope's tutor, blamed Maurice for bringing such a person into my company, which really Maurice could not help.

I could not have believed that even a 'brave Belge' could speak to a woman of my age as he habitually spoke to me. Moreover, I was in constant anxiety about Maurice as Monsieur Soubre always was going to the [women] and trying to persuade Maurice to go with him. I overheard his conversation at dinner as I lay in my cabin and I told Maurice plainly that I dreaded the worst diseases and that if he *must* have an outbreak, I would give him a pound or two now and then to have a good dancing girl, rather than a lot of fourpenny women. I fear it was not moral, but it has worked well and Maurice looks as blooming as a rose now and is getting fat with early hours and a quiet life.

I believe Monsieur Soubre was glad to go as he had always grumbled at the idea of going above Luxor into savage countries where there was no amusement. He was quite incapable of liking anything but a town life. Did you ever read *Ten Thousand a Year* by Warren?[1] You may have a correct idea of Monsieur Joseph Soubre under the name of Tittlebat Titmouse. A more illiterate, vulgar, impudent little beast I never saw, and always wanting to drag Maurice out to the sixpenny women who frequent the places for the sailors and servants.

Reis Mohammed clawed Maurice at Girgeh and told him he would show him better girls than the Belgian knew and walked him round and round all manner of deserted streets and home to the *dahabieh re infecta* and quite tired. Maurice could not help telling me the pious fraud as a good joke. 'There is no God but God!' said the Reis to me in great excitement. 'Shall that unclean fornicator and son of a burnt father and unchaste mother, lead the produce of thy noble bowels among harlots? Are there not pimps enough in Egypt (I ask pardon of God) without him to bring uncleanness into our boat which has always been like a mosque.'

'Praise be to God *sacré cochon* is gone', say all my people. He was always calling them *sacré cochon* and so they picked up the phrase without understanding it and called him so too. Darfur's joy at Monsieur Soubre's departure is unspeakable. To be relieved from eternal pinches and slaps and especially from being ordered twenty

---

[1] Published in 1839 by Samuel Warren, barrister and novelist, 1807–77.

times a day to fill the chibouque, make coffee, etc., which the boy resented as an infringement of my rights as 'master of the house'. He never failed to say aloud 'that is from the lady's tobacco' whereon he got pinched. Darfur's cheek is, however, indomitable and he persisted in taking every occasion to show up the Belgian's greediness and meanness with such an unconscious air that I could say nothing. I never saw such a case of an *enfant terrible* and of 'malice prepense'.

I never did have a row in my life before and I would not have written to Monsieur Soubre as I did even after all his shameless ways, but I was warned that he wanted to get me to give him a certificate of good conduct to use against me. If he bothers you, Coope and his friends and others in Cairo are all ready to say what his conduct was and that they advised me to turn him out summarily in Cairo. I was miserably ill for ten days, but felt quite different as soon as I was quit of the nuisance.

One great deliverance in the Belgian's departure is having the boat sweet again. As you may suppose, a man who never washed for two months and shut up every door and window was not agreeable in this climate. Of course Maurice has learned nothing. I will endeavour to find someone to replace Monsieur Soubre and meanwhile Maurice will do better alone with me. He is the most dutiful and obedient son to me and, if he does not learn much, at any rate I think he is beginning to see that all the 'fun' he was led into at Brussels was likely to be bad fun enough in the end.

He says he is thoroughly happy and that he was never more amused than when with me, which I think very flattering. He is beginning to pick up a little Arabic, and has got a fancy to stay on with me and learn French, Arabic and Turkish with a view to the Foreign Office. For many reasons I think it would be a very good thing for him, if he continues as steady and good as he is now. There will be time enough to think of this while we are in Nubia.

XLVIII

Etonians have such 'baronial views of life'

December 1867. Dearest Janet. I fear that the money of the Egyptian Trading Company is being much 'eaten'. The way in which Bedel's sons are sent on tours of inspection with one pound a day pay and *dahabiehs* [to take them]—they being utterly useless—seems very like a job. I wish Henry could look into the way things are going. I don't like what I have heard at all; the outgoings in salaries must be very great indeed.

Hoseyn Bey, the Mudir of Keneh, beat all the Shaikhs el-Beled awfully; one died under the stick and the Shaikh of the Abab'deh died of resentment at the insult of being ordered to be beaten, although it was not done. Nevertheless the Mudir failed to get the money for the taxes and has been turned off and replaced by a new man. Nobody has any money; I don't know where it has all gone.

Dearest Alick. I think of starting for Nubia directly after Christmas Day, which we must keep here. We have lovely weather. Maurice is going with a friend of my friends, a Bedawee, to shoot; I hope among the Abab'deh he will get some gazelle shooting. I shall stop at Syaleh to visit the Shaikh's mother, and with them Maurice could go for some days into the desert.

As to crocodiles, *Inshallah*, we will eat their hearts, and not they ours. You may rely on it that Maurice is 'on the head and in the eye' of all my crew, and will not be allowed to bathe in 'unclean places'. Reis Mohammed stopped him at Gebel Abu'l Foda. You would be delighted to see how different he looks.

Half of the old house at Luxor fell down into the temple beneath six days before I arrived; so there is an end of the *Maison de France*, I suppose. It might be made very nice again at a small expense, but I suppose the Consul will not do it, and certainly I shall not unless I want it again. Nothing now remains solid but the three small front rooms and the big hall with two rooms off it. All the part I lived in is gone, and the steps, so one cannot get in. Luckily Yussuf had told Mohammed to move my little furniture to the part which is solid, having a misgiving of the rest. He has the most exquisite baby, an exact miniature of himself. He is in a manner my godson, being named Noor ed-Deen Hishan Abu-l-Hajjaj, to be called *Noor* like me.

On Board the Urania, *January 1868.* Your letter of the 10 December most luckily came on to Edfu by the American Consul-General, who overtook us there in his steamer and gave me a lunch. Maurice was as usual up to his knees in a distant swamp trying to shoot wild geese. Now we are up close to Aswan, and there are no more marshes; but *en revanche* there are quails and *kata*, the beautiful little sand grouse. I eat all that Maurice shoots, which I find very good for me; and as for Maurice he has got back his old round boyish face; he eats like an ogre, walks all day, sleeps like a top, bathes in the morning and has laid on flesh so that his clothes won't button. At Esneh we fell in with handsome Hassan, who is now Shaikh of the Abab'deh, as his elder brother died. He gave us a letter to his brother at Syaleh, up in Nubia; ordering him to get up a gazelle hunt for Maurice, and I am to visit his wife. I think it will be pleasant, as the Beduin women don't veil or shut up, and to judge by the men ought to be very handsome. Both Hassan and Abu Goord, who was with him, preached the same sermon as my learned friend Abdurrachman had done at Luxor. 'Why, in God's name, left I my son without a wife?' They are sincerely shocked at such indifference to a son's happiness.

I enjoyed Nubia immensely, and long to go and live with the descendants of a great *Ras* (head, chief), who entertained me at Ibreem, and who said, like Ravenswood, 'Thou art come to a fallen house, and there is none to serve thee left save me'. It was a paradise of a place, and the Nubian had the grand manners of a very old, proud nobleman. I had a letter to him from Shaikh Yussuf.

I have no almanack, but you will be able to know the date by your own red pocketbook, which determined the beginning of Ramadan at Luxor this year. They received a telegram fixing it for Thursday, but Shaikh Yussuf said that he was sure the astronomers in London knew best, and made it Friday. Tomorrow we shall make our bargain, and next day go up the Cataract—*Inshallah*, in safety. The water is very good, as Jesus the black pilot tells me. He goes to the second Cataract and back, as I intend to stay nearly two months in Nubia. The weather here is perfect now, we have been lucky in having a lovely mild winter hitherto. We are very comfortable with a capital crew, who are all devoted to Maurice. The Shaikh of the Abab'deh has promised to join us if he can, when he has convoyed some 400 Bashibazouks up to Wadi Halfa, who are being sent up because the English are in Abyssinia.

I think another week will see us start downstream. Janet talks of coming up the Nile with me next year, which would be pleasant. I am a little better than I have been the last two months. I was best in Nubia but I got a cold at Esneh, second hand from Maurice, which made me very seedy. I cannot go about at all for want of breath. Could you send me a chair such as people are carried in by two men? A common chair is awkward for the men when the banks are steep, and I am nervous, so I never go out. I wish you could see your son bare-legged and footed, in a shirt and a pair of white Arab drawers, rushing about with the fellaheen. He is everybody's 'brother' or 'son'.

Luxor, April 1868. Dearest Alick. I have been too weak to write, but the heat set in three days ago and took away my cough, and I feel much better. Maurice also flourishes in the broil, and protests against moving yet. He speaks a good deal of Arabic and is friends with everyone. It is *Salaam aleykoum ya maris* on all sides. He has got as far as learning his letters and I hope will learn more. You would rejoice to see his fat rose cheeks and increased breadth and vigour. I never beheld such a change for the better in any human being. Really Omar has done good service in keeping him out of mischief and teaching him to be more careful of money.

A Belgian has died here, and his two slaves, a very nice black boy and an Abyssinian girl, got my little valet, Darfur, to coax me to take them under my protection, which I have done, as there appeared a strong probability that they would be 'annexed' by a rascally Copt who is a Consular agent at Keneh. I believe the Belgian has left money for them, which of course they would never get without someone to look after it, and so I have Ramadan, the boy, with me, and shall take the girl when I go, and carry them both to Cairo, settle their little business, and let them present a sealed-up book which they have to their Consul there, according to their master's desire, and then marry the girl to some decent man. I have left her in Mustapha's hareem till I go.

Since I wrote the above it has turned quite chilly again, so we agreed to stay till the heat really begins. Maurice is so charmed with Luxor that he does not want to go, and we mean to let the boat and live here next winter.

Minieh, May. We are just arriving at Minieh whence the railway will take letters quickly. We dined at Keneh and at Assiut with some friends, and had fantasia at Keneh. Omar desires his dutiful salaams to you and hopes you will be satisfied with the care he has taken of 'the child'. How you would have been amused to hear the girl who came to dance for us at Esneh lecture Maurice about evil ways, but she was an old friend of mine, and gave good and sound advice.

The Abyssinian affair is an awful disappointment to the Pasha; he had laid his calculations for something altogether different, and is furious. The Coptic clergy are ready to murder us. The Arabs are all in raptures. 'God bless the English general, he has frightened our Pasha. He will fear the English more than before, and the Sultan also', and when I lamented the expense, they all exclaimed, 'Never mind the expense, it is worth more than ten millions to you; your faces are whitened and your power enlarged before all the world; but why don't you take us on your way back?'[1]

I saw a very interesting man at Keneh, one Faam, a Copt, who has turned Presbyterian, and has induced a hundred others at Koos to do likewise: an American missionary is their minister. Faam was sent off to the Sudan by the Patriarch, but brought back. He is a splendid old fellow, and I felt I looked on the face of a Christian martyr, a curious sight in the nineteenth century: the calm, fearless, rapt expression was like what you see in noble old Italian pictures, and he had the perfect absence of 'doing pious' which shows the undoubting faith. He and the Mufti, also a noble fellow, sparred about religion in a jocose and friendly tone which would be quite unintelligible in Exeter Hall. When he was gone the Mufti said, 'Ah! we thank them,

---

[1] In July 1867 the British Government decided to send an army from India to make the Emperor Theodore release the prisoners. Aden was for the first time used as an important army staging post for a force of 16,000 fighting men and over 12,000 in the transport services. They landed at Annesley Bay in January 1868 and stormed the strong position of Magdala on April 13. The prisoners were released, the Emperor Theodore committed suicide and the troops returned to India.

for though they know not the truth of Islam, they are good men, and walk straight, and would die for their religion: their example is excellent; praise be to God for them'.

Boulaq, June 14. The climate has been odious—to shiver in cold winds of June on the Nile seems hard. All the crew kissed him [Maurice] on both cheeks and swore to come back again in the winter; and up the country he was hand and glove with all the fellaheen, eating a good deal of what he called 'muck' with great enjoyment, walking arm in arm with a crazy dervish, fetching home a bride at night and swearing lustily by the Prophet.

Would you be shocked if a nigger taught Maurice? One Hajji Daboos I know to be a capital Arabic scholar and he speaks French like a Parisian, and Italian also, only he is a real nigger and so is the best music-master in Cairo. *Que faire?* it's not catching, as Lady Morley said, and I won't present you with a young mulatto any more than with a young *brave Belge.* I may, however, find someone at Beirut. Cairo is in such a state of beggary that all educated young men have fled. Maurice has no sort of idea why a nigger should not be as good as anyone else, but thinks perhaps you might not approve. If you think Maurice would be better elsewhere I am not so selfish as to wish to keep him. Would he be less idle and might he not be dissipated if you again sent him to such places as Brussels?

He knows nothing and the education he has had is such as effectually to prevent his ever learning. He is so deeply imbued with the idea that it is 'snobbish' to read and to know, and that nothing on earth is worth living for but animal pleasures. That nothing can change. He says he likes being with me, but he is rather ashamed of my being supposed to be 'blue'; he says, 'why you know even the governor says you talk like a governess'. However he is a dear boy and you must make the best of him as he is.

I observe all the 'Eton fellows' of his age have exactly the same *baronial* views of life and hate the 'cads' who are base enough to read books. The good manners of the Arab *canaille* has greatly improved Maurice's manners, which smelt terribly strong of the billiard room and brandy. He has all my faculty for getting on capitally with savages and niggers of all sorts and likes Upper Egypt and its rude ways far better than Cairo.

I will talk over your Indian idea with Maurice. It might be as well to let him go and let him see. I had had ideas of colonial life for

Maurice for decidedly the animal predominates so utterly over the intellectual activity that he will never be fit for any desk or book work. Not that he is stupid; he talks Arabic quite fluently which is rather a feat to achieve in seven or eight months.

You would have stared to see old Ahmad Agha Abd el-Sadig, a very good friend of ours at Aswan, coaxing and patting the *weled* (boy) when he dined here the other day, and laughing immoderately at Maurice's nonsense. He is one of the M.P.'s for Aswan, and a wealthy and much respected man in the Said.

Giafar Pasha backsheeshed me an *abbayeh* of crimson silk and gold, also a basket of coffee. I was obliged to accept them as he sent his son with them, and to refuse would have been an insult, and as he is the one Turk I do think highly of I did not wish to affront him. It was at Luxor on his way to Khartum. He also invited Maurice to Khartum, and proposed to send a party to fetch him from Korosko, on the Nile. Giafar is Viceroy of the Sudan, and a very quiet man, who does not 'eat the people'.

I do hope you will arrange some place for Maurice to live when he leaves me. I really do not think he can be expected to do well if you keep him in Hertford Street. I am sure when you were young you would not have liked to live with Aunty Ponty. I hope you will not think me unkind, but Maurice will do all he can to please you I hope and believe, unless his back is put up by old maidenly interference. Try not to show this to your mother and sisters and to put yourself for a minute in the place of a lad who is conscious of his own great shortcomings and sore at being continually reminded of them.

He says that if you will give him a moderate allowance, he will go to Germany or France and learn the language in some out of the way place, and I don't think the plan a bad one. I hope you will not think me meddling if I beg you not to hand over Lord Lansdowne's £5,000 to Maurice when he comes of age. He has got the wildest ideas of making impossible percentages from the young Bedels and fellows of the mercantile swell genus with whom he has foregathered. I told Maurice bluntly that if I should chance to be alive when he comes of age I should resist such a measure by all means in my power during my life, unless, of course, it were in order to invest it in some good business. My mother's money is quite enough to play ducks and drakes with. Maurice is not extravagant but he is careless and helpless, not with money so much as with other things, but the money, too, slips through his fingers he can't tell how.

XLIX

'The English have taken to doing very odd things about paying'

Dearest Alick. I fear you will think I am always in a bother but I send you a letter which I received from Mohammed Gazowee. When Mr Coope and his party came, I recommended him to them as I had always known him please all his employers for six years as well as Dean Stanley. I advised them to contract with him for the whole of their expenses. Instead of that they hired a boat for £80 a month— a high price as she had no canteen, that is kitchen utensils, crockery, linen, etc. They also hired servants and then agreed to pay him £15 a month wages and £4 a day for food for themselves and four servants, for the use of his canteen, fuel, candles, washing, etc. He told me what he had done and said that they did not like to draw up an agreement before the Consul, did I feel sure he would be paid. I foolishly told him 'I would answer for them', and you see the result.

It seems that they found one or two parties who had done it cheaper, but that is no reason for breaking one's word. I have heard very strong remarks on the affair from Englishmen; one man said he would advise Gazowee to put it in the papers. As for me, the receipt of his letter made me really ill. I feel that I ought to pay the money. What am I to do? I know that what Gazowee says about the excellence of his provisions is true and that the price, though high, is not more than other good dragomans [charge] and less than several. Besides if they did not like the price, they should have refused it and I would have found them a cheaper. But Mr Coope never mentioned a price and only seemed to want to have everything very good. If a man goes to a good hotel, he knows he will pay more than at a lodging house, and cannot refuse to pay the bill on the plea that someone else keeps a cheaper house. Gazowee is one of those helpless mild men who is afraid of everybody, and it is a cruel thing for him to lose £120. Will you remonstrate with Mr Coope.

Cairo, June 5. My dear Alexander. You say that I 'must have known that Gazowee had not an immaculate reputation' when I recommended him to your friends. This is a serious imputation which I do not at all feel that anyone has the right to lay to my charge. I recommended Gazowee because I *did know* that he had never been before any court, consular or Egyptian, and I can send you about fifty testimonials of unusual weight. I shall also write to Dean Stanley to tell you what he knows about him.

If it is true that Lady Herbert has printed so purposeless a falsehood, I shall certainly advise Gazowee to proceed against her for defamation. I must get her book and see how it is.[1] She never saw him and can have no intelligible motive for so maligning him. I will not drop the matter until I have cleared myself from the imputation of wilfully recommending a man who had been condemned in a consular court.

June 14. I am exceedingly sorry you are annoyed about Mohammed el Gazowee, but I could do no less. I had always made a rule never to recommend a dragoman, but you must remember that you wrote to me that it was your desire that I should do so, and I, therefore, being asked for the best, recommended him. Of course, if people are content to live as I do, they can spend much less, but English people don't like coarse bread, lentils and *melocheea,* and exotic food is expensive. The Consul, Mr Reade, is quite ready to testify that he considers the charge a very fair one. The English have taken to doing very odd things about paying. I know I shall insist on a deposit when I let my boat for fear of having the money withheld on account of two champagne glasses short of the inventory as happened this year.

Dr Patterson is appointed to direct the hospital at Galata [in Constantinople] and is making enquiries about the climate. He offers us rooms in his house if we will go to Constantinople. Maurice, too,

[1] Lady Herbert stated in *Cradle Lands,* published 1867: 'Your dragoman cheats and robs you without mercy; and, in fact, the one who had accompanied our travellers, although the bearer of a certificate stating that he had previously served H.R.H. the Prince of Wales, to whom he had given great satisfaction, was obliged to be brought before the English Consul on their return to Cairo, and threatened with being taken to the Pasha, before he would disgorge a portion of his ill-gotten gains.'

wishes it very much, just for two months. Dr Patterson wants me to have two months out of Egypt in order to profit by the change back in September. He suggests also Beirut or one of the Greek islands. I am very feeble and short of breath, but I will try the experiment. Don't think I am going to die directly. Dr Patterson says I have a good bit of breathing power left yet and wonderful vitality. My first bad place in the right lung is, in fact, cured, but the left, which got a damage at Soden, is a good deal worse and my heart is hindered and bothered. But I have no pain and can lie down all right, only I am so bent as to be almost deformed, I fancy, and quite like an old hag.

My best love to Janet, I'll write soon to her, but I am lazy and Maurice is worse. Omar nearly cried when Maurice went to Alexandria for a week. 'I seem to feel how dull we shall be without him when he goes away for good', said he, and Darfur expresses his intention of going with Maurice. 'Thou must give me to the young man back-sheesh', as he puts it, 'because I have plenty of sense and shall tell him what to do.' That is the little rascal's sauce. Terence's slaves are true to the life here.

Arabs advise me to stop at Beirut and go on to Constantinople if I like. We wouldn't spend much. I hope in a few days to find a teacher for Maurice. My breath is so bad I cannot read or correct reading, still less dictate; often I cannot speak much.

Alexandria, July 3 1868. Dearest Alick. We have settled to go to Beirut on Saturday by a Russian steamer, which is said to be very good. I am very weak of course, but perhaps the change may do me good. Dr Patterson wrote from Stamboul an account by no means encouraging, which settled the question. I take Omar and little Darfur. My men are delighted with the chair you have sent and say they can carry me like a Sultan.

Boulaq, October 22. The unlucky journey to Syria almost cost me my life. The climate is absolute poison to consumptive people. In ten days after I arrived the doctor told me to settle my affairs, for I had probably only a few days to live, and certainly should never recover. However I got better, and was carried on board the steamer, but am too weak for anything. We were nearly shipwrecked coming back owing to the Russian captain having his bride on board and not minding his ship. We bumped and scraped and rolled very unpleasant-ly. At Beirut the Sisters of Charity wouldn't nurse a Protestant, nor the Prussians a non-Lutheran. But Omar and Darfur nursed me better than Europeans ever do. Little Blackie was as sharp about the physic as a born doctor's boy when Omar was taking his turn of sleep. I did not like the few Syrians I saw at all.

Cairo, November 6. Dearest Alick. I am sure that you will rejoice to hear that I at last feel really better. Luckily I found two bottles of cod-liver oil, and have taken one with excellent effect, as well as porter. I was so weak I thought I could not be much worse and this unorthodox treatment did me good and has greatly stopped the terrible spitting of matter which nearly killed me in Syria.

I have got Maurice to take a French lesson every morning from Miss Mathews[1] and when we go up the river I will get a shaikh for his Arabic. I have not been able to find a man to go with us.

After paying up all here and advancing Miss Mathews six months of her salary in order that she might invest it safely and have something in the event of my death, I shall start with £300 which shall last until next May or June. But should Maurice leave me earlier he must borrow off Ross for his journey home as I could not afford to give it him for all the way to London. If I were forced to borrow up the river it is at about £60 per cent. To Omar I owe wages since the 1st October. I mention this in case of my death.

Mr Elliot refuses me a protection which I got Mr Francis to beg him for for Omar. I feel it to be unfair, considering that he gave one to Rames Bey, the favourite mameluke of Halim Pasha, who clearly cannot be in as much danger as a poor Arab. It is all of a piece.

I now feel so much like living on a bit longer that I will ask you to send me a cargo of medicines. I didn't think it worth while before to ask for anything to be sent to me that could not be forwarded to Hades, but my old body seems very tough and I fancy I have still one or two of my nine lives left.

I hope to sail in a very few days, Maurice is going up to Cairo so I send this by him. Yesterday was little Rainie's birthday, and I thought very longingly of her.

---

[1] Engaged by Lucie at Beirut.

L

Farewell to Upper Egypt

Aswan, January 22 1869. Dearest Janet. We are here up at 'far Syene' and I find the climate quite the best for me. But I am more ill, I believe, than you quite suppose. I do not like your father to be worried, but I may tell *you* that I think it hardly possible I can last much longer. However, it is hard to say.

When the Prince of Wales[1] comes I will see his doctor and let you know what he says. I think Maurice had better go home soon. His health is excellent so I have no longer any fear on that score and he ought to do something, and I have no influence with him at all. I believe you are the only person he will not utterly set at defiance.

I wish I could hope to see any of you once more, but I do not see any possibility of reaching Europe. My breathing is now so painful that I cannot walk the length of the *dahabieh* without gasping for breath, and I am so feeble that I can do nothing without help. Omar is more patient and careful than one could think a man could be in saving me every exertion; I can't think where he learnt such good nursing. When I have got rid of Miss Mathews and her clamour I shall be very comfortable and you need have no fear that I am not taken well care of.

Aswan, January 25 1869. Dearest Alick. We have been here ten days, and I find the air quite the best for me. I cough much less, only I am weak and short of breath. I have got a most excellent young Reis for my boat, and a sailor who sings like a nightingale, indeed he is not a sailor at all, but a professional Cairo singer who came up with me for fun. He draws crowds to hear him, and at Esneh the congre-

[1] Later Edward VII. He was doing a tour with Princess Alexandra to Egypt and Constantinople in the winter of 1869.

358

gation prayed for me in the mosque that God might reward me for the pleasure I had provided for them. If prayers could avail to cure I ought to get well rapidly. At Luxor Omar killed the sheep he had vowed, and Mustapha and Mohammed each killed two, as thank-offerings for my life, and all the derweeshes held two great *Zikrs* in a tent pitched behind the boat, and drummed and chanted and called on the Lord for two whole nights; and every man in my boat fasted Ramadan severely, from Omar and the crew to the little boys. I think Darfur was the most meritorious of all, because he has such a Gargantuan appetite, but he fasted his thirty days bravely and rubbed his little nose in the dust energetically in prayer.

If I die, dearest Alick, pray have something done for Darfur. He is the best and merriest of all little boys and I love him dearly. He is clever, brave and honest and very affectionate and careful to me, and more droll than anything you could conceive. As to Omar, he is the same as ever—the best of nurses and the pleasantest person about one. Miss Mathews is a terrible nuisance. The clever old woman who put her off on me at Beirut evidently 'brayed her well in the mortar', whereof Suleyman speaks, but when the vigorous use of the pestle was discontinued her natural folly burst forth in full force and she is a weariness and a trouble. At first she pretended to be willing 'to make herself useful' (if only she knew how), only Mrs Robertson had always made all her clothes for her and cut her nails and brushed her hair, etc., etc. But now she has developed into the timid and playful little dear. (A hideous woman of thirty with false teeth) and wants more waiting on than I do.

I shall send her back to be petted at Beirut as soon as I can do so without being unkind. If I were ill she would be a fearful aggravation of the evil, as she is always cackling and screeching and calling Omar and Darfur to find her worsted needle or lace her boots. She is very sulky because I can't chaperone her about and give her gaieties.

Aswan, January 25 1869. On Christmas day I was at Esneh, it was warm and fine, and I made fantasia and had the girls to dance. Zeyneb and Hillaleah claim to be my own special *Ghaɀawee,* so to speak my *Ballerine da camera,* and they did their best. How I did long to transport the whole scene before your eyes—Ramadan warbling intense love songs, and beating on a tiny tambourine, while Zeyneb danced before him and gave the pantomime to his song; and the sailors, and girls, and respectable merchants sat *pêle-mêle* all round on the deck, and the player on the rabab drew from it a wail like that of Isis for dead Osiris. I never quite know whether it is now or four thousand years ago, or even ten thousand, when I am in the dreamy intoxication of a real Egyptian fantasia; nothing is so antique as the Ghazawee— the *real* dancing girls. They are still subject to religious ecstasies of a very curious kind, no doubt inherited from the remotest antiquity. Ask any learned pundit to explain to you the *Zar*—it is really curious.

Now that I am too ill to write I feel sorry that I did not persist and write on the beliefs of Egypt in spite of your fear that the learned would cut me up, for I honestly believe that knowledge will die with me which few others possess. You must recollect that the learned know books, and I know men, and what is still more difficult, women.

The Cataract is very bad this year, owing to want of water in the Nile, and to the shameful conduct of the Maōhn here. The cataract men came to me, and prayed me to 'give them my voice' before the Mudir, which I will do. Allah ed-Deen Bey seems a decent man and will perhaps remove the rascal, whose robberies on travellers are notorious, and his oppression of the poor savages who pull the boats up odious. Two boats have been severely damaged, and my friend the Reis of the Cataract (the one I threatened to shoot last year, and who has believed in me ever since) does not advise me to go up, though he would take me for nothing, he swears, if I wished. So as the air is good here and Maurice is happy with his companions, I will stay here.

I meant to have discharged my men, but I have grown so fond of them (having so good a set), that I can't bring myself to save £20 by turning them adrift when we are all so happy and comfortable, and the poor fellows are just marrying new wives with their wages. Good-bye dearest Alick, forgive a scrawl, for I am very weak all over, fingers and all. Best love to my darling Rainie. Three boats have little girls of five to eight on board, and I do envy them so. I think Maurice had better go home to you, when we get to Cairo. He ought to be doing something.

LI

'I only pray for the end'

Boulaq, June 15 1869. Dearest Alick. Do not think of coming here. Indeed it would be almost too painful to me to part from you again; and as it is, I can patiently wait for the end among people who are kind and loving enough to be comfortable, without too much feeling of the pain of parting. The leaving Luxor was rather a distressing scene, as they did not think to see me again.

The kindness of all the people was really touching, from the Cadi who made ready my tomb among his own family, to the poorest fellaheen. Omar sends you his most heartfelt thanks, and begs that the boat may remain registered at the Consulate in your name for his use and benefit. The Prince has appointed him his own dragoman. But he is sad enough, poor fellow, all his prosperity does not console him for the loss of 'the mother he found in the world'. Mohammed at Luxor wept bitterly and said, 'poor I, my poor children, poor all the people', and kissed my hand passionately, and the people at Esneh, asked leave to touch me 'for a blessing', and everyone sent delicate bread, and their best butter, and vegetables and lambs. They are kinder than ever now that I can no longer be of any use to them.

If I live till September I will go up to Esneh, where the air is softest and I cough less. I would rather die among my own people in the Said than here.

You must forgive this scrawl, dearest. Don't think please of sending Maurice out again, he must begin to work now or he will never be good for anything.

Can you thank the Prince of Wales for Omar, or shall I write? He was most pleasant and kind, and the Princess too. She is the most perfectly simple-mannered girl I ever saw. She does not even try to be civil like other great people, but asks blunt questions, and looks at one so heartily with her clear, honest eyes, that she must win all hearts, but she is not pretty. They were more considerate than any people I have seen, and the Prince, instead of being gracious, was, if I may say so, quite respectful in his manner: he is very well bred and pleasant. I wish he did not drink so much and was more dignified, but he, too, has the honest eyes that makes one sure he has a kind heart.

My sailors were so proud at having the honour of rowing him *in our own boat,* and of singing to him. I had a very good singer in the boat. Please send some little present for my Reis: he is such a good man; he will be pleased at some little thing from you. He is half Turk, and seems like a whole one. Maurice will have told you all about us. Good-bye for the present, dearest Love. I can't say any more.

Cairo, Helwan opposite Bedreshayn, July 9 1869. Dearest Alick. Don't make yourself unhappy and don't send out a nurse. Miss Mathews has come out excellent and I am nursed as well as possible. My two reises, Ramadan and Yussuf, are strong and tender, and Omar is as ever. I am too absorbed in mere bodily suffering to wish anyone else to witness it. The worst is I am so strong. I rehearsed my death two days ago and came back again after being a whole night insensible.

I repeat I could not be better cared for anywhere than by my good loving crew. Tell Maurice how they all cried and how Abd el-Haleem forswore drink and hashish. He is very good, too, but the Reises are incomparable.

God bless you, my dearest of all loves. How sad that your Nile project was too late.

Kiss my darlings all, and dear Charly. I grieve for her eyes. I don't write very well, I suppose, being worn out with want of sleep and incessant suffocation.

Forgive me all my faults toward you. I wish I had seen your dear face once more—but not now. I would not have you here now on any account.

*   *   *

On July 13, before Alexander Duff Gordon had received her last letters, she asked Miss Mathews to bring her a telegraph form and she wrote an announcement of her death to her husband, leaving the time to be filled in. She could not, she said, last longer than the following day; she had not been in bed for twelve days and could only find relief from the pain of coughing and suffocation in a dentist's reclining chair.

She read again the last letter she had received from her daughter Rainie and cried bitterly at the thought of not seeing her again, but then she said how wrong it was to complain against the will of God or to give pain to others. Omar, little Darfur and the crew kept vigil on deck praying by the dark Nile while Emma Mathews sat by her.

At midnight Lucie said that she was very cold and blankets were brought but they made no difference. At two in the morning she asked for some café au lait and when it was given to her she said: 'How nice it smells. You know what is coming, do not be afraid.' Omar and the crew came into her cabin and she had just enough strength to bless and embrace them and to thank them for all their kindness. One of them said he hoped she would get better. 'That is not kind to wish me to linger on in pain,' she replied. 'I only pray for the end.' Heartbroken they stood there as dawn broke on the river and Omar knelt by her bedside in utter misery, powerless now to help her.

'Her wish,' wrote Miss Mathews, 'was to have seen her husband, but as it could not be done she resigned herself saying "Thy Will be done".' She died just before seven in the morning of July 14 at the age of forty-eight. The telegram reached Alexander and Janet in London just as they were preparing to leave for Egypt.

* * *

Caroline Norton wrote in *The Times* of her friend, Lucie: 'Those who remember her in her youth and beauty, before disease rather than time had altered the pale heroic face, and bowed the slight, stately figure, may well perceive some strange analogy between soul and body in the Spartan firmness which enabled her to pen that last farewell so quietly. [The letter of June 15.]

'But to the last her thought was for others, and for the services she could render . . . The long exile she endured for the sake of a better climate has failed to arrest, though it delayed, the doom foretold by her physicians.

'To that exile we owe the most popular, perhaps, of her contributions to the literature of her country, *Letters from the Cape*, and *Letters from Egypt*, the latter more especially interesting from the vivid, life-like descriptions of the people among whom she dwelt, her aspirations for their better destiny, and the complete amalgamation of her own pursuits and interests with theirs. She was a settler, not a traveller among them.

'Unlike Lady Hester Stanhope, whose fantastic and half-insane notions of rulership and superiority have been so often recorded for our amazement, Lady Duff Gordon kept the simple frankness of heart and desire to be of service to her fellow-creatures without a thought of self or a taint of vanity in her intercourse with them . . .

'The source of her popularity was in the liberal kindliness of spirit with which she acted on all occasions, more especially towards those she considered the victims of bad government and oppressive laws. Sympathizing, helping, doctoring their sick, teaching their children, learning the language, Lady Duff Gordon lived in Egypt, and in Egypt she has died, leaving a memory of her greatness and goodness such as no other European woman ever acquired in that country. It is touching to trace her lingering hopes of life and amended health in her letters to her husband and her mother, and to see how, as they faded out, there rose over those hopes, the grander light of fortitude and submission to the will of God.

'Gradually, hope departs, and she begins bravely to face the inevitable destiny. And then comes the end of all, the strong yet tender announcement of her own conviction that there would be no more meetings, but a grave opened to receive her in a foreign land. . .

'Who shall say what seeds of kindly intercommunion that dying Englishwoman . . . may have planted in the arid Eastern soil?'[1]

'She lies among strangers; but it will be long before her memory is forgotten in the land of her birth, where her monument is not of marble or stone or brass, but of thought; and where those who read her works, and the brief transcript of her life in exile, will comprehend the long regret that lies like a slant shadow across the scenes once brightened by her presence.'[2]

[1] *The Times*, July 26 1869.
[2] *Macmillan's Magazine*, vol. 20, May to October 1869. Both were written by Caroline Norton.

Brief Bibliography

Caroline Norton published an article 'Lady Duff Gordon and her Works' in *Macmillan's Magazine*, vol. 20, May to October 1869 and in *The Times* of July 26, 1869, she wrote: 'Lady Duff Gordon's printed works were many. She was an excellent German scholar, and had the advantage in her translations from that difficult language of her labours being shared by her husband . . . She was also a classic scholar of no mean pretensions.'

Following are some of the books Lady Duff Gordon translated. *Mary Schweidler, the Amber Witch*, from the German of William Meinhold, 1844; Leopold von Ranke's *History of Prussia* in 3 vols; a selection from *Criminal Trials* by the German jurist Ritter von Feuerbach; *Ferdinand I and Maximilian II of Austria; State of Germany after the Reformation*, by *Leopold von Ranke*, 1853, and also, with her husband, Ranke's *Memoirs of the House of Brandenburg and History of Prussia during the 17th and 18th centuries, 1849*; *The Russo-Turkish Campaign in Europe, in 1828–29*, by Baron von Moltke, Major on the Prussian Staff; *Stella and Vanessa* from the French of Leon de Wailly, 1850, and an account of the poet Heinrich Heine in Lord Houghton's *Monographs Personal and Social*.

Letters from the Cape, 1864, and 1875, new editions 1921 and 1927; *Letters from Egypt*, edited by Sarah Austin, 1865; *Last Letters from Egypt*, with a memoir by her daughter, Janet Ross, 1875, and a fuller edition in 1902. *Letters from the Cape* and *Letters from Egypt* were used in a biography, *Lucie Duff Gordon*, by Gordon Waterfield, London 1937.

Sarah Austin was the first to introduce Leopold von Ranke to the British public through her translations of his *History of the Reformation in Germany* and his *History of the Popes*. Among her other translations were *Report on the State of Public Instruction in Prussia* from the French of Victor Cousin; she edited *Memoirs of Sydney Smith* and John Austin's *Lectures on Jursprudence*.

Articles on Lady Duff Gordon and on each of her parents, John and Sarah Austin, are published in the Dictionary of National Biography and in the Encyclopedia Britannica, 13th edition.

Among the books referred to in *Letters from Egypt* are: *Cradle Lands*, by Lady Herbert, London 1867; *Eothen*, by A. W. Kinglake, London 1844; *Manners and Customs of the Modern Egyptians*, by Edward Lane, London 1836; *The English Governess in Egypt* and *Nights in the Hareem*, by Emmeline Lott, 1866 and 1867, London; *Eastern Life Present and Past*, by Harriet Martineau, London 1848; *The Crescent and the Cross*, by E. Warburton, London 1845.

Index

Index